Project Management

ALL-IN-ONE

by Nick Graham; Mark C. Layton, MBA^2, CST, PMP, SAFe SPC; David Morrow, CSP, ICP-ACC; Steven J. Ostermiller, CSP, PMP; Stanley E. Portny, PMP; Doug Rose, CSP-SM, PMI-ACP, PMP, SAFe SPC; and Cynthia Snyder Dionisio

Project Management All-in-One For Dummies®

Published by: **John Wiley & Sons, Inc.**, 111 River Street, Hoboken, NJ 07030-5774, www.wiley.com

Copyright © 2020 by John Wiley & Sons, Inc., Hoboken, New Jersey

Published simultaneously in Canada

No part of this publication may be reproduced, stored in a retrieval system or transmitted in any form or by any means, electronic, mechanical, photocopying, recording, scanning or otherwise, except as permitted under Sections 107 or 108 of the 1976 United States Copyright Act, without the prior written permission of the Publisher. Requests to the Publisher for permission should be addressed to the Permissions Department, John Wiley & Sons, Inc., 111 River Street, Hoboken, NJ 07030, (201) 748-6011, fax (201) 748-6008, or online at http://www.wiley.com/go/permissions.

Trademarks: Wiley, For Dummies, the Dummies Man logo, Dummies.com, Making Everything Easier, and related trade dress are trademarks or registered trademarks of John Wiley & Sons, Inc., and may not be used without written permission. All other trademarks are the property of their respective owners. John Wiley & Sons, Inc., is not associated with any product or vendor mentioned in this book.

LIMIT OF LIABILITY/DISCLAIMER OF WARRANTY: WHILE THE PUBLISHER AND AUTHOR HAVE USED THEIR BEST EFFORTS IN PREPARING THIS BOOK, THEY MAKE NO REPRESENTATIONS OR WARRANTIES WITH RESPECT TO THE ACCURACY OR COMPLETENESS OF THE CONTENTS OF THIS BOOK AND SPECIFICALLY DISCLAIM ANY IMPLIED WARRANTIES OF MERCHANTABILITY OR FITNESS FOR A PARTICULAR PURPOSE. NO WARRANTY MAY BE CREATED OR EXTENDED BY SALES REPRESENTATIVES OR WRITTEN SALES MATERIALS. THE ADVICE AND STRATEGIES CONTAINED HEREIN MAY NOT BE SUITABLE FOR YOUR SITUATION. YOU SHOULD CONSULT WITH A PROFESSIONAL WHERE APPROPRIATE. NEITHER THE PUBLISHER NOR THE AUTHOR SHALL BE LIABLE FOR DAMAGES ARISING HEREFROM.

For general information on our other products and services, please contact our Customer Care Department within the U.S. at 877-762-2974, outside the U.S. at 317-572-3993, or fax 317-572-4002. For technical support, please visit https://hub.wiley.com/community/support/dummies.

Wiley publishes in a variety of print and electronic formats and by print-on-demand. Some material included with standard print versions of this book may not be included in e-books or in print-on-demand. If this book refers to media such as a CD or DVD that is not included in the version you purchased, you may download this material at http://booksupport.wiley.com. For more information about Wiley products, visit www.wiley.com.

Library of Congress Control Number: 2020937968

ISBN 978-1-119-70026-5 (pbk); ISBN 978-1-119-70027-2 (ebk); ISBN 978-1-119-70028-9 (ebk)

Manufactured in the United States of America

SKY10031635_042122

Contents at a Glance

Table of Contents

Introduction

No matter where you work or what you do, chances are you need to start, plan, execute, monitor, and complete projects smoothly. *Project Management All-in-One For Dummies* is your guide to effectively developing and using the skills you need.

About This Book

Project Management All-in-One For Dummies helps you acquire and cultivate some of the most important attributes needed for carrying out successful projects. Here, you get pointers on starting, planning, controlling, and finishing projects; using checklists and software to help you work; trying popular new project management methods like agile and scrum; and preparing for Project Management Professional (PMP) certification.

A quick note: Sidebars (shaded boxes of text) dig into the details of a given topic, but they aren't crucial to understanding it. Feel free to read them or skip them. You can pass over the text accompanied by the Technical Stuff icon, too. The text marked with this icon gives some interesting but nonessential information about increasing influence.

One last thing: Within this book, you may note that some web addresses break across two lines of text. If you're reading this book in print and want to visit one of these web pages, simply key in the web address exactly as it's noted in the text, pretending as though the line break doesn't exist. If you're reading this as an e-book, you've got it easy — just click the web address to be taken directly to the web page.

Foolish Assumptions

Here are some assumptions about you, dear reader, and why you're picking up this book:

- You're an experienced project manager who wants to take your skills to new heights.
- You're new to project management and you've never been on a project team, but you're eager to find out more.
- You're interested in finding out about different tools you can use to manage projects.
- You're curious about different types of project management methods, such as agile, scrum, and enterprise agility.
- You want to brush up on some basics as you prepare for the PMP exam.

Icons Used in This Book

Like all *For Dummies* books, this book features icons to help you navigate the information. Here's what they mean.

REMEMBER

If you take away anything from this book, it should be the information marked with this icon.

TECHNICAL STUFF

This icon flags information that digs a little deeper than usual into a particular topic.

TIP

This icon highlights especially helpful advice about developing and using project management skills.

WARNING

This icon points out situations and actions to avoid in your role as a project manager.

Beyond the Book

In addition to the material in the print or e-book you're reading right now, this product comes with some access-anywhere goodies on the web. Check out the free Cheat Sheet for info on the phases of a project life cycle, project management processes, and a project manager's basic tasks. To get this Cheat Sheet, simply go to `www.dummies.com` and search for "*Project Management All-in-One For Dummies* Cheat Sheet" in the Search box.

Where to Go from Here

You don't have to read this book from cover to cover, but if you're an especially thorough person (and you probably are if you're a project manager!), go right ahead. If you just want to find specific information and then get back to your projects, take a look at the table of contents or the index, and then dive into the chapter or section that interests you.

For example, if you want the basics on starting, planning, and managing a project, flip to Books 1 and 2. If you want to build your scrum skills, check out Book 5. Or if you're considering earning your PMP certification, Book 7 is the place to be.

No matter where you start, you'll find the information you need to more effectively manage your work projects. Good luck!

1

In the Beginning: Project Management Basics

Contents at a Glance

» Breaking down project management

» Identifying the project manager's role

Chapter 1 Achieving Results with Project Management

Successful organizations create projects that produce desired results in established time frames with assigned resources. As a result, businesses are increasingly driven to find individuals who can excel in this project-oriented environment.

Because you're reading this book, chances are good that you've been asked to manage a project. So, hang on tight — you're going to need a new set of skills and techniques to steer that project to successful completion. But not to worry! This chapter gets you off to a smooth start by showing you what projects and project management really are and by helping you separate projects from non-project assignments. This chapter also offers the rationale for why projects succeed or fail and gets you into the project-management mindset.

Determining What Makes a Project a Project

No matter what your job is, you handle a myriad of assignments every day. For example, you may prepare a memo, hold a meeting, design a sales campaign, or move to new offices. Or you may make the information systems more user-friendly, develop a research compound in the laboratory, or improve the organization's public image. Not all these assignments are projects. How can you tell which ones are and which ones aren't? This section is here to help.

TIP

People often confuse the following two terms with *project:*

- **Process:** A *process* is a series of routine steps to perform a particular function, such as a procurement process or a budget process. A process isn't a one-time activity that achieves a specific result; instead, it defines *how* a particular function is to be done every time. Processes, like the activities that go into buying materials, are often parts of projects.
- **Program:** This term can describe two different situations:
  - First, a *program* can be a set of goals that gives rise to specific projects, but, unlike a project, a program can never be completely accomplished. For example, a health-awareness program can never completely achieve its goal (the public will never be totally aware of all health issues as a result of a health-awareness program), but one or more projects may accomplish specific results related to the program's goal (such as a workshop on minimizing the risk of heart disease).
  - Second, a *program* sometimes refers to a group of specified projects that achieve a common goal.

Understanding the three main components that define a project

A *project* is a temporary undertaking performed to produce a unique product, service, or result. Large or small, a project always has the following three components:

- **Specific scope:** Desired results or products.
- **Schedule:** Established dates when project work starts and ends. (See Chapter 1 in Book 2 for how to develop responsive and feasible project schedules.)
- **Required resources:** Necessary number of people and funds and other resources.

As illustrated in Figure 1-1, each component affects the other two. For example: Expanding the type and characteristics of desired outcomes may require more time (a later end date) or more resources. Moving up the end date may necessitate paring down the results or increasing project expenditures (for instance, by paying overtime to project staff). Within this three-part project definition, you perform work to achieve your desired results.

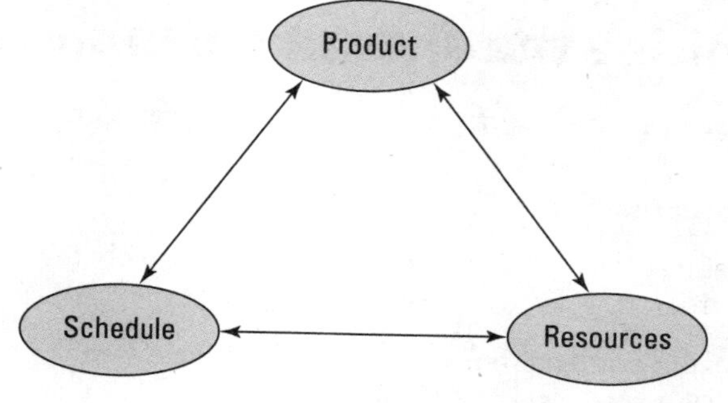

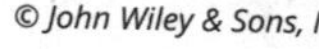
© John Wiley & Sons, Inc.

FIGURE 1-1: The relationship between the three main components of a project.

REMEMBER

Although many other considerations may affect a project's performance (see the later section "Defining Project Management" for details), these three components are the basis of a project's definition for the following three reasons:

- The only reason a project exists is to produce the results specified in its scope.
- The project's end date is an essential part of defining what constitutes successful performance; the desired result must be provided by a certain time to meet its intended need.
- The availability of resources shapes the nature of the products the project can produce.

A Guide to the Project Management Body of Knowledge, 6th Edition *(PMBOK 6)*, elaborates on these components by

- Emphasizing that *product* includes both the basic nature of what is to be produced (for example, a new training program or a new prescription drug) and its required characteristics (for example, the topics that the training program must address), which are defined as the product's *quality*
- Noting that *resources* refers to funds, as well as to other, nonmonetary resources, such as people, equipment, raw materials, and facilities

PMBOK 6 also emphasizes that *risk* (the likelihood that not everything will go exactly according to plan) plays an important role in defining a project and that guiding a project to success involves continually managing tradeoffs among the three main project components — the products to be produced and their characteristics, the schedule, and the resources required to do the project work.

Recognizing the diversity of projects

Projects come in a wide assortment of shapes and sizes. For example, projects can

- **Be large or small**
  - Installing a new subway system, which may cost more than $1 billion and take 10 to 15 years to complete, is a project.
  - Preparing an ad hoc report of monthly sales figures, which may take you one day to complete, is also a project.
- **Involve many people or just you**
  - Training all 10,000 of your organization's staff in a new affirmative-action policy is a project.
  - Rearranging the furniture and equipment in your office is also a project.
- **Be defined by a legal contract or by an informal agreement**
  - A signed contract between you and a customer that requires you to build a house defines a project.
  - An informal promise you make to install a new software package on your colleague's computer also defines a project.
- **Be business-related or personal**
  - Conducting your organization's annual blood drive is a project.
  - Having a dinner party for 15 people is also a project.

REMEMBER

No matter what the individual characteristics of your project are, you define it by the same three components described in the previous section: results (or scope), start and end dates, and resources. The information you need to plan and manage your project is the same for any project you manage, although the ease and the time to develop it may differ. The more thoroughly you plan and manage your projects, the more likely you are to succeed.

Describing the four phases of a project life cycle

REMEMBER

A project's *life cycle* is the series of phases that the project passes through as it goes from its start to its completion. A *phase* is a collection of logically related project activities that culminates in the completion of one or more project deliverables (see Chapter 3 in Book 1 for more on project deliverables). Every project, whether large or small, passes through the following four life-cycle phases:

- **Starting the project:** This phase involves generating, evaluating, and framing the business need for the project and the general approach to performing it and agreeing to prepare a detailed project plan. Outputs from this phase may include approval to proceed to the next phase, documentation of the need for the project and rough estimates of time and resources to perform it (often included in a project charter), and an initial list of people who may be interested in, involved with, or affected by the project.
- **Organizing and preparing:** This phase involves developing a plan that specifies the desired results; the work to do; the time, cost, and other resources required; and a plan for how to address key project risks. Outputs from this phase may include a project plan that documents the intended project results and the time, resources, and supporting processes needed to create them.
- **Carrying out the work:** This phase involves establishing the project team and the project support systems, performing the planned work, and monitoring and controlling performance to ensure adherence to the current plan. Outputs from this phase may include project results, project progress reports, and other communications.
- **Closing the project:** This phase involves assessing the project results, obtaining customer approvals, transitioning project team members to new assignments, closing financial accounts, and conducting a post-project evaluation. Outputs from this phase may include final, accepted, and approved project results and recommendations and suggestions for applying lessons learned from this project to similar efforts in the future.

For small projects, this entire life cycle can take just a few days. For larger projects, it can take many years! In fact, to allow for greater focus on key aspects and to make it easier to monitor and control the work, project managers often subdivide larger projects into separate phases, each of which is treated as a mini-project and passes through these four life-cycle phases. No matter how simple or complex the project is, however, these four phases are the same.

REMEMBER

In a perfect world, you complete one phase of your project's life cycle before you move on to the next one, and after you complete that phase, you never return to it again. But the world isn't perfect, and project success often requires a flexible approach that responds to real situations that you may face, such as the following:

- **You may have to work on two (or more) project phases at the same time to meet tight deadlines.** Working on the next phase before you complete the current one increases the risk that you may have to redo tasks, which may cause you to miss deadlines and spend more resources than you originally planned. If you choose this strategy, be sure people understand the potential risks and costs associated with it.

» **Sometimes you learn by doing.** Despite doing your best to assess feasibility and develop detailed plans, you may realize you can't achieve what you thought you could. When this situation happens, you need to return to the earlier project phases and rethink them in light of the new information you've acquired.

» **Sometimes things change unexpectedly.** Your initial feasibility and benefits assessments are sound, and your plan is detailed and realistic. However, certain key project team members leave the organization without warning during the project. Or a new technology emerges, and it's more appropriate to use than the one in your original plans. Because ignoring these occurrences may seriously jeopardize your project's success, you need to return to the earlier project phases and rethink them in light of these new realities.

Defining Project Management

Project management is the process of guiding a project from its beginning through its performance to its closure. Project management includes five sets of processes, which is described in more detail in the following sections:

» **Initiating processes:** Clarifying the business need, defining high-level expectations and resource budgets, and beginning to identify audiences that may play a role in your project

» **Planning processes:** Detailing the project scope, time frames, resources, and risks, as well as intended approaches to project communications, quality, and management of external purchases of goods and services

» **Executing processes:** Establishing and managing the project team, communicating with and managing project audiences, and implementing the project plans

» **Monitoring and controlling processes:** Tracking performance and taking actions necessary to help ensure project plans are successfully implemented and the desired results are achieved

» **Closing processes:** Ending all project activity

As illustrated in Figure 1-2, these five process groups help support the project through the four phases of its life cycle. Initiating processes support the work to be done when starting the project, and planning processes support the organizing and preparing phase. Executing processes guide the project tasks performed when carrying out the work, and closing processes are used to perform the tasks that bring the project to an end.

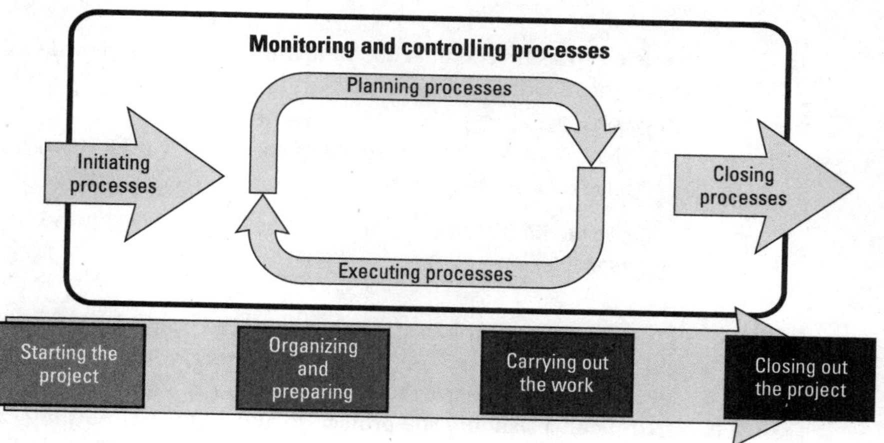

FIGURE 1-2: The five project-management process groups that support the four project life-cycle phases.

© John Wiley & Sons, Inc.

Figure 1-2 highlights how you may cycle back from executing processes to planning processes when you have to return to the organizing and preparing phase to modify existing plans to address problems you encounter or new information you acquire while carrying out the project work. Finally, you use monitoring and controlling processes in each of the four phases to help ensure that work is being performed according to plans.

REMEMBER

Successfully performing these processes requires the following:

- **Information:** Accurate, timely, and complete data for the planning, performance monitoring, and final assessment of the project
- **Communication:** Clear, open, and timely sharing of information with appropriate individuals and groups throughout the project's duration
- **Commitment:** Team members' personal promises to produce the agreed-upon results on time and within budget

Starting with the initiating processes

All projects begin with an idea. Perhaps your organization's client identifies a need, or maybe your boss thinks of a new market to explore, or maybe you think of a way to refine your organization's procurement process.

Sometimes the initiating process is informal. For a small project, it may consist of just a discussion and a verbal agreement. In other instances, especially for larger projects, a project requires a formal review and decision by your boss and/or other members of your organization's senior management team.

Decision-makers consider the following two questions when deciding whether to move ahead with a project:

- ***Should* we do it?** Are the benefits we expect to achieve worth the costs we'll have to pay? Are there better ways to approach the issue?
- ***Can* we do it?** Is the project technically feasible? Are the required resources available?

REMEMBER

If the answer to both questions is "Yes," the project can proceed to the organizing and preparing phase (see the following section), during which a project plan is developed. If the answer to either question is a definite, ironclad "No," under no circumstances should the project go any further. If nothing can be done to make it desirable and feasible, the decision-makers should stop all work on the project immediately. Doing anything else guarantees wasted resources, lost opportunities, and a frustrated staff.

Outlining the planning processes

When you know what you hope to accomplish and you believe it's possible, you need a detailed plan that describes how you and your team will make it happen. Include the following in your project-management plan:

- An overview of the reasons for your project.
- A detailed description of intended results.
- A list of all constraints the project must address.
- A list of all assumptions related to the project.
- A list of all required work. (Chapter 3 in Book 1 discusses how to identify all required project work.)
- A breakdown of the roles you and your team members will play.
- A detailed project schedule. (Chapter 1 in Book 2 explains how to develop your schedule.)
- Needs for personnel, funds, and non-personnel resources (such as equipment, facilities, and information).
- A description of how you plan to manage any significant risks and uncertainties.
- Plans for project communications.
- Plans for ensuring project quality. (Chapter 3 in Book 2 covers how to track progress and maintain control of your project throughout its life cycle so as to achieve success.)

TIP

Always put your project plans in writing; doing so helps you clarify details and reduces the chances that you'll forget something. Plans for large projects can take hundreds of pages, but a plan for a small project can take only a few lines on a piece of paper (or a tablecloth!).

The success of your project depends on the clarity and accuracy of your plan and on whether people believe they can achieve it. Considering past experience in your project plan makes your plan more realistic; involving people in the plan's development encourages their commitment to achieving it.

WARNING

Don't let the pressure to get fast results convince you to skip the planning and get right to the tasks. Although this strategy can create a lot of immediate activity, it also creates significant chances for waste and mistakes.

TIP

Be sure your project's drivers and supporters review and approve the plan in writing before you begin your project (see Chapter 2 in Book 1). For a small project, you may need only a brief email or someone's initials on the plans. For a larger project, though, you may need a formal review and sign-off by one or more levels of your organization's management.

Examining the executing processes

After you've developed your project-management plan and set your appropriate project baselines, it's time to get to work and start executing your plan. This is often the phase when management gets more engaged and excited to see things being produced.

Preparing

Preparing to begin the project work involves the following tasks (see Chapter 2 in Book 2 for details):

- **Assigning people to all project roles:** Confirm the individuals who'll perform the project work and negotiate agreements with them and their managers to make sure they'll be available to work on the project team.
- **Introducing team members to each other and to the project:** Help people begin developing interpersonal relationships with each other. Help them appreciate the overall purpose of the project and explain how the different parts will interact and support each other.
- **Giving and explaining tasks to all team members:** Describe to all team members what work they're responsible for producing and how the team members will coordinate their efforts.

» **Defining how the team will perform its essential functions:** Decide how the team will handle routine communications, make different project decisions, and resolve conflicts. Develop any procedures that may be required to guide performance of these functions.

» **Setting up necessary tracking systems:** Decide which system(s) and accounts you'll use to track schedules, work effort, and expenditures, and then set them up.

» **Announcing the project to the organization:** Let the project audiences know that your project exists, what it will produce, and when it will begin and end.

REMEMBER

Suppose you don't join your project team until the actual work is getting underway. Your first task is to understand how people decided initially that the project was possible and desirable. If the people who participated in the start of the project and the organizing and preparing phases overlooked important issues, you need to raise them now. When searching for the project's history, check minutes from meetings, memos, letters, emails, and technical reports. Then consult with all the people involved in the initial project decisions.

Performing

Finally, you get to perform the project work! The performing subgroup of the executing processes includes the following tasks:

» **Doing the tasks:** Perform the work that's in your plan.

» **Assuring quality:** Continually confirm that work and results conform to requirements and applicable standards and guidelines.

» **Managing the team:** Assign tasks, review results, and resolve problems.

» **Developing the team:** Provide needed training and mentoring to improve team members' skills.

» **Sharing information:** Distribute information to appropriate project audiences.

Surveying the monitoring and controlling processes

As the project progresses, you need to ensure that plans are being followed and desired results are being achieved. The monitoring and controlling processes include the following tasks (see Chapter 3 in Book 2 for specific activities):

- **Comparing performance with plans:** Collect information on outcomes, schedule achievements, and resource expenditures; identify deviations from your plan; and develop corrective actions.
- **Fixing problems that arise:** Change tasks, schedules, or resources to bring project performance back on track with the existing plan, or negotiate agreed-upon changes to the plan itself.
- **Keeping everyone informed:** Tell project audiences about the team's achievements, project problems, and necessary revisions to the established plan.

Ending with the closing processes

Finishing your assigned tasks is only part of bringing your project to a close. In addition, you must do the following (see Chapter 4 in Book 2 for a discussion of each of these points):

- Get your clients' approvals of the final results.
- Close all project accounts (if you've been charging time and money to special project accounts).
- Help team members move on to their next assignments.
- Hold a post-project evaluation with the project team to recognize project achievements and to discuss lessons you can apply to the next project. (At the very least, make informal notes about these lessons and your plans for using them in the future.)

Knowing the Project Manager's Role

The project manager's job is challenging. For instance, she often coordinates technically specialized professionals — who may have limited experience working together — to achieve a common goal. Although the project manager's own work experience is often technical in nature, her success requires a keen ability to identify and resolve sensitive organizational and interpersonal issues. This section describes the main tasks that a project manager handles and note potential challenges she may encounter.

Looking at the project manager's tasks

Historically, the performance rules in traditional organizations were simple: Your boss made assignments; you carried them out. Questioning your assignments was a sign of insubordination or incompetence.

But these rules have changed. Today your boss may generate ideas, but you assess how to implement them. You confirm that a project meets your boss's (and your organization's) real need and then determine the work, schedules, and resources you require to implement it.

Handling a project any other way simply doesn't make sense. The project manager must be involved in developing the plans because she needs the opportunity to clarify expectations and proposed approaches and then to raise any questions she may have *before* the project work begins.

REMEMBER

The key to project success is being proactive. Instead of waiting for others to tell you what to do,

- Seek out information because you know you need it.
- Follow the plan because you believe it's the best way.
- Involve people whom you know are important for the project.
- Identify issues and risks, analyze them, and elicit support to address them.
- Share information with the people you know need to have it.
- Put all important information in writing.
- Ask questions and encourage other people to do the same.
- Commit to your project's success.

Staving off excuses for not following a structured project-management approach

Be prepared for other people to fight your attempts to use proven project-management approaches. You need to be prepared for everything! The following list provides a few examples of excuses you may encounter as a project manager and the appropriate responses you can give:

- **Excuse:** Our projects are all crises; we have no time to plan.

  Response: Unfortunately for the excuse giver, this logic is illogical! In a crisis, you have limited time and resources to address the critical issues, and you definitely can't afford to make mistakes. Because acting under pressure and emotion (the two characteristics of crises) practically guarantees that mistakes will occur, you can't afford not to plan.

- **Excuse:** Structured project management is only for large projects.

  Response: No matter what size the project is, the information you need to perform it is the same. What do you need to produce? What work has to be done? Who's going to do that work? When will the work end? Have you met expectations?

  Large projects may require many weeks or months to develop satisfactory answers to these questions. Small projects that last a few days or less may take only 15 minutes, but either way, you still have to answer the questions.

- **Excuse:** These projects require creativity and new development. They can't be predicted with any certainty.

  Response: Some projects are more predictable than others. However, people awaiting the outcomes of any project still have expectations for what they'll get and when. Therefore, a project with many uncertainties needs a manager to develop and share initial plans and then to assess and communicate the effects of unexpected occurrences.

Even if you don't encounter these specific excuses, you can adapt the response examples provided here to address your own situations.

Avoiding shortcuts

The short-term pressures of your job as a project manager may encourage you to act today in ways that cause you, your team, or your organization to pay a price tomorrow. Especially with smaller, less formal projects, you may feel no need for organized planning and control.

WARNING

Don't be seduced into the following, seemingly easier shortcuts:

- **Jumping directly from starting the project to carrying out the work:** You have an idea and your project is on a short schedule. Why not just start doing the work? Sounds good, but you haven't defined the work to be done!

  Other variations on this shortcut include the following:

  - **"This project's been done many times before, so why do I have to plan it out again?"** Even though projects can be similar to past ones, some elements are always different. Perhaps you're working with some new people, using a new piece of equipment, and so on. Take a moment now to be sure your plan addresses the current situation.

- **"Our project's different than it was before, so what good is trying to plan?"** Taking this attitude is like saying you're traveling in an unknown area, so why try to lay out your route on a road map? Planning for a new project is important because no one's taken this particular path before. Although your initial plan may have to be revised during the project, you and your team need to have a clear statement of your intended plan from the outset.

» **Failing to prepare in the carrying-out-the-work phase:** Time pressure is often the apparent justification for this shortcut. However, the real reason is that people don't appreciate the need to define procedures and relationships before jumping into the actual project work. See Chapter 2 in Book 2 for a discussion of why this preparation step is so important — and get tips on how to complete it.

» **Jumping right into the work when you join the project in the carrying-out-the-work phase:** The plan has already been developed, so why go back and revisit the starting-the-project and the organizing-and-preparing phases? Actually, you need to do so for two reasons:

- To identify any issues that the developers may have overlooked
- To understand the reasoning behind the plan and decide whether you feel the plan is achievable

» **Only partially completing the closing phase:** At the end of one project, you often move right on to the next. Scarce resources and short deadlines encourage this rapid movement, and starting a new project is always more challenging than wrapping up an old one.

However, you never really know how successful your project is if you don't take the time to ensure that all tasks are complete and that you've satisfied your clients. If you don't take positive steps to apply the lessons this project has taught you, you're likely to make the same mistakes you made in this project again or fail to repeat this project's successful approaches.

Staying aware of other potential challenges

Projects are temporary; they're created to achieve particular results. Ideally, when the results are achieved, the project ends. Unfortunately, the transitory nature of projects may create some project-management challenges, including the following:

- **Additional assignments:** People may be asked to accept an assignment to a new project in addition to — not in lieu of — existing assignments. They may not be asked how the new work might affect their existing projects. (Higher management may just assume the project manager can handle everything.) When conflicts arise over a person's time, the organization may not have adequate guidelines or procedures to resolve those conflicts (or they may not have any guidelines at all).
- **New people on new teams:** People who haven't worked together before and who may not even know each other may be assigned to the same project team. This lack of familiarity with each other may slow the project down because team members may
  - Have different operating and communicating styles.
  - Use different procedures for performing the same type of activity.
  - Not have time to develop mutual respect and trust.

  Flip to Chapter 2 in Book 2 for guidance on how to put together a successful team and get off on the right foot.
- **No direct authority:** For most projects, the project manager and team members have no direct authority over each other. Therefore, the rewards that usually encourage top performance (such as salary increases, superior performance appraisals, and job promotions) aren't available. In addition, conflicts over time commitments or technical direction may require input from a number of sources. As a result, they can't be settled with one unilateral decision.

register

- » Identifying your drivers, supporters, and observers
- » Using an effective format for your stakeholder register
- » Determining who has authority in your project
- » Prioritizing your stakeholders by their levels of power and interest

Chapter 2

Involving the Right People

Often a project is like an iceberg: Nine-tenths of it lurks below the surface. You receive an assignment and think you know what it entails and who needs to be involved. Then, as the project unfolds, new people emerge who may affect your goals, your approach, and your chances for project success.

You risk compromising your project in the following ways when you don't involve key people or groups in your project in a timely manner:

- » You may miss important information that can affect the project's performance and ultimate success.
- » You may insult someone. And you can be sure that when someone feels you have slighted or insulted them, they'll take steps to make sure you don't do it again!

As soon as you begin to think about a new project, start to identify people who may play a role directly and indirectly. This chapter shows you how to identify these candidates; how to decide whether, when, and how to involve them; and how to determine who has the authority, power, and interest to make critical decisions.

Understanding Your Project's Stakeholders

A *project stakeholder* is any person or group that supports, is affected by, or is interested in your project. Your project's stakeholders can be inside or outside your organization, and knowing who they are helps you

- Plan whether, when, and how to involve them.
- Determine whether the scope of the project is bigger or smaller than you originally anticipated.

You may hear other terms used in the business world to describe project stakeholders, but these terms address only some of the people from your complete project stakeholder register. Here are some examples:

- **A *distribution list* identifies people who receive project communications.** These lists are often out-of-date for a couple of reasons. Some people remain on the list simply because no one removes them; other people are on the list because no one wants to run the risk of insulting them by removing them. In either case, having their names on this list doesn't ensure that these people actually support, are affected by, or are interested in your project.
- ***Team members* are people whom the project manager directs.** All team members are stakeholders, but the stakeholder register includes more than just team members.

Developing a Stakeholder Register

As you identify the different stakeholders for your project, record them in a stakeholder register. Check out the following sections for information on how to develop this register.

Starting your stakeholder register

A project stakeholder register is a living document, which should be updated regularly throughout the project. You need to start developing your register as soon as you begin thinking about your project.

Begin your project's stakeholder register by considering the initial version of the register that's generated upon completion of the development of the project charter. (This charter authorizes the existence of a project and provides the project manager with the authority to use organizational resources to support the performance of project activities.)

Next, write down any other names that occur to you. When you discuss your project with other people, ask them who they think may be affected by or interested in your project. Then select a small group of the stakeholders you identify and conduct a formal brainstorming session. Continue to add and subtract names to your stakeholder register until you can't think of anyone else.

The following sections explain how to refine your stakeholder register by dividing it into specific categories and recognizing important potential stakeholders. You also find a sample to show you how to put your own register together.

Using specific categories

To increase your chances of identifying all appropriate people, develop your stakeholder register in categories. You're less likely to overlook people when you consider them department by department or group by group instead of trying to identify everyone from the organization individually at the same time.

REMEMBER

Start your stakeholder register by developing a hierarchical grouping of categories that covers the universe of people who may be affected by, be needed to support, or be interested in your project. You can start with the following groups:

- **Internal:** People and groups inside your organization
  - **Upper management:** Executive-level management responsible for the general oversight of all organization operations
  - **Requesters:** The person who came up with the idea for your project and all the people through whom the request passed before you received it
  - **Project manager:** The person with overall responsibility for successfully completing the project
  - **End users:** People who will use the goods or services the project will produce

- Team members: People assigned to the project whose work the project manager directs

  - **Groups normally involved:** Groups typically involved in most projects in the organization, such as the human resources, finance, contracts, and legal departments
  - **Groups needed just for this project:** Groups or people with special knowledge related to this project

- **External:** People and groups outside your organization
  - **Clients or customers:** People or groups that buy or use your organization's products or services
  - **Collaborators:** Groups or organizations with whom you may pursue joint ventures related to your project
  - **Vendors, suppliers, and contractors:** Organizations that provide personnel, raw materials, equipment, or other resources required to perform your project's work
  - **Regulators:** Government agencies that establish regulations and guidelines that govern some aspect of your project work
  - **Professional societies:** Groups of professionals that may influence or be interested in your project
  - **The public:** The local, national, and international community of people who may be affected by or interested in your project

Continue to subdivide these categories further until you arrive at job titles (or position descriptions) and the names of the people who occupy them. (The process of systematically separating a whole into its component parts is called *decomposition*, which you can read about in Chapter 3 of Book 1.)

Considering stakeholders that are often overlooked

As you develop your stakeholder register, be sure not to overlook the following potential stakeholders:

- **Support groups:** These people don't tell you what you should do (or help you deal with the trauma of project management); instead, they help you accomplish the project's goals. If support groups know about your project early, they can fit you into their work schedules more readily. They can also tell you information about their capabilities and processes that may influence what your project can accomplish and by when. Such groups include

* Facilities
* Finance
* Human resources
* Information technology (IT)
* Legal services
* Procurement or contracting
* Project management office
* Quality
* Security
* Help desks
* Call centers

» **End users of your project's products:** *End users* are people or groups who will use the goods and services your project produces. Involving end users at the beginning of and throughout your project helps ensure that the goods and services produced are as easy as possible to implement and use, and are most responsive to their true needs. It also confirms that you appreciate the fact that the people who will use a product may have important insights into what it should look like and do, which increases the chances that they'll work to implement the products successfully.

  In some cases, you may omit end users on your stakeholder register because you don't know who they are. In other situations, you may think you have taken them into account through *liaisons* — people who represent the interests of the end users.

» **People who will maintain or support the final product:** People who will service your project's final products affect the continuing success of these products. Involving these people throughout your project gives them a chance to make your project's products easier to maintain and support. It also allows them to become familiar with the products and effectively build their maintenance into existing procedures.

Examining the beginning of a sample stakeholder register

Suppose you're asked to coordinate your organization's annual blood drive. Figure 2-1 illustrates some of the groups and people you may include in your project's stakeholder register as you prepare for your new project.

Category			
Level 1	Level 2	Level 3	Level 4
Internal	Upper Management	Executive Oversight Committee	
		VP, Sales and Marketing	
		VP, Operations	
		VP, Administration	
	Requester	VP, Sales and Marketing	
		Manager, Community Relations	
	Project Team	Project Manager	
		Team Members	Customer Service Rep
			Community Relations Rep
			Human Resources Rep
	Groups Normally Involved	Finance	
		Facilities	
		Legal	
		Human Resources	
	Groups Just for This Project	Project Manager and Team Members from last year's blood drive	
External	Clients/Customers	Donors	Prior
			New
		Hospital and medical centers receiving blood from the drive	
	Vendors, Contractors	Attending nurses, food-service provider, facility's landlord, local blood center	
	Regulatory Agencies	Local board of health	
	Professional Societies	American Medical Association	
		American Association of Blood Banks	
	Public	Local community	
		Local media	Local newspapers
			Local TV stations
			Local radio stations

© John Wiley & Sons, Inc.

FIGURE 2-1: The beginning of a sample stakeholder register for an annual blood drive.

Ensuring your stakeholder register is complete and up to date

Many different groups of people may influence the success of or have an interest in your project. Knowing who these people are allows you to plan to involve them at the appropriate times during your project. Therefore, identifying all project stakeholders as soon as possible and reflecting any changes in those stakeholders as soon as you find out about them are important steps to take as you manage your project.

REMEMBER

To ensure your stakeholder register is complete and up to date, consider the following guidelines:

- **Eventually identify each stakeholder by position description and name.** You may, for example, initially identify people from sales and marketing as stakeholders. Eventually, however, you want to specify the particular people from that group — such as *brand manager for XYZ product, Sharon Wilson* — and their contact information.
- **Speak with a wide range of people.** Check with people in different organizational units, from different disciplines, and with different tenures in the organization. Ask every person whether she can think of anyone else you should speak with. The more people you speak with, the less likely you are to overlook someone important.
- **Allow sufficient time to develop your stakeholder register.** Start to develop your register as soon as you become project manager. The longer you think about your project, the more potential stakeholders you can identify. Throughout the project, continue to check with people to identify additional stakeholders.
- **Include stakeholders who may play a role at any time during your project.** Your only job at this stage is to identify names so you don't forget them. At a later point, you can decide whether, when, and how to involve these people (see the later section "Determining Whether Stakeholders Are Drivers, Supporters, or Observers").
- **Include team members' functional managers.** Include the people to whom the project manager and team members directly report. Even though functional managers usually don't perform project tasks themselves, they can help ensure that the project manager and team members devote the time they originally promised to the project and that they have the resources necessary to perform their project assignments.
- **Include a person's name on the stakeholder register for every role she plays.** Suppose your boss plans to provide expert technical advice to your project team. Include your boss's name twice — once as your direct supervisor and once as the technical expert. If your boss is promoted but continues to serve as a technical advisor to your project, the separate listings remind you that a new person now occupies your direct supervisor's slot.
- **Continue to add and remove names from your stakeholder register throughout your project.** Your stakeholder register evolves as you understand more about your project and as your project changes. Plan to review your register at regular intervals throughout the project to identify names that should be added or deleted. Encourage people involved in your project to continually identify new stakeholders as they think of them.

» **When in doubt, write down a person's name.** Your goal is to avoid overlooking someone who may play an important part in your project. Identifying a potential audience member doesn't mean you have to involve that person; it simply means you have to consider her. Eliminating the name of someone who won't be involved is a lot easier than trying to add the name of someone who should be.

Using a stakeholder register template

A *stakeholder register template* is a predesigned stakeholder register that contains typical categories and stakeholders for a particular type of project. You may develop and maintain your own stakeholder register templates for tasks you perform, functional groups may develop and maintain stakeholder register templates for tasks they typically conduct, or your organization's project management office may develop and maintain templates for the entire organization.

Regardless of who maintains the template, it reflects people's cumulative experiences. As the organization continues to perform projects of this type, stakeholders that were overlooked in earlier efforts may be added and stakeholders that proved unnecessary removed. Using these templates can save you time and improve your accuracy.

Suppose you prepare the budget for your department each quarter. After doing a number of these budgets, you know most of the people who give you the necessary information, who draft and print the document, and who have to approve the final budget. Each time you finish another budget, you revise your stakeholder register template to include new information from that project. The next time you prepare your quarterly budget, you begin your stakeholder register with your template. You then add and subtract names as appropriate for that particular budget preparation.

REMEMBER

When using stakeholder register templates, keep the following guidelines in mind:

» **Develop templates for frequently performed tasks and for entire projects.** Stakeholder register templates for kicking off the annual blood drive or submitting a newly developed drug to the Food and Drug Administration are valuable. But so are templates for individual tasks that are part of these projects, such as awarding a competitive contract or printing a document. Many times, projects that appear totally new actually contain some tasks that you've done before. You can still reap the benefits of your prior experience by including the stakeholder register templates for these tasks in your overall project stakeholder register.

» **Focus on position descriptions rather than the names of prior stakeholders.** Identify a stakeholder as *accounts payable manager* rather than *Bill Miller.* People come and go, but functions endure. For each specific project, you can fill in the appropriate names.

» **Develop and modify your stakeholder register template from previous projects that actually worked, not from initial plans that looked good but lacked key information.** Often you develop a detailed stakeholder register at the start of your project but don't revise the register during the project or add stakeholders whom you overlooked in your initial planning. If you update your template with information from an initial list only, your template can't reflect the discoveries you made throughout the earlier project.

» **Encourage your team members to brainstorm possible stakeholders before you show them an existing stakeholder register template.** Encouraging people to identify stakeholders without guidance or restrictions increases the chances that they'll think of stakeholders who were overlooked on previous projects.

» **Use templates as starting points, not ending points.** Make clear to your team that the template isn't the final register. Every project differs in some ways from similar ones. If you don't critically examine the template, you may miss people who weren't involved in previous projects but whom you need to consider for this one.

» **Reflect your different project experiences in your stakeholder register templates.** The post-project evaluation is an excellent time to review, critique, and modify your stakeholder register for a particular project (see Chapter 4 in Book 2 for details on the post-project evaluation).

WARNING

Templates can save time and improve accuracy. However, starting with a template that's too polished can suggest you've already made up your mind about the contents of your final list, which may discourage people from freely sharing their thoughts about other potential stakeholders. In addition, their lack of involvement in the development of the project's audience list may lead to their lack of commitment to the project's success.

Determining Whether Stakeholders Are Drivers, Supporters, or Observers

After you identify every one of your stakeholders, you need to determine which group those people fall into: drivers, supporters, or observers. Then you can decide whether to involve them and, if so, how and when. The following sections help you identify when you need to involve drivers, supporters, and observers, and how to keep them involved.

Distinguishing the different groups

Separating stakeholders into the following three categories helps you decide what information to seek from and share with each group, as well as to clarify the project decisions in which to involve them.

- **Drivers:** People who have some say in defining the results of your project. You're performing your project for these people.
- **Supporters:** The people who help you perform your project. Supporters include individuals who authorize or provide the resources for your project as well as those who actually work on it.
- **Observers:** People who are neither drivers nor supporters but who are interested in the activities and results of your project. Observers have no say in your project, and they're not actively involved in it. However, your project may affect them at some point in the future.

Suppose an IT group has the job of modifying the layout and content of a monthly sales report for all sales representatives. The vice president of sales requested the project, and the *chief information officer* (CIO — the boss of the head of the IT group) approved it. As the project manager for this project, consider categorizing your project's stakeholders as follows:

- **Drivers:** The vice president of sales is a driver because he has specific reasons for revising the report. The CIO is a potential driver because she may hope to develop certain new capabilities for her group through this project. Individual sales representatives are all drivers for this project because they'll use the redesigned report to support their work.
- **Supporters:** The systems analyst who designs the revised report, the training specialist who trains the users, and the vice president of finance who authorizes the funds for changing the manual are all supporters.
- **Observers:** The head of the customer service department is a potential observer because he hopes your project will lead to an improved problem-tracking system this year.

Beware of supporters who try to act like drivers. In the preceding example, the analyst who finalizes the content and format of the report may try to include certain items that she thinks are helpful. However, only the real drivers should determine the specific data that go into the report. The analyst just determines whether including the desired data is possible and what doing so will cost.

REMEMBER

Keep in mind that the same person can be both a driver and a supporter. For example, the vice president of sales is a driver for the project to develop a revised monthly sales report, but he's also a supporter if he has to transfer funds from the sales department budget to pay for developing the report.

TIP

A *project champion* (also known as a *project sponsor*) is a person in a high position in the organization who strongly supports your project; advocates for your project in disputes, planning meetings, and review sessions; and takes whatever actions are necessary to help ensure the successful completion of your project. As soon as you start planning, find out whether your project has a champion. If it doesn't, try to recruit one. An effective project champion has the following characteristics:

- Sufficient power and authority to resolve conflicts over resources, schedules, and technical issues
- A keen interest in the results of your project
- A willingness to have his or her name cited as a strong supporter of your project

Deciding when to involve your stakeholders

Projects pass through the following four phases as they progress from an idea to completion (see Chapter 1 in Book 1 for detailed explanations of these phases):

- Starting the project
- Organizing and preparing
- Carrying out the work
- Closing the project

Plan to involve drivers, supporters, and observers in each phase of your project's life cycle. The following sections tell you how you can do so. See the later section "Assessing Your Stakeholders' Power and Interest" for information on what to consider when deciding how to involve different stakeholders.

Drivers

Keeping drivers involved in your project from start to finish is critical because they define what your project should produce, and they evaluate your project's success when it's finished. Their desires and your assessment of feasibility can influence whether you should pursue the project. Check out Table 2-1 to see how to involve drivers during the four phases of your project.

TABLE 2-1 Involving Drivers in the Different Project Phases

Phase	Involvement Level	How to Involve
Starting the project	Heavy	Identify and speak with as many drivers as possible. If you uncover additional drivers later, explore with them the issues that led to the project; ask them to identify and assess any special expectations they may have.
Organizing and preparing	Moderate to heavy	Consult with drivers to ensure your project plan addresses their needs and expectations. Have them formally approve the plan before you start the actual project work.
Carrying out the work	Moderate	As the project gets underway, introduce the drivers to the project team. Have the drivers talk about their needs and interests to reinforce the importance of the project and help team members form a more accurate picture of project goals. In addition, have the team members talk to the drivers to increase the drivers' confidence that the team members can successfully complete the project. While performing the project work, keep drivers apprised of project accomplishments and progress to sustain their ongoing interest and enthusiasm. Continually confirm that the results are meeting their needs.
Closing the project	Heavy	Have drivers assess the project's results and determine whether their needs and expectations were met. Identify their recommendations for improving performance on similar projects in the future.

Supporters

Involving supporters from start to finish is important since they perform and support the project work; supporters need to know about changing requirements so they can promptly identify and address problems. Keeping them actively involved also sustains their ongoing motivation and commitment to the project. Check out Table 2-2 to see how to involve supporters during your project's four phases.

Observers

After you choose the observers with whom you want to actively share project information, involve them minimally throughout the project because they neither tell you what should be done nor help you do it. Table 2-3 shows how you may keep observers involved.

TABLE 2-2 Involving Supporters in the Different Project Phases

Phase	Involvement Level	How to Involve
Starting the project	Moderate	Wherever possible, have key supporters assess the feasibility of meeting driver expectations. If you identify key supporters later in the project, have them confirm the feasibility of previously set expectations.
Organizing and preparing	Heavy	Supporters are the major contributors to the project plan. Because they facilitate or do all the work, have them determine necessary technical approaches, schedules, and resources. Also have them formally commit to all aspects of the plan.
Carrying out the work	Heavy	Familiarize all supporters with the planned work. Clarify how the supporters will work together to achieve the results. Have supporters decide how they'll communicate, resolve conflicts, and make decisions during the course of the project. Throughout the project, keep supporters informed of project progress, encourage them to identify performance problems they encounter or anticipate, and work with them to develop and implement solutions to these problems.
Closing the project	Heavy	Have supporters conclude their different tasks. Inform them of project accomplishments and recognize their roles in project achievements. Elicit their suggestions for handling similar projects more effectively in the future.

TABLE 2-3 Involving Observers in the Different Project Phases

Phase	Involvement Level	How to Involve
Starting the project	Minimal	Inform observers of your project's existence and its main goals.
Organizing and preparing	Minimal	Inform observers about the project's planned outcomes and time frames.
Carrying out the work	Minimal	Tell observers that the project has started and confirm the dates for planned milestones. Inform observers of key project achievements.
Closing the project	Minimal	When the project is done, inform observers about the project's products and results.

TIP

Because observers don't directly influence or affect your project, be sure to carefully manage the time and effort you spend sharing information with them. When deciding whom to involve and how to share information with them, consider the following:

- Their level of interest in your project
- The likelihood that your project will affect them at some point in the future
- The need to maintain a good working relationship with them

Using different methods to involve your stakeholders

Keeping drivers, supporters, and observers informed as you progress in your project is critical to the project's success. Choosing the right method for involving each stakeholder group can stimulate that group's continued interest and encourage its members to actively support your work. Consider the following approaches for keeping your project stakeholders involved throughout your project:

- **One-on-one meetings:** *One-on-one meetings* (formal or informal discussions with one or two other people about project issues) are particularly useful for interactively exploring and clarifying special issues of interest with a small number of people.
- **Group meetings:** These meetings are planned sessions for some or all team members or stakeholders. Smaller meetings are useful to brainstorm project issues, reinforce team member roles, and develop mutual trust and respect among team members. Larger meetings are useful to present information of general interest.
- **Informal written correspondence:** Informal written correspondence (notes, memos, letters, and emails) helps you document informal discussions and share important project information.
- **More formal information-sharing vehicles:** Information resources such as project newsletters or sites on the organization's intranet may be useful for sharing nonconfidential and noncontroversial information with larger groups of stakeholders.

» **Written approvals:** Written approvals (such as a technical approach to project work or formal agreements about a product, schedule, or resource commitment) serve as records of project decisions and achievements.

Making the most of your stakeholders' involvement

To maximize your stakeholders' involvement and contributions, follow these guidelines throughout your project:

» **Involve stakeholders early in the project planning if they have a role later on.** Give your stakeholders the option to participate in planning even if they don't perform until later in the project. Sometimes they can share information that'll make their tasks easier. At the least, they can reserve time to provide their services when you need them.

» **If you're concerned with the legality of involving a specific stakeholder, check with your legal department or contracts office.** Suppose you're planning to award a competitive contract to buy certain equipment. You want to know whether prospective bidders typically have this equipment on hand and how long it'll take to receive it after you award the contract. However, you're concerned that speaking to potential contractors in the planning phase may tip them off about the procurement and lead to charges of favoritism by unsuccessful bidders who didn't know about the procurement in advance.

  Instead of ignoring this important stakeholder, check with your contracts office or legal department to determine how you can get the information you want and still maintain the integrity of the bidding process.

» **Develop a communication plan with all key stakeholders to meet their information needs and interests as well as yours.** Determine the information they want and the information you believe they need. Also decide when to provide that information and in what format. Finally, clarify what you want from them and how and when they can provide it.

» **Always be sure you understand each stakeholder's *"what's in it for me"* (WIIFM).** Clarify why seeing your project succeed is in each stakeholder's interest. Throughout your project, keep reminding your stakeholders of the benefits they'll realize when your project's complete and the progress your project has made toward achieving those benefits.

Displaying Your Stakeholder Register

You're concerned with two issues when developing the format and content of your stakeholder register:

- Increasing your confidence that you identified all appropriate stakeholders
- Helping others suggest people not on the register who should be included and people on the register who possibly should not

Figure 2-2 shows a sample stakeholder register format you may use for your stakeholder register. The format includes three major categories of information:

- The hierarchical structure of the categories in which stakeholders are located
- The specific identifiers of each stakeholder (job title and name)
- The stakeholder's role with regard to the project (driver, supporter, or observer; see the earlier section "Determining Whether Stakeholders Are Drivers, Supporters, or Observers")

Note: You can add columns on the right for optional information, such as email, phone, and so on.

Category				Job Title (or Position)	Name (Last, First)	Role *(D, S, O)	...
Level 1	Level 2	Level 3	...				

Add additional columns as needed

* D = Driver S = Supporter O = Observer

© John Wiley & Sons, Inc.

FIGURE 2-2: A sample stakeholder register format.

Confirming Your Stakeholders' Authority

In project terms, *authority* refers to the overall right to make project decisions that others must follow, including the right to apply project resources, expend funds, or give approvals. Having opinions about how an aspect should be addressed is different from having the authority to decide how it will be addressed. Mistaking a person's level of authority can lead to frustration as well as wasted time and money.

REMEMBER

Confirm that the people you've identified as stakeholders have the authority to make the decisions they need to make to perform their tasks. If they don't have that authority, find out who does and how to bring those people into the process.

At the beginning of the carrying-out-the-work phase in your projects, take the following steps to define each stakeholder's authority:

1. **Clarify each stakeholder's tasks and decisions.**

   Define with each person his tasks and his role in those tasks. For example, will he just work on the task, or will he also approve the schedules, resource expenditures, and work approaches?

2. **Ask each stakeholder what his authority is regarding each decision and task.**

   Ask about individual tasks rather than all issues in a particular area. For example, a person can be more confident about his authority to approve supply purchases up to $5,000 than about his authority to approve all equipment purchases, no matter the type or amount.

   REMEMBER

   Clarify decisions that the stakeholder can make himself. For decisions needing someone else's approval, find out whose approval he needs. (Ask — never assume!)

3. **Ask each stakeholder how he knows what authority he has.**

   Does a written policy, procedure, or guideline confirm the authority? Did the person's boss tell him in conversation? Is the person just assuming? If the person has no specific confirming information, encourage him to get it.

4. **Check out each stakeholder's history of exercising authority.**

   Have you or other people worked with this person in the past? Has he been overruled on decisions that he said he was authorized to make? If so, ask him why he believes he won't be similarly overruled this time.

5. Verify whether anything has recently changed regarding each stakeholder's authority.

Do you have any reason to believe that this person's authority has changed? Is he new to his current group or position? Has he recently started working for a new boss? If any of these situations exists, encourage the person to find specific documentation to confirm his authority for his benefit as well as yours.

REMEMBER

Reconfirm the information in these steps when a particular stakeholder's decision-making assignments change. Suppose, for example, that you initially expect all individual purchases on your project to be at or under $2,500. Bill, the team representative from the finance group, assures you that he has the authority to approve such purchases for your project without checking with his boss. Midway through the project, you find that you have to purchase a piece of equipment for $5,000. Be sure to verify with Bill that he can personally authorize this larger expenditure. If he can't, find out whose approval you need and plan how to get it.

Assessing Your Stakeholders' Power and Interest

A stakeholder's potential impact on a project depends on the power she can exercise and the interest she has in exercising that power. Assessing the relative levels of each helps you decide with whom you should spend your time and effort to realize the greatest benefits.

Power is a person's ability to influence the actions of others. This ability can derive either from the direct authority the person has to require people to respond to her requests (*ascribed power;* refer to the preceding section for more about authority) or the ability she has to induce others to do what she asks because of the respect they have for her professionally or personally (*achieved power*). In either case, the more power a person has, the better able she is to marshal people and resources to support your project. Typically, drivers and supporters have higher levels of power over your project than observers do.

On the other hand, a person's *interest* in something is how much she cares or is curious about it or how much she pays attention to it. The more interested a person is in your project, the more likely she is to want to use her power to help the project succeed.

You can define a stakeholder's relative levels of power and interest related to your project as being either *high* or *low*. You then have four possible combinations for each stakeholder's relative levels of power and interest. The particular values of a stakeholder's power and interest ratings suggest the chances that the stakeholder may have a significant impact on your project and, therefore, the relative importance of keeping that stakeholder interested and involved in your project.

TIP

Most often, you base the assessments of a stakeholder's power over and interest in your project on the aggregated individual, subjective opinions of several parties: you, your team members, your project's other stakeholders, people who have worked with the stakeholder on other projects, subject matter experts, and/or the stakeholder himself or herself. If you assign a value of 1 to each individual rating of *high* and 0 to each individual rating of *low*, you'd rate a stakeholder's power or interest as *high* if the average of the individual assessments were 0.5 or greater and *low* if the average were below 0.5.

Figure 2-3 depicts a *Power-Interest Grid*, which represents these four possible power-interest combinations as distinct quadrants on a two-dimensional graph. As the project manager, you should spend a minimal amount of time and effort with stakeholders who have low levels of both power and interest (Quadrant I). Spend increasingly greater amounts of time and effort with stakeholders who have a low level of power and a high level of interest (Quadrant II) and a low level of interest and a high level of power (Quadrant III), respectively. You should spend the most time and effort keeping stakeholders with high degrees of both power and interest (Quadrant IV) informed and involved.

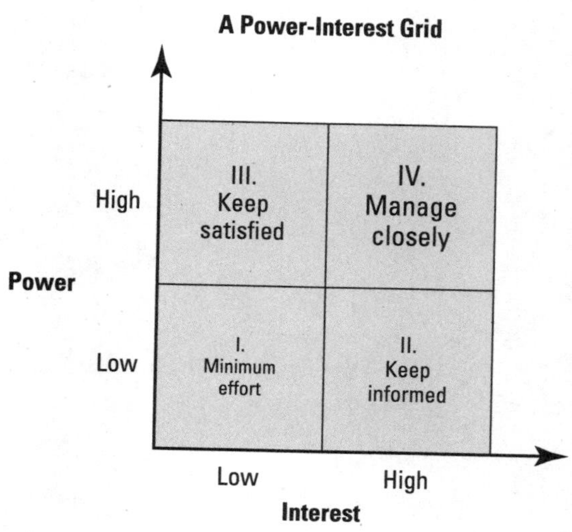

FIGURE 2-3: Involving stakeholders with different levels of power and interest in your project.

IN THIS CHAPTER

» Breaking your work into manageable pieces

» Creating a work breakdown structure

» Dealing with unknown circumstances

» Keeping project information in a WBS dictionary

Chapter 3
Developing Your Game Plan

The keys to successful project planning and performance are completeness and continuity. You want to identify all important information in your project plan and address every aspect of your plan when performing the project.

Describing in detail all the work required to complete your project helps you accomplish these tasks. Your description of project work provides the basis for scheduling, planning resources, defining roles and responsibilities, assigning work to team members, capturing key project performance data, and reporting on completed project work. This chapter helps you break down your project work into manageable pieces.

Divide and Conquer: Breaking Your Project into Manageable Chunks

Two major concerns at the start of a new project are remembering to plan for all important pieces of work and accurately estimating the time and resources required to perform that work. To address both issues, you can develop a logical framework to define all work that is necessary to complete the project.

Suppose you're asked to design and present a training program. You and a colleague work intensely for a couple of months developing the content and materials, arranging for the facilities, and inviting the participants. A week before the session, you ask your colleague whether he has made arrangements to print the training manuals. He says that he thought you were dealing with it, and you say that you thought he was dealing with it. Unfortunately, neither of you arranged to have the manuals printed because you each thought the other person was handling it. Now you have a training session in a week, and you don't have the time or money to print the needed training notebooks.

How can you avoid situations like this one in the future? By using a structured approach in the planning stage of your project to identify all required project work. The following sections explain how to accomplish this task by subdividing your project's intermediate and final products into finer levels of detail and specifying the work required to produce them.

Thinking in detail

REMEMBER

The most important guideline to remember when identifying and describing project work is this: Think in detail! People consistently underestimate the time and resources they need for their project work because they just don't recognize everything they have to do to complete it.

Suppose you have to prepare a report of your team's most recent meeting. Based on your past experience with preparing many similar reports, you quickly figure you'll need a few days to do this one. But how confident are you that this estimate is correct? Are you sure you've considered all the work that writing this particular report will entail? Will the differences between this report and others you've worked on mean more time and work for you? How can you tell?

The best way to determine how long and how much work a project will take to complete is to break down the required project work into its component deliverables, a process called *decomposition.* (A *deliverable* is an intermediate or final product, service, and/or result your project will produce. Project deliverables are often called *objectives.*)

The greater the detail in which you decompose a project, the less likely you are to overlook anything significant. For example, creating the report in the preceding example actually entails producing three separate deliverables: a draft, reviews of the draft, and the final version. Completing the final version of the report, in turn, entails producing two deliverables: the initial version and the edited version. By decomposing the project into the deliverables necessary to generate the final report, you're more likely to identify all the work you need to do to complete the project.

TIP

Follow these two guidelines when decomposing your project:

- **Allow no gaps.** Identify all components of the deliverable you're decomposing. In the example of creating a meeting report, if you have *allowed no gaps,* you'll have the desired final product in hand after you've produced the draft, the reviews of the draft, and the final version. However, if you feel that you'll have to do additional work to transform these three subproducts into a final product, you need to define the subproduct(s) that this additional work will produce.
- **Allow no overlaps.** Don't include the same subproduct in your decomposition of two or more different deliverables. For example, don't include completed reviews of the draft by your boss and the vice president of your department as parts of the draft (the first deliverable) if you've already included them with all other reviews under reviews of the draft (the second deliverable).

Using these guidelines as you specify the parts and subparts of your project decreases the chance that you'll overlook something significant, which, in turn, helps you develop more accurate estimates of the time and resources needed to do the project.

Identifying necessary project work with a work breakdown structure

Thinking in detail is critical when you're planning your project, but you also need to consider the big picture. If you fail to identify a major part of your project's work, you won't have the chance to detail it! Thus, you must be both comprehensive and specific.

Consider the example of someone putting together a 5,000-piece jigsaw puzzle of the United States. He can count the pieces before assembling the puzzle to determine whether any pieces are missing. However, knowing that he has only 4,999 pieces can't help him determine which piece is missing. He needs to divide the 5,000 pieces into smaller groups that he can examine and understand. Say that he divides the puzzle of the United States into 50 separate 100-piece puzzles, one for each of the 50 states. Because he knows the United States has 50 states, he's confident that each piece of the puzzle should be in one and only one box.

Suppose he takes it a step further and divides each state into four quadrants, each comprised of 25 pieces. Again, he can count the pieces in each box to see whether any are missing. However, determining which one of 25 pieces is missing from the northeast sector of New Jersey is easier than figuring out which piece is missing from the 5,000-piece puzzle of the entire United States.

Figure 3-1 shows how you can depict necessary project work in a *work breakdown structure* (WBS), a deliverable-oriented decomposition of the work required to produce the necessary project products and achieve the project's objectives. The different levels in a WBS have had many different names. The top element is typically called a *project* and the lowest level of detail is typically called a *work package*. However, the levels in between have been called *phases, subprojects, work assignments, tasks, subtasks,* and *deliverables.* In this book, the top-level box (the Level 1 component) is a *project,* the lowest level of detail is a *work package,* and the elements in between are *Level 2 components, Level 3 components,* and so forth. A work package is comprised of activities that must be performed to produce the deliverable it represents.

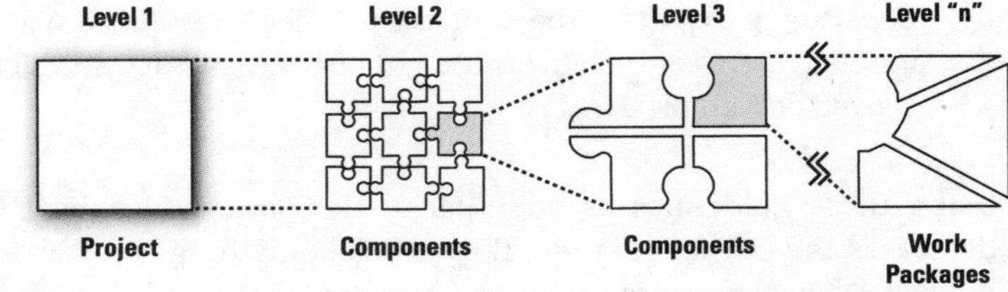

FIGURE 3-1: Developing a work breakdown structure.

© John Wiley & Sons, Inc.

Specifically, Figure 3-1 shows that you can subdivide the entire project, represented as a Level 1 component, into Level 2 components and then subdivide some or all Level 2 components into Level 3 components. You can continue to subdivide all the components you create in the same manner until you reach a point at which you think the components you defined are sufficiently detailed for planning and management purposes. These Level "n" components, where *n* is the number of the lowest-level component in a particular WBS branch, are called *work packages.*

Suppose you're responsible for a project titled *Training Program Creation and Presentation* that entails creating and presenting a new training program for your organization. To get started, you develop a WBS for this project as follows:

1. **Determine the major deliverables or products to be produced.**

   Ask yourself, "What major intermediate or final products or deliverables must be produced to achieve the project's objectives?"

   You may identify the following items:

   - Training program needs statement
   - Training program design
   - Participant notebooks

- Trained instructor
- Program testing
- Training program presentation

REMEMBER

Creating the WBS with deliverables rather than activities is important because

- It reinforces that in almost all instances, you achieve project success by producing desired outcomes, not by performing certain activities.
- It creates a link between the scope statement (a written confirmation of the results your project will produce and the constraints and assumptions under which you will work) and the WBS, which helps ensure that you identify and perform all required work (and only work that is, in fact, required).

2. **Divide each major deliverable from Step 1 into its component deliverables.**

   If you start with *Training program needs statement,* ask, "What intermediate deliverables must I have so I can create the needs statement?"

   You may determine that you require the following:

   - Interviews of potential participants
   - A review of materials discussing the needs for the program
   - A report summarizing the needs this program will address

3. **Divide each intermediate deliverable from Step 2 into its component parts.**

   If you start with *Interviews of potential participants,* ask, "What deliverables must I have to complete these interviews?"

   You may decide that you have to produce the following deliverables:

   - Selected interviewees
   - Interview questionnaire
   - Interview schedule
   - Completed interviews
   - Report of interview findings

   But why stop here? You can break each of these five items into its component parts and then break those pieces into even more parts. How far should you go? The following sections can help you answer that question.

Asking four key questions

Determining how much detail you need isn't a trivial task. You want to describe your work in sufficient detail to support accurate planning and meaningful tracking. But the benefits of this detail must justify the additional time you spend developing and maintaining your plans and reporting your progress.

REMEMBER

Asking the following four questions about each WBS component can help you decide whether you've defined it in enough detail:

- Do you require two or more intermediate deliverables to produce this deliverable?
- Can you accurately estimate the resources you need to perform the work to produce this deliverable? (Resources include personnel, equipment, raw materials, money, facilities, information, and so on.)
- Can you accurately estimate how long producing this deliverable will take?
- If you have to assign the work to produce this deliverable to someone else, are you confident that person will understand exactly what to do?

If you answer yes to the first question or no to any one of the other three, break down the deliverable into the components necessary to produce it. Each WBS component that you decide is sufficiently detailed is called a *work package.*

Your answers to these questions depend on how familiar you are with the work required to produce the WBS component, how critical the component is to the success of your project, what happens if something goes wrong, whom you may assign to be responsible for producing the component, how well you know that person, and so on. In other words, the correct level of detail for your WBS depends on your judgment.

TIP

If you're a little uneasy about answering these four questions, try this even simpler test: Subdivide your WBS component into additional deliverables if you think either of the following situations applies:

- The component will take longer than two calendar weeks to complete.
- The component will require more than 80 person-hours to complete.

Keep in mind that these estimates are just guidelines. For example, if you estimate that it'll take two weeks and two days to prepare a report, you've probably provided sufficient detail. But if you think it'll take two to three months to finalize requirements for your new product, you need to break the deliverable *finalized requirements* into more detail because

» Experience has shown that there can be so many different interpretations of what is supposed to occur during these two to three months that you can't be sure your time and resource estimates are correct, and you can't confidently assign the task to someone to perform.
» You don't want to wait two or three months to confirm that work is on schedule by verifying that a desired product has been produced on time.

Making assumptions to clarify planned work

Sometimes you want to break down a particular WBS component further, but certain unknowns stop you from doing so. How do you resolve this dilemma? You can make assumptions regarding the unknowns or, better yet, ask a subject matter expert (SME) for advice.

Regarding the *Training Program Creation and Presentation* project example that is introduced earlier in this chapter — suppose you decide that the *Completed interviews* deliverable from Step 3 needs more detail so you can estimate its required time and resources. However, you don't know how to break it down further because you don't know how many people you'll interview or how many separate sets of interviews you'll conduct. If you assume you'll interview five groups of seven people each, you can then develop specific plans for arranging and conducting each of these sessions. In most situations, it's best to consider a guess in the middle of the possible range. To determine how sensitive your results are to the different values, you may want to analyze for several different assumptions.

Be sure to write down your assumption so you remember to change your plan if you conduct more or less than five interview sessions.

Focusing on results when naming deliverables

Whenever possible, name a deliverable based on the result you need to achieve rather than the activity you need to perform to achieve that result. For example, you might title a deliverable that signifies completion of a needs assessment survey you have to conduct in one of two ways:

» Survey completed
» Needs assessment finished

Both options state that something has been finished. However, although the deliverable *Survey completed* indicates that a survey was performed, it doesn't explain what type of information the survey was supposed to obtain or whether it successfully obtained that information. On the other hand, *Needs assessment finished* confirms that the information from the completed survey successfully fulfilled the purpose for which it was intended.

Using action verbs to title activities

If you want to provide additional insight into the contents of a work package, you can define the activities that must be performed in order to produce it. An *activity* is defined as the work performed to produce a deliverable. Use action verbs in the titles of activities that comprise a work package to clarify the nature of the work the activities entail. Action verbs can improve your time and resource estimates, your work assignments to team members, and your tracking and reporting because they provide a clear picture of the work included in the activities and, thereby, the work packages of which they are a part.

Consider the assignment to prepare a report after a team meeting. Suppose you choose *Draft report* to be one of its work packages. If you don't break down *Draft report* further, you haven't indicated clearly whether it includes any or all of the following actions:

- Collecting information for the draft
- Determining length and format expectations and restrictions
- Writing the draft
- Reviewing the draft yourself before officially circulating it to others

But if you simply break down the work package into two components that are titled "Design the draft report" and "Write the draft report," your scope of work is instantly clearer. A few well-chosen words at this level go a long way.

Developing a WBS for large and small projects

You need to develop a WBS for very large projects, very small projects, and everything in between. Building a skyscraper, designing a new airplane, researching and developing a new drug, and revamping your organization's information systems all need a WBS. So, too, do writing a report, scheduling and conducting a meeting, coordinating your organization's annual blood drive, and moving into your new office. The size of the WBS may vary immensely depending on the project, but the hierarchical scheme used to develop each one is the same.

REMEMBER

Occasionally, your detailed WBS may seem to make your project more complex than it really is. Seeing 100 tasks (not to mention 10,000) on paper can be a little unnerving! However, the WBS doesn't create a project's complexity; it just displays that complexity. In fact, by clearly portraying all aspects of your project work, the WBS actually simplifies your project and increases the odds of the project being completed on time.

Check out the nearby sidebar "Conducting a survey: Using the work breakdown structure" for an illustration of how a WBS helps you develop a more accurate estimate of the time you need to complete your work.

CONDUCTING A SURVEY: USING THE WORK BREAKDOWN STRUCTURE

Suppose your boss asks you to estimate how long it'll take to survey people regarding the characteristics they would like to see in a new product your company may develop. Based on your experience with doing similar types of assessments in the past, you figure you'll need to contact people at the company headquarters, at two regional activity centers, and from a sampling of current clients. You tell your boss the project will take you between one and six months to complete.

Have you ever noticed that bosses aren't happy when you respond to their question of "How long will it take?" with an answer of "Between one and six months"? You figure that finishing any time before six months meets your promise, but your boss expects you to be done in one month, given some (okay, a lot of) hard work. The truth is, though, you don't have a clue how long the survey will take because you have no idea how much work you have to do to complete it.

Developing a WBS encourages you to define exactly what you have to do and thereby improves your estimate of how long each step will take. In this example, you decide to conduct three different surveys: personal interviews with people at your headquarters, phone conference calls with people at the two regional activity centers, and a mail survey of a sample of your company's clients. Realizing you need to describe each survey in more detail, you begin by considering the mail survey and decide it includes five deliverables:

- **A sample of clients to survey:** You figure you need one week to select your sample of clients if the sales department has a current record of all company clients. You check with that department, and, thankfully, it does.
- **A survey questionnaire:** As far as this deliverable is concerned, you get lucky. A colleague tells you she thinks that the company conducted a similar survey of a different target population a year ago and that extra questionnaires from that effort may still be around. You find that a local warehouse has 1,000 of these questionnaires and — yes! — they're perfect for your survey. How much time do you need to allow for designing and printing the questionnaires? Zero!

(continued)

Developing Your Game Plan

(continued)

- **Survey responses:** You determine that you need a response rate of at least 70 percent for the results to be valid. You consult with people who've done these types of surveys before and find out that you have to use the following three-phased approach to have an acceptable chance of achieving a minimum response rate of 70 percent:

  1. Initial mailing out and receiving of questionnaires (estimated time = four weeks)
  2. Second mailing out and receiving of questionnaires to non-respondents (estimated time = four weeks)
  3. Phone follow-ups with people who still haven't responded, encouraging them to complete and return their surveys (estimated time = two weeks)

- **Data analyses:** You figure you'll need about two weeks to enter and analyze the data you expect to receive.
- **A final report:** You estimate you'll need two weeks to prepare the final report.

Now, instead of one to six months, you can estimate the time you need to complete your mail survey to be 15 weeks. Because you've clarified the work you have to do and how you'll do it, you're more confident you can reach your goal, and you've increased the chances that you will!

Note: To develop the most accurate estimates of your project's duration, in addition to the nature of the work you do, you need to consider the types and amounts of resources you require, together with their capacities and availabilities (see Chapter 1 in Book 2 for more on how to estimate durations). However, this example illustrates that using just a WBS to refine the definition of your project's work components significantly improves your estimates.

Understanding a project's deliverable/activity hierarchy

Figure 3-2 shows a portion of the *deliverable/activity hierarchy* for the project of surveying people to determine what characteristics a new product your organization may develop should have (refer to the nearby sidebar "Conducting a survey: Using the work breakdown structure" for details on this example). As illustrated in the figure, three types of components make up a project's deliverable/activity hierarchy:

» **Deliverables:** Intermediate or final products created during the performance of the project

» **Work packages:** Deliverables at the lowest point in each branch of the hierarchy that can be further subdivided into activities

» **Activities:** Work that's performed to produce a deliverable

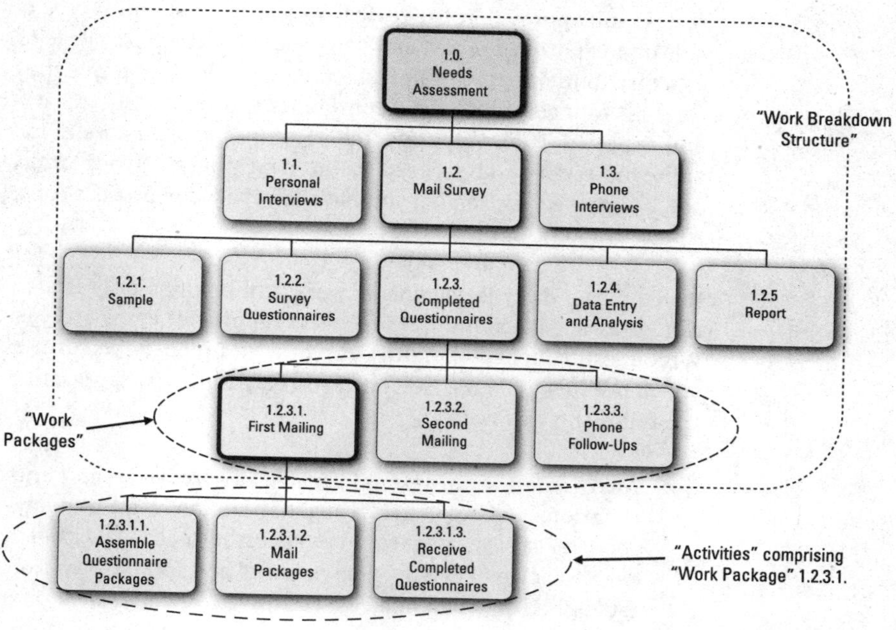

FIGURE 3-2: The hierarchy of deliverables and activities for surveying people to determine the characteristics of a new product your organization may develop.

© John Wiley & Sons, Inc.

The WBS is the portion of the hierarchy that contains the deliverables (from the topmost level down to and including all the work packages) that will be produced during the project. The activities that comprise the work packages are recorded in a comprehensive activity list. While not considered to be part of the WBS, each activity is a component of a work package, so you need to identify it as such. (For convenience, you should include activities in the WBS dictionary under the work package to which they relate; see the later section "Documenting What You Need to Know about Your Planned Project Work" for details on the WBS dictionary.)

Dealing with special situations

With a little thought, you can break most WBS elements into components. However, in some situations, like the ones that are explained in the following sections, you have to get creative.

Representing conditionally repeating work

Suppose your project contains a deliverable (such as an approved report) that requires an unknown number of repetitive cycles (such as reviewing and revising the latest version of the draft report) to produce, each of which generates at least one intermediate deliverable. In reality, you write the report and submit it for review and approval. If the reviewers approve the report, you obtain your deliverable of an approved report and you proceed to the next phase of your project (such as a distributed report). But if the reviewers don't approve the report, you have to revise it to incorporate their comments and then resubmit it for a second review and approval. If they approve the second draft, you obtain your deliverable of an approved report and proceed to the next phase of your project. But if they still don't approve your report, you have to repeat the process (or try to catch them in a better mood).

Revising the draft is *conditional work*; it'll be done only if a certain condition (in this case, not receiving the reviewers' approval) comes to pass. Unfortunately, a WBS doesn't include conditional work; you plan to perform every piece of work you detail in your WBS. However, you can indirectly represent conditional work in the following two ways:

- **You can define a single deliverable as *Approved report* and assign it a duration.** In effect, you're saying that you can create as many *Reviewed but not approved versions of the report* as necessary (each of which is an intermediate deliverable) to obtain the final reviewed and approved version within the established time period.
- **You can assume that you'll need a certain number of revisions and include the intermediate deliverable created after each one (a different *Reviewed but not approved version of the report*) in your WBS.** This approach allows more meaningful tracking.

REMEMBER

Whichever approach you choose, be sure to document it in your project plan.

Assuming that your project needs three reviews and two revisions doesn't guarantee that your draft will be good to go only after the third review. If your draft is approved after the first review, congratulations! You can move on to the next piece of work immediately (that is, you don't perform two revisions just because the plan assumed you would have to!).

However, if you still haven't received approval after the third review, you continue to revise it and submit it for further review until you do get the seal of approval you need. Of course, then you have to reexamine your plan to determine the impact of the additional reviews and revisions on the schedule and budget of future project activities.

REMEMBER

A plan isn't a guarantee of the future; it's your statement of what you'll work to achieve. If you're unable to accomplish any part of your plan, you must revise it accordingly (and promptly).

Handling work with no obvious break points

Sometimes you can't see how to break a piece of work into two-week intervals. Other times that amount of detail just doesn't seem necessary. Even in these situations, however, you want to divide the work into smaller chunks to remind yourself to periodically verify that your current schedule and resource estimates are still valid.

In these instances, arbitrarily define intermediate milestones to occur every two weeks that are defined as "progress confirmed as being on schedule" or "expenditures confirmed as being on budget." Here's an illustration of why it's important to have frequent milestones to support project tracking and how to deal with WBS components that have no obvious break points.

Soon after a young engineer joined his organization, he was asked to design and build a piece of equipment for a client. He submitted a purchase request to his procurement department for the raw materials he needed and was told that, if they didn't arrive by the promised delivery date in six months, he should notify the procurement specialist he was working with so she could investigate the situation. He was uneasy about waiting six months without checking periodically to see whether everything was still on schedule, but being young, inexperienced, and new to the organization, he wasn't comfortable trying to fight this established procedure. So he waited six months.

When he didn't receive his raw materials by the promised delivery date, he notified the procurement specialist, who, in turn, checked with the vendor. Apparently, there had been a major fire in the vendor's facilities five months earlier, and production had just resumed the previous week. The vendor estimated his materials would be shipped in about five months!

The engineer could've divided the waiting time into one-month intervals and called the vendor at the end of each month to see whether anything had occurred that changed the projected delivery date. Although checking periodically wouldn't have prevented the fire, the engineer would've known about it five months sooner and could've made other plans immediately.

Planning a long-term project

A long-term project presents an entirely different challenge. Often the work you perform a year or more in the future depends on the results of the work you do between now and then. Even if you can accurately predict the work you'll perform later, the further into the future you plan, the more likely it is that something will change and require you to modify your plans.

When developing a WBS for a long-term project, use a *rolling-wave approach*, in which you continually refine your plans throughout the life of your project as you discover more about the project and its environment. This approach acknowledges that uncertainties may limit your plan's initial detail and accuracy, and it encourages you to reflect more-accurate information in your plans as soon as you discover it. Apply the rolling-wave approach to your long-term project by taking the following steps:

1. **Break down the first three months' work into components that take two weeks or less to complete.**
2. **Plan the remainder of the project in less detail, perhaps describing the work in packages you estimate to take between one and two months to complete.**
3. **Revise your initial plan at the end of the first three months to detail your work for the next three months in components that take two weeks or less to complete.**
4. **Modify any future work as necessary, based on the results of your first three months' work.**
5. **Continue revising your plan in this way throughout the project.**

REMEMBER

No matter how carefully you plan, something unanticipated can always occur. The sooner you find out about such an occurrence, the more time you have to minimize any negative impact on your project.

Issuing a contract for services you will receive

Generally speaking, you use a WBS that you include in a contract for services to be provided to you by another person or organization differently from the way you use one to guide project work that you or your organization performs itself. When you perform the project yourself, the WBS provides the basis for developing detailed project schedules, estimating personnel and other resource requirements, detailing the project roles and responsibilities of project team members, and assessing all aspects of the ongoing work. However, when you manage a contract with an external organization that's performing the project for you, you use the WBS to

- Support responsive progress assessment to help ensure that the overall project is on track to finish on time and within budget.

» Provide the contractor with a framework for tracking and reporting periodic assessments of project schedule achievement and resource expenditures.

» Confirm that product, schedule, and resource performance is sufficient to justify the making of scheduled progress payments.

In addition, you don't want the WBS to unduly restrict the contractor's ability to use his experience, skills, and professional judgment to achieve the results detailed in the contract. Typically, developing the WBS to two or three levels of detail is sufficient to meet the preceding needs without creating unnecessary restrictions.

Creating and Displaying Your Work Breakdown Structure

You can use several schemes to develop and display your project's WBS; each one can be effective under different circumstances. This section looks at a few of the most common schemes and provides some examples and advice on how and when to apply them.

Considering different schemes to create your WBS hierarchy

The following five schemes (and their examples) can help you subdivide project work into WBS components:

» **Project phases:** Initiation, design, or construction

» **Product components:** Floor plan, training manuals, or screen design

» **Functions:** Design, launch, review, or test

» **Geographical areas:** Region 1 or the northwest

» **Organizational units:** Marketing, operations, or facilities

Project phases, product components, and functions are the most often used.

When you choose a scheme to organize the subelements of a WBS component, continue to use that same scheme for all the subelements under that component to prevent possible overlap in categories. For example, consider that you want to develop finer detail for the WBS component titled *Report*. You may choose to break out the detail according to function, such as *Draft report*, *Reviews of draft report*, and *Final report*. Or you may choose to break it out by product component, such as *Section 1*, *Section 2*, and *Section 3*.

WARNING

Don't define a WBS component's subelements by using some items from two different schemes. For instance, for the component *Report*, don't use the subelements *Section 1*, *Section 2*, *Reviews of draft report*, and *Final report*. Combining schemes in this way increases the chances of either including work twice or overlooking it completely. For example, the work to prepare the final version of Section 2 could be included in either of two subelements: *Section 2* or *Final report*.

TIP

Consider the following questions when choosing a scheme:

- **What higher-level milestones will be most meaningful when reporting progress?** For example, is it more helpful to report that *Section 1* is completed or that the entire *Draft report* is done?
- **How will you assign responsibility?** For example, is one person responsible for the draft, reviews, and final report of Section 1, or is one person responsible for the drafts of Sections 1, 2, and 3?
- **How will you and your team members actually do the work?** For example, is the drafting, reviewing, and finalizing of Section 1 separate from the same activities for Section 2, or are all chapters drafted together, reviewed together, and finalized together?

Using one of two approaches to develop your WBS

How you develop your WBS depends on how familiar you and your team are with your project, whether similar projects have been successfully performed in the past, and how many new methods and approaches you'll use. Choose one of the following two approaches for developing your WBS based on your project's characteristics:

- **Top-down:** Start at the top level in the hierarchy and systematically break WBS elements into their component parts.

  This approach is useful when you have a good idea of the project work involved before the actual work begins. The top-down approach ensures that you thoroughly consider each category at each level, and it reduces the chances that you overlook work in any of your categories.

» **Brainstorming (also called bottom-up):** Generate all possible work and deliverables for this project and then group them into categories.

Brainstorming is helpful when you don't have a clear sense of a project's required work at the outset. This approach encourages you to generate any and all possible pieces of work that may have to be done, without worrying about how to organize them in the final WBS. After you decide that a proposed piece of work is a necessary part of the project, you can identify any related work that is also required.

TIP

Whichever approach you decide to use, consider using stick-on notes to support your WBS development. As you identify pieces of work, write them on the notes and put them on the wall. Add, remove, and regroup the notes as you continue to think through your work. This approach encourages open sharing of ideas and helps all people appreciate — in detail — the nature of the work that needs to be done.

The top-down approach

Use the following top-down approach for projects that you or others are familiar with:

1. **Specify all Level 2 components for the entire project.**
2. **Determine all necessary Level 3 components for each Level 2 component.**
3. **Specify the Level 4 components for each Level 3 component as necessary.**
4. **Continue in this way until you've completely detailed all project intermediate and final deliverables.**

   The lowest-level components in each WBS chain are your project's work packages.

The brainstorming approach

Use the following brainstorming approach for projects involving untested methods or for projects you and your team members aren't familiar with:

1. **Identify all the intermediate and final deliverables that you think your project will produce.**

   Don't worry about overlap or level of detail.

   Don't discuss wording or other details of the work items.

   Don't make any judgments about the appropriateness of the work.

2. **Group these items into a few major categories with common characteristics and eliminate any deliverables that aren't required.**

   These groups are your Level 2 categories.

3. **Divide the deliverables under each Level 2 category into groups with common characteristics.**

   These groups are your Level 3 categories.

4. **Use the top-down method described in the preceding section to identify any additional deliverables that you overlooked in the categories you created.**

5. **Continue in this manner until you've completely described all project deliverables and work components.**

   The lowest-level components in each WBS chain are your project's work packages.

Categorizing your project's work

Although you eventually want to use only one WBS for your project, early in the development of your WBS, you can look at two or more different hierarchical schemes. Considering your project from two or more perspectives helps you identify work you may have overlooked.

Suppose a local community wants to open a halfway house for substance abusers. Figures 3-3 and 3-4 depict two different schemes to categorize the work for this community-based treatment facility. The first scheme classifies the work by product component, and the second classifies the work by function:

- Figure 3-3 defines the following components as Level 2 categories: staff, facility, residents (people who'll be living at the facility and receiving services), and community training.
- Figure 3-4 defines the following functions as Level 2 categories: planning, recruiting, buying, and training.

Both WBSs contain the same lowest-level components or work packages.

When you think about your project in terms of major functions (rather than final product components), you realize that you forgot the following work:

- Planning for staff recruiting
- Buying staff supplies
- Planning for your community training

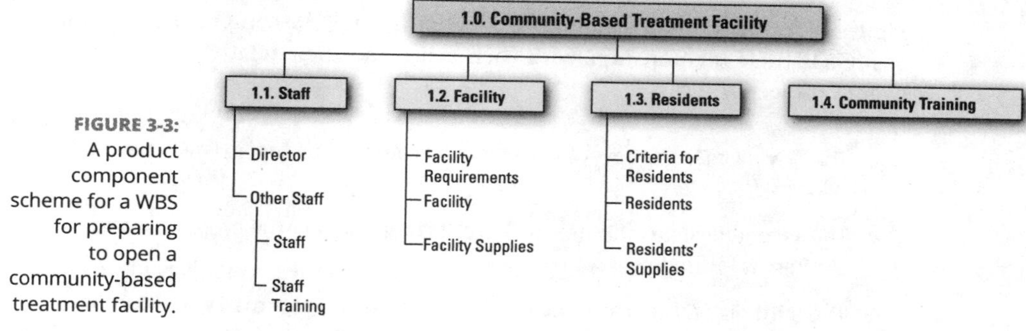

FIGURE 3-3: A product component scheme for a WBS for preparing to open a community-based treatment facility.

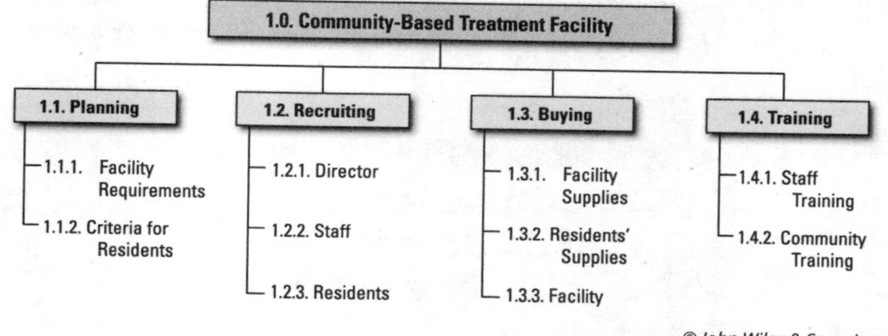

FIGURE 3-4: A functional scheme for a WBS for preparing to open a community-based treatment facility.

After you identify the work components you overlooked, you can include them in either of the two WBSs.

WARNING

Be sure you choose only one WBS before you leave your project's planning phase. Nothing confuses people faster than trying to use two or more different WBSs to describe the same project.

Labeling your WBS entries

As the size of a project grows, its WBS becomes increasingly complex. Losing sight of how a particular piece of work relates to other parts of the project is easy to do. Unfortunately, this problem can lead to poor coordination between related work efforts and a lack of urgency on the part of people who must perform the work.

Figure 3-5 illustrates a scheme for labeling your WBS components so you can easily see their relationships with each other and their relative positions in the overall project WBS:

- The first digit *(1)*, the Level 1 identifier, indicates the project in which the item is located.
- The second digit *(5)* indicates the Level 2 component of the project in which the item is located.
- The third digit *(7)* indicates the Level 3 component under the Level 2 component in which the item is located.
- The fourth and last digit *(3)* is a unique identifier assigned to distinguish this item from the other Level 4 components under the Level 3 component *1.5.7.* If *1.5.7.3. Materials Ordered* isn't subdivided further, it's a work package.

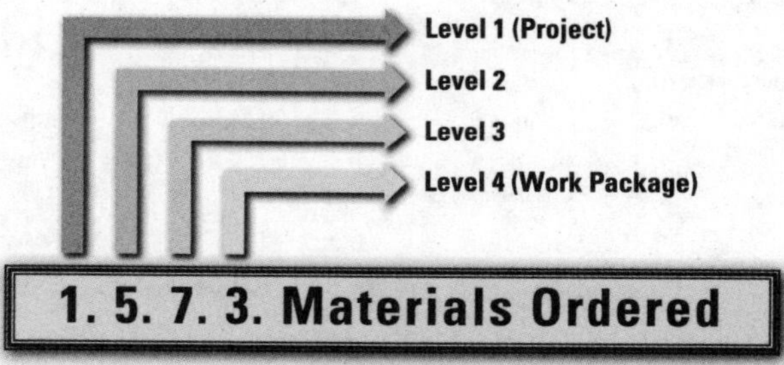

FIGURE 3-5: A useful scheme for identifying your WBS components.

© John Wiley & Sons, Inc.

TIP

When you're ready to label the activities that fall under a given work package, use a combination of the WBS code of the work package and a unique code that specifically refers to each activity. For example, suppose an activity under the work package 1.5.7.3. is *Prepare list of items to order.* You may give this activity the identifier code depicted in Figure 3-6. In this instance, the first four digits of the activity code are the WBS code for the work package of which this activity is a part. The fifth digit distinguishes this activity from the others that comprise work package 1.5.7.3.

Displaying your WBS in different formats

You can display your WBS in several different formats. This section looks at three of the most common ones.

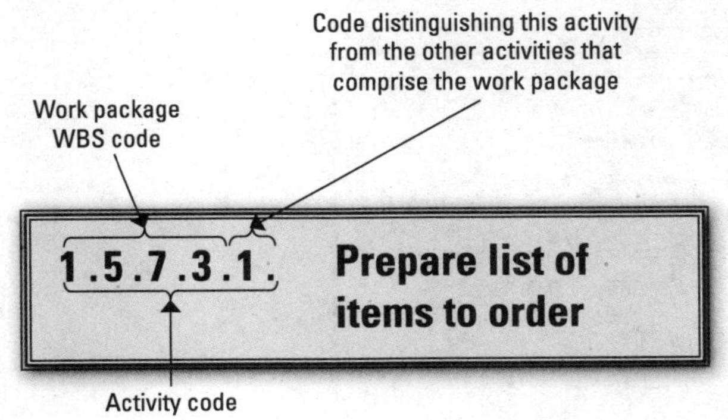

FIGURE 3-6: The components of an activity code.

© John Wiley & Sons, Inc.

The organization-chart format

Figure 3-7 shows a WBS in the *organization-chart format* (also referred to as a *hierarchy diagram* or *graphical view*). This format effectively portrays an overview of your project and the hierarchical relationships of different WBS components at the highest levels. However, because this format generally requires a lot of space, it's less effective for displaying large WBSs.

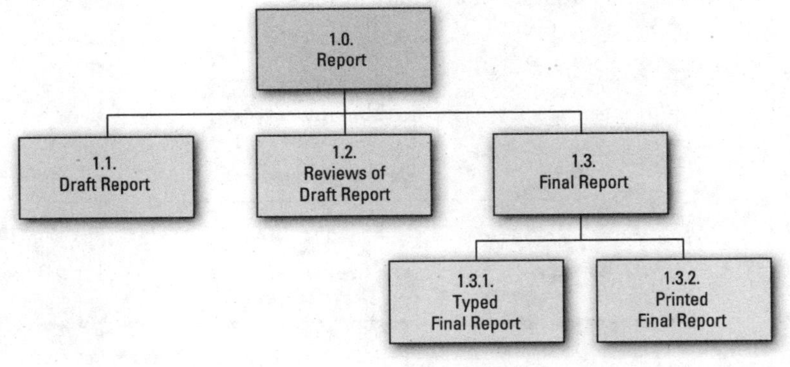

FIGURE 3-7: Drawing your WBS in the organization-chart format.

© John Wiley & Sons, Inc.

The indented-outline format

The *indented-outline format* in Figure 3-8 is another way to display your WBS. This format allows you to read and understand a complex WBS with many components. However, you can easily get lost in the details of a large project with this format and forget how the pieces all fit together.

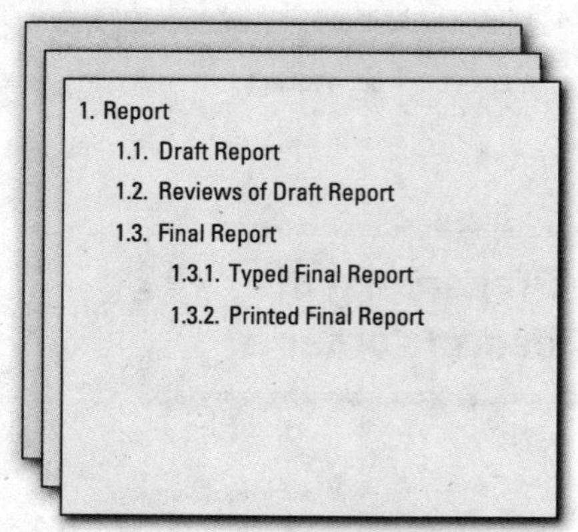

FIGURE 3-8: Drawing your WBS in the indented-outline format.

© John Wiley & Sons, Inc.

TIP

Both the organization-chart format and the indented-outline format can be helpful for displaying the WBS for a small project. For a large project, however, consider using a combination of the organization-chart and the indented-outline formats to explain your WBS. You can display the Level 1 and Level 2 components in the organization-chart format and portray the detailed breakout for each Level 2 component in the indented-outline format. Figure 3-9 contains an example of a combined organization-chart format.

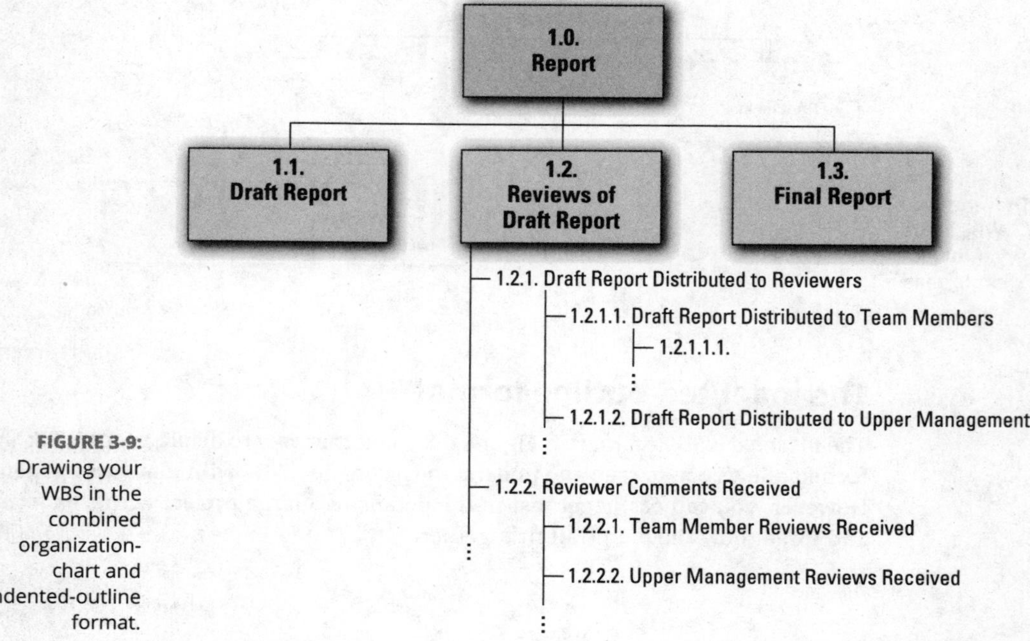

FIGURE 3-9: Drawing your WBS in the combined organization-chart and indented-outline format.

© John Wiley & Sons, Inc.

The bubble-chart format

The *bubble-chart format* in Figure 3-10 is particularly effective for displaying the results of the brainstorming approach to develop your WBS for both small and large projects (see the earlier section "The brainstorming approach"). You interpret the bubble-chart format as follows:

- The bubble in the center represents your entire project (in this case, *Report*).
- Lines from the center bubble lead to Level 2 breakouts (in this case, *Draft report, Reviews of draft,* and *Final report*).
- Lines from each Level 2 component lead to Level 3 components related to the Level 2 component. (In this case, the Level 2 component *Final report* consists of the two Level 3 components *Typed final report* and *Printed final report.*)

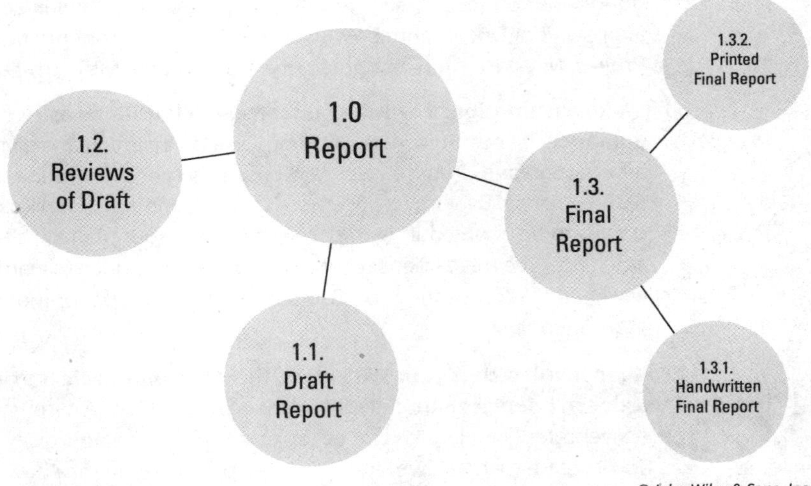

FIGURE 3-10: Drawing your WBS in the bubble-chart format.

The free-form nature of the bubble-chart format allows you to easily record thoughts generated during a brainstorming session. You can also easily rearrange components as you proceed with your analysis.

The bubble-chart format isn't effective for displaying your WBS to audiences who aren't familiar with your project. Use this format to develop your WBS with your team, but convert it into an organization-chart or indented-outline format when you present it to people outside your team.

Improving the quality of your WBS

You increase the chances for project success when your WBS is accurate and complete *and* when people who will be performing the work understand and agree with it. The following guidelines suggest some ways to improve your WBS's accuracy and acceptance:

- **Involve the people who'll be doing the work.** When possible, involve them during the initial development of the WBS. If they join the project after the initial planning, have them review and critique the WBS before they begin work.
- **Review and include information from WBSs from similar projects.** Review plans and consult people who've worked on projects similar to yours that were successful. Incorporate your findings into your WBS.
- **Keep your WBS current.** When you add, delete, or change WBS elements during your project, be sure to reflect these changes in your WBS. (See the later section "Documenting What You Need to Know about Your Planned Project Work" for more about sharing the updated WBS with the team.)
- **Make assumptions regarding uncertain activities or ask an SME for guidance.** If you're not sure whether you'll do a particular activity, make an assumption and prepare your WBS based on that assumption or based on SME guidance. Be sure to document that assumption. If your assumption proves to be wrong during the project, change your plan to reflect the true situation. (See the earlier sections "Making assumptions to clarify planned work" and "Representing conditionally repeating work" for more about assumptions.)

REMEMBER

- **Keep in mind that your WBS identifies only your project's deliverables; it doesn't depict their chronological order.** Nothing is wrong with listing deliverables from left to right or top to bottom in the approximate order that you'll create them. However, in complex projects, you may have difficulty showing detailed interrelationships among intermediate and final deliverables in the WBS format. *The purpose of the WBS is to ensure that you identify all project deliverables.* Check out Chapter 1 in Book 2 for more on developing your project schedule.

Using templates

A *WBS template* is an existing WBS that contains deliverables typical for a particular type of project. This template reflects people's cumulative experience from performing many similar projects. As people perform more projects, they add deliverables to the template that were overlooked and remove deliverables that weren't needed. Using templates can save you time and improve your accuracy.

WARNING

Don't inhibit people's active involvement in the development of the WBS by using a template that's too polished. Lack of people's involvement can lead to missed activities and lack of commitment to project success.

This section looks at how you can develop a WBS template and improve its accuracy and completeness.

Drawing on previous experience

By drawing on previous experience, you can prepare your WBS in less time than it takes to develop a whole new WBS and be more confident that you've included all essential pieces of work.

Suppose you prepare your department's quarterly budget. After doing a number of these budgets, you know most of the work you have to perform. Each time you finish another budget, you revise your WBS template to include new information you gleaned from the recently completed project.

The next time you start to plan a quarterly budget, begin with the WBS template you've developed from your past projects. Then add and subtract elements as appropriate for this particular budget preparation.

Improving your WBS templates

The more accurate and complete your WBS templates are, the more time they can save on future projects. This section offers several suggestions for continually improving the quality of your WBS templates.

TIP

When using templates, keep in mind the following guidelines:

- **Develop templates for frequently performed tasks as well as for entire projects.** Templates for the annual organization blood drive or the submission of a newly developed drug to the Food and Drug Administration are valuable. So are templates for individual tasks that are part of these projects, such as awarding a competitive contract or having a document printed. You can always incorporate templates for individual pieces of work into a larger WBS for an entire project.
- **Develop and modify your WBS template from previous projects that worked, not from initial plans that looked good.** Often you develop a detailed WBS at the start of your project, but you may forget to add intermediate or final deliverables that you overlooked in your initial planning. If you update your template from a WBS that you prepared at the *start* of your project, it won't reflect what you discovered *during* the actual performance of the project.

- **Use templates as starting points, not ending points.** Clarify to your team members and others involved in the project that the template is only the start for your WBS, not the final version. Every project differs in some ways from similar ones performed in the past. If you don't critically examine the template, you may miss work that wasn't done in previous projects but that needs to be done in this one.
- **Continually update your templates to reflect your experiences from different projects.** The post-project evaluation (also called lessons learned) is a great opportunity to review and critique your original WBS. (See Chapter 4 in Book 2 for information on how to plan and conduct this evaluation.) At the end of your project, take a moment to revise your WBS template to reflect what you found.

Identifying Risks While Detailing Your Work

In addition to helping you identify work you need to complete, a WBS helps you identify unknowns that may cause problems when you attempt to perform that work. As you think through the work you have to do to complete your project, you often identify considerations that may affect how or whether you can perform particular project activities. Sometimes you have the information you need to assess and address a consideration and sometimes you don't. Identifying and dealing effectively with information you need but don't have can dramatically increase your chances for project success.

Unknown information falls into one of two categories:

- **Known unknown:** Information you know you need that someone else has
- **Unknown unknown:** Information you know you need that neither you nor anyone else has because it doesn't exist yet

REMEMBER

You deal with known unknowns by finding out who has the information you need and then getting it. You deal with unknown unknowns by using one or more of the following strategies:

- Buying insurance to minimize damage that occurs if something doesn't turn out the way you expected

» Developing contingency plans to follow if something doesn't turn out the way you expected

» Trying to influence what the information eventually turns out to be

In the project *Conducting a survey* discussed in the earlier sidebar "Conducting a survey: Using the work breakdown structure," you figure you'll need a week to select a sample of clients to survey if the sales department has a current data tape listing all the company's clients. At this point, whether the data tape exists is a *known unknown* — it's unknown to you, but, if it exists, someone else knows about it. You deal with this unknown by calling people to find someone who knows whether such a data tape does or doesn't exist.

You experience a different situation when you become aware that twice in the past month, computer operators at your company accidentally destroyed a data tape when they spilled coffee on it as they were preparing to mount it on a tape drive. As part of your *Conducting a survey* project, you need to have a computer operator mount a tape on a tape drive. Not surprisingly, you're now concerned that the operator may spill coffee on your tape and destroy it, too.

Whether or not the operator will spill coffee on your tape is an unknown unknown when you prepare the WBS for your project plan. You can't determine beforehand whether the operator will spill coffee on your tape because it's an unintended, unplanned act (at least you hope so!).

Because you can't find out for certain whether or not this occurrence will happen, you consider taking one or more of the following approaches to address this risk:

» **Develop a contingency plan.** For example, in addition to developing a scheme for the computerized selection of names directly from the data tape, have the statistician who guides the selection of the sample develop a scheme for selecting names randomly by hand from the hard copy of the data tape.

» **Take steps to reduce the likelihood that coffee is spilled on your data tape.** For example, on the morning that your data tape is to be run, check beforehand for open cups of coffee in the computer room.

Of course, if you feel the chances the operator will spill coffee on your data tape are sufficiently small, you can always choose to do nothing beforehand and just deal with the situation if and when it actually occurs.

Developing the WBS helps you identify a situation that may compromise your project's success. You then must decide how to deal with that situation.

Documenting What You Need to Know about Your Planned Project Work

After preparing your project WBS, take some time to gather essential information about all your work packages (lowest-level WBS components), and keep it in the *WBS dictionary* that's available to all project team members. You and your team will use this information to develop the remaining parts of your plan, as well as to support the tracking, controlling, and replanning of activities during the project. The project manager (or her designee) should approve all changes to information in this dictionary.

The WBS dictionary can contain but isn't limited to the following information for all WBS components:

- **WBS component title and WBS identification code:** Descriptors that uniquely identify the WBS component
- **Activities included:** List of all the activities that must be performed to create the deliverable identified in the work package
- **Work detail:** Narrative description of work processes and procedures
- **Schedule milestones:** Significant events in the component's schedule
- **Quality requirements:** Desired characteristics of the deliverables produced in the WBS component
- **Acceptance criteria:** Criteria that must be met before project deliverables are accepted
- **Required resources:** People, funds, equipment, facilities, raw materials, information, and so on that these activities need

TIP

For larger projects, you maintain the whole WBS — including all its components from Level 1 down to and including the work packages — in the same hierarchical representation, and you keep all the activities that comprise the work packages in an activity list and/or the WBS dictionary. Separating the WBS components in this way helps you more easily see and understand the important interrelationships and aspects of the project deliverables and work.

On smaller projects, however, you may combine the deliverable-oriented WBS components and the activities that comprise each work package in the same hierarchical display.

2

Steering the Ship: Planning and Managing a Project

Contents at a Glance

project

» Using your network diagram to determine schedule possibilities

» Approximating activity durations and forming your project's initial schedule

» Presenting your project's schedule

Chapter 1
You Want This Project Done When?

Project assignments always have deadlines. So even though you're not sure what your new project is supposed to accomplish, you want to know when it has to be finished. Unfortunately, when you find out the desired end date, your immediate reaction is often one of panic: "But I don't have enough time!"

The truth is, when you first receive your project assignment, you usually have no idea how long it'll take to complete. Initial reactions tend to be based more on fear and anxiety than on facts, especially when you're trying to juggle multiple responsibilities and the project sounds complex.

To help you develop a more realistic estimate of how long your project will take, you need an organized approach that clarifies how you plan to perform your project's activities, what schedules are possible, and how you'll meet deadlines that initially appear unrealistic. This chapter describes a technique that helps you proactively develop an achievable schedule (while keeping your anxiety in check).

REMEMBER

Even though the technique of using network diagrams takes about ten minutes to master, the explanations and illustrations can appear overwhelming at first glance. If this chapter is your first contact with flowcharts, initially scan it for the main points and then read the different sections several times. The more you read the text, the more logical the explanations become. However, if you get frustrated with the technical details, take a break and come back to it later. You'll be surprised how much clearer the details are the second or third time around!

Picture This: Illustrating a Work Plan with a Network Diagram

To determine the amount of time you need for any project, you have to determine the following two pieces of information:

- **Sequence:** The order in which you perform the activities
- **Duration:** How long each individual activity takes

For example, suppose you have a project consisting of ten activities, each of which takes one week to complete. How long will you take to complete your project? The truth is, you can't tell. You may finish the project in one week if you have the ability and resources to perform all ten activities at the same time. You may take ten weeks if you have to do the activities one at a time in sequential order. Or you may take between one and ten weeks if you have to do some but not all activities in sequence.

To develop a schedule for a small project, you can probably consider the durations and sequential interdependencies in your head. But projects with 15 to 20 activities or more — many of which you can perform at the same time — require an organized method to guide your analysis.

This section helps you develop feasible schedules by showing you how to draw network diagrams and then how to choose the best one for your project.

Defining a network diagram's elements

A *network diagram* is a flowchart that illustrates the order in which you perform project activities. It's your project's test laboratory — it gives you a chance to try out different strategies before performing the work.

No matter how complex your project is, its network diagram has the following three elements: milestones, activities, and durations.

Milestone

A *milestone*, sometimes called an *event*, is a significant occurrence in the life of a project. Milestones take no time and consume no resources; they occur instantaneously. Think of them as signposts that signify a point in your trip to project completion. Milestones mark the start or end of one or more activities or the creation of deliverables. (See Chapter 3 in Book 1 for more on deliverables.) Examples of milestones are *draft report approved* and *design begun.*

Activity

An *activity* (also called a *task*) is a component of work performed during the course of a project. Activities take time and consume resources; you describe them by using action verbs. Examples of activities are *design report* and *conduct survey.*

REMEMBER

Make sure you clearly define activities and milestones. The more clearly you define them, the more accurately you can estimate the time and resources needed to perform them, the more easily you can assign them to someone else, and the more meaningful your reporting of schedule progress becomes.

Duration

Duration is the total number of work periods completing an activity takes. Several factors can affect duration:

- The amount of *work effort* (the amount of time a person needs to work full-time on the activity to complete it) required.
- People's availability to work on the project.
- Whether multiple people can work on the activity at the same time.
- Capacity of non-personnel resources (for example, a computer's processing speed and the pages per minute that a copier can print) and their availability.
- Delay. For example, if your boss spends one hour reading your memo after it sat in her inbox for four days and seven hours, the activity's duration is five days, even though your boss spends only one hour reading it.

REMEMBER

The units of time describe two related but different activity characteristics. *Duration* is the number of work periods required to perform an activity; *work effort* is the amount of time a person needs to complete the activity. For example, suppose four people have to work together full time for five days to complete an activity. The activity's duration is five days. The work effort is 20 person-days (4 people times 5 days).

Understanding the basis of a duration estimate helps you figure out ways to reduce it. For example, suppose you estimate that testing a software package requires that it run for 24 hours on a computer. If you can use the computer only six hours in any one day, the duration for your software test is four days. Doubling the number of people working on the test doesn't reduce the duration to two days, but getting approval to use the computer for 12 hours a day does.

Drawing a network diagram

Determining your project's end date requires you to choose the dates that each project activity starts and ends and the dates that each milestone is reached. You can determine these dates with the help of a network diagram.

REMEMBER

The *activity-on-node* technique (also called *activity-in-box* or *precedence diagramming method*) for drawing a network diagram uses the following three symbols to describe the diagram's three elements:

- **Boxes:** Boxes represent activities and milestones. If the duration is *0,* it's a milestone; if it's greater than *0,* it's an activity. Note that milestone boxes are sometimes highlighted with lines that are bold, double, or otherwise more noticeable.
- **Letter *t*:** The letter *t* represents duration.
- **Arrows:** Arrows represent the direction work flows from one activity or milestone to the next. Upon completing an activity or reaching a milestone, you can proceed either to a milestone or directly to another activity as indicated by the arrow(s) leaving that box.

Figure 1-1 presents a simple example of an activity-on-node network diagram. When you reach Milestone A (the box on the left), you can perform Activity 1 (the box in the middle), which you estimated will take two weeks to complete. Upon completing Activity 1, you reach Milestone B (the box on the right). The arrows indicate the direction of workflow.

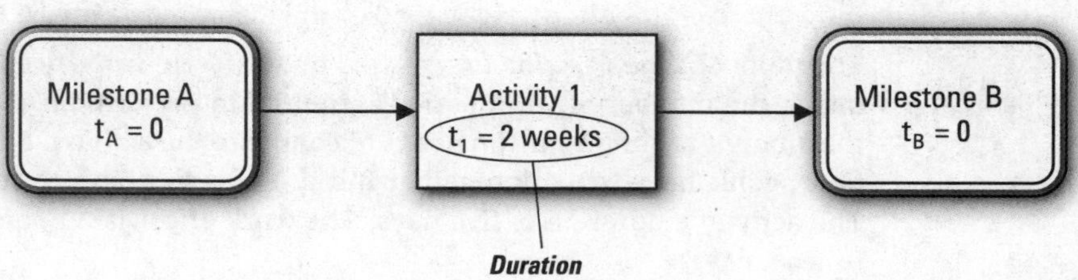

FIGURE 1-1: The three symbols in an activity-on-node network diagram.

© John Wiley & Sons, Inc.

Note: If you've worked with network diagrams in the past, you may have seen them drawn in another format called *activity-on-arrow,* also called the *classical approach,* an *arrow diagram,* or a *PERT chart* (see the later section "Improving activity duration estimates" for an explanation of PERT analysis). This format represents milestones with circles and activities with arrows. However, because the activity-on-node technique is the one most used today, all network diagrams in this chapter are drawn in this format.

Analyzing a Network Diagram

Think of your project as a trip you and several friends are planning to take. Each of you has a car and will travel a different route to the final destination. During the trip, two or more of your routes will cross at certain places. You agree that all people who pass through a common point must arrive at that point before anyone can proceed on the next leg of the journey. The trip is over when all of you reach the final destination.

You certainly don't want to undertake a trip this complex without planning it out on a road map. After all, planning your trip allows you to

- Determine how long the entire trip will take
- Identify potential difficulties along the way
- Consider alternate routes to get to your final destination more quickly

This section helps you plan your project schedule by telling you how to read and interpret a road map (your network diagram) so you can determine the likely consequences of your possible approaches.

Reading a network diagram

REMEMBER

Use the following two rules as you draw and interpret your network diagram. After you understand these rules, analyzing the diagram is a snap:

- **Rule 1:** After you finish an activity or reach a milestone, you can proceed to the next activity or milestone, as indicated by the arrow(s).
- **Rule 2:** Before you can start an activity or reach a milestone, you must first complete all activities and reach all milestones with arrows pointing to the activity you want to start or the milestone you want to reach.

Figure 1-2 illustrates a network diagram. According to Rule 1, from *Project Started,* you can proceed to work on either Activity 1 or 3, which means you can do either Activity 1 or Activity 3 by itself or both Activities 1 and 3 at the same time. In other words, these two activities are independent of each other.

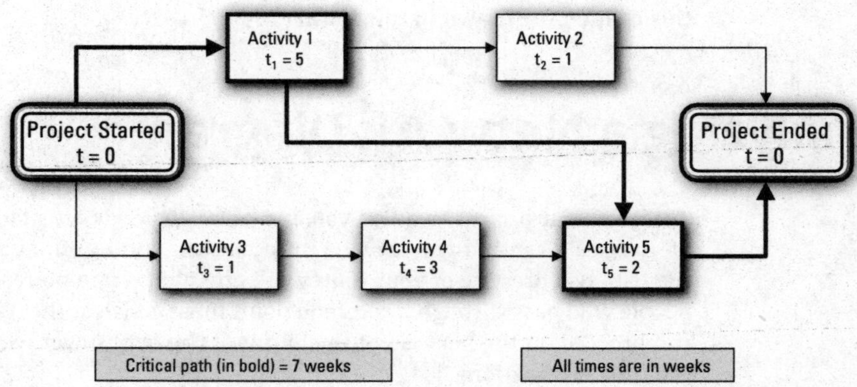

FIGURE 1-2: An example of a network diagram.

© John Wiley & Sons, Inc.

You may also choose to do neither of the activities. Rule 1 is an *allowing* relationship, not a *forcing* (or requiring) relationship. In other words, you can work on any of the activities that the arrows from *Project Started* lead to, but you don't have to work on any of them.

For example, suppose a part of your plan includes two activities to build a device: *receive parts* and *assemble parts.* As soon as you receive the parts, you can start to assemble them; in fact, you can't start to assemble them until you receive them. But after you receive all the parts you ordered, neither rule says you must start to assemble them immediately; you can assemble them if you want to, or you can wait. Of course, if you wait, the completion of the assembly will be delayed. But that's your choice.

According to Rule 2, you can start working on Activity 2 in Figure 1-2 as soon as you complete Activity 1 because the arrow from Activity 1 is the only one leading to Activity 2. Rule 2, therefore, is a forcing relationship, because it forces you to wait until you complete Activity 1 before you can begin working on Activity 2. If arrows from three activities led to Activity 2, you'd have to complete all three activities before starting Activity 2. (The diagram wouldn't indicate that you could start working on Activity 2 by completing only one or two of the three activities that led to it.)

Interpreting a network diagram

You can use your network diagram to figure out when to start and end activities and when you'll finish the entire project if you perform the activities in this way. To find out the schedule that your approach will allow, you need the following information:

- **Critical path:** A sequence of activities that takes the longest time to complete (this is also the shortest time in which you can complete your project)
- **Noncritical path:** A sequence of activities in which you can delay activities and still finish your project in the shortest possible time
- **Slack time (also called *float*):** The maximum amount of time you can delay an activity and still finish your project in the shortest possible time
- **Earliest start date:** The earliest date you can start an activity
- **Earliest finish date:** The earliest date you can finish an activity
- **Latest start date:** The latest date you can start an activity and still finish your project in the shortest possible time
- **Latest finish date:** The latest date you can finish an activity and still finish your project in the shortest possible time

You can use the *critical path method (CPM)* to determine this information and to build your project's overall schedule. The following sections illustrate how this method works.

The importance of the critical path

The length of your project's critical path(s) in your network diagram defines your project's length (hence, the critical path method for determining your project's schedule). If you want to finish your project in less time, consider ways to shorten its critical path.

WARNING

Monitor critical-path activities closely during performance because any delay in critical-path activities delays your project's completion. Also closely monitor any activities on paths that are close to being critical, because any minor delay on those paths can also delay your project's completion.

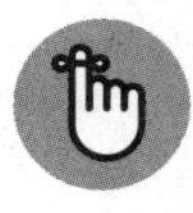

REMEMBER

Your project can have two or more critical paths at the same time. In fact, every path in your project can be critical if every one of them takes the same amount of time. However, when every path is critical, you have a high-risk situation; a delay in any activity immediately causes a delay in the completion of the project.

Critical paths can change as your project unfolds. Sometimes activities on a critical path finish so early that the path becomes shorter than one or more other paths that were initially considered noncritical. Other times, activities on an initially noncritical path are delayed to the point where the sum of their completion times becomes greater than the length of the current critical path (which turns the initially noncritical path into a critical one).

The forward pass: Determining critical paths, noncritical paths, and earliest start and finish dates

Your first step in analyzing your project's network diagram is to start at the beginning and see how quickly you can complete the activities along each path. You should determine this information without taking into account any effects that constraints on the availability of personnel or other resources may have. This start-to-finish analysis is called the *forward pass.*

To help you understand what a forward pass is, you can perform one through the diagram in Figure 1-2. According to Rule 1, you can consider working on either Activity 1 or Activity 3 (or both together) as soon as the project starts (check out the earlier section "Reading a network diagram" for more info on the two rules of network diagram analysis). First, consider Activities 1 and 2 on the upper path:

- The earliest you can start Activity 1 is the moment the project starts (the beginning of week 1).
- The earliest you can finish Activity 1 is the end of week 5 (add Activity 1's estimated duration of five weeks to its earliest start time, which is the start of the project).
- According to Rule 2, the earliest you can start Activity 2 is the beginning of week 6 because the arrow from Activity 1 is the only one leading to Activity 2.
- The earliest you can finish Activity 2 is the end of week 6 (add Activity 2's estimated duration of one week to its earliest start time at the beginning of week 6).

So far, so good. Now consider Activities 3 and 4 on the lower path of the diagram:

- The earliest you can start Activity 3 is the moment the project starts (the beginning of week 1).
- The earliest you can finish Activity 3 is the end of week 1.
- The earliest you can start Activity 4 is the beginning of week 2.
- The earliest you can finish Activity 4 is the end of week 4.

You have to be careful when you try to determine the earliest you can start Activity 5. According to Rule 2, the two arrows entering Activity 5 indicate you must finish both Activity 1 and Activity 4 before you begin Activity 5. Even though you can finish Activity 4 by the end of week 4, you can't finish Activity 1 until the end of week 5. Therefore, the earliest you can start Activity 5 is the beginning of week 6.

REMEMBER

If two or more activities or milestones lead to the same activity, the earliest you can start that activity is the latest of the earliest finish dates for those preceding activities or milestones.

Is your head spinning yet? Take heart; the end is in sight.

- The earliest you can start Activity 5 is the beginning of week 6.
- The earliest you can finish Activity 5 is the end of week 7.
- The earliest you can finish Activity 2 is the end of week 6. Therefore, the earliest you can finish the entire project (and reach the milestone called *Project Ended*) is the end of week 7.

So far, you have the following information about your project:

- The length of the critical path (the shortest time in which you can complete the project) is seven weeks. Only one critical path takes seven weeks; it includes the milestone *Project Started,* Activity 1, Activity 5, and the milestone *Project Ended.*
- Activity 2, Activity 3, and Activity 4 aren't on critical paths.

The backward pass: Calculating the latest start and finish dates and slack times

You're halfway home. In case resource conflicts or unexpected delays prevent you from beginning all the project activities at their earliest possible start times, you want to know how much you can delay the activities along each path and still finish the project at the earliest possible date. This finish-to-start analysis is called the *backward pass.*

To expand on the example introduced in the preceding section, the forward pass indicates that the earliest date you can reach the milestone *Project Ended* is the end of week 7. However, Rule 2 in the earlier section "Reading a network diagram" says you can't reach the milestone *Project Ended* until you've completed Activities 2 and 5. Therefore, to finish your project by the end of week 7, the latest you can finish Activities 2 and 5 is the end of week 7. Consider the lower path on the diagram in Figure 1-2 with Activities 3, 4, and 5:

- You must start Activity 5 by the beginning of week 6 to finish it by the end of week 7 (because Activity 5's estimated duration is two weeks).
- According to Rule 2, you can't start Activity 5 until you finish Activities 1 and 4. So you must finish Activities 1 and 4 by the end of week 5.
- You must start Activity 4 by the beginning of week 3.
- You must finish Activity 3 before you can work on Activity 4. Therefore, you must finish Activity 3 by the end of week 2.
- You must start Activity 3 by the beginning of week 2.

Finally, consider the upper path on the network diagram in Figure 1-2:

- You must start Activity 2 by the beginning of week 7.
- You can't work on Activity 2 until you finish Activity 1. Therefore, you must finish Activity 1 by the end of week 6.

Be careful in your calculations. You must finish Activity 1 by the end of week 5 to start Activity 5 at the beginning of week 6. But to start work on Activity 2 at the beginning of week 7, you must finish Activity 1 by the end of week 6. So finishing Activity 1 by the end of week 5 satisfies both requirements.

REMEMBER

If two or more arrows leave the same activity or milestone, the latest date you can finish the activity or reach the milestone is the earliest of the latest dates that you must start the next activities or reach the next milestones.

In Figure 1-2, the latest start dates for Activities 2 and 5 are the beginnings of week 7 and week 6, respectively. Therefore, the latest date to finish Activity 1 is the end of week 5. The rest is straightforward: You must start Activity 1 by the beginning of week 1 at the latest.

TIP

To organize the dates you calculate in the forward and backward passes, consider writing the earliest and latest start dates and the earliest and latest finish dates at the top of each milestone or activity box in the project's network diagram. Figure 1-3 illustrates how this looks for the example in Figure 1-2.

Now that you have all the earliest and latest start and finish dates for your milestones and activities, you need to determine the slack time for each activity or milestone. You can determine slack time in one of two ways:

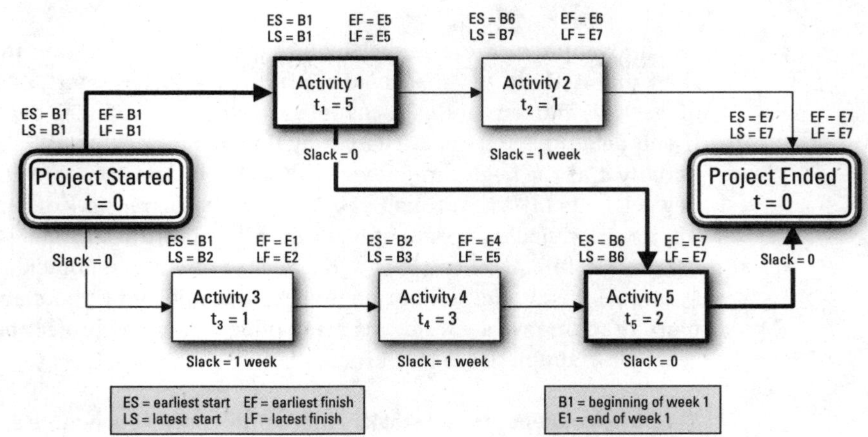

© John Wiley & Sons, Inc.

FIGURE 1-3: An example of a network diagram with earliest and latest start and finish dates as well as slack times.

- Subtract the earliest possible start date from the latest allowable start date.
- Subtract the earliest possible finish date from the latest allowable finish date.

Thus, you can determine that Activities 2, 3, and 4 have slack times of one week, while Activities 1 and 5 have no slack time. Figure 1-3 displays this information.

REMEMBER

If an activity's slack time is zero, the activity is on a critical path.

REMEMBER

Although slack time is defined as the amount of time an activity or milestone can be delayed without delaying your project's completion date, slack time is actually associated with a path of activities rather than with an individual activity. The information in Figure 1-3 indicates that both Activity 3 and Activity 4 (which are on the same path) have slack times of one week. However, if the start of Activity 3 is delayed by a week to the beginning of week 2, the earliest that Activity 4 can start will be the beginning of week 3, and it will have zero slack time.

A Guide to the Project Management Body of Knowledge, 6th Edition *(PMBOK 6)* identifies the following two types of slack:

- **Total slack (also called total float):** The amount of time a schedule activity may be delayed from its earliest start date without delaying the project's end date or violating a schedule constraint. This type is the same as what I refer to as *slack.*
- **Free slack (also called free float):** The amount of time a schedule activity may be delayed without delaying the earliest start date of any immediately following schedule activities or violating a schedule constraint.

As an example of these terms, look at the network diagram in Figure 1-3. Consider that Activity 3 is scheduled to start at its earliest start, or ES (the beginning of week 1), and Activity 4 is scheduled to start at its ES (the beginning of week 2). If you delay the start of Activity 3 by up to one week, you'll still be able to start Activity 4 at the beginning of week 3 (its LS, or latest start) and end it by the end of week 5, its LF (latest finish). So Activity 3 has a *free slack* of zero (because delaying its scheduled start date of ES at all will cause the start date of Activity 4 to be delayed), while Activity 4 has a *free slack* of one week. Coincidently, each activity (3 and 4) has a *total slack* of one week, since delaying the start of either one by more than one week will delay the completion of the project beyond the current scheduled completion date of the end of week 7.

Note: The concept of total slack is more often used in schedule analyses, and that's the concept used in this book. For simplicity, this information item is referred to simply as *slack* rather than *total slack.*

Working with Your Project's Network Diagram

The preceding sections explain the general rules and procedures for drawing and analyzing any network diagram. This section tells you how to create and analyze the network diagram for your own project.

Determining precedence

To draw your project's network diagram, you first have to decide the order of your project's activities. This section tells you different reasons you may need to perform activities in a particular order.

Looking at factors that affect predecessors

A *predecessor* to an activity (Activity A, for example) is an activity or milestone that determines when work on Activity A can begin. *PMBOK 6* identifies the following four relationships that can exist between a predecessor and the activity or milestone coming immediately after it (termed its *successor*):

- **Finish-to-start:** The predecessor must finish before the successor can start.
- **Finish-to-finish:** The predecessor must finish before the successor can finish.

» **Start-to-start:** The predecessor must start before the successor can start.

» **Start-to-finish:** The predecessor must start before the successor can finish.

The finish-to-start precedence relationship is the one most commonly used, so it's the one addressed in this book. In other words, in this book, a *predecessor* is an activity that must be completed before its successor activity can start or its successor milestone can be reached.

Sometimes an activity can't start precisely when its predecessor is finished. A *lag* is the amount of time after its predecessor is completed that you must wait before an activity can start. A *lead* is the amount of time before its predecessor is finished that an activity can begin. This book considers only situations where lead and lag times are zero.

An activity is an *immediate predecessor* to Activity A if you don't have any other activities between it and Activity A. When you determine the immediate predecessors for every activity, you have all the information you need to draw your project's network diagram. The following considerations affect the order in which you must perform your project's activities:

» **Mandatory dependencies:** These relationships must be observed if project work is to be a success. They include
   - **Legal requirements:** Federal, state, and local laws or regulations require that certain activities be done before others. As an example, consider a pharmaceutical company that has developed a new drug in the laboratory and demonstrated its safety and effectiveness in clinical trials. The manufacturer wants to start producing and selling the drug immediately but can't. Federal law requires that the company obtain Food and Drug Administration (FDA) approval of the drug before selling it.
   - **Procedural requirements:** Company policies and procedures require that certain activities be done before others. Suppose you're purchasing new furniture for your company's offices. You've finished selecting and pricing the furniture you want and would like to begin the process of selecting a vendor and placing the order. However, your organization follows a procurement process for large purchases, which requires that the vice president of finance formally approve the expenditure of the funds required before you can proceed.
   - **Hard logic:** Certain processes must logically occur before others. For example, when building a house, you must pour the concrete for the foundation before you erect the frame.

- **Discretionary dependencies:** You may choose to establish these relationships between activities, but they aren't required. They include
  - **Logical dependencies:** Performing certain activities before others sometimes seems to make the most sense. Suppose you're writing a report. Because much of Chapter 3 depends on what you write in Chapter 2, you decide to write Chapter 2 first. You can write Chapter 3 first or work on both at the same time, but that plan increases the chance that you'll have to rewrite some of Chapter 3 after you finish Chapter 2.
  - **Managerial choices:** Sometimes you make arbitrary decisions to work on certain activities before others. Consider that you have to perform both Activity C and Activity D. You can't work on them at the same time, and you know of no legal or logical reason why you should work on one or the other first. You decide to work on Activity C first.
- **External dependencies:** Starting a project activity may require that certain work external to the project be completed first. For example, imagine that your project includes an activity to test a device you're developing. You want to start testing right away, but you can't start this activity until your organization's test laboratory receives and installs a new piece of test equipment they plan to order.

Choosing immediate predecessors

You can decide on the immediate predecessors for your project's activities in one of two ways:

- **Front-to-back:** Start with the activities you can perform as soon as your project begins and work your way through to the end. To use this method, follow these steps:
  1. **Select the first activity or activities to perform as soon as your project starts.**
  2. **Decide which activity or activities you can perform when you finish the first ones (from Step 1).**
  3. **Continue in this way until you've considered all activities in the project.**
- **Back-to-front:** Choose the activity or activities that will be done last on the project and continue backward toward the beginning. To use this method, follow these steps:
  1. **Identify the last project activity or activities you'll conduct.**
  2. **Decide which activity or activities you must complete right before you can start to work on the last activities (from Step 1).**
  3. **Continue in this manner until you've considered all activities in your project.**

Regardless of which method you use to find your project's immediate predecessors, record the immediate predecessors in a simple table like Table 1-1. (This table lists the immediate predecessors in the example shown in Figure 1-2.)

TABLE 1-1 **Immediate Predecessors for Figure 1-2**

Activity Code	Activity Description	Immediate Predecessors
1	Activity 1	None
2	Activity 2	1
3	Activity 3	None
4	Activity 4	3
5	Activity 5	1, 4

TIP

Determine precedence based on the nature and requirements of the activities, not on the resources you think will be available. Suppose Activities A and B of your project can be performed at the same time but you plan to assign them to the same person. In this case, don't make Activity A the immediate predecessor for B, thinking that the person can work on only one activity at a time. Instead, let your diagram show that A and B can be done at the same time. Later, if you find out you have another person who can help out with this work, you can evaluate the impact of performing Activities A and B at the same time.

TIP

When you create your network diagram for simple projects, consider writing the names of your activities and milestones on sticky-back notes and attaching them to chart paper or a wall. For more complex projects, consider using an integrated project-management software package. See Chapters 3 and 4 in Book 3 for a discussion of how to use software to support your project planning, and check out *Microsoft Project 2019 For Dummies* by Cynthia Snyder Dionisio (Wiley) for the lowdown on Microsoft Project, the most popular project-management software package.

Using a network diagram to analyze a simple example

Consider the following example of preparing for a picnic to illustrate how to use a network diagram to determine possible schedules while meeting project expectations and satisfying project constraints. (You shouldn't plan all your picnics this way, but the situation does illustrate the technique rather nicely!)

Deciding on the activities

It's Friday evening, and you and your friend are considering what to do during the weekend to unwind and relax. The forecast for Saturday is for sunny and mild weather, so you decide to go on a picnic at a local lake. Because you want to get the most enjoyment possible from your picnic, you decide to plan the outing carefully by drawing and analyzing a network diagram. Table 1-2 illustrates the seven activities you decide you must perform to prepare for your picnic and get to the lake.

TABLE 1-2 **Activities for Your Picnic at the Lake**

Activity Code	Activity Description	Who Will Be Present	Duration (In Minutes)
1	Load car	You and your friend	5
2	Get money from bank	You	5
3	Make egg sandwiches	Your friend	10
4	Drive to the lake	You and your friend	30
5	Decide which lake to go to	You and your friend	2
6	Buy gasoline	You	10
7	Boil eggs (for egg sandwiches)	Your friend	10

In addition, you agree to observe the following constraints:

- You and your friend will start all activities at your house at 8 a.m. Saturday — you can't do anything before that time.
- You must perform all seven activities to complete your project.
- You can't change who must be present during each activity.
- The two lakes you're considering are in opposite directions from your house, so you must decide where you're going to have your picnic before you begin your drive.

Setting the order of the activities

Now that you have all your activities listed, you need to decide the order in which you'll do them. In other words, you need to determine the immediate predecessors for each activity. The following dependencies are required: Your friend must boil the eggs before he can make the egg sandwiches (duh!), and both of you must load the car and decide which lake to visit before you start your drive.

The order of the rest of the activities is up to you. You may consider the following approach:

- Decide which lake before you do anything else.
- After you both agree on the lake, you drive to the bank to get money.
- After you get money from the bank, you get gasoline.
- At the same time, after you agree on the lake, your friend starts to boil the eggs.
- After the eggs are boiled, your friend makes the egg sandwiches.
- After you get back with the gas and your friend finishes the egg sandwiches, you both load the car.
- After you both load the car, you drive to the lake.

Table 1-3 depicts these predecessor relationships.

TABLE 1-3 **Predecessor Relationships for Your Picnic**

Activity Code	Activity Description	Immediate Predecessors
1	Load car	3, 6
2	Get money from bank	5
3	Make egg sandwiches	7
4	Drive to lake	1
5	Decide which lake	None
6	Buy gasoline	2
7	Boil eggs (for egg sandwiches)	5

Creating the network diagram

Now that you have your immediate predecessors in mind, you can draw the network diagram for your project from the information in Table 1-3.

TIP

Observe the following guidelines when drawing your network diagram:

- Begin your diagram with a single milestone (a commonly used name for this milestone is *Project Started*).
- Clearly specify all conditions that must be met for a milestone to be reached.

» Don't leave activities or events hanging; have them all come together in a common milestone that represents the end of the project (a commonly used name for this milestone is *Project Ended*).

» If your network diagram is excessively complex, look for groups of activities that are self-contained (that is, have only each other as predecessors). Define each of these groups as a subproject, where the duration of the subproject is equal to the length of the critical path(s) of the diagram representing the order in which the self-contained activities will be performed.

To create the network diagram for the picnic example, follow these steps:

1. **Begin your project with a single milestone and label it *Project Started.***
2. **Find all activities in the table that have no immediate predecessors — they can all start as soon as you begin your project.**

   In this case, only Activity 5 has no immediate predecessors.
3. **Begin your diagram by drawing the relationship between *Project Started* and the beginning of Activity 5 (see Figure 1-4).**

   Depict Activity 5 with a box and draw an arrow to it from the *Project Started* box.
4. **Find all activities that have your first activity as an immediate predecessor.**

   In this case, Table 1-3 shows that Activities 2 and 7 have Activity 5 as an immediate predecessor. Draw boxes to represent these two activities and draw arrows from Activity 5 to Activities 2 and 7 (see Figure 1-5).
5. **Continue in the same way with the remaining activities.**

   Recognize from Table 1-3 that only Activity 6 has Activity 2 as an immediate predecessor. Therefore, draw a box to represent Activity 6 and draw an arrow from Activity 2 to that box.

   Table 1-3 also shows that only Activity 3 has Activity 7 as an immediate predecessor. So draw a box to represent Activity 3 and draw an arrow from Activity 7 to Activity 3. Figure 1-5 depicts your diagram in progress.

   Now realize that Activity 1 has both Activities 3 and 6 as immediate predecessors. Therefore, draw a box representing Activity 1 and draw arrows from Activities 3 and 6 to this box.

   The rest is pretty straightforward. Because only Activity 4 has Activity 1 as its immediate predecessor, draw a box representing Activity 4 and draw an arrow from Activity 1 to Activity 4.
6. **After adding all the activities to the diagram, draw a box to represent *Project Ended* and draw an arrow from Activity 4 (the last activity you have to complete) to that box (see Figure 1-6 for the complete network diagram).**

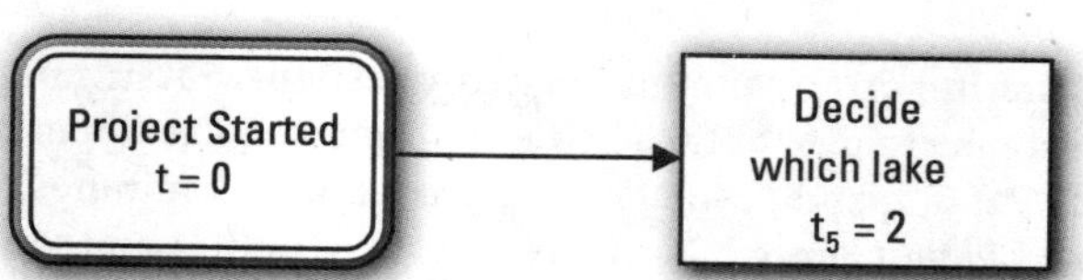

FIGURE 1-4: Starting your picnic-at-the-lake network diagram.

© John Wiley & Sons, Inc.

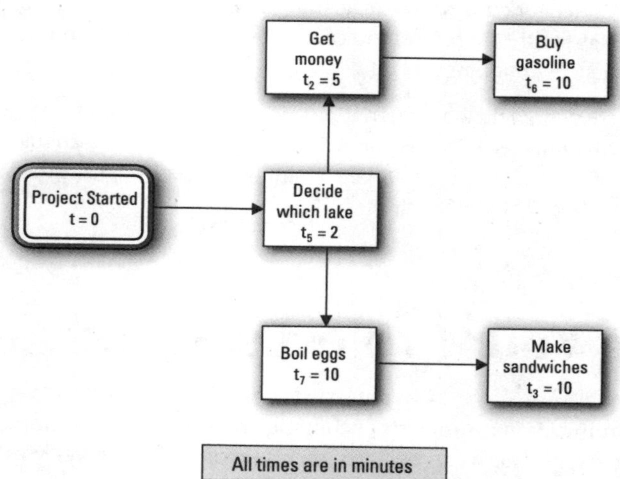

FIGURE 1-5: Continuing your picnic-at-the-lake network diagram.

© John Wiley & Sons, Inc.

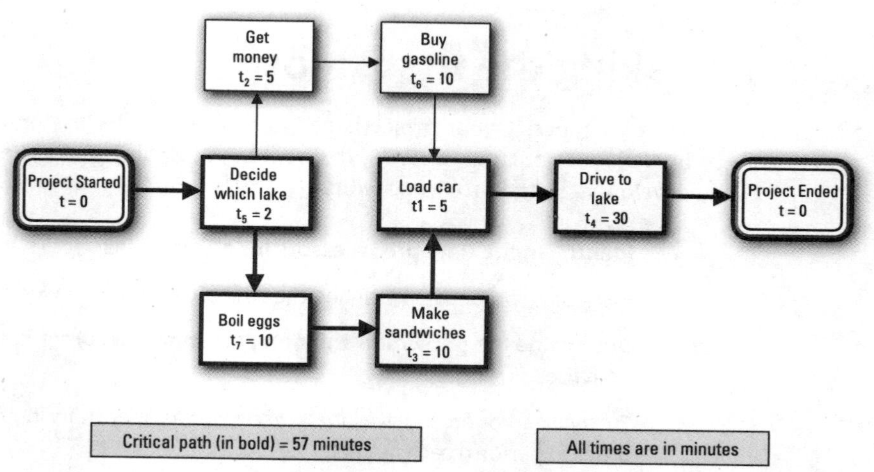

FIGURE 1-6: The completed picnic-at-the-lake network diagram.

© John Wiley & Sons, Inc.

Now for the important timing-related questions. First, how long will you and your friend take to get to the lake for your picnic? The upper path (*Project Started*; Activities 5, 2, 6, 1, and 4; and *Project Ended*) takes 52 minutes to complete, and the lower path (*Project Started*; Activities 5, 7, 3, 1, and 4; and *Project Ended*) takes 57 minutes to complete. Thus, the trip will take 57 minutes from the time you start until you arrive at the lake for your picnic, and the lower path is the critical path.

The second timing-related question you have to answer is whether you can delay any activities and still get to the lake in 57 minutes. If so, which ones can you delay and by how much? To answer these questions, consider the following:

- The network diagram reveals that Activities 5, 7, 3, 1, and 4 are all on the critical path. Therefore, you can't delay any of them if you want to get to the lake in 57 minutes.
- Activities 2 and 6 aren't on the critical path, and they can be performed at the same time as Activities 7 and 3. Activities 7 and 3 take 20 minutes to perform, while Activities 2 and 6 take 15 minutes. Therefore, Activities 2 and 6 have a total slack time of 5 minutes.

Developing Your Project's Schedule

Developing your project's schedule requires the combination of activities, resources, and activity-performance sequences that gives you the greatest chance of meeting your client's expectations with the least amount of risk. This section helps you start making a project schedule. It also focuses on some potential pitfalls and solutions for meeting time crunches.

Taking the first steps

After you specify your project's activities (see the discussion on creating a work breakdown structure, or WBS, in Chapter 3 of Book 1), take the following steps to develop an initial project schedule:

1. **Identify immediate predecessors for all activities.**

   Immediate predecessors define the structure of your network diagram.

2. **Determine the personnel and non-personnel resources required for all activities.**

   The type, amount, and availability of resources affect how long you need in order to perform each activity.

3. **Estimate durations for all activities.**

   See the later section "Estimating Activity Duration" for details on how to do so.

4. **Identify all intermediate and final dates that must be met.**

   These dates define the criteria that your schedule must meet.

5. **Identify all activities or milestones outside your project that affect your project's activities.**

   After you identify these external activities and milestones, you can set up the appropriate dependencies between them and your project's activities and milestones.

6. **Draw your network diagram.**

   Use the network diagram to determine what schedules your project can achieve.

7. **Analyze your project's network diagram to identify all critical paths and their lengths and to identify the slack times of noncritical paths.**

   This information helps you choose which project activities to monitor and how often to monitor them. It also suggests strategies for getting back on track if you encounter unexpected schedule delays. (See the earlier section "Interpreting a network diagram" for additional information on critical and noncritical paths.)

If the completion date is acceptable to your client, you're done with your scheduling. However, if your client wants you to finish faster than your initial schedule allows, your analyses are just beginning.

Avoiding the pitfall of backing in to your schedule

WARNING

Beware of developing a schedule by *backing in* — that is, starting at the end of a project and working your way back toward the beginning to identify activities and estimate durations that allow you to meet your client's desired end date. Using this approach substantially decreases the chances that you'll meet the schedule for the following reasons:

- You may miss activities because your focus is on meeting a time constraint, not on ensuring that you've identified all required work.
- You base your duration estimates on what you can allow activities to take rather than what they'll require.
- The order for your proposed activities may not be the most effective one.

One project manager had allowed one week for her final report's review and approval. When she was asked whether she thought this estimate was realistic, she replied that it certainly wasn't realistic but that she had to use that estimate for the project plan to work out. In other words, she was using time estimates that totaled to the number she *wanted* to reach rather than ones she thought she *could* meet.

REMEMBER

A project plan is a road map that, if followed, will lead to project success. To have the greatest chance of achieving that success, the following must happen:

- The plan must be complete and accurate (that is, performing all parts of the project in accordance with the plan will actually result in project success).
- The plan must be feasible (in other words, there can be no instances where performing one or more parts of the project in accordance with the plan is determined to be impossible).
- People must believe the plan is complete, accurate, and feasible (it's not enough that the plan is complete, accurate, and feasible; people must know it and believe it, too).
- People must commit to following the plan (in other words, people must decide to make every effort to perform their project work in accordance with the plan).
- People must make every effort to follow the plan (people must follow through on their commitment).

Basing a project schedule on estimates of activity durations you know are impossible to achieve may allow you to produce a schedule that makes it appear you can finish the project by the required end date. However, as soon as people have difficulty meeting an established date, they'll stop trying to meet it, rationalizing that they knew before they began that meeting that date would be impossible.

Meeting an established time constraint

Suppose your initial schedule has you finishing your project in three months, but your client wants the results in two months. Consider the following options for reducing the length of your critical paths:

- **Recheck the original duration estimates.**
  - Be sure you've clearly described the activity's work.
  - If you used past performance as a guide for developing the durations, recheck to be sure all characteristics of your current situation are the same as those of the past performance.

- Ask other experts to review and validate your estimates.
- Ask the people who'll actually be doing the work on these activities to review and validate your estimates.

» **Consider using more-experienced personnel.** Sometimes more-experienced personnel can get work done in less time. Of course, using more-experienced people may cost you more money. Further, you're not the only one in your organization who needs those more-experienced personnel; they may not always be available to help with your project!

» **Consider different strategies for performing the activities.** As an example, if you estimate a task you're planning to do internally to take three weeks, see whether you can find an external contractor who can perform it in two weeks.

» **Consider *fast tracking* — performing tasks that are normally done sequentially at the same time.** Although fast tracking can shorten the overall time to perform the tasks, it also increases the risk of having to redo portions of your work, so be ready to do so.

REMEMBER

As you reduce the lengths of critical paths, monitor paths that aren't initially critical to ensure that they haven't become critical. If one or more paths have become critical, use these same approaches to reduce their lengths.

Applying different strategies to arrive at your destination in less time

Consider the example of preparing for a picnic (which is introduced in the earlier section "Using a network diagram to analyze a simple example") to see how you can apply these approaches for reducing a project's time to your own project.

Figure 1-6 earlier in this chapter illustrates your initial 57-minute plan. If arriving at the lake in 57 minutes is okay, your analysis is done. But suppose you and your friend agree that you must reach the lake no later than 45 minutes after you start preparing on Saturday morning. What changes can you make to save you 12 minutes?

WARNING

You may be tempted to change the estimated time for the drive from 30 minutes to 18 minutes, figuring that you'll just drive faster. Unfortunately, doing so doesn't work if the drive really takes 30 minutes. Keep in mind that your plan represents an approach that you believe has a chance to work (though not necessarily one that's guaranteed). If you have to drive at speeds in excess of 100 miles per hour over dirt roads to get to the lake in 18 minutes, reducing the duration estimate has no chance of working (though it does have an excellent chance of getting you a speeding ticket).

To develop a more realistic plan to reduce your project's schedule, take the following steps:

1. **Start to reduce your project's time by finding the critical path and reducing its time until a second path becomes critical.**
2. **To reduce your project's time further, shorten both critical paths by the same amount until a third path becomes critical.**
3. **To reduce the time still further, shorten all three critical paths by the same amount of time until a fourth path becomes critical, and so on, until every path in the project is critical.**

Performing activities at the same time

One way to shorten the time it takes to do a group of activities is by taking one or more activities off the critical path and doing them in parallel with the remaining activities. However, often you have to be creative to simultaneously perform activities successfully.

Consider the 57-minute solution to the picnic example in Figure 1-6. Assume an automatic teller machine (ATM) is next to the gas station that you use. If you use a full-service gas island, you can get money from the ATM while the attendant fills your gas tank. As illustrated in Figure 1-7, this strategy allows you to perform Activities 2 and 6 at the same time — in a total of 10 minutes rather than the 15 minutes you indicated in the initial network diagram.

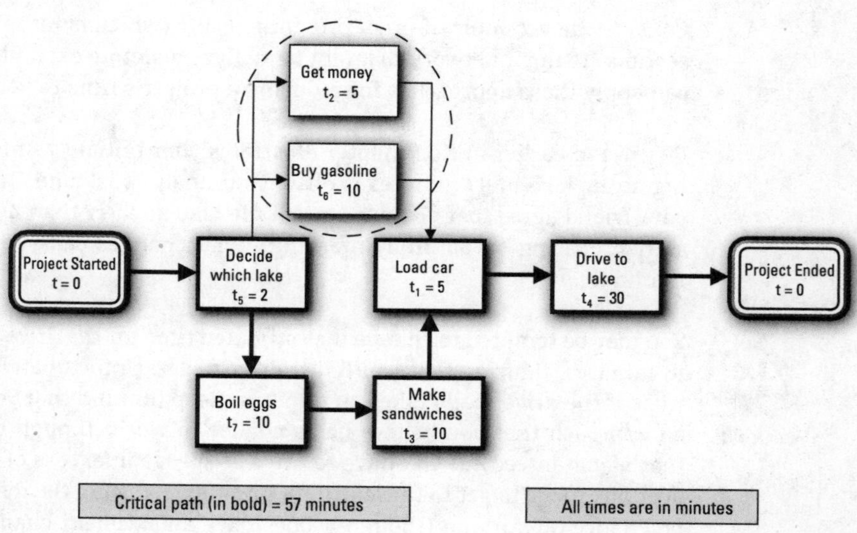

FIGURE 1-7: Getting gas at the full-service island and cash at the nearby ATM.

At first glance, it appears you can cut the total time down to 52 minutes by making this change. But look again. These two activities aren't on the critical path, so completing them more quickly has no impact on the overall project schedule. (Before you think you can save five minutes by helping your friend make the sandwiches, remember that you agreed you can't swap jobs.)

Now you have to try again. This time, keep in mind you must reduce the length of the *critical path* if you want to save time. Here's another idea: On your drive to the lake, you and your friend are both in the car, but only one of you is driving. The other person is just sitting there. If you agree to drive, your friend can load the fixings for the sandwiches into the car and make the sandwiches while you drive. This adjustment appears to take ten minutes off the critical path. But does it really?

The diagram in Figure 1-6 shows that the upper path (Activities 2 and 6) takes 15 minutes and the lower path (Activities 7 and 3) takes 20 minutes. Because the lower path is the critical path (and the upper path has five minutes of slack), removing up to five minutes from the lower path can reduce the time to complete the overall project by the same amount. However, reducing the lower path by five minutes makes it the same length (15 minutes) as the upper path, which means that both paths are now critical.

Figure 1-8 reveals that taking five more minutes off the lower path (to reflect that the sandwiches take ten minutes to make) doesn't save more time for the overall project because the upper path still takes 15 minutes. However, removing the extra five minutes from the lower path does give it five minutes of slack.

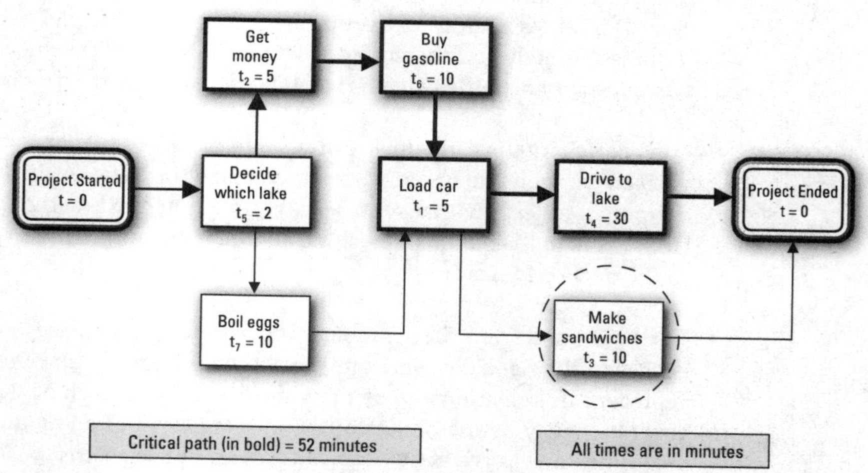

FIGURE 1-8: Making sandwiches while driving to the lake.

You Want This Project Done When?

Now you can consider using your first idea to get money at the ATM while an attendant fills your car with gas. This time, this move can save you five minutes because the upper path is now critical. Figure 1-9 reflects this change in your network diagram.

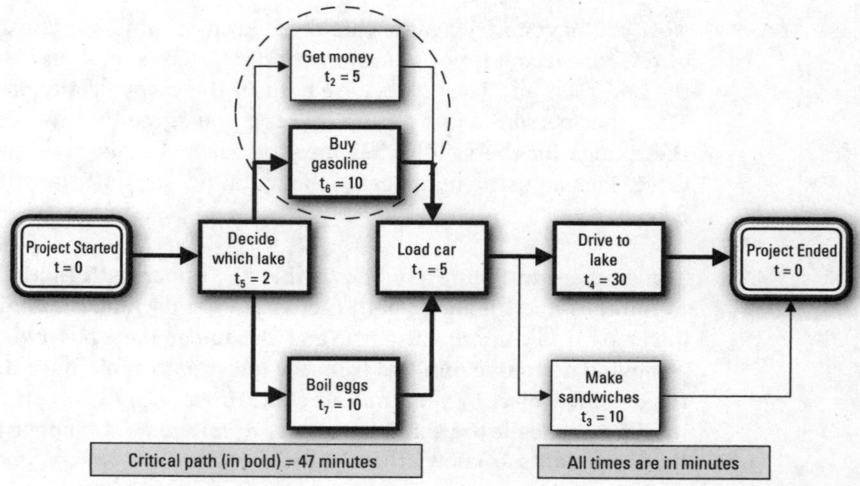

© John Wiley & Sons, Inc.

FIGURE 1-9: Getting gas at the full-service island while getting cash at the nearby ATM and making sandwiches while driving to the lake.

Finally, you can decide which lake to visit and load the car at the same time, which saves you an additional two minutes. Figure 1-10 illustrates the final 45-minute solution. ***Note:*** For clarity, four milestones (Project Started, Project Ended, Ready to Load Car and Ready to Drive) and two summary activities (Preparation and Travel) have been added to the original list of activities. Neither summary activity is linked directly to other project activities, because the subactivities under the two summary activities are already linked to other activities or milestones.

TIP

Consider a situation in which you have to complete two or more activities before you can work on two or more new ones. Show this relationship in your diagram by defining a milestone that represents completion of the activities, drawing arrows from the activities to this milestone and then drawing arrows from that milestone to the new activities (refer to Figure 1-9).

In the example, you first complete the activities *Get money, Buy gasoline,* and *Boil eggs,* and then you can perform the activities *Load car* and *Decide which lake.* You represent this relationship by drawing arrows from each of the first three activities to a newly defined milestone, *Ready to load car,* and by drawing arrows from that milestone to the activities *Load car* and *Decide which lake.*

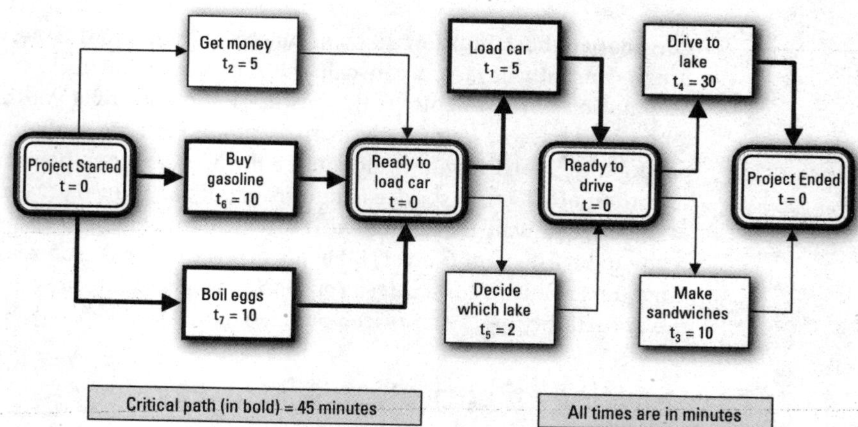

FIGURE 1-10: Getting to your picnic at the lake in 45 minutes.

© John Wiley & Sons, Inc.

REMEMBER

If you think this analysis is getting complicated, you're right. You pay a price to perform a group of activities faster. This price includes

- **Increased planning time:** You have to precisely detail all the activities and their interrelationships because you can't afford to make mistakes.
- **Increased risks:** The list of assumptions grows, increasing the chances that one or more will turn out to be wrong.

In the picnic-at-the-lake example, you make the following assumptions to arrive at a possible 45-minute solution:

- You can get right into the full-service island at a little after 8 a.m.
- Attendants are available to fill up your tank as soon as you pull into the full-service island.
- The ATM is free and working when you pull into the full-service island.
- You and your friend can load the car and make a decision together without getting into an argument that takes an hour to resolve.
- Your friend can make sandwiches in the moving car without totally destroying the car's interior in the process.

While making assumptions can increase the risk that you may not meet your project schedule, identifying the assumptions you make can improve your ability to increase the chances that they will come true — or at least convince you to develop contingency plans in case they don't.

Consider your assumption that you can get right into a full-service island at about 8 a.m. on Saturday. You can call the gas station owner and ask whether your assumption is reasonable. If the gas station owner tells you he has no idea how long you'll have to wait for someone to pump your gas, you may ask him whether paying him $200 in cash would make a difference. When he immediately promises to cordon off the full-service island from 7:55 a.m. until 8:20 a.m. and assign two attendants to wait there, one with a nozzle and the other with a charge receipt ready to be filled out (so you'll be out in ten minutes), you realize you can reduce most uncertainties for a price! Your job is to determine how much you can reduce the uncertainty and what price you have to pay to do so.

Devising an entirely new strategy

So you have a plan for getting to the lake in 45 minutes. You can't guarantee the plan will work, but at least you have a chance. However, suppose your friend now tells you he really needs to get to the lake in 10 minutes, not 45! Your immediate reaction is probably "Impossible!" You figure creative planning is one thing, but how can you get to the lake in 10 minutes when the drive alone takes 30 minutes?

By deciding that you absolutely can't arrive at the lake in 10 minutes when the drive alone takes 30 minutes, you've forgotten that the true indicator of success in this project is arriving at the lake for your picnic, not performing a predetermined set of activities. Your original seven activities were fine, as long as they allowed you to get to the lake within your set constraints. But if the activities won't allow you to achieve success as you now define it (arriving at the lake in ten minutes), consider changing the activities.

Suppose you decide to find a way other than driving to get from your home to the lake. After some checking, you discover that you can rent a helicopter for $500 per day that'll fly you and your friend to the lake in ten minutes. However, you figure that you both were thinking about spending a total of $10 on your picnic (for admission to the park at the lake). You conclude that it makes no sense to spend $500 to get to a $10 picnic, so you don't even tell your friend about the possibility of renting the helicopter. Instead, you just reaffirm that getting to the lake in ten minutes is impossible. Unfortunately, when you decided not to tell your friend about the helicopter option, you didn't know he'd found out that he could make a $10,000 profit on a business deal if he could get to the lake in ten minutes. Is it worth spending $500 to make $10,000? Sure. But you didn't know about the $10,000 when you gave up on getting to the lake in ten minutes.

REMEMBER

When developing schedule options, it's not your job to preempt someone else from making a decision. Instead, you want to present all options and their associated costs and benefits to the decision-maker so he can make the best decision. In this instance, you should've told your friend about the helicopter option so he could've considered it when he made the final decision.

Subdividing activities

You can often reduce the time to complete a sequence of activities by subdividing one or more of the activities and performing parts of them at the same time. In the picnic-at-the-lake example, your friend can save seven minutes when boiling the eggs and preparing the egg sandwiches by using the approach illustrated in Figure 1-11. Here's what your friend needs to do:

- **Divide the activity of boiling the eggs into two parts:**
  - **Prepare to boil the eggs.** Remove the pot from the cupboard, take the eggs out of the refrigerator, put the water and eggs in the pot, put the pot on the stove, and turn on the heat — estimated duration of three minutes.
  - **Boil the eggs in water.** Allow the eggs to boil in a pot until they're hard — estimated duration of seven minutes.
- **Divide the activity of making the egg sandwiches into two parts:**
  - **Perform the initial steps to make the sandwiches.** Take the bread, mayonnaise, lettuce, and tomatoes out of the refrigerator; take the wax paper out of the drawer; put the bread on the wax paper; put the mayonnaise, lettuce, and tomatoes on the bread — estimated duration of seven minutes.
  - **Finish making the sandwiches.** Take the eggs out of the pot; shell, slice, and put them on the bread; slice and finish wrapping the sandwiches — estimated duration of three minutes.
- **First prepare to boil the eggs; next boil the eggs in water and perform the initial steps to make sandwiches at the same time; finally, finish making the sandwiches.**

As Figure 1-11 illustrates, the total time to boil the eggs and prepare the sandwiches is 3 minutes plus 7 minutes plus 3 minutes for a total of 13 minutes. ***Note:*** The total time for the original activity to boil the eggs is still ten minutes (three minutes to prepare and seven minutes in the water), and the total time for the original activity to make the sandwiches is also still ten minutes (seven minutes for the initial steps and three minutes to finish up). But by subdividing the activities and scheduling them in greater detail, you can complete them in 13 minutes rather than 20.

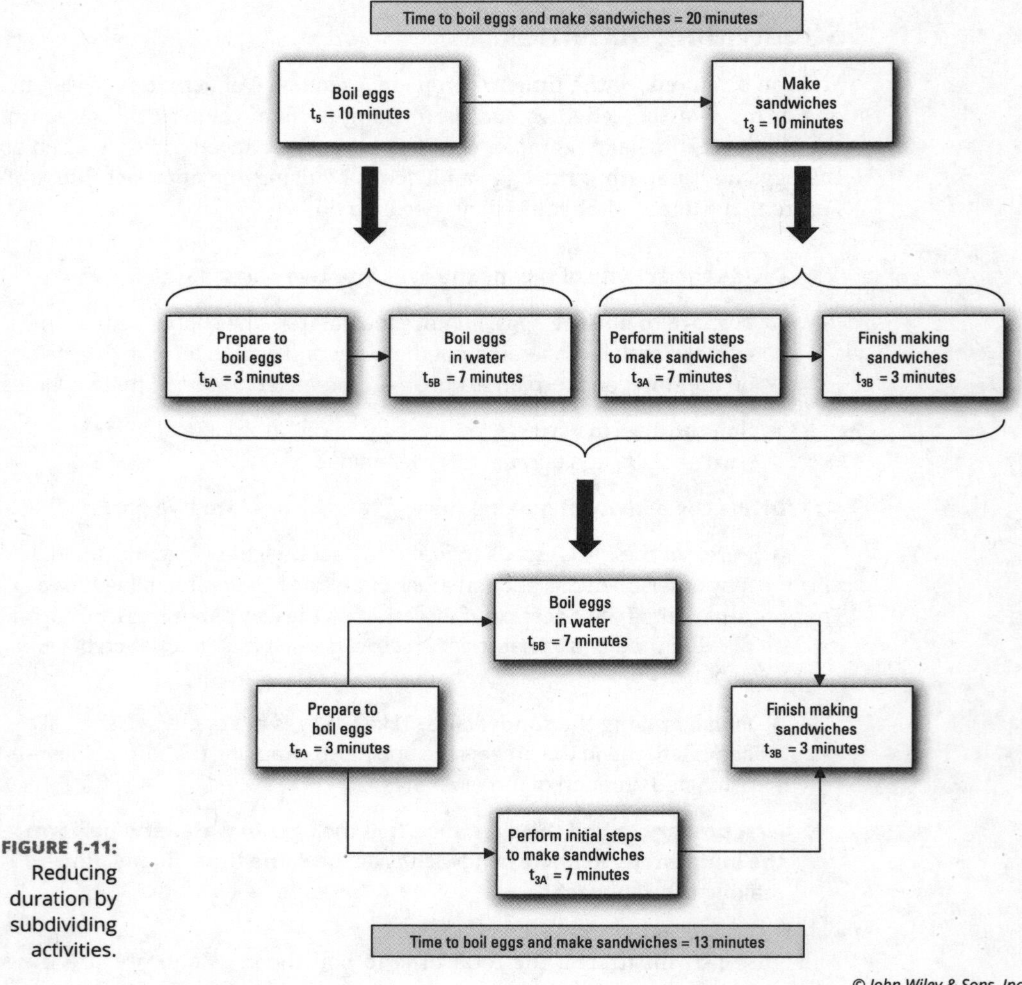

FIGURE 1-11: Reducing duration by subdividing activities.

© John Wiley & Sons, Inc.

Estimating Activity Duration

A *duration estimate* is your best sense of how long you need in order to actually perform an activity. The estimate isn't how long you want the activity to take or how long someone tells you it must take; the estimate is how long you think it really will take.

WARNING

Overly optimistic or unrealistically short duration estimates can cause an activity to take longer than necessary for the following two reasons:

- Because unrealistic estimates appear to meet your schedule targets, you don't seek realistic alternative strategies that increase the chances of accomplishing activities in their declared durations.
- If people believe duration estimates are totally unrealistic, they'll stop trying to achieve them. When delays occur during an activity, people will accept them as inevitable instead of seeking ways to overcome them.

This section looks more closely at what you need to estimate activity duration accurately, including an understanding of the activity's components and processes and the resources required to support these processes.

Determining the underlying factors

The underlying makeup of an activity determines how long it will take to complete. Therefore, accurately estimating that activity's duration requires you to describe its different aspects and determine the effect of each one on the activity's length.

REMEMBER

When estimating an activity's duration, consider past experience, expert opinion, and other available sources of information to clarify the following components of the activity:

- **Work performed by people:** Physical and mental activities that people perform, such as writing a report, assembling a piece of equipment, and thinking of ideas for an ad campaign.
- **Work performed by nonhuman resources:** Activities that computers and other machines perform, such as testing software on a computer and printing a report on a high-speed copy machine.
- **Physical processes:** Physical or chemical reactions, such as concrete curing, paint drying, and chemical reactions in a laboratory.
- **Time delays:** Time during which nothing is happening, such as needing to reserve a conference room two weeks before holding a meeting. (Time delays are typically due to the unavailability of resources.)

Considering resource characteristics

Knowing the types of resources an activity requires can help you improve your estimate of the activity's duration. For example, not all copy machines generate copies at the same rate. Specifying the characteristics of the particular machine you'll use to make copies can improve the activity's duration estimate.

To support project work, you may need the following types of resources: personnel, equipment, facilities, raw materials, information, and funds. For each resource you need, you have to determine its

- **Capacity:** Productivity per unit time period
- **Availability:** When a resource will be available

For example, a copy machine that produces 1,000 copies per minute can complete a job in half the time a machine that produces 500 copies per minute requires. Likewise, a large printing job can take half as long if you have access to a copy machine for four hours a day rather than two hours a day.

Finding sources of supporting information

The first step toward improving your estimate's accuracy is to take into account the right kinds of information, such as determining how long similar activities have actually taken in the past rather than how long people thought they would or should take. However, your estimate's accuracy also depends on the accuracy of the information you use to derive it.

REMEMBER

The information you need often has no single authoritative source. Therefore, compare information from the following sources as you prepare your duration estimates:

- Historical records of how long similar activities have taken in the past
- People who've performed similar activities in the past
- People who'll be working on the activities
- Experts familiar with the type of activity, even if they haven't performed the exact activity before

Improving activity duration estimates

In addition to ensuring accurate and complete data, do the following to improve the quality of your duration estimates (see Chapter 3 in Book 1 for more details about how to define and describe your project's activities):

» **Clearly define your activities.** Minimize the use of technical jargon and describe work processes fully.

» **Subdivide your activities until your lowest-level activity estimates are two weeks or less.**

» **Clearly define activity start and end points.**

» **Involve the people who'll perform an activity when estimating its duration.**

» **Minimize the use of fudge factors.** A *fudge factor* is an amount of time you add to your best estimate of duration "just to be safe." Automatically estimating your final duration estimates to be 50 percent greater than your initial ones is an example. Fudge factors compromise your project planning for the following reasons:

- Work tends to expand to fill the allotted time. If you're able to finish an activity in two weeks but use a 50-percent fudge factor to indicate a duration of three weeks, the likelihood that you'll finish in less than three weeks is almost zero.
- People use fudge factors to avoid studying activities in sufficient depth; as a result, they can't develop viable performance strategies.
- Team members and other project audiences lose faith in your plan's accuracy and feasibility because they know you're playing with numbers rather than thinking activities through in detail.

TIP

No matter how hard you try, accurately estimating duration can be next to impossible for some activities. For example, you may have an exceptionally difficult time coming up with accurate duration estimates for activities you haven't done before, activities you'll perform in the distant future, and activities with a history of unpredictability. In these cases,

» Make the best estimate you can by following the approaches and guidelines in this section.

» Closely monitor activities as your project unfolds to identify details that may affect your initial estimate.

» Reflect any changes in your project schedule as soon as you become aware of them.

In situations where you've performed an activity many times before and have historical data on how long it took each time, you may be able to estimate with confidence how long the activity will take the next time you perform it. In less-certain situations, however, you may choose to consider the activity's duration as a random variable that can have a range of values with different probabilities.

The *program evaluation and review technique* (PERT) is a network analysis methodology that treats an activity's duration as a random variable with the probability of the variable having different values being described by a Beta distribution. According to the characteristics of a Beta distribution, you determine the *average value* (also called the *expected value*) of the activity's duration from the following three time estimates:

- **Optimistic estimate (t_o):** If you perform the activity 100 times, its duration would be greater than or equal to this number 99 times.
- **Most likely estimate (t_m):** If you perform the activity 100 times, the duration would be this number more times than any other.
- **Pessimistic estimate (t_p):** If you perform this activity 100 times, its duration would be less than or equal to this number 99 times.

The expected value of the duration (t_e) is then defined by the following formula: Expected value = $t_e = (t_o + 4t_m + t_p) \div 6$.

REMEMBER

If only a small number of activities in your network is uncertain, you may assign their durations to be equal to their expected values and determine the critical path, earliest and latest start and finish times, and slack times as described earlier in this chapter. However, if all activities in your network are uncertain, you may choose to develop three time estimates for each activity. In this case, you can use the properties of the Beta distribution to determine the probability that the length of the critical path falls within specified ranges on either side of its expected value.

Displaying Your Project's Schedule

Unless all your activities are on a critical path, your network diagram doesn't specify your exact schedule. Rather, it provides information for you to consider when you develop your schedule. After you select your actual dates, choose one of the following commonly used formats in which to present your schedule:

- **Milestone list:** A table that lists milestones and the dates you plan to reach them
- **Activity list:** A table that lists activities and the dates you plan to start and end them
- **Combined milestone and activity report:** A table that includes milestone and activity dates

» **Gantt (or bar) chart:** A timeline that illustrates when each activity starts, how long it continues, and when it ends

» **Combined milestone and Gantt chart:** A timeline that illustrates when activities start, how long they continue, when they end, and when selected milestones are achieved

Figure 1-12 presents the 45-minute schedule for your picnic at the lake (from Figure 1-10 earlier in this chapter) in a combined milestone and activity report.

Picnic-at-the-Lake Project (45-Minute Solution)						
Activity/Milestone			People Present	Start Date (minutes after start)	End Date (minutes after start)	Comments
ID	WBS Code	Name				
8	**1.0**	**Project Started**	**You and friend**	**0**	**0**	**Critical path**
10	2.0	Preparation	You and friend	0	25	
2	**2.1**	**Get money**	**You**	**0**	**5**	**Critical path**
6	**2.2**	**Buy gasoline**	**You**	**0**	**10**	**Critical path**
7	**2.3**	**Boil eggs**	**Your friend**	**0**	**10**	**Critical path**
3	**2.4**	**Make sandwiches**	**Your friend**	**15**	**25**	**Critical path**
12	3.0	Ready to load car	You and friend	10	10	
5	**4.0**	**Decide which lake**	**You and friend**	**10**	**12**	**Critical path**
13	5.0	Ready to drive	You and friend	15	15	
11	6.0	Travel	You and friend	10	45	
1	**6.1**	**Load car**	**You and friend**	**10**	**15**	**Critical path**
4	**6.2**	**Drive to lake**	**You and friend**	**15**	**45**	**Critical path**
9	**7.0**	**Project Ended (arrival at lake)**	**You and friend**	**45**	**45**	**Critical path**

Note: Milestones and activities that are on a critical path are highlighted in bold.

© John Wiley & Sons, Inc.

FIGURE 1-12: Representing your picnic-at-the-lake schedule in a combined milestone and activity report.

You may combine two or more formats into a single display. Figure 1-13 illustrates a combined WBS, responsibility assignment matrix (a table that depicts each project audience's role in the performance of different project activities), and Gantt chart (in which triangles represent milestones) for the picnic-at-the-lake example. In addition to requiring less paperwork to prepare and being easier to update and maintain than separate information documents, a combined display can provide greater insight into the plan by presenting two or more aspects together for ready comparison.

Picnic-at-the-Lake Project (45-Minute Solution)

Work Breakdown Structure			Responsibility Assignment Matrix		Gantt Chart
Activity/Milestone			Personnel		Time (in minutes after start)
ID	WBS Code	Name	You	Friend	0 5 10 15 20 25 30 35 40 45
8	**1.0**	**Start**	**P**	**S**	
10	2.0	Preparation	P	S	
2	**2.1**	**Get money**	**P**		
6	**2.2**	**Buy gasoline**	**P**		
7	**2.3**	**Boil eggs**		**P**	
3	**2.4**	**Make sandwiches**		**P**	
12	3.0	Ready to load car	S	P	
5	**4.0**	**Decide which lake**	**S**	**P**	
13	5.0	Ready to drive	S	P	
11	6.0	Travel	P	S	
1	**4.1**	**Load car**	**S**	**P**	
4	**4.2**	**Drive to lake**	**P**	**S**	
9	**5.0**	**End**	**P**	**S**	

P = Primary Responsibility S = Supporting Responsibility

Critical path milestones and activities are highlighted in bold

© John Wiley & Sons, Inc.

FIGURE 1-13: Representing your picnic-at-the-lake schedule in a combined WBS, responsibility assignment matrix, and Gantt chart.

You may also choose to display your project schedule with an Interface Gantt chart. In addition to including all the information you find in a simple Gantt chart, the Interface Gantt chart represents dependencies between the project's activities and milestones with arrows drawn between the bars. The picnic-at-the-lake 45-minute schedule is presented in Figure 1-14 with an Interface Gantt chart.

TIP

Each format can be effective in particular situations. Consider the following guidelines when choosing the format in which to display your schedule:

- Milestone lists and activity lists are more effective for indicating specific dates.
- The Gantt chart provides a clearer picture of the relative lengths of activities and times when they overlap.
- The Gantt chart provides a better high-level overview of a project.
- The Interface Gantt chart has all the benefits of the plain Gantt chart plus it illustrates the order in which the activities are performed.

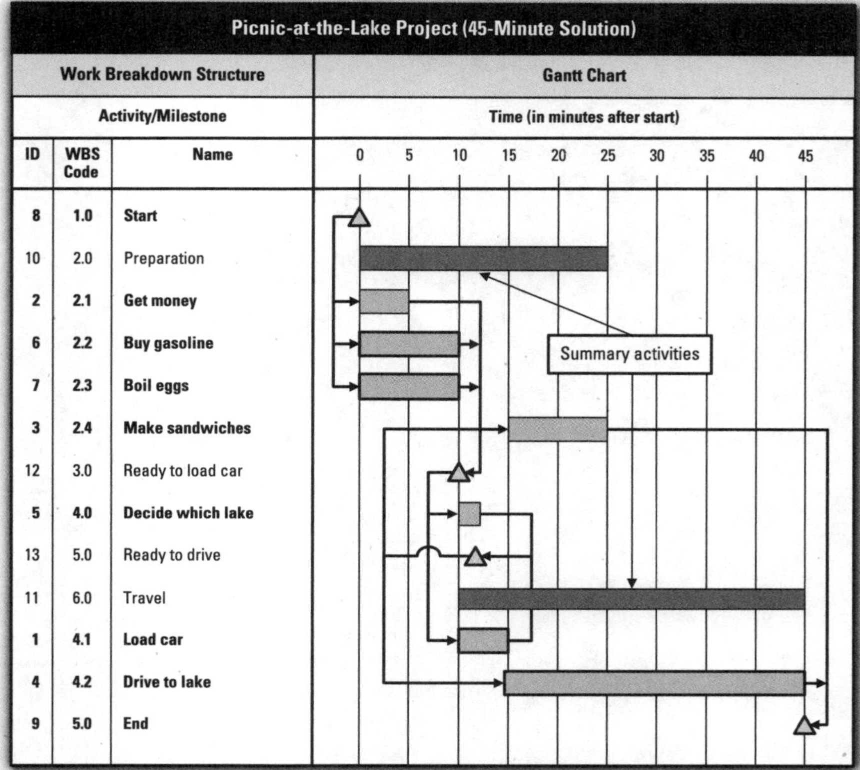

© John Wiley & Sons, Inc.

FIGURE 1-14: Representing your picnic-at-the-lake schedule in an Interface Gantt chart.

» Developing your team's identity along with its operating procedures

» Creating systems and schedules for project control

» Introducing your project with an official announcement

» Laying the groundwork for the post-project review

Chapter 2

Starting Your Project Team Off on the Right Foot

After intense work on a tight schedule, you submit your project plan (the single document that integrates and consolidates your project's scope statement, stakeholder register, work breakdown structure, responsibility assignment matrix, schedule, resource requirements, budget, and all subsidiary plans for providing project support services) for review and approval. A few days later, your boss comes to you and says,

"I have some good news and some bad news. Which would you like to hear first?"

"Tell me the good news," you respond.

"Your plan's been approved."

"So, what's the bad news?" you ask.

"Now you have to do the project!"

Starting off your project correctly is a key to ultimate success. Your project plan describes what you'll produce, the work you'll do, how you'll do it, when you'll do it, and which resources you'll need to do it. When you write your project plan, you base it on the information you have at the time, and, if information isn't available, you make assumptions. The more time between your plan's completion and its approval, the more changes you're likely to find in your plan's assumptions as you actually start your project.

As you prepare to start your project, you need to reconfirm or update the information in your plan, determine or reaffirm which people will play roles in your project, their time commitment, and exactly what those roles will be, and prepare the systems and procedures that will support your project's performance. This chapter tells you how to accomplish these tasks and get your project off to a strong start.

Finalizing Your Project's Participants

A *project stakeholder* is a person or group that supports, is affected by, or is interested in your project. (See Chapter 2 in Book 1 for details on how to identify project stakeholders.) In your project plan, you describe the roles you expect people to play and the amount of effort you expect team members to invest. You identify the people by name, by title or position, or by the skills and knowledge they need to have.

This section shows you how to reaffirm who will be involved in your project. It also helps you make sure everyone's still on board — and tells you what to do if some people aren't.

Are you in? Confirming your team members' participation

To confirm the identities of the people who'll work to support your project, you have to verify that specific people are still able to uphold their promised commitments and, if necessary, recruit new people to fulfill the remaining needs.

REMEMBER

As you contact the people who will support your project, be sure to do the following:

1. **Inform them that your project has been approved and when work will start.**

   Not all project plans get approved. You rarely know in advance how long the approval process will take or how soon your project can start. Inform team members as soon as possible so they can schedule the necessary time.

2. **Confirm that they're still able to support your project.**

   People's workloads and other commitments may change between the time you prepare your plan and your project's approval. If a person is no longer able to provide the promised support, recruit a replacement as soon as possible (see the later section "Filling in the blanks" for guidelines).

3. **Explain what you'll do to develop the project team and start the project work.**

   Provide a list of all team members and others who will support the project. Also mention the steps you'll take to introduce members and kick off the project.

4. **Reconfirm the work you expect them to perform, the schedules and deadlines you expect them to keep, and the amount of time you expect them to spend on the work.**

   Clarify specific activities and the nature of the work.

TIP

Depending on the size and formality of your project, you can use any format from a quick email to a formal work-order agreement to share this information with the people who will be involved in your project.

As Figure 2-1 illustrates, a typical *work-order agreement* includes the following information:

- **Identifiers:** The identifiers include the project name, project number, and work breakdown structure (WBS) code and component name. (For more on the WBS, see Chapter 3 in Book 1.) The project name and number confirm that your project is now official. You use the WBS code and component name to record work progress as well as time and resource charges.
- **Work to be performed and deliverables or results to be produced:** These details describe the different activities and procedures involved in the project, as well as outputs of the project.
- **Activity start date, end date, and number of hours to be spent:** Including this information reaffirms
  - The importance of doing the work within the schedule and budget
  - Acknowledgment from the person who'll do the work that he expects to do the described work within these time and resource constraints
  - The criteria you'll use to assess the person's performance
- **Written approvals from the person who'll do the work, his supervisor, and the project manager:** Including these written approvals increases the likelihood that everyone involved has read and understood the project's elements and is committed to support it.

Work-Order Agreement		
Project name:		Project number:
WBS component name:		Work Breakdown Structure code:
Description of work to be performed:		
Deliverables or results to be produced:		
Start date	End date	Number of hours to be spent
Approvals		
Project manager: Name (Print) Name (Signature) Date	Team member: Name (Print) Name (Signature) Date	Team member's supervisor: Name (Print) Name (Signature) Date

FIGURE 2-1: A typical work-order agreement.

© John Wiley & Sons, Inc.

TIP

Be sure you specify all this information when reconfirming a person's commitment to your project. The longer you wait to specify these details, the greater the chances are that the person won't provide the support you had hoped for.

REMEMBER

If you choose not to use a formal work-order agreement, be sure to write down all key information that clarifies your agreement and get signed approvals from the team member and his supervisor. Asking for signed approvals encourages people to consider carefully before they make any commitments and serves as a reference and reminder of exactly what was promised.

Assuring that others are on board

Other people may also play a role in your project's success, even though they may not officially be members of your project team. Two such groups are *drivers* (people who have a say in defining the results of your project) and *supporters* (people who will perform a service or provide resources for your team).

Two other special stakeholders are your *project champion* and your *project executive sponsor.* Both are people in high positions in the organization who strongly support your project; who will advocate for your project in disputes, planning meetings, and review sessions; and who will take necessary actions to help ensure your project's success. (See Chapter 2 in Book 1 for more on these different types of project stakeholders.)

Contact your project champion and all other drivers and supporters to

- Inform them that your project has been approved and when work will start.
- Reaffirm your project's objectives.
- Confirm with identified drivers that the project's planned results still address their needs.
- Clarify with supporters exactly how you want them to help your project.
- Develop specific plans for involving each stakeholder throughout the project and keeping them informed of progress. This is also called the stakeholder management plan.

TIP

Some people will be interested in your project but won't define its planned results or directly support your efforts. As you identify these *observers,* as they're often called, choose those individuals you want to keep informed of your progress throughout the project and plan how you'll do so. (See Chapter 2 in Book 1 for tips on how to identify project observers.)

Filling in the blanks

If your plan identifies proposed project team members only by job title, position description, or skills and knowledge (and not by specific names), you have to find actual people to fill the specified roles. You can fill the empty roles by assigning responsibility to someone already on your organization's staff, by recruiting a person from outside your organization, or by contracting with an external organization. If you don't have the authority to hire a person yourself, work with the functional manager to whom the new hire will report.

Whichever method you choose, prepare a written description of the activities you want each person to perform. This description can range from a simple memo for informal projects to a written job description for more formal ones.

REMEMBER

Write down your needs for each category of personnel separately. At a minimum, include the following information in your role descriptions:

- Project name, number, and start date
- Necessary skills and knowledge
- Supervision to be provided
- Activities to be performed and start and end dates
- Anticipated level of effort

If you plan to look inside your organization to recruit team members for roles not yet filled, do the following:

- Identify potential candidates by working with your human resources (HR) department and area managers.
- Meet with the candidates to discuss your project, describe the work involved, and assess their qualifications.
- Choose the best candidates and ask them to join your team.
- Document the agreements you make with the new team members.

Also, if you plan to obtain the support of external consultants, work with your organization's contracts office. Provide the contracts office with the same information that you provide your HR office. Review the contract document before your contracting officer signs it.

In addition to filling your empty team-member roles, work with people in key organizational units to identify people, other than team members, who will support your project (for example, a contracts specialist or a procurement specialist, as long as he isn't officially on your project team). After you identify these people, do the following:

- Meet with them to clarify your project's goals and anticipated outputs and the ways in which they will support your performance.
- Develop plans for involving them and keeping them informed of progress throughout your project.

Developing Your Team

Merely assigning people to tasks doesn't create a project team. A *team* is a collection of people who are committed to common goals and who depend on one another to do their jobs. Project teams consist of members who can and must make a valuable and unique contribution to the project.

A team is different from other associations of people who work together. For example,

- A *group* consists of people who work individually to accomplish their particular assignments on a common task.

- **A** *committee* consists of people who come together to review and critique issues, propose recommendations for action, and, on occasion, implement those recommendations.

REMEMBER

As soon as you identify your project team members, take steps to define and establish your team's identity as well as its operating practices. Develop the following elements, making sure your team understands and accepts them:

- **Goals:** What the team as a whole and members individually hope to accomplish
- **Roles:** Each member's areas of specialty, position on the team, assignments, authority, responsibilities, and accountability
- **Processes:** The techniques that team members will use to perform their project tasks
- **Relationships:** The attitudes and behaviors of team members toward one another

This section discusses how to begin creating your team's identity by having members review and discuss the project plan, examine overall team and individual team-member goals, agree on everyone's roles, and start to establish productive working relationships.

Reviewing the approved project plan

REMEMBER

As soon as people join the team, have them review the approved project plan to reinforce the project's goals, clarify the work planned, confirm the feasibility of time and resource estimates and methods of communication, and identify any potential problems. Meet as a group to discuss people's thoughts and reactions after they've reviewed the plan.

Team members who contributed to the proposal can remind themselves of the project's background and purpose, their planned roles, and the work to be done. They can also identify situations and circumstances that may have changed since the proposal was prepared and then review and reassess project risks and risk-management plans.

New team members can understand the project's background and purpose, find out about their roles and assignments, raise concerns about time frames and budgets, and identify issues that may affect the project's success.

Developing team and individual goals

Team members commit to your project when they believe their participation can help them achieve worthwhile professional and personal goals. Help team members develop and buy into a shared sense of the project goals by doing the following:

- » Discuss the reasons for the project, its supporters, and the impact of its results.
- » Clarify how the results may benefit your organization's clients.
- » Emphasize how the results may support your organization's growth and viability.
- » Explore how the results may impact each team member's job.

REMEMBER

Encourage people to think about how their participation may help them achieve personal goals, such as acquiring new skills and knowledge, meeting new people, increasing their visibility in the organization, and enhancing their opportunities for job advancement. Obviously, projects aren't only about helping team members achieve personal benefits. However, when team members can realize personal benefits while performing valued services for the organization, the members' motivation and commitment to project success will be greater.

Specifying team-member roles

Nothing causes disillusionment and frustration faster than bringing motivated people together and then giving them no guidance on how to work with one another. Two or more people may start doing the same activity independently, and other activities may be overlooked entirely. Eventually, these people find tasks that don't require coordination, or they gradually withdraw from the project to work on more rewarding assignments.

To prevent this frustration from becoming a part of your project, work with team members to define the activities that each member works on and the nature of their roles. Possible team member roles include the following:

- » **Primary responsibility:** Has the overall obligation to ensure the completion of an activity
- » **Secondary or supporting responsibility:** Has the obligation to complete part of an activity
- » **Approval:** Must approve the results of an activity before work can proceed

- **Consultation resource:** Can provide expert guidance and support if needed
- **Required recipient of project results:** Receives either a physical product from an activity or a report of an activity

TIP

A responsibility assignment matrix (RAM) is a table that depicts each project audience's role in the performance of different project activities. If you prepared a RAM as part of your project plan, use it to start your discussions of project roles with your team members. Make sure you don't just present the RAM; take the time to encourage questions and concerns from team members until they're comfortable that the roles are feasible and appropriate.

Defining your team's operating processes

Develop the procedures that you and your team will use to support your day-to-day work. Having these procedures in place allows people to effectively and efficiently perform their tasks; it also contributes to a positive team atmosphere. At a minimum, develop procedures for the following:

- **Communication:** These processes involve sharing project-related information in writing and through personal interactions. Communication procedures may include
  - When and how to use email to share project information
  - Which types of information should be in writing
  - When and how to document informal discussions
  - How to set up regularly scheduled reports and meetings to record and review progress
  - Scheduled team meetings and the communication platform the team will be using
  - How to address special issues that arise
- **Decision-making:** These processes involve deciding among alternative approaches and actions. Develop guidelines for making the most appropriate choice for a situation, including consensus, majority rule, unanimous agreement, and decision by technical expert. Also develop escalation procedures — the steps you take when the normal decision-making approaches get bogged down.
- **Conflict resolution:** These processes involve resolving differences of opinion between team members. (See the later section "Resolving conflicts" for details on two conflict-resolution procedures.)

Supporting the development of team-member relationships

On high-performance project teams, members trust each other and have cordial, coordinated working relationships. But developing trust and effective work practices takes time and concerted effort.

TIP

Help your team members get to know and be comfortable with one another as soon as your project starts by encouraging them to do the following:

- » Work through conflicts together (see the next section for more on conflict resolution).
- » Brainstorm challenging technical and administrative issues.
- » Spend informal personal time together, such as having lunch or participating in non-wor k-related activities after hours.

Resolving conflicts

With most projects, the question isn't *if* disagreements will occur between team members; it's *when.* So you need to be prepared to resolve those differences of opinion with a conflict-resolution plan that includes one or both of the following:

- » **Standard approaches:** Normal steps that you take to encourage people to develop a mutually agreeable solution
- » **Escalation procedures:** Steps you take if the people involved can't readily resolve their differences

Minimizing conflict on your team

Throughout the life of a project, conflicts may arise around a myriad of professional, interpersonal, technical, and administrative issues. The first step toward minimizing the negative consequences of such conflicts is to avoid them before they occur. The following tips can help you do just that:

- » Encourage people to participate in the development of the project plan.
- » Get commitments and expectations in writing.
- » Frequently monitor work in progress to identify and resolve any conflicts that arise before they become serious.

If a conflict does arise, one or more of the participants in the conflict or one or more people with knowledge of the issues around which the conflict arose need to take an active role to resolve the conflict. The person or people chosen for this task should have knowledge of the conflict and the issues surrounding it, the techniques of proactive conflict resolution, the respect of the people involved in the conflict, and no preconceived preferences for any of the solutions of the people involved in the conflict. Whether they informally assume the responsibility to help resolve the conflict or are assigned by the project manager or another member of management to do so, they should do the following:

- Study the conflict and gather all related background information to identify the likely and underlying reasons for it.
- Select and follow an appropriate resolution strategy.
- Maintain an atmosphere of mutual cooperation when trying to find an acceptable solution.

As you work to understand the reasons for a conflict, note that conflicts can arise over one or more of the following:

- **Facts:** Objective data that describe a situation
- **Methods:** How a person responds to particular values of data
- **Goals:** What someone is ultimately trying to accomplish when she resolves the conflict
- **Values:** The basic personal feelings and principals that motivate someone's behavior

Keep in mind that personal beliefs about each of these four types of information can be due to

- Incorrect information
- Different perceptions or inferences based on the same information
- Different reactions to the same information based on the position a person occupies or the role she plays on the team

Acting out conflict resolution with a simple example

Suppose that Sarah and Jimmy have been assigned to develop recommendations for how to improve the production of a poorly performing unit in their company.

After reviewing some related reports and having a few discussions, Sarah has decided the best way to improve performance is to fire two of the four people in the unit and retrain the other two. In contrast, Jimmy has decided the only way to improve the unit's performance is to fire all four people.

At the moment, Sarah and Jimmy are at a standoff, but if they're willing, they can take one of the following approaches to resolve their conflict:

- **Competition (Forcing):** Both people assertively act to have their solution to the conflict chosen. (There's a winner and a loser.)
- **Accommodation (Smoothing):** One person chooses to go with the other person's solution. (There's a winner and a loser.)
- **Avoidance (Withdrawing):** One person chooses not to acknowledge the conflict at all. For example, Sarah may draft a memo that two people in the unit can be trained and the other two fired, ignoring the fact that Jimmy wants all four people to be fired. (There's a winner and a loser.)
- **Compromise (Giving a little, getting a little):** Both people give in a little to the other person's proposed solution. (Each person wins and loses in some way.)
- **Collaboration (Problem-solving):** Both people get what they want. (There are two winners and no losers.)

As you consider these possible resolutions, keep in mind the following two points:

- **Conflict is not necessarily "bad."** Conflict that focuses on the merits of alternative solutions and maintains respect for the parties involved can result in a solution that's better than the original choice of either of the participants.
- **Most people understand that they may have to "lose" a conflict every once in a while, and they learn to absorb the blow to their psyche.** However, if they lose a disproportionate number of the conflicts in which they choose to participate, they may decide to withdraw from the team and not share their true feelings.

REMEMBER

To increase the chances of achieving a successful collaborative resolution on your team, follow these guidelines:

- Suggest that participants develop sets of criteria for rating solutions instead of just arguing strongly for one solution.
- Encourage participants to develop additional possible solutions instead of just arguing that their original solution should be selected.

- Allow sufficient time to explore the different alternatives proposed.
- Don't take sides during the discussions. If one person senses that you're predisposed to the other person's solution, she'll think the decision process was unfair and not accept any solution but her own.

All together now: Helping your team become a smooth-functioning unit

When team members trust each other, have confidence in each other's abilities, can count on each other's promises, and communicate openly, they can devote all their efforts to performing their project work instead of spending their time dealing with interpersonal frustrations. Help your team achieve this high-performance level of functioning by guiding it through the following stages:

- **Forming:** This stage involves identifying and meeting team members and politely discussing project objectives, work assignments, and so forth. During this stage, you share the project plan, introduce people to each other, and discuss each person's background, organizational responsibilities, and areas of expertise.
- **Storming:** This stage involves raising and resolving personal conflicts about the project or other team members. As part of the storming stage, do the following:
  - Encourage people to discuss any concerns they have about the project plan's feasibility and make sure you address those concerns.
  - Encourage people to discuss any reservations they may have about other team members or team members' abilities.
  - Focus these discussions on ways to ensure successful task performance; you don't want the talks to turn into unproductive personal attacks.

  REMEMBER

  Initially, you can speak privately with people about issues you're uncomfortable bringing up in front of the entire team. Eventually, though, you must discuss their concerns with the entire team to achieve a sense of mutual honesty and trust.
- **Norming:** This stage involves developing the standards and operating guidelines that govern team-member behavior. Encourage members to establish these team norms instead of relying on the procedures and practices they use in their functional areas. Examples of these norms include
  - **How people present and discuss different points of view:** Some people present points of view politely, while others aggressively debate their opponents in an attempt to prove their points.

- **Timeliness of meeting attendance:** Some people always show up for meetings on time, while others are habitually 15 minutes late.
- **Participation in meetings:** Some people sit back and observe, while others actively participate and share their ideas.

TIP

At a team meeting, encourage people to discuss how team members should behave in different situations. Address the concerns people express and encourage the group to adopt team norms.

» **Performing:** This stage involves doing project work, monitoring schedules and budgets, making necessary changes, and keeping people informed.

REMEMBER

As you guide your team through these developmental stages, keep in mind the following guidelines:

» **Your team won't automatically pass through these stages; you'll have to guide them.** Left on their own, teams often fail to move beyond the forming stage. Many people don't like to confront thorny interpersonal issues, so they simply ignore them. Your job is to make sure your team members address what needs to be addressed and become a smooth-functioning team.

» **Your involvement as project manager in your team's development needs to be heavier in the early stages and lighter in the later ones.** During the forming stage, you need to take the lead as new people join the team. Then, in the storming stage, you take a strong facilitative role as you guide and encourage people to share their feelings and concerns. Although you can help guide the team as it develops its standards and norms during the norming stage, your main emphasis is to ensure that everyone participates in the process. Finally, if you've navigated the first three stages successfully, you can step back in the performing stage and offer your support as the team demonstrates its ability to function as a high-performing unit.

» **On occasion, you may have to revisit a stage you thought the team had completed.** For example, a new person may join the team, or a major aspect of the project plan may change.

» **If everything goes smoothly on your project, it doesn't matter whether the team has successfully gone through the forming, storming, and norming stages.** But when the project runs into problems, your team may become dysfunctional if it hasn't progressed successfully through each stage. Suppose, for example, that the team misses a major project deadline. If team members haven't developed mutual trust for one another, they're more likely to spend time searching for someone to blame than working together to fix the situation.

» **As the project manager, you need to periodically assess how the team feels it's performing; you then have to decide which, if any, issues the team needs to work through.** Managing your team is a project in and of itself!

Laying the Groundwork for Controlling Your Project

Controlling your project throughout its performance requires that you collect appropriate information, evaluate your performance compared with your plan, and share your findings with your project's stakeholders. This section highlights the steps you take to prepare to collect, analyze, and share this information. (See Chapter 3 in Book 2 for full details on maintaining control of your project.)

Selecting and preparing your tracking systems

Effective project control requires that you have accurate and timely information to help you identify problems promptly and take appropriate corrective action. This section highlights the information you need and explains how to get it.

Throughout your project, you need to track performance in terms of the following:

» **Schedule achievement:** The assessment of how well you're meeting established dates

» **Personnel resource use:** The levels of effort people are spending on their assignments

» **Financial expenditures:** The funds you're spending for project resources

See Chapter 3 in Book 2 for a detailed discussion of the information systems you can use to track your project's progress.

If you use existing, enterprise-wide information systems to track your project's schedule performance and resource use, set up your project on these systems as follows (see Chapter 3 in Book 2 for information on how to decide whether to use existing information systems to support your project's monitoring and control):

- **Obtain your official project number.** Your *project number* is the official company identifier for your project. All products, activities, and resources related to your project are assigned that number. Check with your organization's finance department or project office to find out your project's number and check with your finance or information technology department to determine the steps you must take to set up your project on the organization's financial tracking system, labor recording system, and/or activity tracking system.
- **Finalize your project's work breakdown structure (WBS).** Have team members review your project's WBS and make any necessary changes or additions. Assign identifier codes to all WBS elements. (Check out Chapter 3 in Book 1 for a complete explanation of the WBS.)
- **Set up charge codes for your project on the organization's labor-tracking system.** If team members record their labor hours by projects, set up charge codes for all WBS activities. Doing so allows you to monitor the progress of individual WBS elements, as well as the total project.

TIP

If your organization's system can limit the number of hours for each activity, enter those limits (see the later section "Setting your project's baseline" as well as Chapter 3 of Book 2 for how to establish targets for your project's schedule, resource needs, and budget). Doing so ensures that people don't mistakenly charge more hours to activities than your plan allows. It is the project manager's responsibility to review the hours spent on the project and that they are billing their time correctly.

- **Set up charge codes for your project on your organization's financial system.** If your organization tracks expenditures by project, set up the codes for all WBS activities that have expenditures. If the system can limit expenditures for each activity, enter those limits.

Establishing schedules for reports and meetings

To be sure you satisfy your information needs and those of your project's stakeholders, set up a schedule of reports you'll prepare and meetings you'll hold during the project. Planning your communications with your stakeholders in advance helps ensure that you adequately meet their individual needs and allows them to reserve time on their calendars to attend the meetings.

Meet with project stakeholders and team members to develop a schedule for regular project meetings and progress reports. Confirm the following details:

- What reports will be issued
- Which meetings will be held and what their specific purposes will be
- When reports will be issued and when meetings will be held
- Who will receive the reports and attend the meetings
- Which formats the reports and meetings will be in and what they'll cover

Setting your project's baseline

The project *baseline* is the version of your project's plan that guides your project activities and provides the comparative basis for your performance assessments. At the beginning of your project, use the plan that was approved at the end of the organizing-and-preparing stage, modified by any approved changes made during the carrying-out-the-work stage, as your baseline (see Chapter 1 in Book 1 for a discussion of the project life-cycle stages). During the project, use the most recent approved version of the project plan as your baseline. (See Chapter 3 in Book 2 for more discussion on setting, updating, and using your project's baseline to control your project.)

Hear Ye, Hear Ye! Announcing Your Project

After you've notified your key project stakeholders (that is, the drivers and supporters) that your project has been approved and when it'll start, you have to introduce it to others who may be interested (known as *observers*; see Chapter 2 in Book 1 for a discussion of how to identify the observers among your project's stakeholders). Consider one or more of the following approaches to announce your project to all interested parties:

- An email to selected individuals or departments in your organization
- An announcement in your organization's newsletter
- A flyer on a prominent bulletin board
- A formal kickoff meeting
- A press release (if your project has stakeholders outside your organization)

REMEMBER

Regardless of how you announce your project, be sure to mention its purpose and scope, your intended outcomes and results, and the key dates. Tell people how they can get in touch with you if they have questions or would like detailed information.

Setting the Stage for Your Post-Project Evaluation

A *post-project evaluation* (also called a *lessons learned session*), described in detail in Chapter 4 of Book 2, is a meeting in which you

- Review the experience you've gained from the project.
- Recognize people for their achievements.
- Plan to ensure that good practices are repeated on future projects.
- Plan to head off problems you encountered on this project on future projects.

TIP

Start laying groundwork for the post-project evaluation as soon as your project begins to make sure you capture all relevant information and observations about the project to discuss at the post-project meeting. Lay the groundwork by doing the following:

- Tell the team you'll hold a post-project review when the project ends.
- Encourage team members to keep records of problems, ideas, and suggestions throughout the project. When you prepare the final agenda for the post-project evaluation session, ask people to review these records and notes to find topics to discuss.
- Clarify the criteria that define your project's success by reviewing the latest version of your project's objectives with team members.
- Describe the details of the situation your project is designed to address before you begin the project work (if the project was designed to change or improve a situation). Doing so enables you to assess the changes in these details when the project ends.
- Maintain your own *project log* (a narrative record of project issues and occurrences) and encourage other team members to do the same.
- The post evaluation documentation will be stored in the project repository upon project closed. This is a valuable document because it can prevent mistakes in the organization's future projects.

IN THIS CHAPTER

» Using information systems to track scheduling, work effort, and expenditures

» Implementing your control process and taking corrective actions

» Managing changes responsibly

Chapter 3

Monitoring Progress and Maintaining Control

A sad reality for many projects is that although they're born accompanied by high hopes and expectations, they die amid frustration and disappointment. Your project plans represent visions that you believe will work; however, those plans don't implement themselves automatically, and they can't predict the future with certainty.

Successful projects require continued care and management to ensure that they follow their plans correctly and, in turn, produce the desired results. When unexpected situations occur, you, as the project manager, must react promptly to adjust your efforts and keep your project on track.

This chapter discusses the steps in the project-control process and focuses on the systems and techniques you can use to collect, analyze, and report on schedule performance, labor hours, and expenditures, as well as the processes for dealing with change requests and taking corrective actions when needed.

Holding the Reins: Project Control

Project control entails the following activities, which you perform throughout your project to ensure it proceeds according to plan and produces the desired results:

- **Reconfirming the plan:** At the beginning of each performance period, reaffirm with team members the following project responsibilities and commitments they made for the coming period:
  - Activities they agreed to perform
  - Dates they agreed they will start and end these activities
  - Amount of person effort they agreed they'll need to perform these activities (*person effort* or *work effort* is the actual time a person spends doing an activity; one person-hour of work effort is equal to the amount of work done by one person working full time for one hour)
- **Assessing performance:** During the performance period, have team members record information on the following:
  - Completed intermediate and final deliverables
  - Dates they reached milestones
  - Dates they started and ended activities
  - Number of hours they worked on each activity
  - Amount of non-personnel resources they used for each activity
  - Expenditures they made for each activity

  Collect this information at the end of the performance period, compare it with the plan, and determine the reasons for any differences.
- **Taking corrective action:** If necessary, take steps to bring your project's performance back into conformance with your plans; if doing so isn't possible, you may have to change the plans to reflect new expectations.
- **Keeping people informed:** Share your achievements, problems, and future plans with your project's stakeholders.

TIP

Choose the periods for monitoring your project's performance based on the overall length of the project, the risk of unexpected occurrences, and your proximity to major milestones. Although you may choose to monitor selected project activities on a daily basis in certain situations, plan to assess your project's overall performance at least once a month to identify promptly any unexpected occurrences or performance problems that must be addressed.

Initially, you may be uncomfortable reconfirming commitments people have made for an upcoming performance period, because you feel doing so

- **Suggests that you don't trust the person:** After all, the person has made a commitment to do the specified work; wouldn't she tell you if she were unable to live up to that commitment?
- **Increases the likelihood that she'll say she can't live up to the original promise:** You're concerned that raising the topic may actually encourage her to say she can't honor her commitments.

In most cases, however, neither concern proves to be warranted, for the following reasons:

- Raising the issue doesn't suggest a lack of trust; if you didn't trust the person, you wouldn't talk to her at all! Checking in with her reflects your understanding that she may not have had a chance to tell you about new circumstances that may make it difficult to honor her commitments.
- Raising the issue doesn't increase the chances that she'll opt out of a commitment; it buys you time. If the person can't perform according to her promises, you'll find that out at the end of the performance period anyway — when she hasn't finished the work. So taking time to reconfirm actually provides an entire performance period to develop alternative ways of dealing with her new restrictions.

REMEMBER

When a person reaffirms her existing commitments for the upcoming performance period, the chances are greater that she'll perform her assignments successfully, on time, and within budget. If she's unable to honor the commitments she made previously (for example, if she has unexpectedly been assigned to work on another high-priority effort during the same time period), you can work with her to develop new plans for how and when she will complete her assignment for your project.

Establishing Project Management Information Systems

A *project management information system* (PMIS) is a set of procedures, equipment, and other resources for collecting, analyzing, storing, and reporting information that describes project performance. A PMIS contains the following three parts:

- **Inputs:** Raw data that describe selected aspects of project performance

» **Processes:** Analyses of the data that compare actual performance with planned performance

» **Outputs:** Reports that present the results of the analyses

Designing a PMIS not only requires that you define which data to collect during the project but also that you specify how to collect the data, who collects it, when they collect it, and how they enter the data into the system. All these factors can affect the timeliness and accuracy of the data and, therefore, of your project performance assessments.

To support your ongoing management and control of the project, you need to collect and maintain information about schedule performance, work effort, and expenditures. The following sections tell you how to collect, analyze, and report on these three parts of your project's performance.

REMEMBER

Many information systems have the technical support of computers, scanners, and printers. But an information system can consist of manual processes and physical storage devices as well. For example, you can record project activities in your notebook or calendar and keep records of project budgets in your file cabinet. However, you still need to monitor your procedures for collecting, storing, analyzing, and reporting your information; they affect the accuracy and timeliness of your performance assessments.

The clock's ticking: Monitoring schedule performance

Regularly monitoring your project's schedule performance can provide early indications of possible activity-coordination problems, resource conflicts, and cost overruns that may occur in the future. The following sections show you what information you need in order to monitor schedule performance, how to collect and evaluate it, and how to ensure its accuracy.

Defining the schedule data to collect

As discussed in Chapter 3 of Book 1, your project's *work breakdown structure* (WBS) is a deliverable-oriented decomposition of the work required to produce your project's deliverables. The lowest level of detail of each branch of the WBS is a *work package*, and each work package, in turn, is composed of *activities* (pieces of work performed during the project).

You can describe an activity's schedule performance either by noting the dates it began and ended or by describing how much of it has been done (in other words, *percent completed*).

If you choose to describe your project's schedule performance by noting the status of individual activities, collect either or both of the following data items to support your analyses:

- The start and end dates for each activity in your project
- The dates when milestones (such as *contract signed, materials received,* or *environmental test completed*) are reached (see Chapter 1 in Book 2 for details about milestones)

WARNING

Be careful if you decide to use percent completed to indicate an activity's progress because most often you have no clear way to determine this percentage. For example, saying that your new product design is 30 percent complete is virtually meaningless because you can't determine objectively how much of the thinking and creating is actually done. Suggesting that you have completed 30 percent of your design because you have expended 30 of the 100 hours budgeted for the task or because three of the ten days allotted for its performance have passed is equally incorrect. The first indicator is a measure of resource use, and the second is a measure of time elapsed. Neither measure indicates the amount of substantive *work* completed.

On the other hand, if your activity has clear segments that take roughly the same amount of time and effort, you may be able to determine an accurate measure of percent completed. For example, if you planned to conduct telephone interviews with 20 different people and you have completed 10, you can argue that the activity is 50 percent complete.

Analyzing schedule performance

Assess your project's schedule status by comparing actual activity start and end dates and actual milestone dates to their planned dates. Figures 3-1 and 3-2 present formats that support ready comparisons of this data.

Figure 3-1 depicts a *combined activity and milestone report.* The following information in this report comes from your project plan:

- The activity or milestone identification code and name
- The person responsible for ensuring the activity or milestone occurs
- The dates the activity should start and end or the milestone should occur

New Product Needs Assessment Project						
Activity/Milestone	Person Responsible	Start Date		End Date		Comments
		Planned	Actual	Planned	Actual	
2.1.1. Design questionnaire	F. Smith	Feb 14	Feb 15	Feb 25	Feb 25	
2.1.1.6. Questionnaire design approved	F. Smith	-	-	Feb 28	Feb 28	
2.2.2. Pilot test questionnaire	F. Smith	Apr 20	Apr 21	Apr 30	Apr 25	Critical Path

FIGURE 3-1: A combined activity and milestone report.

© John Wiley & Sons, Inc.

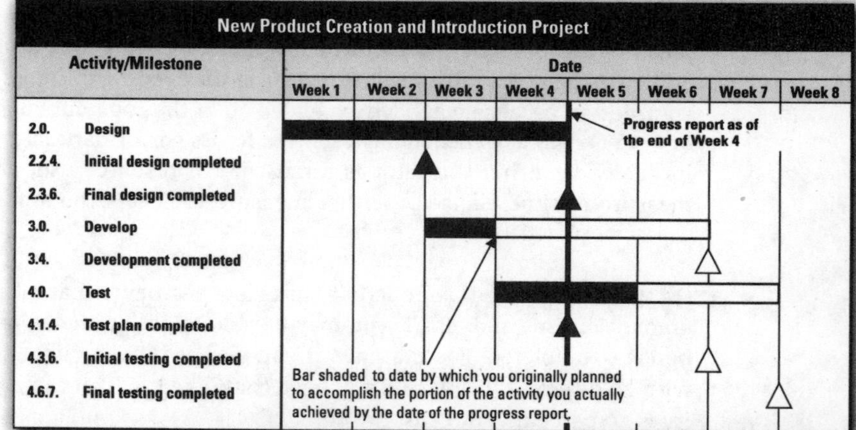

FIGURE 3-2: A progress Gantt chart.

© John Wiley & Sons, Inc.

Compare this information from your plan with the following data to describe performance during the period of the report:

- The actual dates activities start and end or the actual dates milestones are reached
- Relevant comments about the activities or milestones

Figure 3-2 illustrates a *progress Gantt chart*. You shade an appropriate portion of each bar to represent deliverable progress (see Chapter 1 in Book 2 for the skinny on Gantt charts). This sample chart presents project performance as of the end of week 4 of the project. According to the Gantt chart, the design phase is complete, the development phase is one week behind schedule, and the testing phase is one week ahead of schedule.

The most meaningful way to assess progress on a WBS component is to note the component's intermediate deliverables that you've achieved to date. The progress Gantt chart in Figure 3-2 really says that, by the end of week 4, you produced all the intermediate deliverables for Task 3.0 — development — that you had planned to produce by the end of week 3 or that Task 3.0 is one week behind schedule.

Note: You can prepare these project schedule reports with any level of detail you choose, depending on your stakeholders' interests and needs. The higher-level report shown in Figure 3-2 presents information for four-week portions of project work, but the detailed data used to determine the status of these four-week portions of work was for activities that were two weeks or less.

WARNING

Not everyone interprets a progress Gantt chart the same way. The chart's creator intended the chart to suggest that Task 3.0 is one week behind schedule. However, some people have said that they interpret the report to mean Task 3.0 is 25 percent complete because one of the four segments for Task 3.0 is shaded. The message is this: Be sure you include a legend with your graph that explains clearly how you want people to interpret it.

Collecting schedule performance data

To collect the schedule performance data, develop a standard format and process for recording your work accomplishments. Standard formats and processes improve the accuracy of your information and take less time to complete.

REMEMBER

Consider the following factors when you schedule your activity monitoring:

- **Is the activity on a critical path?** All other things being equal, delayed activities on a critical path will delay your overall project schedule (see Chapter 1 in Book 2 for a discussion of critical paths). Therefore, consider monitoring critical-path activities more frequently to identify actual or potential delays as soon as possible so you can minimize their effect on the remainder of the project schedule.
- **Is the activity on a path that's close to being critical?** Activities on noncritical paths can have some delays before their paths become critical. The maximum delay for noncritical activities is called *slack time* or *float* (see Chapter 1 in Book 2). If an activity's slack time is very short, a small delay can cause the path to become critical. Therefore, consider monitoring activities that have very small slack times more often (again, to identify actual or potential problems as soon as possible).

- **Is the activity risk high?** If you feel that an activity is likely to encounter problems, consider monitoring it more frequently to identify those problems as soon as they occur.
- **Have you already encountered problems with this activity?** Consider monitoring activities more frequently if you've already had problems with them. Past problems often increase the chances of future problems.
- **Are you approaching the activity's planned completion date?** Consider monitoring activities approaching completion more frequently to ensure all final details are addressed and the schedule is met.

TIP

At the beginning of every performance period, print separate reports for all team members that include their planned activities and milestones for the period. Ask them to verify the information and reaffirm their commitments to the dates contained in the reports. Discuss and resolve any issues that they identify.

Then ask them to record during the performance period the dates on which they actually start and end activities and reach milestones in the appropriate columns, along with any pertinent comments they want to share. Finally, have them send you a copy of the completed report on the first business day after the end of the performance period.

Recording and reporting on progress this way has several advantages:

- Recording achievements at the time they occur increases the likelihood that the data are accurate.
- The agreed-upon submission schedule reduces the chances that you'll surprise people with unexpected requests for progress data.
- Having people continuously review their proposed schedules and record their accomplishments and their errors (for the lessons learned session and the repository) their mistakes heightens their awareness of goals and increases the chances that they'll meet their commitments.
- The purpose of project control is to encourage people to perform according to your plan, not just to collect data. The more aware team members are of their work in relation to the overall schedule, the greater the likelihood that they'll hit the schedule. If they don't know or care about the target date, they're unlikely to hit it.

WARNING

Monitor schedule performance at least once a month. Experience has shown that waiting longer does the following:

- Allows people to lose focus and commitment to the activity and increases the chances that the activity won't end on schedule
- Provides more time for small problems to go undetected and, thus, evolve into bigger problems

Improving the accuracy of your schedule performance data

TIP

Collecting the right data is the first requirement for effectively controlling your project's schedule. However, your analyses will be meaningless if the data are incorrect. Follow these tips to improve the accuracy of your schedule performance data:

- **Tell the team members how you plan to use their schedule performance data.** People are always more motivated to perform a task if they understand the reasons for it.
- **Provide schedule performance reports to the people who give you the data.** People are even more motivated to perform a task if they get direct benefits from it.
- **Publicly acknowledge those people who give you timely and accurate data.** Positive reinforcement of desired behavior confirms to people that they're meeting your expectations; it also emphasizes that desirable behavior to other people.
- **Clearly define activities and milestones.** Clear definitions help you confirm when an event or activity does or doesn't occur.
- **Use all the data that you collect; don't collect more data than you'll use.** Collect only the data that you know you'll use to assess schedule performance.

Choosing a vehicle to support your schedule tracking system

Check to see whether your organization uses an enterprise-wide project planning and tracking system. The best places to look for this information are your organization's project management office (PMO), information technology department, and finance department. If your organization has such a system, check to see whether you can use it to monitor your project, whether it provides the information you need, and whether its information is timely and accurate.

If your organization doesn't have an existing tracking system you can use, you need to develop your own. You can use either a manual system or a computer-based system; both offer advantages and disadvantages:

- **Manual tracking systems:** These systems include day planners, personal calendars, and handwritten project logs. If you use any of these systems to record your activities and achievements, you don't need special computers or software, which may save you money.

  However, manual systems have these disadvantages:

  - Storing your data requires physical space. The more data you have, the more space you need.
  - Comparing and analyzing the data by hand can be time-consuming, and the chances for errors are greater.
  - Preparing reports by hand is time-consuming.

- **Computer-based tracking systems:** These systems offer the advantages of faster processing, more efficient data storage, and professionally designed reports. The following types of software can support a computer-based tracking system:

  - Integrated project-management software, such as Microsoft Project (discussed in Chapters 3 and 4 of Book 3) and Microsoft Project Server
  - Database software, such as Microsoft Access
  - Spreadsheet software, such as Microsoft Excel
  - Word-processing software, such as Microsoft Word

  However, computer-based systems are more difficult to learn to use, more difficult to maintain, and more expensive to rent or buy.

TIP

Many manufacturers offer software packages in these categories, but many organizations use Microsoft software for these functions. Check to see whether this software is available on your organization's local area network (LAN).

All in a day's work: Monitoring work effort

Comparing work effort expended with work effort planned can highlight when people are incorrectly expanding or reducing the scope of an activity, are more or less qualified than you anticipated, are encountering unexpected difficulties performing the work, or are in danger of using up allocated work effort before your project ends.

Monitoring work effort requires that you collect the actual effort spent on each WBS work package or activity. The following sections discuss what data to collect, how to collect it, how to improve its accuracy, and how to analyze it.

Collecting work-effort data

Having people complete time sheets is the most effective way to collect work-effort expenditure data. (The term *time sheet* refers to a record of the effort spent by a person doing a particular piece of work, whether it's maintained on a sheet of paper, an electronic record, a computer's memory, or any other medium.) You need to include the following information on each time sheet (see Figure 3-3 for an example of a typical time sheet):

- » The number of hours a team member worked on each work package each day
- » The team member's signature verifying that the information is correct
- » An approval signature (typically the project manager or someone he designates) verifying that the time charges are valid and appropriate

(Name of) Project

From: Apr 3, 201_ to Apr 10, 201_
Time Period

Employee: Name ________ Signature ________ Approval: Name ________ Signature ________

Work Package			Sun	Mon	Tue	Wed	Thu	Fri	Sat	Total
Project No.	WBS Code	Name	Apr 3	Apr 4	Apr 5	Apr 6	Apr 7	Apr 8	Apr 9	
		Total Hours								

FIGURE 3-3: A typical weekly time sheet.

© John Wiley & Sons, Inc.

Generally, recording work on activities to the nearest half-hour is sufficient.

Note: Some people may record their time in intervals smaller than half-hours. Lawyers, for example, often allocate their time in six-minute segments. Their clients would have it no other way — given that a lawyer may charge $500 or more per hour!

A *time log* is a form that breaks the day into intervals and allows a team member to record the specific activity he worked on in each interval. For example, to record time in half-hour intervals for a member who begins work at 8:30 a.m., the first interval on the log is 8:30 to 9 a.m., the second is 9 to 9:30 a.m., and so on.

If team members fill out time logs conscientiously, they provide more-accurate data because the log allows them to account for every segment of the day. However, maintaining a time log is far more time-consuming than filling out a time sheet. Normally, recording on a time sheet the total time a person spends working on different activities each day is sufficient.

Choosing a vehicle to support your work-effort tracking system

Before you choose a method for tracking your work effort, check whether your organization has a time-recording system in place that can accurately record data the way you need it. When assessing an existing time-recording system, consider the following:

- Time-recording systems typically allocate a person's pay to regular work, vacation time, sick leave, and holiday leave. As such, the system may require exempt employees (that is, employees who aren't paid for overtime) to record no more than 40 hours per week. Additionally, these systems are often unable to track work by detailed WBS categories.
- People are often uncomfortable recording the hours they spend on different assignments because they aren't sure how the organization will use the information.
- A time-recording system's standard reports may not present information the way you need it to support your work-effort tracking.

If you decide to create your own work-effort recording and storage method, you have to decide whether to develop a manual or computer-based system. As you decide, consider the following:

- Manual systems typically involve having people note in their daily calendars or personal diaries the hours they spent on different activities. Unfortunately, data recorded this way are often incomplete and inaccurate. In addition, you'll have difficulty pulling the data together to perform organized assessments and prepare meaningful reports.

- You can support a computer-based system with the following software:
  - Project-management software, such as Microsoft Project (covered in Chapters 3 and 4 of Book 3)
  - Database software, such as Microsoft Access
  - Spreadsheet software, such as Microsoft Excel

Improving the accuracy of your work-effort data

TIP

Just as with schedule performance data, the more accurate your work-effort expenditure data are, the more meaningful your analyses will be. Take the following steps to increase the accuracy of the work-effort expenditure data you collect:

- **Explain to people that you're using their labor-effort expenditures to help you determine when you may need to change aspects of the plan.** When you ask people to detail the hours they spend on specific assignments, they often fear that you'll criticize them for not spending time exactly in accordance with the plan — no matter what the reason — or for not spending enough hours on project work as opposed to other administrative duties. Unfortunately, if they believe these are your motives, they'll allocate their work-hours among activities to reflect what they think you want to see rather than what they're really doing.
- **Encourage people to record the actual hours they work instead of making their total hours equal 40 hours per week.** If people must record a total of 40 hours per week and they work overtime, they'll omit hours here and there or try to reduce them proportionately. You want workers to record accurate data.
- **Include categories for time on non-project activities, such as *unallocated, administrative overhead,* and so on.** If you want people to record their time expenditures honestly, you must provide them with appropriate categories.
- **Encourage people to fill out their own time sheets.** Some people ask a third person, such as a secretary, to fill out time sheets for them. But people have a hard-enough time remembering what they themselves did the past day or the past week; expecting someone else to accurately remember it for them is totally unrealistic.

» **Collect time sheets weekly, if possible, or at least once every two weeks.** No matter how often you ask people to fill out their time sheets, many people wait until the sheet is due to complete it. If you collect sheets once a month, those people will be sitting there at the end of the month trying to remember what they did four weeks ago!

» **Don't ask people to submit their time sheets before the period is over.** On occasion, managers ask workers to submit time sheets on Thursday for the week ending on Friday. But this practice immediately reduces the accuracy of the data because a worker can't be certain what he'll do tomorrow. More importantly, though, this practice suggests to workers that if guessing at Friday's allocation is acceptable, maybe they don't have to be too concerned with the accuracy of the rest of the week's data, either.

Analyzing work effort expended

Evaluate your project's work-effort expenditures by comparing the actual expenditures with those in your plan. Figure 3-4 depicts a portion of a typical labor report that describes the work effort expended by two team members on work package 3.1.2 (questionnaire design) for each of the first four weeks of the project. For each team member, the figure displays the following information:

» **Planned:** The number of person-hours the team member was supposed to work on the work package this week (an existing number obtained from the latest approved version of the project plan, also called the *current baseline*)

» **Actual:** The number of person-hours the team member did work on the work package this week (an existing number obtained from the team member's time sheet for the week)

» **Remaining:** The number of person-hours the team member has left to work on the work package at the end of this week (a calculated number: the Remaining number from last week minus the Actual number from this week)

» **Difference:** The difference between the number of person-hours the team member was supposed to have remaining at the end of this week and the actual number of person-hours she has remaining (a calculated number: the Difference number from last week plus [the Planned number minus the Actual number from this week])

» **Budget:** The total number of person-hours planned for each team member to work on the work package and the number of person-hours planned for each team member to work on the work package each week (existing numbers obtained from the latest approved version of the project plan)

Work Package		Employee		Work Effort Expended (Person-hours)					
WBS Code	Name			Budget	Week 1	Week 2	Week 3	Week 4	...
3.1.2.	Questionnaire design	H. Jones	Planned	130	20	40	30	30	...
			Actual	0	10	30	20	25	...
			Remaining	130	120	90	70	45	...
			Difference	0	+10	+20	+30	+35	...
		F. Smith	Planned	70	0	20	20	15	...
			Actual	0	0	25	10	15	...
			Remaining	70	0	45	35	20	...
			Difference	0	0	-5	+5	+5	...

New Product Needs Assessment Project

FIGURE 3-4: A labor report.

© John Wiley & Sons, Inc.

REMEMBER

Actual labor expenditures rarely agree 100 percent with the planned amounts. (In fact, if the number of hours for each task each month is identical to the number in your plan for several months, you may wonder whether people are copying the numbers from the plan onto their time sheets! See the earlier section "Collecting work-effort data" for more info on time sheets.) Typically, variances of up to 10 percent above or below the expected numbers in any month are normal.

Consider the work-effort expenditures for the two team members in the labor report in Figure 3-4. Smith appears to be working in accordance with the plan. He charged more hours in week 2 than planned, fewer than planned in week 3, and the same as planned in week 4. Jones's situation is very different. Each week, Jones spends less time on the project than planned, and the total shortfall of hours increases steadily. Whether or not this shortfall indicates a problem isn't clear from the report, but the systematic undercharging does point to a situation that needs further investigation.

Follow the money: Monitoring expenditures

You monitor your project's expenditures to verify that they're in accordance with the project plan and, if they're not, to address any deviations. You may think you can determine project funds used to date and funds remaining just by reading the balance in your project's financial account (the project's *checkbook*). However, spending project funds entails several steps before you actually pay for an item. After each step, you have a better sense of whether you'll incur the expenditure and, if you do, its exact amount.

The process leading up to and including the disbursement of funds for goods and services includes the following steps:

1. **You include a rough estimate of the item's cost in your project's budget.**

   You can develop this rough estimate by using your prior experience, by checking with others who have purchased similar items in the past, or by checking with your procurement department. Usually, you don't check with specific vendors or supplies when developing this rough estimate.

2. **You submit a written, approved request for the item to your procurement department.**

   This request specifies the rough estimate of the cost included in your project budget and any upper limit that the actual cost can't exceed. The project manager or his designee approves it, and then anyone else who controls the expenditure of project funds (such as the finance department) approves it.

3. **Your procurement department selects a vendor and submits a purchase order.**

   The purchase order formally requests the vendor to furnish you the item and specifies the procurement department's estimate of the price.

4. **The vendor agrees to provide the item you requested.**

   The vendor provides written confirmation that he will sell you the item along with the item's price (including applicable taxes and shipping and handling charges) and the projected delivery date.

5. **You receive and accept the item but aren't yet billed for it.**

   You receive the item and verify that it meets the agreed specifications. If you don't accept the item after the vendor makes repeated attempts to fix any problems you have with it, your procurement department cancels the purchase order, and you begin looking for a different vendor or a different item that will meet your needs.

6. **You or your finance department receives a bill for the item.**

   This bill details the item's final cost and any associated discounts, taxes, and shipping and handling charges.

7. **Your finance department disburses funds to pay for the item.**

   The bill for your item is paid with money from your project's funds.

Depending on the size of your purchase and the size and formality of your organization, you may handle some of these stages informally for some purchases. As you proceed from the first step to the last, your estimate of the item's price becomes more accurate, and the likelihood that you'll actually make the purchase increases.

Responsible project monitoring requires that you have a clear idea of available project funds at each stage of the process. To do so, you typically need to monitor purchase requisitions, purchase orders, commitments (that is, purchase orders or contracts that you and the contractor or vendor agreed to), accounts payable, and expenditures.

The following sections discuss how to analyze your project's expenditures, how to get the expenditure data you need for your analyses and improve the accuracy of that data, and how to choose the right vehicle to support your expenditure tracking system.

Analyzing expenditures

You evaluate your project's financial performance by comparing actual expenditures with planned expenditures. Figure 3-5 depicts a typical cost report that presents expenditures for the current performance period and from the beginning of the project for different levels of WBS components. The following information in this report comes from your project plan:

- The codes and names for each WBS component
- The funds budgeted for each WBS component in the performance period
- The cumulative funds budgeted to date for each WBS component
- The total budget for each WBS component

(Name of) Project									
WBS Component		Performance Period			To Date			Total	
WBS Code	Name	Budget	Actual	Difference	Budget	Actual	Difference	Budget	Remaining
1.0	Total	$12,500	$11,200	$1,300	$27,500	$25,500	$2,000	$200,000	$174,500
1.1	Requirements	5,000	4,400	600	12,300	11,400	900	45,000	33,600
1.2	Focus Groups	3,000	2,900	100	7,500	7,100	400	10,000	2,900
1.3	Document Reviews	1,500	1,200	300	4,000	3,800	200	5,000	1,200
1.4	Requirements Report	500	300	200	800	500	300	4,000	3,500
⋮	⋮	⋮	⋮	⋮	⋮	⋮	⋮	⋮	⋮

FIGURE 3-5: A cost report.

© John Wiley & Sons, Inc.

The actual numbers for the period come from the data you obtain during that period. *Actual* in this illustration may mean the value of purchase requisitions, purchase orders, commitments, accounts payable, and/or expenditures. Total remaining funds are the difference between the total budget and the actual amounts expended to date.

Collecting expenditure data and improving its accuracy

Typically, you obtain your expenditure data from purchase requisitions, purchase orders, vendor bills, and written checks. You normally see all purchase requisitions because, as the project manager, you probably have to approve them. The procurement department typically prepares purchase orders, and you may be able to get copies. Vendor bills usually go directly to the accounts payable group in the finance department, and these people pay the checks. You may be able to have the finance department send copies of bills to you to verify the amounts and so forth, and you can request reports of all payments from your project's account if they're tracked by project code.

REMEMBER

Follow these guidelines to increase the accuracy of your project's expenditure data:

- Remove purchase orders from your totals after you receive the bill (or verify that payment has been made) to avoid double-counting an expenditure.
- Be sure to include the correct work package charge code on each purchase requisition and purchase order.
- Periodically remove voided or canceled purchase requisitions and purchase orders from your lists of outstanding documents.

Choosing a vehicle to support your expenditure tracking system

Before developing your own system to monitor your project's expenditures, first check the nature and capabilities of your organization's financial tracking system. Most organizations have a financial system that maintains records of all expenditures. Often the system also maintains records of accounts payable. Unfortunately, many financial systems categorize expenses by cost center but don't have the capacity to classify expenses by project or WBS component within a project.

If you have to develop your own system for tracking project expenditures, consider using the following types of software:

- Integrated project-management software, such as Microsoft Project (discussed in Chapters 3 and 4 of Book 3)
- Accounting software, such as QuickBooks
- Database software, such as Microsoft Access
- Spreadsheet software, such as Microsoft Excel

REMEMBER

Even if your organization's financial system can classify expenditures by work package within a project, you'll probably have to develop your own system for tracking purchase requisitions and purchase orders. Consider using a spreadsheet program or database software to support this tracking.

Putting Your Control Process into Action

The first part of this chapter tells you how to set up the systems that provide you the necessary information to guide your project. This section explains how to use those systems to consistently monitor and guide your project's performance.

Heading off problems before they occur

Great project plans often fall by the wayside when well-intentioned people try to achieve the best-possible results on their own. They may spend more hours than planned, hoping the additional work can produce better results. They may ask people who weren't in the original plan to work on the project or spend more money for an item than the budget allowed, believing these choices will result in higher-quality outcomes.

At the start of your project, set up procedures that prevent people from exceeding established budgets without prior approval. For example, if people record the number of hours they spend on each project activity,

- Confirm with them the maximum number of hours they may charge to each activity before they start it.
- Arrange for the time-recording system to reject attempts to charge more hours than planned for an activity unless the person has your prior written approval.
- Arrange for the time-recording system to reject any project hours charged by unauthorized people.

For purchases of equipment, materials, supplies, and services,

- Confirm anticipated purchases, the upper limits for cost of individual items (if any), and the upper limit on the total expenditures.
- Arrange for the procurement office or financial system to reject attempts to overspend these limits without your prior written approval.

REMEMBER

A change to your project's budget may be necessary and desirable. However, you have to make that decision with full awareness of the change's effect on other aspects of the project.

Formalizing your control process

To guide your project throughout its performance, establish procedures to collect and submit required progress data, to assess work and results, to take corrective actions when needed, and to keep stakeholders informed of your project's status. Follow these procedures throughout your project's life by taking these steps:

1. **At the start of each performance period, reconfirm with people their commitments and your expectations.**

   See the earlier section "Holding the Reins: Project Control" for more details on how to do so.

2. **During the performance period, have people record schedule performance data, work-effort expenditures, and any purchase requisitions and purchase orders they issue.**

   See the earlier sections "Collecting schedule performance data," "Collecting work-effort data," and "Collecting expenditure data and improving its accuracy" for details.

3. **At agreed-upon intervals during or at the end of the performance period, have people submit their activity performance, expenditures, and work-effort data either to all relevant organizational systems or to systems specially maintained for your project.**
4. **At the end of the performance period, enter people's tracking data into the appropriate PMIS, compare actual performance for the period with planned performance, identify any problems, formulate and take corrective actions, and keep people informed.**

   See the later sections "Identifying possible causes of delays and variances," "Identifying possible corrective actions," and "Getting back on track: Rebaselining" for more details.

5. **At the beginning of the next performance period, repeat Steps 1 through 4.**

REMEMBER

Monitoring project performance doesn't identify problems; it identifies symptoms and trends. When you identify a symptom, you must investigate the situation to determine the nature of any underlying problems, the reasons for the problems, and ways to fix them. But you can't get an accurate picture of where your project stands by monitoring only one or two aspects of your project. You must consider your project's performance in all three of its dimensions — outcomes produced, time spent to perform activities, and resources used — to determine the reasons for any inconsistencies you identify.

Suppose a member of your project team spent half as much time working on a project activity during the period as you had planned. Does this discrepancy mean you have a problem? You really can't tell. If the person reached all her planned milestones and the quality of her deliverables met the established standards, perhaps you don't have a problem. However, if she didn't reach some milestones or the quality of her deliverables was subpar, a problem may exist. You must consider product quality and schedule achievement together with the discrepancy between planned and actual work-hours to determine whether your project actually has a problem.

Identifying possible causes of delays and variances

After you confirm that a problem exists, you have to understand what caused the problem before you can bring your project back on track. The following circumstances may cause schedule delays:

- During the performance period, people spend less time on the activity than they agreed to.
- The activity requires more work effort than you planned.
- People are expanding the scope of the activity without the necessary reviews and approvals.
- Completing the activity requires steps you didn't identify in your plan.
- The people working on the activity have less experience with similar activities than you anticipated.

The following situations may result in people charging more or less time to activities than you planned:

- The person is more or less productive than you assumed when you developed the plan.
- You allowed insufficient time for becoming familiar with the activity before starting to work on it.

» The person is more or less efficient than you considered.

» The activity requires more or less work than you anticipated.

You may spend more or less money on your project activities than you planned for the following reasons:

» You receive the bills for goods or services later than you planned, so they're paid later than you planned.

» You prepay for certain items to receive special discounts.

» You don't need certain goods or services that you budgeted for in your plan.

» You need goods or services that you didn't budget for in your plan.

Identifying possible corrective actions

When your project's performance deviates from your plan, first try to bring your project back in accordance with the existing plan. Then, if necessary, investigate the option of formally changing some of the commitments in the existing plan to create a new plan.

REMEMBER

Consider the following approaches for bringing a project back in line with its existing plan:

» **If the variance results from a one-time occurrence, see whether it will disappear on its own.** Suppose you planned to spend 40 person-hours searching for and buying a piece of equipment, but you actually spent 10 person-hours because you found exactly what you wanted for the price you wanted to pay at the first store. Don't immediately change your plan to reallocate the 30 person-hours you saved on this activity. Most likely, you'll wind up overspending slightly on some future activities, and the work-effort expenditures will even each other out.

» **If the variance suggests a situation that will lead to similar variances in the future, consider changing your plan to prevent the future variances from occurring.** Suppose a team member requires twice the allotted work effort to finish her assignment because she's less experienced than the plan anticipated. If her lack of experience will cause her to be less productive on future assignments, revise the plan to allow her to spend more effort on those assignments. (See Chapter 1 in Book 2 for information on how to reduce the time it takes to complete a project.)

Getting back on track: Rebaselining

Your project's *baseline* is the accepted or approved version of your project plan that was set in the planning stage of the project. It guides project performance and provides a standard against which to compare your actual project performance. *Rebaselining* is officially adopting a new project plan to guide activities and serve as the comparative basis for future performance assessments. In general, rebaselining isn't performed without a formal change request.

If you think adopting a new baseline is necessary, do the following:

- Consult with your project sponsor and key project stakeholders to explain why the changes are necessary and to solicit the stakeholders' approval and support.
- Make sure all key project stakeholders know about the new baseline.
- Keep a copy of your original plan and all subsequent modifications to support your final performance assessment when the project is over.

WARNING

Rebaselining is a last resort when project work isn't going according to plan. Exhaust all possible strategies to get back on track before you attempt to change the plan itself. (Chapter 1 in Book 2 has information about changing the order and duration of activities to make up for unexpected delays.)

Reacting Responsibly When Changes Are Requested

No matter how carefully you plan, occurrences you don't anticipate will likely happen at one point or another during your project. Perhaps an activity turns out to be more involved than you figured, your client's needs and desires change, or new technology evolves. When these types of situations arise, you may need to modify your project plan to respond to them.

Even though change may be necessary and desirable, it always comes at a price. Furthermore, different people may have different opinions about which changes are important and how to implement them.

This section helps you manage changes in your project. It provides some helpful steps to follow when considering and acting on a change request. It also looks at gradual and unapproved project expansion and steps you can take to avoid it.

Responding to change requests

On large projects, formal change-control systems govern how you can receive, assess, and act on requests for changes. But whether you handle change requests formally or informally, always follow these steps:

1. **When you receive a request for change to some aspect of your project, clarify exactly what the request is asking you to do.**
2. **If possible, ask for the request in writing or confirm your understanding of the request by writing it down yourself.**

   In a formal change-control system, people must submit every request for change on a change-request form.
3. **Assess the change's potential effects on all aspects of your project.**

   Also consider what may happen if you don't make the change.
4. **Decide whether you'll implement the change.**

   If this change affects other people, involve them in the decision, too.
5. **If you decide not to make the change, tell the requester and explain the reason(s).**
6. **If you decide to make the change, write down the necessary steps to implement the change.**

   In a formal change-control system, you detail all aspects of the change in a written change order.
7. **Update your project's plan to reflect any adjustments in schedules, outcomes, or resource budgets as a result of the change.**
8. **Tell team members and appropriate stakeholders about the change and the effect you expect it to have on your project.**

REMEMBER

The following guidelines can help you smoothly incorporate changes into your project:

- **Don't use the possibility of changes as an excuse for not being thorough in your original planning.** Make your project plan as accurate and complete as possible to reduce the need for future changes.
- **Remember that change always has a cost.** Don't ignore that cost, figuring you have to make the change anyway. Determine the cost of the change so you can plan for it and, if possible, minimize it.
- **Assess the effect of change on all aspects of your project.** Maintain a broad perspective — a change early in your project may affect your project from beginning to end.

Creeping away from scope creep

Scope creep is the gradual expansion of project work without formal consideration and acceptance of these changes or their associated costs and effects. Scope creep can occur as a result of any of the following:

- » Lack of clarity and detail in the original description of project scope, objectives, and work
- » Willingness to modify a project without formal review and approval
- » Willingness to let people who don't do the work associated with the changes decide whether to make changes
- » The feeling that you should never say "no" to a client
- » Personal pride that encourages you to believe you can do anything

Control scope creep by doing the following:

- » Include detailed descriptions of all project objectives in your plan.
- » Always assess the effect of requested changes on project products, schedules, and resources.
- » Share your true feelings about whether you can implement the requested changes.
- » Develop honest and open relationships with your clients so they're more receptive when you raise issues associated with their requested changes.

IN THIS CHAPTER

- » Planning for a successful project completion
- » Addressing any remaining administrative issues
- » Helping your team transition to the end of your project
- » Evaluating successes and failures with the post-project evaluation

Chapter 4

Bringing Your Project to Closure

One characteristic that distinguishes a project from other work assignments is its distinct end — the point at which all work is complete and the results are achieved. However, with intense demands pulling you to your next assignment, you may be compelled to let your completed projects languish and eventually fade away instead of clearly ending them with an announcement, recognition of the results, and a thank-you to all the people who made those results possible.

Unfortunately, not bringing your projects to full closure hurts both the organization and the people who performed the work. When you don't assess the extent to which your project achieved the desired outcomes, you can't determine whether you conceived, planned, and performed the project well. Furthermore, team members don't have the chance to experience closure, achievement, and a job well done.

This chapter shows you how to close your project successfully by finishing all substantive work, performing the final administrative tasks, and helping team members complete their association with your project and move on. In addition, this chapter helps you announce your project's end and conduct a post-project evaluation.

TIP

As Chapter 1 in Book 1 discusses, very large projects are often subdivided into phases, and each phase is treated as a separate mini-project. The discussions in this chapter apply to the closing-the-project stage of each mini-project as well as to the closing-the-project stage of the entire project.

Staying the Course to Completion

Following your project all the way through to completion helps ensure that everyone gets the maximum benefits from your project's results. You also get the chance to compare your project's benefits with the costs incurred, confirm the company's return on investment, and validate its process for selecting projects.

WARNING

Bringing a project to an end typically entails wrapping up a multitude of small details and open issues. Dealing with these numerous assignments can be frustrating under the best of circumstances. However, the following situations can make the end of a project even more difficult:

- You don't have a detailed, written list of all the activities you must perform during closeout.
- Some team members transferred to new assignments during your project's course, forcing the remaining members to assume new responsibilities in addition to their original ones.
- The project staff loses motivation as general interest in the project wanes and people look forward to new assignments.
- The project staff wants the project to continue because they don't want to end the personal and professional relationships they've developed or they're not excited about their next assignments.
- Your customers (internal and/or external) aren't overly interested in completing the final details of the project.

Reduce the impact of difficult situations like these and increase the chances for your project's success by planning for closure at the outset of your project, identifying and attending to all closure details and tasks, and refocusing your team. This section shows you how to do this (and more).

Planning ahead for your project's closure

If you wait until the end of your project to start thinking in detail about its closure, it may be too late to gather all the necessary information and resources. Instead, start planning for your project's completion at the same time that you prepare your initial project plan by doing the following (see Chapter 1 in Book 1 for details of what goes into the project plan):

- **Describe your project objectives completely and clearly, and identify all relevant objective measures and specifications.** If one of the project objectives is to change an existing situation, describe that situation before you perform the project so you have a comparative basis for assessment at the end of your project.
- **Prepare a checklist of everything you must do before you can officially close your project.** Here are some examples of closure items to include on your checklist:
  - Complete any unfinished project activities.
  - Complete all required deliverables.
  - Obtain all necessary acceptances and approvals of project results, including those of the client(s).
  - Assess the extent to which project results met expectations.
  - Perform all required administrative tasks.
  - Terminate all related contracts for goods and services.
  - Transition team members to their new assignments.
  - Ensure that all project documentation and deliverables are archived in the appropriate storage locations.

  REMEMBER

  For each item on the project-closure checklist, specify who will perform it, when it will be done, and what resources will be required.
- **Include closure activities in your project plan.** In your project's work breakdown structure (WBS), specify all activities you'll have to perform to close out your project and then plan for sufficient time and resources to perform them (see Chapter 3 in Book 1 for more on this tool).

Updating your initial closure plans when you're ready to wind down the project

Encourage your team members to consider the closing-the-project stage of your project to be a separate assignment with its own objectives, tasks, and resource requirements (see Chapter 1 in Book 1 for more on the closing-the-project stage). As you complete the main project's work, review and update the preliminary closure plans you developed in your initial project plan (see the preceding section for details on these preliminary plans).

Charging up your team for the sprint to the finish line

As team members work hard to fulfill project obligations, their focus often shifts from accomplishing the project's overall objectives to completing their individual assignments. In addition, other audiences who were initially very interested in the project's results may become involved with other priorities and activities as the project continues (which means they likely lose interest and enthusiasm for your project). However, successful project completion requires a coordinated effort by all key participants.

REMEMBER

To reinforce your team's focus and interest, do the following:

- **Remind people of the value and importance of the project's final results.** Frequently discuss the benefits the organization will realize from your project's final results as well as the individual benefits your team members will gain. People are more likely to work hard to successfully complete a project when they realize the benefits they'll achieve by doing so.
- **Call your team together and reaffirm your mutual commitment to bring the project to successful completion.** Discuss why you feel the project is important and describe your personal commitment to completing it successfully. Encourage other people to make similar commitments. People overcome obstacles and perform difficult assignments more effectively when they're committed to succeed.
- **Monitor final activities closely and give each team member frequent feedback on performance.** Set up frequent milestones and progress-reporting times with team members. Staying in close touch with team members provides you and them up-to-date info on how close you are to final closure. This close contact also provides the opportunity to identify and deal with any issues and problems that may arise throughout the course of your project.
- **Be accessible to all team members.** Make yourself available when team members want to confer with you. Consider having lunch periodically with them and letting them see you around their office area. Being accessible affirms your interest in and the importance of their work.

Handling Administrative Issues

Just as you must have authorization for people to legally spend time, effort, and resources to perform work on your project, you must rescind this authorization when you close the project to ensure that people won't continue to spend time, effort, or resources on it in the future. You can officially terminate this authorization by doing the following:

- **Obtain all required approvals.** Obtain written approval that your project has passed all performance tests and adhered to applicable standards and certifications. In addition, be sure you've obtained customer or client acceptances. This step confirms that no additional work is necessary on the project.
- **Reconcile any outstanding transactions.** If you've made project purchases from outside sources, resolve any disputes with vendors and suppliers, pay all outstanding bills, and make sure the contracts are officially closed. Make sure you adjust any project work effort or expenditures that were posted to incorrect accounts.
- **Close out all charge categories.** Get official confirmation that no future labor or financial charges can be made to your project accounts.

Providing a Smooth Transition for Team Members

As part of successfully finishing your own project, you need to help your team members complete their project responsibilities and move on to their next assignments. Handling this transition in an orderly and agreed-upon fashion allows people to focus their energies on completing their tasks on your project instead of wondering where and when their next assignments will be. In particular, do the following:

- **Acknowledge and document team members' contributions.** Express your appreciation to people for their assistance on your project and share with them your assessment of their performance. Take a moment to thank their supervisors for making them available to your project and provide the supervisors with an assessment of their performance.

REMEMBER

As a general rule, share positive feedback in public; share constructive criticisms and suggestions for improvement in private. In both cases, be sure to share your comments with team members personally and follow up your conversation in writing.

- **Help people plan for their transition to new assignments.** If appropriate, help people find their next project assignments. Help them develop a schedule for winding down their involvement with your project while making sure they fulfill all their remaining obligations. Consider holding a final project meeting or lunch to provide your team members closure on their work and project relationships.
- **Announce to the organization that your project is complete.** You can make this announcement in an email, in an announcement on the company intranet, in a meeting, or through an organization-wide publication, such as a newsletter. You need to make this announcement for the following three reasons:
  - To alert people in your organization that the planned outcomes of your project are now available
  - To confirm to people who supported your project that their efforts led to a successful result
  - To let people know they can no longer charge time or resources to your project
- **Take a moment to let team members and others who supported your project know the true results of the time and work they invested.** Nothing can give your team members stronger motivation to jump into the next assignment and provide continued high-quality support than telling them about the positive results of their previous hard work.

Surveying the Results: The Post-Project Evaluation

Lay the groundwork for repeating on future projects what worked on past ones (and avoiding what didn't) by conducting a post-project evaluation. A *post-project evaluation* (also called a *post-project review* or *lessons learned*) is an assessment of project results, activities, and processes that allows you to

- Recognize project achievements and acknowledge people's work.
- Identify techniques and approaches that worked and devise steps to ensure you and others use them again in the future.
- Identify techniques and approaches that didn't work and devise steps to ensure you and others don't use them again in the future.

This section helps you plan for, conduct, and follow up on a post-project, or lessons learned, evaluation.

Preparing for the evaluation throughout the project

Take steps in each stage of your project's evolution (starting the project, organizing and preparing, carrying out the work, and closing the project) to lay the groundwork for your post-project evaluation (see Chapter 1 in Book 1 for more on the four stages of a project):

- **Starting the project:**
  - Determine the benefits your project's *drivers* wanted to realize when they authorized your project. (See Chapter 2 in Book 1 for a discussion of drivers and the other types of project stakeholders.)
  - If your project is designed to change an existing situation, take *before* measures to describe the existing situation so you have something to compare to the *after* measures you take when the project is completed.
- **Organizing and preparing:**
  - Identify additional project drivers you may have overlooked in the first stage of your project. Your project drivers' expectations serve as the criteria for defining your project's success, so you want to know who they are before you begin your project's work.
  - Develop clear and detailed descriptions of all project objectives.
  - Include the activity "Conduct a post-project evaluation" in your work breakdown structure (WBS) and allow time and resources to perform it. (See Chapter 3 in Book 1 for a discussion of the WBS.)
- **Carrying out the work:**
  - Tell team members that the project will have a post-project evaluation.
  - Encourage team members to record issues, problems, and successes throughout their project involvement in a handwritten or computerized project log. Review the log when proposing topics for discussion at the post-project evaluation meeting.
  - Maintain files of cost, labor-hour charges, and schedule performance reports throughout the project. (See Chapter 3 in Book 2 for details on how to track and report this information.)

» **Closing the project:**
  - If changing an existing situation was a project objective, take *after* measures of that situation's key characteristics to see whether you successfully met that objective.
  - Obtain final cost, labor-hour, and schedule performance reports for the project.
  - Survey key stakeholders to determine how well they feel the project addressed their needs and their assessments of project team and project manager performance.

Setting the stage for the evaluation meeting

A post-project evaluation lessons learned is only as good as the results, expenditures, and performance information it's based on. The information must be complete, detailed, and accurate. Prepare for your post-project evaluation meeting by collecting information about the following:

- Project results
- Schedule performance
- Resource expenditures
- Problems that arose during the project
- Changes during the project in objectives, schedules, and budgets
- Unanticipated occurrences or changes in the environment during the project
- Customers' satisfaction with the project results
- Management's satisfaction with the project results
- Effectiveness of the project-management processes
- Lessons learned

You can collect this information from the following sources:

- Progress reports
- Project logs
- Cost reports

- Schedule reports
- Project memos, correspondence, and meeting minutes
- Interviews and surveys of customers, managers, and team members

REMEMBER

Prepare a detailed agenda for the post-project evaluation meeting that specifies the times when topic discussions will start and end. Consider including the following topics on your agenda:

- Statement of the meeting's purpose
- Specific meeting outcomes to be accomplished
- Highlights of project performance, including the following:
  - The project's original /current SOW/ scope statement
  - Results, schedules, and resources
  - Approaches to project planning
  - Project tracking systems and procedures
  - Project communications
  - Project team practices and effectiveness
- Recognition and discussion of special achievements
- Review of customer and management reactions to the project
- Discussion of problems and issues
- Discussion of how to reflect experiences from this project in future efforts

TIP

Circulate a draft agenda, related background materials, and a list of attendees to all expected attendees at least one week before the meeting. This advance notice gives people time to suggest additions, deletions, and other changes to the agenda. Revise the agenda to address these suggestions, and distribute the final agenda to all meeting participants at least one day before the meeting.

Conducting the evaluation meeting

A successful post-project evaluation meeting (which you can hold in person, via videoconference, or through most other meeting methods) requires that you address the right topics and that people share their project thoughts and experiences openly and honestly.

At the post-project (a.k.a. lesson learned) evaluation meeting, explore the following issues:

- Did you accomplish all the project objectives?
- Did you meet the project schedule?
- Did you complete the project within budget?
- With regard to problems during the project,
  - Could you have anticipated and planned for them in advance? If so, how?
  - Did you handle them effectively and efficiently when they arose?
- Did you use the organization's project-management systems and procedures effectively?

REMEMBER

To ensure you get the most accurate information and the best recommendations for future actions, do the following before and during your post-project evaluation meeting:

- **Invite the right people.** Invite all the people who participated in your project at all points throughout its life. If the list of potential invitees is too long, consider meeting separately with select subgroups and then holding a general session at which everyone reviews the results of the smaller meetings and you solicit final comments and suggestions.
- **Declare at the beginning of the meeting that it's supposed to be a learning experience rather than a finger-pointing session.** As the project manager, you run the post-project evaluation meeting. At its outset, you need to declare that the session is a time for self-examination and suggestions for ensuring the success of future projects. If people start to attack or criticize other participants, you can immediately bring the discussion back on track by asking the participants the following questions:
  - What can you do in the future to deal more effectively with such situations?
  - What can you do in the future to head off such situations?

  If people resist your attempts to redirect their conversations, you can mention actions that you, as project manager, can take in the future to head off or deal with similar situations more effectively and then ask people to share additional ideas.
- **Encourage people to**
  - Identify what other people did well.
  - Examine their own performance and see how they could've handled situations differently.

» **Consider holding the session away from your office.** People often feel more comfortable critiquing existing practices and discussing new approaches when they're away from their normal work environments.

TIP

Be sure to assign a person to take notes during the post-project evaluation meeting. In addition to a list of attendees and highlights of information, the notes should list all the agreed-on activities to implement the lessons learned from the meeting and the people responsible for those activities.

Following up on the evaluation

Often your busy schedule pulls you to new projects before you've had a chance to analyze and benefit from previous ones. However, even when people do take a few moments to review previous project experiences, they seldom incorporate the lessons learned in their future operating practices.

REMEMBER

As soon as possible after your post-project evaluation meeting, you, as project manager, need to prepare and distribute a wrap-up report that's based on the meeting minutes and that addresses the following topics:

» Practices to incorporate in future projects

» Steps to take to encourage these practices

» Practices to avoid in future projects

» Steps to take to discourage these practices

Consider this wrap-up report as you plan future projects to make sure you apply the lessons you learned.

3 Helping Out: Using Tools on a Project

Contents at a Glance

» Surveying types of checklists

» Using project templates

» Going over a project's structure

Chapter 1
Considering Checklists and Templates

So you're managing a new project and thinking about making some checklists and templates to help you out. You may think that you just want to get going with your project and start ticking some boxes. However, to get the best out of checklists and templates and use them really effectively, you need to appreciate how to use them and also how not to. This chapter explains what you need to know.

Checklists are designed to help you make sure that you have got everything right at different points in a project and haven't missed out anything important. It's so easy to make mistakes that are actually avoidable. As well as helping you think things through for each project, checklists also draw on lots of experience and help you make sure that you get it right for "this" project, whether "this" project is your first one or just your latest.

TIP

If you're new to projects, it will also pay you to go through the last part of this chapter to understand the project structure that checklists are designed to fit in with. If you're already familiar with project structure, you can skip that section if you prefer and head to Chapter 2 of Book 3, which covers the key documents for managing a project.

...cklists Properly

...unning any project you'll find that checklists are a very powerful tool. They ...u to ensure that you produce sound, well thought-out plans and control ...ts the first time around. That will not only save time and trouble later, ... also help you develop a deserved reputation as a thorough and effective project manager.

This section gives you a few pointers on using checklists, including tackling problems where you want other staff to use them too, but they are less than enthusiastic. Some don't like things like project methods and checklists, and say that they have no need of them because of their experience and knowledge.

Consider the example of an airline pilot Imagine that you're standing in an airport waiting to check in for your flight over the Atlantic Ocean. The captain and co-pilot for your flight happen to walk past you and you overhear what the Captain is saying: "I'm not bothering with the pre-flight checklist on this trip. I've been flying aircraft for years, I'm very experienced and I'm sure I'll remember everything important." You might feel slightly unhappy about that and start scanning the departure board to see if you can find an alternative flight. You certainly wouldn't take the captain's words as a sign of expertise and professionalism.

Using checklists is not unprofessional; rather the reverse. As much as you possibly can, you want to be sure that you get things right and that you don't miss anything important. Quite apart from the consequences for the project if you get things wrong, avoiding problems will also save you a lot of time and potential loss of resources later.

REMEMBER

Here are a few pitfalls to avoid when you use checklists:

- **Use the checklists thoughtfully:** Adjust them to the needs of your project, then use them. Otherwise you may be in danger of, for example, applying large project controls to a small project that simply doesn't need them. Continuing with the aircraft analogy from the start of this section, different aircraft have different pre-flight checklists.
- **Be extra careful in audit:** Following on from the last point, if you're using checklists to check up on someone else's project (Project Audit) don't apply some generic checklist to every project and ignore the individual project characteristics and specific control needs.
- **Don't get "check happy":** The objective is not to fill up all the boxes with checkmarks, but to do the project work so that you can check the boxes — if you see the difference. When you check a box it should mean that the item is properly dealt with.

» **Add to the checklists:** If you need extra things on the checklists because of the nature of those projects, then add them.

» **Take away from the checklists:** As a reverse of the last point, if you never need to do something that's on a checklist then take it off. Always keep the checklists relevant to what you are doing.

In short, keep your brain in gear and don't drive up project overheads by doing unnecessary work because you haven't thought through whether everything on a checklist is relevant to your project.

TIP

You'll find checklists useful if you're a project expert — back to the analogy of an experienced aircraft pilot. You'll also find them useful if you are less experienced in project management and need a bit of help. One format you can consider for checklists looks like this:

❑ **Item:** Explanation and help.

If you're very experienced, you can just run down the bold headed items to be sure that you've covered everything you need to. If you're less experienced, or just unsure of a particular point, a short explanation after each checklist item can help you see why that item may be important in your project.

Understanding Checklist Types

You can use several different types of checklists. The following list explains up front what the types of checklists are:

» **Activity checklists:** The activity checklists are to make sure that you are doing, or have done, everything you need to at a particular point in the project. For example, if you're approaching the end of a Deliverables Due stage, have you done all the necessary checking and preparation for the review of deliverables due?

» **Completion checklists:** The completion type of checklist is to make sure that you've got everything. So, when you're doing the organization chart of who is needed for the project, have you got all of the management roles covered or have you missed one?

- **Information checklists:** These tell you about the range of things in a particular area. For example, if when you're writing the Business Case for your project, you have to be very clear about the three types of benefits that the project will produce, because they're very different. There's a checklist to describe what the three types of benefits of the project are and to briefly explain them.

Trying Templates

Templates are helpful, but you should use them intelligently as you do the checklists. In fact the same do's and don'ts apply that are in the earlier section "Using Checklists Properly." Templates can work powerfully for you in four ways:

- To save you significant time and effort "re-inventing the wheel," such as in designing a document from scratch when it would be much quicker to use a template.
- Even if you can't quite use a template as is, you can use it as a starting point and adapt it. That's usually a whole lot faster and much less effort than starting from scratch. You're bound to want quite a few of the sections in a template even if you take a few out and add one or two others in.
- To help instruct others on how documents should be completed, improving the relevance, consistency and accuracy of the information that they enter.
- To help make sure that you haven't missed anything.

Following on from the second point in the list, many people assume that their organization and its projects are going to be very different from everyone else's. In fact the core of project management is very similar, so you may well find that you only need minor changes to the templates, or even none at all, in which case you can relax and go home early today.

TIP

On the *For Dummies* website, you can find some project management templates available in Microsoft Word format. That way you can load a template straight into your computer. Helpful and sensible, don't you think? But then that's why you bought a *For Dummies* title in the first place. Check out `www.dummies.com/store/product/Project-Management-Checklists-For-Dummies.productCd-1118931432,navId-322439,descCd-DOWNLOAD.html`.

Reviewing Project Structure

The main parts, or *phases*, of any project are introduced in Chapter 1 of Book 1: starting the project, organizing and preparing, carrying out the work, and closing the project. The following sections cover how you can use checklists and templates during various points of a project.

Kicking off the project

Some people say that just about everything is a project: Even, they claim, making a cup of tea. That's a common myth and it's absolutely untrue, so don't be fooled for a moment. Projects have overheads, such as the work needed for planning, risk management, quality management and progress control. Not all work justifies such overheads. Sometimes you can do things as "normal" work, perhaps even using a few project techniques, and it doesn't justify putting in full project controls and structure. If that's the case it's not a problem, it just isn't a project.

REMEMBER

Before starting a project, you need to do three important things:

1. **Get an understanding of what will be involved and make sure that the work is worth doing — one way or another. Develop a business case for the project that includes ROI or savings to the organization.**
2. **If the job is worth doing, decide whether it's a project or should be tackled as "business as usual" type work. Is it a project or operational?**
3. **If it does look like a project, get some idea of what resource will be needed, find out whether that resource is available and then when the project could start. This information is provided in the business case for the project.**

And guess what? A lot of the pre-project work in Kick Off is about those three exact things in the preceding list. Too many projects start. Many get a long way into planning or, even worse, begin the delivery work and then find out that actually the project isn't worth doing. Getting into that position is bad news for two reasons:

- First, all of the people involved feel — very understandably — disappointed that all their hard work was a complete waste of effort.
- Second, your organization has wasted valuable staff time and money. There may even be a strategic dimension to the impact. Another project may have been ruled out in favor of investing time and money in this one, and that project would have been genuinely worth doing. The strategic part of the impact can be very significant and it's easy to underestimate it.

You'll know from your own experience that most ideas sound great at first. It's only when you start working on an idea that you begin to realize that it's not quite as shiny and wonderful as you first thought and, to be brutally honest, there are an awful lot of drawbacks and problems. The idea of the Kick Off is to do a limited amount of work early on to investigate the idea and stop the project before it's even started if you discover that it isn't worthwhile after all. The business case will describe in detail the risks and benefits.

REMEMBER

A good approach in Kick Off is to take it in three sequential steps. Don't think that all this pre-project work is going to take a long time, though, because almost always it won't. The approach actually reflects normal business handling of ideas.

1. **Rough out the idea on a single sheet of paper.**

   Set down what it is and the advantages of doing the work. If that looks good when discussed with an organizational manager, then move to Step 2.

2. **Work up the idea into a bit more detail and create a Business Case.**

   Your task here may include looking into a few different options for the way that the work is done and getting a bit of expert input if it's needed to make sure that the recommendation is realistic and technically sound. When the recommendation is reviewed by organizational managers, if it still looks good then you can move to Step 3.

3. **Develop a Scope Statement (sometimes known as a Project Brief or a Statement of Work).**

   This is a more detailed view and should be done by people including some with project experience not just business expertise. If, when the Scope Statement is reviewed, it still looks good then the project can be started, a project team appointed and work begun in earnest on the full planning. If you're not sure what documents like the Scope Statement are all about, then don't worry a bit because they're covered in Chapter 2 of Book 3.

The three steps can normally be completed in the space of two or three days, even for quite substantial projects. Notice too how the work increases through the steps. You only put more effort in if the idea is still looking good. If it turns out to be not such a good idea after all then the earlier you drop it the better, when less resource has been used investigating it.

TIP

When the project starts it's important to have project roles filled and defined clearly, so that people know who will be doing what and when will they be doing it. The roles and responsibilities of the team members should be distributed to all team members. Check out Chapter 2 in Book 1 to find out more about involving the right people in a project.

Doing the planning

If the Business Plan and the Scope statement shows that it's worth starting the project off, then the next stage of the project should be a planning stage. It's a bad mistake to rush into the work without proper plans. You'll only waste time and get confused when things start to go wrong, such as when you discover additional work that you hadn't realized would be needed. Also, you won't be able to control the project. If you don't know where you are supposed to be (because you haven't got a plan) how can you tell whether you're on track or not?

You'll normally need to develop a number of plans in the Planning Stage. Flip to Chapter 3 in Book 1 to help you develop a work breakdown structure (WBS) for your project. Chapter 1 in Book 2 is useful for mapping out a project schedule.

WARNING

It's easy to get plans wrong and, as touched on earlier in this chapter, that can so easily be because you've missed things. If you fail to spot part of the work needed in the project, then clearly it can cause you big problems later on. The project will get delayed while that extra, but essential, work is done. Perhaps you'll need additional people to do the extra work too — even specialists. But what if those people aren't available at short notice? No, it's a lot better to have a good plan at the start and one that's both complete and clear. What's that you say? A checklist or two might help? Now there's an idea.

Unless your project is particularly small and straightforward, you'll usually need other plans as well. For example, how will you manage risk in the project? To explain that and to put the necessary controls in place you can write a Risk Plan.

TIP

Before you start to think that the planning sounds like a huge amount of electronic "paperwork" remember that some of the plans may be quite short and simple, though still necessary. However, you always need to be careful to only produce what you really need to control the project. Clearly a small, simple, low-risk project will need much less in terms of planning and control than a large, high-risk and business critical one. The documentation should reflect those different control needs.

Delivering project products

The next stage of the project, carrying out the work, is where all the main project work gets done. You will give one or more teams work assignments to build the project deliverables. Book 2 has details on this phase of a project's life cycle (in particular Chapters 2 and 3).

TIP

The heading for this section refers to products. Before you start to think about the activities and resources you need in the project, you first investigate what it is that you are going to produce — the project deliverables. So, you have to build a wall. What exactly do you mean by 'wall' then? Is it something like the Great Wall of China, or a small wall around a flower bed in your back garden? Until you're clear on what you have to produce (the products), you can't be accurate with planning the activities and resources, and using the right checklists and templates.

Closing the project

In many projects you'll find it sensible to have a Closure Stage. Some take the view that once the final delivery has been made at the end of the "carrying out the work" phase then that's it, you turn the lights out and everyone can go home. More often than not though, there's still work to be done and you'll still need people on the project to do it.

Typical closure work involves transitioning the product to the end users. Then there are often adjustments needed to project deliverables to fine-tune them. You'll still need your project team members around to carry out those adjustments. On the project management side of things, you'll also need checklists and templates to record how the project went and report things like the final cost.

Only when that "tidy-up" work is all complete can you shut the project down and finally disband the teams. See Chapter 4 in Book 2 for more about bringing your project to closure.

Evaluating the project

After a project is closed, there's still another job to be done and that's the evaluation. Sadly the evaluation work (or lessons learned) is often neglected but that doesn't mean it's unimportant. You can often do the final evaluation after a few weeks and you'll normally be checking out two aspects with the help of a few checklists and templates:

- **Measuring benefits:** A check to see whether the benefits originally claimed for the project when it was started have actually materialized. You can think of this as the "Return on Investment." What was the return in terms of business benefits?

» **Looking at operational effectiveness:** Do the project deliverables work well and have they proved appropriate for those using them after a period of time? For example, staff can be very happy with a new building at first. However, after a few weeks they've discovered that the layout is wrong and the building is very hard to work in. Equally, sometimes an initial negative reaction to deliverables can be reversed after a few weeks when staff find that actually the products are really excellent, but that they just took a bit of getting used to.

Find out more about the post-project evaluation in Chapter 4 of Book 2.

» Using documents for control, including progress reports

» Balancing the amount of documentation against the control needs

Chapter 2
The Key Documents for Managing a Project

Chapter 1 of Book 3 contains a warning about not creating a "paper mountain" in your project. However, unless you have a particularly good memory and nobody else will ever need to document any project information, you're going to have to write some stuff down.

This chapter explains the range of documents you may want to think about for your project. You may not need all of them, but you can use the checklists to think through what you will need, and then how much detail you should go into, which in turn will depend on the control needs of the project.

REMEMBER

A document needn't always be a document. To keep things simple, this chapter refers to documents, but a document needn't always be a document. For example, a progress report may be presented verbally in a meeting and captured in the meeting minutes or given in the form of a short business presentation with visuals. In the early part of Kick Off, the Idea and Recommendation may each be an agenda item in a management meeting where someone explains the proposed project. The content is the same; it's just the medium that's different. In each case, think through the best way of communicating; the answer isn't always a document.

Kicking Off

The three documents in Kick Off work up the idea for a project from a one-side overview. You add more detail at each point when you have established that it's worth progressing. The information from the earlier documents is not duplicated because in the later ones you expand on the information in the earlier ones.

- **The Project Idea:** A one-page overview of the basics of the idea for the project.
- **Exploratory and Business Case Development:** Typically five to ten sides of paper, exploring options and costs, recommending one, recommending not to go ahead after all or perhaps recommending that while the work should be done, it doesn't need a project to do it. Also called the exploratory phase and business case development.
- **Review of the Business Case:** Okay, it's looking like a viable project now. The review states the scope and an overview of the Business Case and is developed using project expertise, not just business expertise.

Project Planning

When the project sponsor receives approval from senior level managers who have an interest in the success of the project and accept the business case with the statement of work, it's time to start the project itself and that begins with the Planning Stage. You'll need some major documents here for project approval and then control, but you'll need to prepare other control documents too, such as a Risk Log and a Project Log.

The major planning documents

There are several major documents here, but the second one — the Project Management Plan — contains quite a few other plans:

- **Project Charter:** The strategic view of the project. This will be maintained throughout. Among other things it contains the scope statement to say what the project is, the objectives and, importantly, the full Business Case.
- **Project Management Plan (PMP):** The tactical view of how you'll manage the project. The following management plans roll up to the Project Management Plan. You'll need some or all of the following:

- **Project Scope Management Plan:** Developed to ensure the project includes all the required work to complete the project successfully. This is also used to guard against scope creep with the product, activity, and resource plans and the budget.
- **Risk Management Plan:** How you will control risk, contingency and response planning and monitoring, and controlling risk throughout the project. This also includes risk included in reporting procedures.
- **Human Resource Management Plan:** Documenting the roles and responsibilities and required skills for the project team.
- **Communications Management Plan:** What information will be needed and how and to whom it will be communicated. This also includes the document repository where all project documents are stored.
- **Stakeholder Management Plan:** If you have a significant amount of Stakeholder management to do, how you will do it. (See Chapter 2 in Book 1 for more information on project stakeholders.)
- **Procurement Management Plan:** If your project will need resources, services and supplies in a significant amount. This shows what will be procured and when, including lead times and cost.

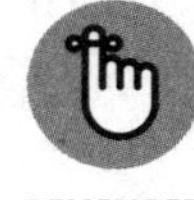

REMEMBER

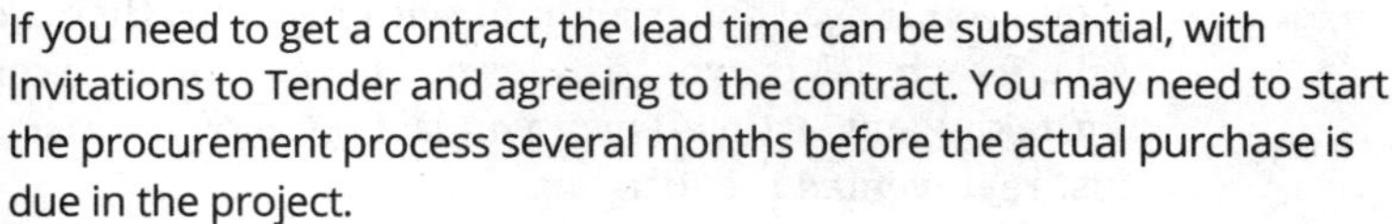

If you need to get a contract, the lead time can be substantial, with Invitations to Tender and agreeing to the contract. You may need to start the procurement process several months before the actual purchase is due in the project.

- **Cost Mangement Plan:** Estimating budgeting and controlling costs so the project can be completed within the approved budget.

» **Other Controls:** Details of any other controls to be used, not covered in the other plans in the PMP.

» **Stage Plan:** The plan for the first Delivery Stage so you can move ahead promptly when the Charter and PMP are approved.

REMEMBER

As always, fit the documentation to the control needs of the document. There are no prizes for producing unnecessarily large documents — they merely drive up project overheads and waste everyone's time in preparing and then reading them.

The logs

Logs are working documents to keep track of things such as risks. You may not need all of the ones in the following checklist, but you'll need most. You set up the logs in the Planning Stage, or sometimes before, ready for use throughout the project.

» **Project Log:** This functions as the Project Manager's journal. It contains reminders, notes, records of important phone calls, lessons being learned from the project, and so on. It's both simple and really useful.

» **Risk Log:** Another simple yet powerful log, the Risk Log has information on each risk and how it is being managed, as well as response plans. It should be made available "read-only" to everyone on the project so that everyone is aware of the risks and is watching out for them.

» **Change Log:** Not mentioned by many of the project approaches, this log is powerful. If you keep a list of changes in this log you can quickly track which changes have been accepted, which have been rejected, who suggested them and, importantly, what they cost.

» **Stakeholder Log:** If you have a significant number of stakeholders in your project, you can keep a list in the log, perhaps grouped according to their interest. For example, operations staff, suppliers, other organizations that you work with and who will be affected.

REMEMBER

Don't dismiss logs as unnecessary and just over-formalized project bureaucracy. They are often logically necessary. For example, you may decide not to bother with a Risk Log. Instead you'll just keep a simple spreadsheet with each risk on a row. Okay, you'll need some columns with headings then. Perhaps things such as how severe each risk is, what actions you have planned to control it, who is responsible for taking any action, when you last checked the risk. You get the point; you've just re-invented the Risk Log.

Control checklists

You'll use two control checklists stage-by-stage, but you should decide the format during the Planning Stage.

» **Quality Checklist:** A list of tests and other quality activities being done in a stage. Each item is then ticked off when it is done. The checklist is a simple but powerful tool for making sure that a planned test hasn't simply been overlooked.

» **Work Checklist:** A list of products to be developed in a stage, and then the date when each is delivered having been completed and successfully passing any tests. This is an extremely powerful progress checking tool.

Controlling a Project

During the delivery stages, closure stage and evaluation of the project you'll need some further documents. This checklist is to help you think through what you'll need, and perhaps what you won't need.

- **Stage Progress Report:** For the project manager to report progress to the Project Steering Group, possibly copied to others such as organizational managers and project managers of any interfacing projects.
- **Team Progress Report:** Where you have a project with multiple teams working, the team leaders will need to inform the project manager of progress on their current work assignments.
- **Stage Completion Report:** Produced at the end of each stage, this report is used by the project manager to inform the project steering group of how the stage went. So, what was the final time and cost? Were there any problems that will affect future stages? This report may be given as a presentation at the stage gate.
- **Project Completion Report:** Produced by the project manager at the end of the project, it reports how the whole project went. It should also record any lessons learned during the project, good and bad, that may be of value to future projects.
- **Project Evaluation Report:** Produced after the end of the project, this sets down information on benefits realization (what the actual benefits were compared to what was expected when the project started) and the suitability of project deliverables after an initial period of use. (See Chapter 4 in Book 2 for an introduction to the post-project evaluation.)
- **Project Issue (or project memo):** A communication from anyone in the project to the project manager, but you may choose to use them for written communications between the project manager and the project steering group too.
- **Work Package:** A work assignment given to a team leader by a project manager. It sets down what work is to be done and how. A project team will work through one or more work packages in a delivery stage. (Find out more about work packages in Chapter 3 of Book 1.)

Thinking About What You Need

REMEMBER

Your decision on the level of documentation in the project is a control decision and it's a balancing act. On the one hand you don't want excessive or unnecessary documents. On the other hand you need to keep the project in control and other people need to check up on it too — they can't check what isn't there. Overall with documentation, follow the KISS principle of Keep It Simple, Stupid.

The control requirements may be dictated in part by your organizational standards. However, even here think hard. If something is set down as mandatory for every project, be prepared to challenge it if there's no value to your project. You may need to get the Project Steering Group (PSG) on board to do that, but it's not in the PSG's interest to incur unnecessary overheads and divert effort from getting the project delivered successfully.

In some cases, it's not so much the organizational standards that are dictating the degree of documentation but a project management office that is getting a bit carried away. As with standards, though, question the value to your particular project of what they're doing. You really have quite enough to do without spending time and effort on unnecessary bureaucracy.

» Exploring the software interface

» Finding help in Project

Chapter 3

Working with Microsoft Project 2019

Welcome to the world of computerized project management with Microsoft Project. If you've never used project management software, you're entering a brave new world.

Everything you used to do with handwritten to-do lists, sticky notes, word processors, and spreadsheets magically comes together in Project. However, this transition doesn't come in a moment, and you need a basic understanding of what project management software can do to get you up to speed. If you've used previous versions of Project, the overview in this chapter can refresh your memory and ease you into a few of the new Project 2019 features.

Even if you're a seasoned project manager, this chapter provides the foundation for how to work with Project.

Connecting Project 2019 to Project Management

You probably handle projects day in and day out. Some are obvious, because your boss named them so that any fool would know that they're projects: Acme Drilling Project or Network Expansion IT Project, for example. Others are less obvious, such as that presentation you need to put together for your director or that how-to guide on planting a vegetable garden in your backyard.

In this book, a project is defined as a unique venture undertaken to produce distinct deliverables, products, or outcomes. In the context of a project, a *deliverable* is an individual component or item that meets the requirements of the project, such as a design document or a prototype. Projects have multiple variables; some are straightforward to define, and others aren't.

Using the information about variables in Table 3-1, you can say that *project management* is the practice of organizing, managing, and controlling project variables to meet the project outcomes and mission.

TABLE 3-1 **Project Variables**

Variable	Description
Defined	
Scope	The work needed to produce the deliverables, products, or outcomes for the project.
Time	The duration required to complete the project work.
Cost	The funds required to complete the project.
Resources	The people, equipment, material, supplies, and facilities needed to accomplish the project.
Undefined	
Change	The type, timing, number, and degree of modifications from a project baseline; can affect the project's scope, time, cost, or resources.
Risk	Uncertainty (associated with the scope, time, cost, resources, stakeholders, or environment) that can threaten the completion of any aspect of the project. Fortunately, risks can also present opportunities to accelerate the schedule or come in under budget.
Stakeholder	A person who can affect, or who is affected by, the project, either positively or negatively.
Environment	The location, culture, or organization in which the project occurs.

Defining "project manager"

Although understanding the role (let alone the usefulness) of certain managers isn't always easy, you can easily spot the value of a *project manager:* This person creates the master plan for a project and ensures that it is implemented successfully. Along the way, the project manager uses technical, business, and leadership skills to manage the completion of tasks and keep the schedule on track.

TIP

A truly professional project manager may have a degree in project management or a professional certification. For example, if you see the initials *PMP* beside a name, that person has been certified as a project management professional by the Project Management Institute, the leading global organization establishing project management standards and credentials. Flip to Book 7 for more about PMP certification.

Identifying what a project manager does

A project manager isn't always the highest authority in a project. Often, that role belongs to whoever manages the project manager — including, possibly, members of senior management. Rather, the project manager is the person who ensures that aspects of the project are integrated and assumes hands-on responsibility for successes as well as failures.

TIP

In project management parlance, the person who champions (and funds) a project is the *project sponsor.* Although the project manager may work for the project sponsor, the project often also has a *customer* — outside the project manager's own company or within it — for whom the end product is produced. See Chapter 2 in Book 1 for more about the people involved in a project.

The project manager manages these essential pieces of a project (introduced in Books 1 and 2):

- **Scope:** Define and organize all work that needs to be done in order to meet the project mission and create deliverables.
- **Schedule:** This element, which you create by working with Project, includes the estimated tasks, duration, and timing involved in reaching the project goal. See Chapter 1 in Book 2 for more about scheduling a project.
- **Resources:** Assign resources and track their activities on the project as well as resolve resource conflicts and build consensus. This part of the job also involves managing physical resources such as materials and equipment.

» **Cost:** Estimate project costs and apply those estimates across the schedule to create a time-phased budget.

» **Communication:** Notify appropriate *stakeholders* (everyone who has a legitimate stake in its success) of the project status.

REMEMBER

Creating a logical balance of the defined variables of scope, time, cost, and resources is at the core of a good project manager's job throughout the life of a project. Managing a project requires overseeing all its variables to ensure that the project goals are accomplished on time, within the limits of the budget, and using the assigned resources while also addressing risks, managing change, and satisfying stakeholders. Sound easy? Maybe not. However, one thing is certain: Having software to help organize and structure the work makes managing the project less daunting. That's where Project 2019 can help.

Introducing Project 2019

Project 2019, which is a scheduling tool, helps you organize, manage, and control defined variables, as identified in the preceding section. Project can also help you manage the undefined variables as well. You can use Project to organize and manage your work, create realistic schedules, and optimize your use of resources.

Take a moment to look at some of the wonderful ways in which Project can help you organize, manage, and control your project. Now that you have, or your company has, bought Project and you're investing your time to understand how to use it, you can enjoy these benefits:

» **Use built-in templates to get a head start on your project.** Project *templates* are prebuilt plans for a typical business project, such as commercial construction, an engineering project, a new product rollout, software development, or an office move.

» **Organize your project by phase, deliverable, geography, or any other method.** The outline format allows you to progressively elaborate the information in greater granularity depending on how detailed you want your plan to be.

» **Determine costs by your chosen method.** Examples are time period, resource type, deliverable, or cost type.

» **Organize resources by resource type.** Level your resources to avoid overallocation, or determine the impact on the duration of a task based on a change in resources.

» **Calculate costs and timing based on your input.** You can quickly calculate what-if scenarios to solve resource conflicts, maintain costs within your budget, or meet a deliverable deadline.

- **Use views and reports with the click of a button.** A wealth of information is now available to you — and those you report to. You no longer have to manually build a report on total costs to date to meet a last-minute request from your boss.
- **Manage complex algorithms** (that you couldn't even begin to figure out on your own) to complete such tasks as leveling resource assignments to solve resource conflicts, filtering tasks by various criteria, modeling what-if scenarios, and calculating the dollar value of work performed to date.

REMEMBER

No matter how cool the tool, you have to take the time to enter meaningful data. Great software doesn't ensure great outcomes; it only makes them easier to achieve.

Getting to Know You

The file you create in Project is a Project *schedule model.* It's a model because it models what you think will happen given what you know at the time. However, for ease of reference, you can refer to it as a schedule. The schedule has a plethora of data about various aspects of your project as well as graphical representations of that information.

REMEMBER

Some people refer to the project schedule as the project plan. In reality, the project plan *contains* the project schedule — plus information such as the budget, work breakdown structure, project life cycle, risk management plan, and many other ingredients necessary to effectively manage a project.

Opening Project 2019

When you first open Project 2019, you see several options for starting a new project, as shown in Figure 3-1.

You can open a blank project, create a new project from an existing project, or create a new project by importing information from Microsoft Excel or SharePoint. You can also take advantage of premade templates for common project types, such as these examples:

- Residential construction
- Software development
- New product launch
- Merger or acquisition evaluation

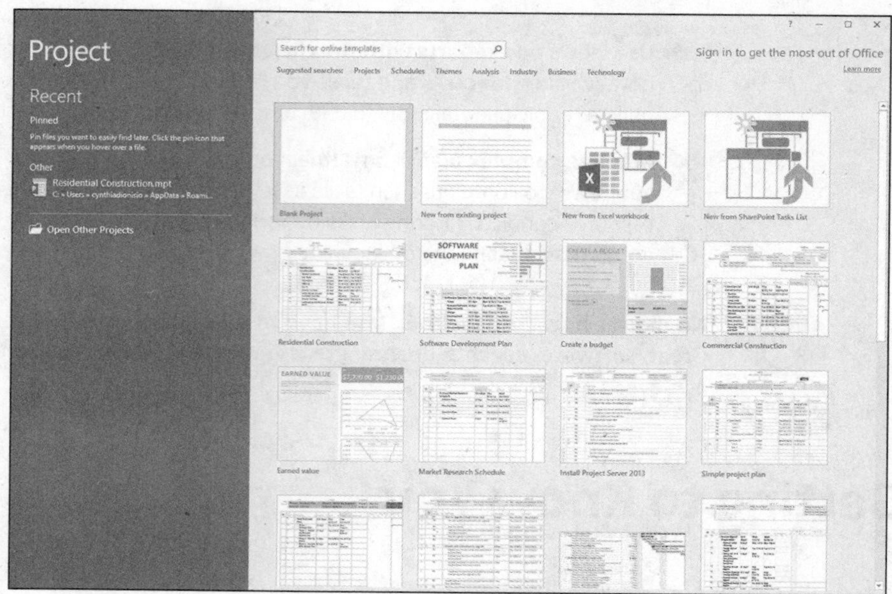

FIGURE 3-1: What you see when you open Project 2019.

If you don't see the template you need, you can search for online templates by entering keywords in the search box at the top of the page. For purposes of this discussion, it's assumed that you're starting with a new, blank project.

When you open a new project, you see the Quick Access toolbar, a few Ribbon tabs, the Ribbon, the Timeline, a pane with a sheet and a chart, and the status bar, as shown in Figure 3-2.

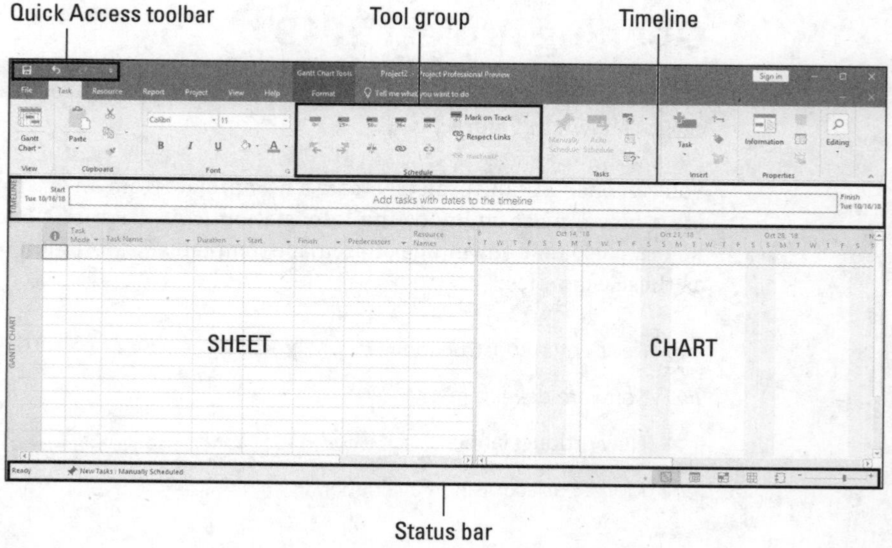

FIGURE 3-2: A blank project.

In Figure 3-2, you see Gantt Chart view. For now, here's an overview of the major elements in Project (refer to Figure 3-2):

- **Quick Access toolbar:** The Quick Access toolbar, above and to the left of the Ribbon, is onscreen at all times and in all views.
- **Ribbon tab:** The Ribbon tabs organize commands based on a particular type of activity. For example, if you're working with resources, you'll likely find the command or setting you want on the Resource tab.
- **Ribbon:** The Ribbon provides easy access to the most commonly used tools and commands. When you change tabs, the available tools on the Ribbon change.
- **Group:** A *group* is a set of related commands or choices on the Ribbon. For example, to format text in a cell on the sheet, first find the formatting information you need in the Font group on the Task tab of the Ribbon.
- **Timeline:** The Timeline provides an overview of the entire project — a graphical view of the project from start to finish. You have the option of showing the Timeline or hiding it.
- **Sheet:** Similar to a spreadsheet, the sheet displays the data in the project. The default fields change depending on the Ribbon tab you're working in. You can customize the columns and fields in the sheet to meet your needs.
- **Chart:** The *chart* is a graphical depiction of the information on the sheet. Depending on the view or Ribbon tab you see, you might also see a bar chart depicting the duration of a task or a resource histogram showing resource usage.
- **Status bar:** The status bar, at the bottom of the Project window, has information on views and zoom level on the right, and information on how newly entered tasks are scheduled on the left.

Navigating Ribbon tabs and the Ribbon

Each of the Ribbon tabs in Project shows different options on the Ribbon. This section provides an overview of each Ribbon tab and of the Ribbon and the Quick Access toolbar.

Each Ribbon tab has a different group of controls or functions. You can navigate from one tab to another by clicking on the tab name.

The first tab on the left is the File Ribbon tab. After you click this tab, you see the Navigation plan down the left side, as shown in Figure 3-3.

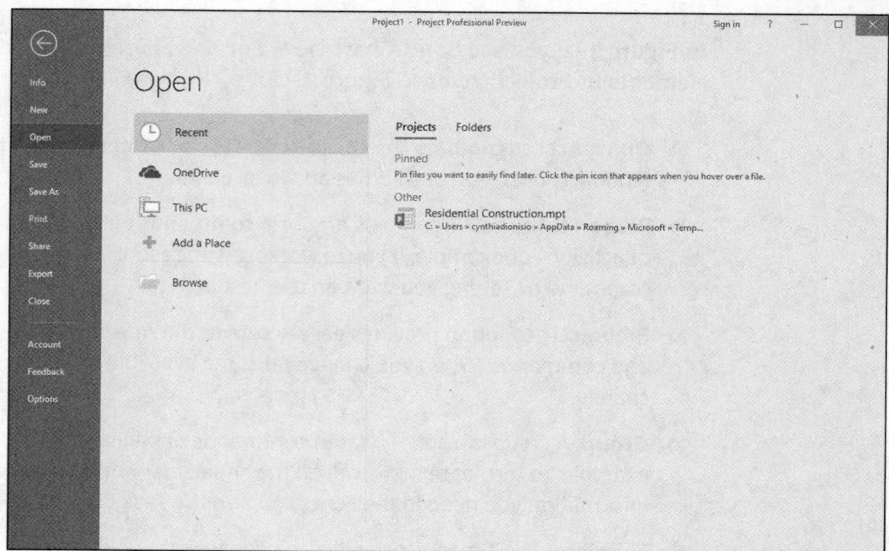

FIGURE 3-3: The File Ribbon tab menu.

The Ribbon tab puts you into Backstage view, where you find choices for working with files and changing options. For example, you can create a new project, open an existing project, save your current project, or print your current project. From Backstage view, you can also share, export, or close your current project. If you're feeling adventurous, you can click Options and customize the Ribbon and the Quick Access toolbar.

The Task Ribbon tab is where you spend a lot of your time in Project. As you can see in Figure 3-4, on the far left side of the Task Ribbon tab is the View. The default view is Gantt Chart view. It shows the task information and the chart that displays a bar chart representing the duration of each task.

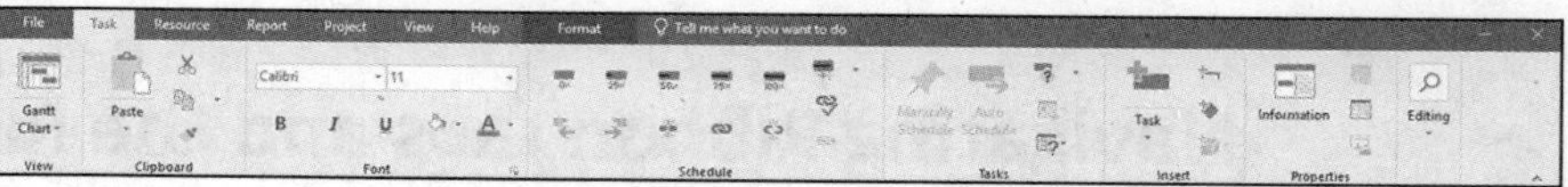

FIGURE 3-4: The Task Ribbon tab.

In addition to Gantt Chart, you can choose these views:

Calendar	Network Diagram
Resource Sheet	Resource Usage
Resource Form	Resource Graph
Task Usage	Task Form

Task Sheet	Team Planner
Timeline	Tracking Gantt

You may recognize some of the groups of commands on the Task Ribbon tab. For example, the Clipboard and Font groups are standard in many Windows applications. Other groups, such as Schedule and Tasks, are specific to a particular view — in this case, Gantt Chart view. Look for the Gantt Chart tools above the Format tab when you see the Task Ribbon tab in Gantt Chart view. In other views, you see different tools above the Format tab.

The Resource Ribbon tab, shown in Figure 3-5, helps you organize resources, such as assigning and leveling resources across tasks. In Project, resources include people, equipment, material, locations, and supplies. You can assign costs and calendars to resources.

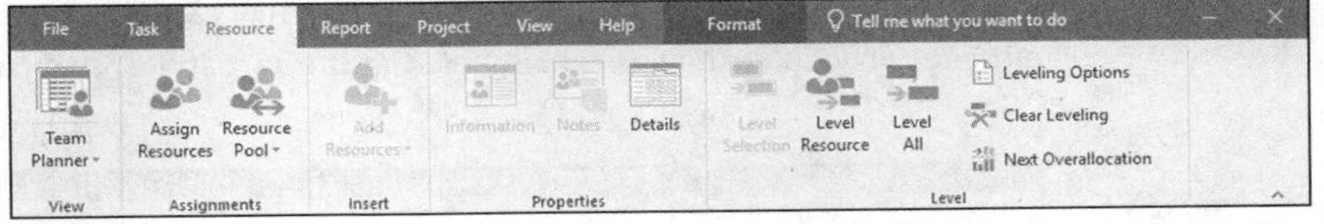

FIGURE 3-5: The Resource Ribbon tab.

The Report Ribbon tab, shown in Figure 3-6, is where you can create reports on resources, costs, or progress, or put them all together in a dashboard report. You can create a report that compares your current status to previous versions of your project.

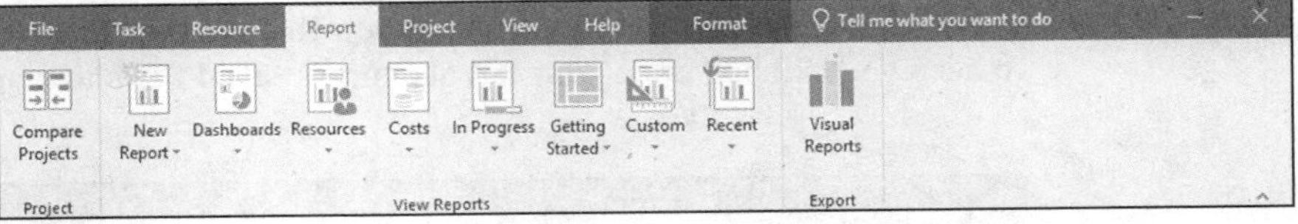

FIGURE 3-6: The Report Ribbon tab.

On the Project Ribbon tab, shown in Figure 3-7, you find commands to help you manage your project as a whole, rather than by task or resource. For example, you can enter or change the project start and finish dates and the baseline. If you need to change working time or add a subproject, this is the place to do it.

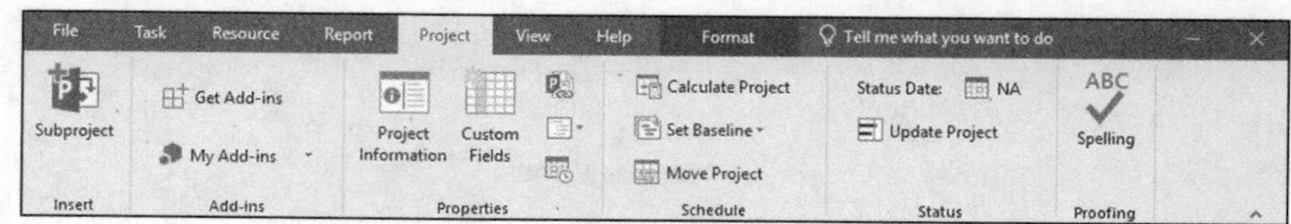

FIGURE 3-7: The Project Ribbon tab.

The View Ribbon tab, shown in Figure 3-8, lets you see some standard views. Examples are Task views, such as Gantt Chart, and Resource views, such as Resource Usage or Team Planner. You can use the View Ribbon tab to look at information sorted by date or a specific period. This tab also lets you see the entire project, show or hide the Timeline, and set the timescale you see.

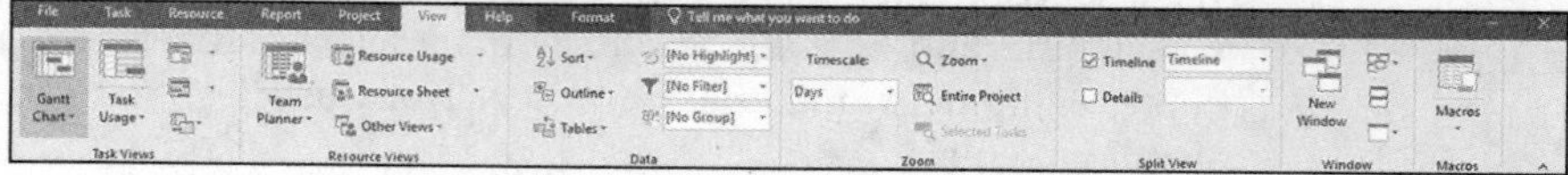

FIGURE 3-8: The View Ribbon tab.

The Format Ribbon tab, shown in Figure 3-9, has commands that help you present your schedule, such as text styles, Gantt Chart styles, and column settings.

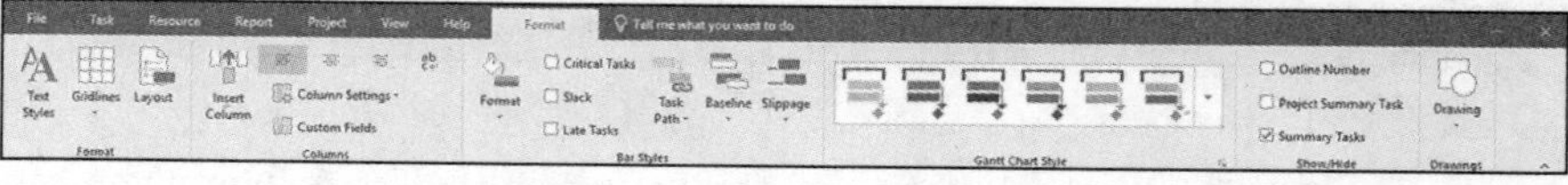

FIGURE 3-9: The Format Ribbon tab.

TIP

You can either show or hide the Ribbon to produce more real estate on your screen. The pushpin to the far right of the Ribbon pins it to your display, keeping it open and visible (as shown in Figure 3-10). The upward-facing arrow (^) on the far-right side hides the Ribbon. If your Ribbon is closed, click on any tab, look in the lower-right corner of the Ribbon and you will see a pushpin. Click on the pushpin to keep your Ribbon open. You can also press Ctrl+F1 to show or hide the Ribbon.

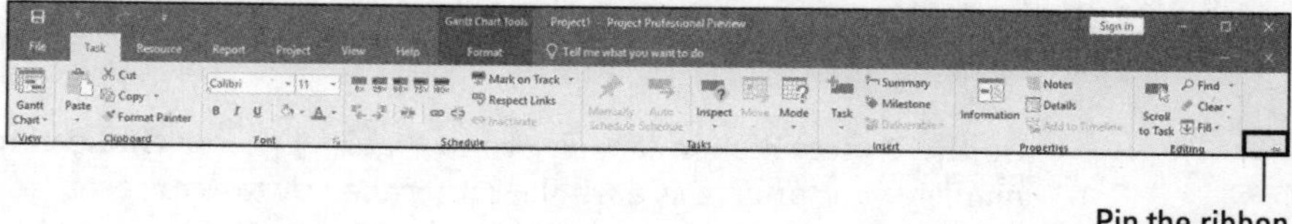

FIGURE 3-10: Keeping your Ribbon visible.

Displaying more tools

The Quick Access toolbar, which appears onscreen at all times, initially contains the Save, Undo, and Redo buttons. You can customize the Quick Access toolbar by clicking the down arrow at the right end of the toolbar and clicking the option you want to hide or display.

If you don't see the option you want, click More Commands near the bottom of the menu to display the Quick Access Toolbar category in the Project Options dialog box. This shows you a full list of commands you can add. Figure 3-11 shows the list of commands you can choose from.

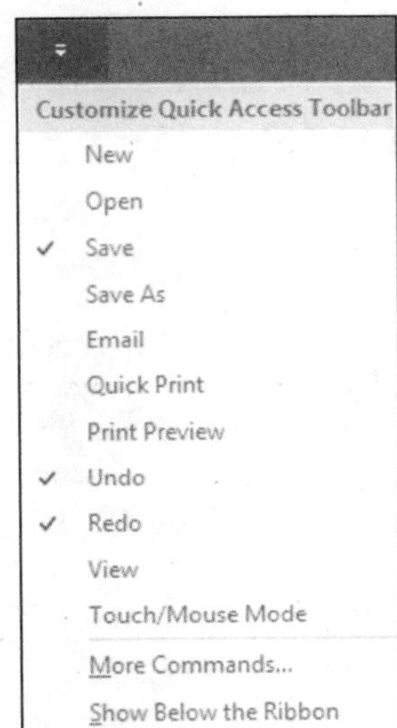

FIGURE 3-11: Customizing the Quick Access toolbar.

The nifty *Timeline* tool shows the entire scaled time span of the project. To show the Timeline, go to the View Ribbon tab (refer to Figure 3-8), in the Split View group and click the check box that says Timeline. You can add tasks or milestones to the Timeline. You can also copy the Timeline and paste it into reports or other presentations. To hide the Timeline, uncheck the Timeline box. You can also work with the Timeline by right-clicking to insert tasks, copy the Timeline, change the font, or view detailed information. Figure 3-12 shows the Timeline with summary tasks and milestones.

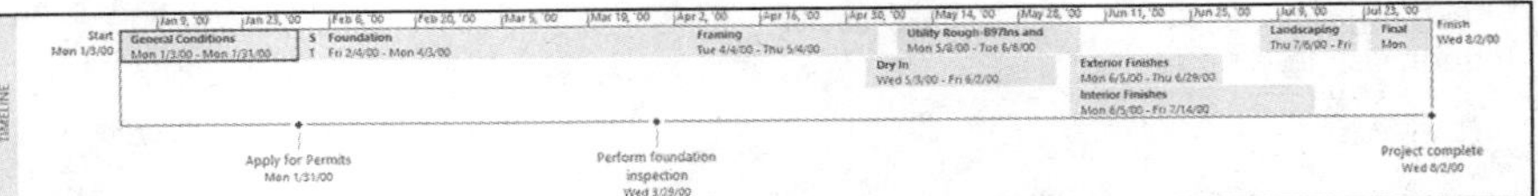

FIGURE 3-12: The Timeline.

The *status bar*, shown in Figure 3-13, sits at the bottom of the project, to indicate whether your tasks are manually or automatically scheduled. The status bar also lets you move quickly to some of the most popular views, such as Gantt, Task Usage, Team Planner, Resource Sheet, and Reports. You can also adjust the time scale from a high-level, time scaled view to a detailed time-scaled view with the View slider, on the far-right end of the status bar.

FIGURE 3-13: The Status bar.

An Updated Feature: Tell Me What You Want to Do

TIP

In previous versions of Microsoft Office, there was a Help function. That has been replaced by the Tell Me What You Want to Do feature. If you want some coaching on how to do something in Project 2019, just click the light bulb next to the Format tab. Enter a keyword, and you have several options to choose from. If you search on "critical path," for example, the information in Figure 3-14 comes up.

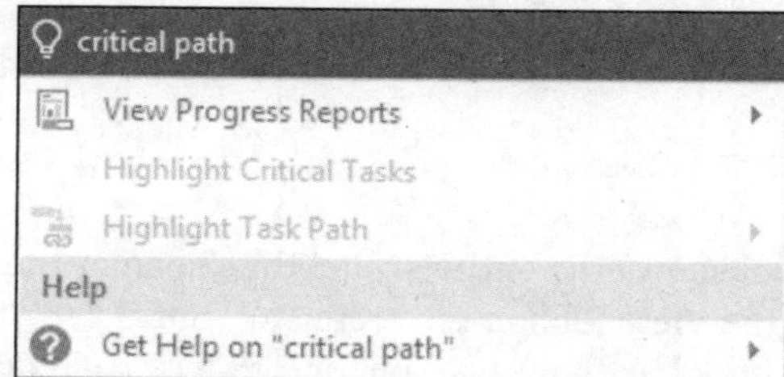

FIGURE 3-14: A search for "critical path."

» Keeping shortcuts close at hand

» Changing the view for better focus

» Adding tasks to the Timeline

Chapter 4
Surveying Cool Shortcuts in Project 2019

Isn't it amazing to watch people work who are adept at using a specific type of software? Their fingers seem to fly over the keyboard; without ever touching the mouse, they create documents, presentations, and other artifacts. This chapter shows you some cool shortcuts that can help you handle Project 2019 like a pro.

Task Information

From Gantt Chart view, you can double-click any task in the project to open the Task Information dialog box. You can then use it, as shown in Figure 4-1, to enter or modify durations, predecessor information, resources, notes, task types, and constraints.

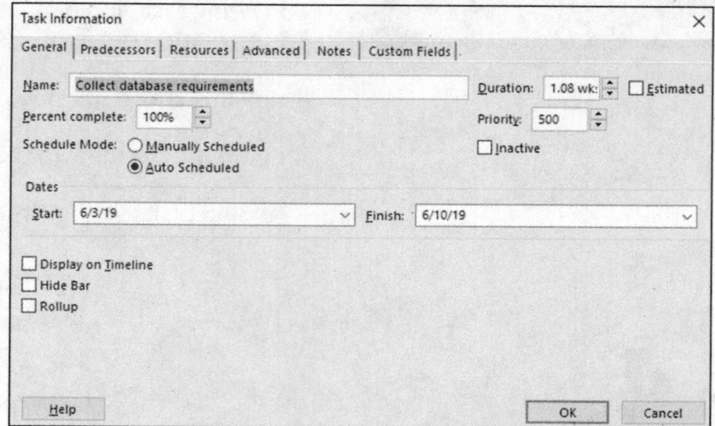

FIGURE 4-1: The Task Information dialog box.

Resource Information

If you want to know anything about a resource, you can find the information in the Resource Information dialog box, as shown in Figure 4-2. From any Resource Sheet view, double-click a resource name to see contact information, availability, cost rates, and any notes you've entered about the resource.

Resource Information

General | Costs | Notes | Custom Fields

Resource Name: Dion Anthony

Cost rate tables

For rates, enter a value or a percentage increase or decrease from the previous rate. For instance, if a resource's Per Use Cost is reduced by 20%, type -20%.

A (Default) | B | C | D | E

Effective Date	Standard Rate	Overtime Rate	Per Use Cost
--	$65.00/h	$0.00/h	$0.00

Cost accrual: Prorated

Help | Details... | OK | Cancel

FIGURE 4-2: The Resource Information dialog box.

You can use the Resource Information dialog box to enter, edit, or update resource information for people, supplies, equipment, and locations considered to be resources.

TIP

When the Assign Resources dialog box is open, double-click a resource name to display the Resource Information dialog box.

Frequently Used Functions

Most user actions in Project are fairly standard, so you shouldn't have to visit the Ribbon every time you want to give a command. Instead, you can simply right-click to display a contextual menu of command options that let you (for example):

- Cut, copy, and paste
- Insert and delete tasks
- Assign resources
- Open the Task Information dialog box
- Add notes
- Add the task to the timeline

Figure 4-3 shows a typical contextual menu you see after right-clicking a task.

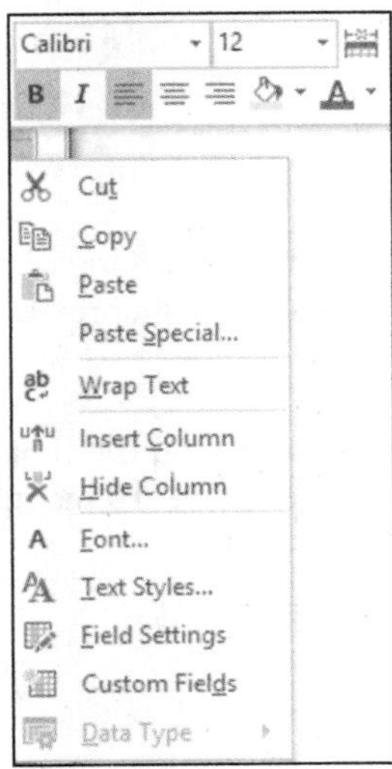

FIGURE 4-3: Contextual menu.

Subtasks

Sometimes, you need to see portions of the project expanded to show all tasks in detail while other portions remain rolled up to a summary task level. In addition to the standard method of clicking the triangle next to the summary task to expand or summarize tasks, you can use keystrokes.

To hide a subtask, press Alt+Shift+hyphen (–). To show subtasks, press Alt+Shift+plus sign (+).

Quick Selections

Say you want to move a row. Place your cursor in any field on the row. You can quickly select the whole row by pressing Shift+Spacebar. To select a whole column, place your cursor anywhere on that column, and press Ctrl+Spacebar.

Fill Down

Suppose that all the tasks in a series have the same resource or the same duration. Rather than repeatedly enter the same resource or duration, you can enter the duration on the topmost task in the list, select the rest of the tasks, and then press Ctrl+D. Project "fills down" the resource to the rest of the selected tasks.

Navigation

The Ctrl key is a helpful tool for navigating to the beginning or end of the project. Simply press Ctrl+Home to move to the beginning of the project or press Ctrl+End to move to the end.

You can also press the Ctrl+Alt keys to navigate around the timescale. To move to the right (forward in time), press Ctrl+Alt+right arrow. To move to the left (backward in time), press Ctrl+Alt+left arrow.

Hours to Years

Sometimes, you want to see the big-picture view of the project by viewing the timescale at the level of months and years. At other times, you need to see details about when tasks will occur. In Project, you can set the timescale to show time in years, all the way down to hours. To show incrementally larger timescale units, press Ctrl+Shift+* (asterisk). To show smaller, more detailed timescale units, press Ctrl+/ (slash).

Timeline Shortcuts

Even the Timeline has shortcuts. When you first show the Timeline, it displays the text "Add tasks with dates to the timeline." Double-click the text to open the Add Tasks to Timeline dialog box (shown in Figure 4-4). Every task is accompanied by a check box; simply select the ones you want to show on the Timeline.

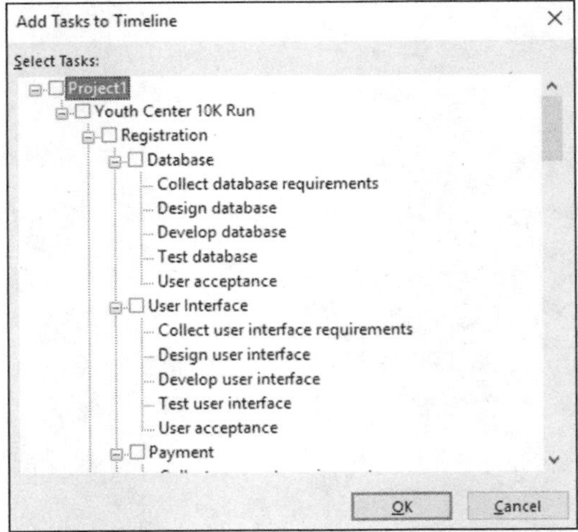

FIGURE 4-4: Adding tasks to the Timeline.

WARNING

Double-clicking the initial text to open the Add Tasks to Timeline dialog box only works the first time you open the Timeline. After you begin entering information on the Timeline, the text that appears on it the first time you open it disappears, and you have to enter tasks by right-clicking them first and choosing Add to Timeline from the shortcut menu.

Quick Undo and Repeat

What if you're typing along and you find the last two rows were entered wrong. Easy! Press Ctrl+Z to undo your last entry. You can press it again to undo the one before that, and the one before that . . . you get the idea. If you want to redo your last entry, just press Ctrl+Y.

4 A New Method: Agile Project Management

Contents at a Glance

» Describing the Platinum Principles

» Understanding what has changed in project management

» Checking out the agile litmus test

Chapter 1
Applying the Agile Manifesto and Principles

This chapter describes the basics of what it means to be agile as outlined in the Agile Manifesto, with its four values, and the 12 Agile Principles behind the Agile Manifesto. It also expands on these basics with three additional Platinum Principles.

This foundation provides product development teams with the information needed to evaluate whether the team is following agile principles, as well as whether their actions and behaviors are consistent with agile values. When you understand these values and principles, you'll be able to ask, "Is this agile?" and be confident in your answer.

Understanding the Agile Manifesto

In the mid-1990s, the Internet was changing the world right before our eyes. The people working in the booming dot-com industry were under constant pressure to be the first-to-market with fast-changing technologies. Development teams worked day and night, struggling to deliver new software releases before competitors made their companies obsolete. The information technology (IT) industry was completely reinvented in a few short years.

Given the pace of change at that time, cracks inevitably appeared in conventional project management practices. Using traditional methodologies such as waterfall didn't allow developers to be responsive enough to the market's dynamic nature and to emerging new approaches to business. Development teams started exploring alternatives to these outdated approaches to project management. In doing so, they noticed some common themes that produced better results.

In February 2001, 17 of these new methodology pioneers met in Snowbird, Utah, to share their experiences, ideas, and practices; to discuss how best to express them; and to suggest ways to improve the world of software development. They couldn't have imagined the effect their meeting would have on the future of project management. The simplicity and clarity of the manifesto they produced and the subsequent principles they developed transformed the world of information technology and continue to revolutionize product development in every industry, not just software.

Over the next several months, these leaders constructed the following:

- **The Agile Manifesto (originally the Manifesto for Agile Software Development):** An intentionally streamlined expression of core development values
- **The Agile Principles:** A set of 12 guiding concepts that support agile teams in delivering value and staying on track
- **The Agile Alliance:** A community development organization focused on supporting individuals and organizations applying agile principles and practices

The group's work was destined to make the software industry more productive, more humane, and more sustainable.

REMEMBER

The Agile Manifesto is a powerful statement, carefully crafted using fewer than 75 words:

> **Manifesto for Agile Software Development**
>
> We are uncovering better ways of developing
> software by doing it and helping others do it.
> Through this work we have come to value:
>
> **Individuals and interactions** over processes and tools
> **Working software** over comprehensive documentation
> **Customer collaboration** over contract negotiation
> **Responding to change** over following a plan

That is, while there is value in the items on
the right, we value the items on the left more.

Agile Manifesto Copyright © 2001: Kent Beck, Mike Beedle, Arie van Bennekum, Alistair Cockburn, Ward Cunningham, Martin Fowler, James Grenning, Jim Highsmith, Andrew Hunt, Ron Jeffries, Jon Kern, Brian Marick, Robert C. Martin, Steve Mellor, Ken Schwaber, Jeff Sutherland, Dave Thomas

This declaration may be freely copied in any form, but only in its entirety through this notice.

No one can deny that the Agile Manifesto is both a concise and an authoritative statement. Whereas traditional approaches emphasize a rigid plan, avoid change, document everything, and encourage hierarchical-based control, the manifesto focuses on

- » People
- » Communications
- » Product
- » Flexibility

REMEMBER

The Agile Manifesto represents a big shift in focus in how products are conceived, conducted, and managed. If you read only the items on the left, you understand the new paradigm that the manifesto signers envisioned. They found that by focusing more attention on individuals and interactions, teams would more effectively produce working software through valuable customer collaboration and by responding well to change. In contrast, the traditional primary focus on processes and tools often produces comprehensive or excess documentation to comply with contract negotiations and to follow an unchanging plan.

Research and experience illustrate why agile values are so important:

- » **Individuals and interactions over processes and tools:** Why? Because research shows a 50 times increase in performance when we get individuals and interactions right. One of the ways to get this right is by collocating a development team with an empowered product owner.
- » **Working software over comprehensive documentation:** Why? Because failure to test for and correct defects during the sprint can take up to 24 times more effort and cost in the next sprint. And after the functionality is deployed to the market, if a production support team that wasn't involved in product development performs the testing and fixing, the cost is up to 100 times more.

» **Customer collaboration over contract negotiation:** Why? Because a dedicated and accessible product owner can generate a fourfold increase in productivity by providing in-the-moment clarification to the development team, aligning customer priorities with the work being performed.

» **Responding to change over following a plan:** Why? Because 80 percent of features developed under a waterfall model are infrequently or never used. Starting with a plan is vital, but the start is when we know the least. Agile teams don't plan less than waterfall teams — they plan as much or more. However, agile teams take a just-in-time approach, planning just enough when needed in support of a strategic product vision and roadmap. Adaptation of the plan to the realities along the way is how agile teams avoid wasteful functionality and deliver products that delight customers.

The creators of the Agile Manifesto originally focused on software development because they worked in the IT industry. However, agile techniques have spread beyond software development and even outside computer-related products. Today, agile approaches such as scrum (see Book 5) are disrupting biotech, manufacturing, aerospace, engineering, marketing, building construction, finance, shipping, automotive, utility, and energy industries with companies such as Apple, Microsoft, and Amazon leading the way. If you want early empirical feedback on the product or service you're providing, you can benefit from agile methods.

The *State of Scrum 2017–2018* report quoted a Scrum Alliance board member who said, "Any organization that does not go through an Agile transformation will die. It is the same as a company refusing to use computers."

REMEMBER

The Agile Manifesto and Agile Principles directly refer to software; this book leaves these references intact when quoting the manifesto and principles. If you create non-software products, try substituting your product as you read on. Agile values and principles apply to all product development activities, not just software.

Outlining the Four Values of the Agile Manifesto

The Agile Manifesto was generated from experience, not from theory. As you review the values described in the following sections, consider what they would mean if you put them into practice. How do these values support meeting time-to-market goals, dealing with change, and valuing human innovation?

TIP

Although the agile values and principles are not numbered, they are numbered here and throughout this book for ease of reference. The numbering matches their order in the manifesto.

Value 1: Individuals and interactions over processes and tools

When you allow each person to contribute his or her unique value to a product, the result can be powerful. When these human interactions focus on solving problems, a unified purpose can emerge. Moreover, the agreements come about through processes and tools that are much simpler than conventional ones.

WARNING

A simple conversation in which you talk through a product issue can solve many problems in a relatively short time. Trying to emulate the power of a direct conversation with email, spreadsheets, and documents results in significant overhead costs and delays. Instead of adding clarity, these types of managed, controlled communications are often ambiguous and time-consuming and distract the development team from the work of creating a product.

Consider what it means if you value individuals and interactions highly. Table 1-1 shows some differences between valuing individuals and interactions and valuing processes and tools.

REMEMBER

If processes and tools are seen as the way to manage product development and everything associated with it, people and the way they approach the work must conform to the processes and tools. Conformity makes it hard to accommodate new ideas, new requirements, and new thinking. Agile approaches, however, value people over process. This emphasis on individuals and teams puts the focus on their energy, innovation, and ability to solve problems. You use processes and tools in agile product management, but they're intentionally streamlined and directly support product creation. The more robust a process or tool, the more you spend on its care and feeding and the more you defer to it. With people front and center, however, the result is a leap in productivity. An agile environment is human-centric and participatory and can be readily adapted to new ideas and innovations.

TABLE 1-1 **Individuals and Interactions Versus Processes and Tools**

	Individuals and Interactions Have High Value	Processes and Tools Have High Value
Pros	Communication is clear and effective. Communication is quick and efficient. Teamwork becomes strong as people work together. Development teams can self-organize. Development teams have more chances to innovate. Development teams can quickly adjust processes as necessary. Development team members can take personal ownership of the product. Development team members can have deeper job satisfaction.	Processes are clear and can be easy to follow. Written records of communication exist.
Cons	To enable more team empowerment and less command and control, managers may have to unlearn traditional leadership tendencies. People may need to let go of ego to work well as members of a team.	People may over-rely on processes instead of finding the best ways to create good products. One process doesn't fit all teams — different people have different work styles. One process doesn't fit all products. Communication can be ambiguous and time-consuming.

Value 2: Working software over comprehensive documentation

A development team's focus should be on producing working functionality. With agile development, the only way to measure whether you are truly finished with a product requirement is to produce the working functionality associated with that requirement. For software products, working software means the software meets the *definition of done:* at the very least, developed, tested, integrated, and documented. After all, the working product is the reason for the investment.

Have you ever been in a status meeting where you reported that you were, say, 75 percent done with your project? What would happen if your customer told you, "We ran out of money. Can we have our 75 percent now?" On a traditional project, you wouldn't have any working software to give the customer; 75 percent done traditionally means you are 75 percent in progress and 0 percent done. With agile product development, however, by using the definition of done, you would have working, potentially shippable functionality for 75 percent of your product requirements — the highest-priority 75 percent of requirements.

Although agile approaches have roots in software development, you can use them for other types of products. This second agile value can easily read, "Working *functionality* over comprehensive documentation."

Tasks that distract from producing valuable functionality must be evaluated to see whether they support or undermine the job of creating a working product. Table 1-2 shows a few examples of traditional project documents and their usefulness. Think about whether documents produced on a recent project you were involved in added value to the functionality being delivered to your customer.

TABLE 1-2 Identifying Useful Documentation

Document	Does the Document Add to Product Value?	Is the Document Barely Sufficient or Gold-Plated?
Project schedule created with expensive project management software, complete with Gantt Chart	No. Start-to-finish schedules with detailed tasks and dates tend to provide more than what is necessary for product development. Also, many of these details change before you develop future features.	Gold-plated. Although project managers may spend a lot of time creating and updating project schedules, team members tend to want to know only key deliverable dates. Management often wants to know only whether the deliverable is on time, ahead of schedule, or behind.
Requirements documentation	Yes. All products have requirements — details about product features and needs. Development teams need to know those needs to create a product.	Possibly gold-plated; should be barely sufficient. Requirements documents can easily grow to include unnecessary details. Agile approaches provide simple ways to enable product requirement conversations.
Product technical specifications	Yes. Documenting how you created a product can make future changes easier.	Possibly gold-plated; should be barely sufficient. Agile documentation includes just what it needs — development teams often don't have time for extra flourishes and are keen to minimize documentation.
Weekly status report	No. Weekly status reports are for management purposes but do not assist product creation.	Gold-plated. Knowing status is helpful, but traditional status reports contain outdated information and are much more burdensome than necessary.
Detailed project communication plan	No. Although a contact list can be helpful, the details in many communication plans are useless to product development teams.	Gold-plated. Communication plans often end up being documents about documentation — an egregious example of busywork.

REMEMBER

With agile product development, *barely sufficient* is a positive description, meaning that a task, document, meeting, or almost anything created includes only what it needs to achieve the goal. Being barely sufficient is practical and efficient — it's sufficient, just enough. The opposite of barely sufficient is *gold-plating,* or adding unnecessary frivolity — and effort — to a feature, task, document, meeting, or anything else.

All development requires some documentation. With agile product development, documents are useful only if they support development and are barely sufficient to serve the design, delivery, and deployment of a working product in the most direct, unceremonious way. Agile approaches dramatically simplify the administrative paperwork relating to time, cost control, scope control, or reporting.

TIP

Stop producing a document and see who complains. After you know the requester of the document, strive to better understand why the document is necessary. The *five whys* work great in this situation — ask "why" after each successive answer to get to the root reason cause for the document. After you know the core reason for the document, see how you can satisfy that need with an agile artifact or streamlined process.

Agile teams produce fewer, more streamlined documents that take less time to maintain and provide better visibility into potential issues. In later chapters, you find out how to create and use simple tools (such as a product backlog, a sprint backlog, and a task board) that allow teams to understand requirements and assess real-time status daily. With agile approaches, teams spend more time on development and less time on documentation, resulting in a more efficient delivery of a working product. See Chapter 2 in Book 4 for more on the product backlog, and see Chapter 3 in Book 4 to learn more about the sprint backlog.

Value 3: Customer collaboration over contract negotiation

The customer is not the enemy. Really.

Historical project management approaches usually limit customer involvement to a few development stages:

- **Start of a project:** When the customer and the project team negotiate contract details.
- **Any time the scope changes during the project:** When the customer and the project team negotiate changes to the contract.

» **End of a project:** When the project team delivers a completed product to the customer. If the product doesn't meet the customer's expectations, the project team and the customer negotiate additional changes to the contract.

This historical focus on negotiation, avoidance of scope change, and limitation of direct customer involvement discourages potentially valuable customer input and can even create an adversarial relationship between customers and project teams.

WARNING

You will never know less about a product than at its start. Locking product details into a contract at the beginning of development means you have to make decisions based on incomplete knowledge. If you have flexibility for change as you learn more about a product and the customer the product is serving, you'll ultimately create better products.

The agile pioneers understood that collaboration, rather than confrontation, produced better, leaner, more useful products. As a result of this understanding, agile methods make the customer part of the product development on an ongoing basis.

Using an agile approach in practice, you'll experience a partnership between the customer and the development team in which discovery, questioning, learning, and adjusting during the course of product development are routine, acceptable, and systematic.

Value 4: Responding to change over following a plan

Change is a valuable tool for creating great products. Teams that can respond quickly to customers, product users, and the market are able to develop relevant, helpful products that people want to use.

Unfortunately, traditional project management approaches attempt to wrestle the change monster and pin it to the ground so it goes out for the count. Rigorous change management procedures and budget structures that can't accommodate new product requirements make changes difficult. Traditional project teams often find themselves blindly following a plan, missing opportunities to create more valuable products or, even worse, unable to react timely to changing market conditions.

Figure 1-1 shows the relationship between time, opportunity for change, and the cost of change on a traditional project. As time — and knowledge about your product — increases, the ability to make changes decrease, and costs more.

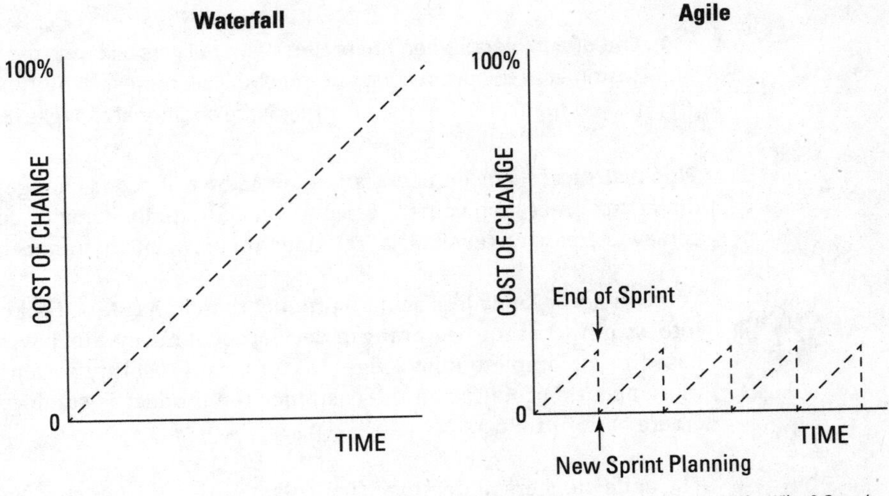

FIGURE 1-1: Traditional project opportunity for change.

By contrast, agile development accommodates change systematically. The flexibility of agile approaches increases stability because product changes are predictable and manageable — in other words, it's expected and non-disruptive to an agile team. In the rest of Book 4, you discover how agile approaches to planning, working, and prioritization allow teams to respond quickly to change.

As new events unfold, the team incorporates these realities into the ongoing work. Any new item becomes an opportunity to provide additional value instead of an obstacle to avoid, giving development teams a greater opportunity for success.

Defining the 12 Agile Principles

In the months following the publication of the Agile Manifesto, the original signatories continued to communicate. To support teams making the transition to agile approaches, they augmented the four values of the Agile Manifesto with 12 principles.

REMEMBER

These principles, along with the Platinum principles (explained in the later section "Adding the Platinum Principles") can be used as a litmus test to see whether the specific practices of your team are true to the intent of the agile movement.

REMEMBER

Following is the text of the original 12 principles, published in 2001 by the Agile Alliance:

1. Our highest priority is to satisfy the customer through early and continuous delivery of valuable software.
2. Welcome changing requirements, even late in development. Agile processes harness change for the customer's competitive advantage.
3. Deliver working software frequently, from a couple of weeks to a couple of months, with a preference to the shorter timescale.
4. Business people and developers must work together daily throughout the project.
5. Build projects around motivated individuals. Give them the environment and support they need and trust them to get the job done.
6. The most efficient and effective method of conveying information to and within a development team is face-to-face conversation.
7. Working software is the primary measure of progress.
8. Agile processes promote sustainable development. The sponsors, developers, and users should be able to maintain a constant pace indefinitely.
9. Continuous attention to technical excellence and good design enhances agility.
10. Simplicity — the art of maximizing the amount of work not done — is essential.
11. The best architectures, requirements, and designs emerge from self-organizing teams.
12. At regular intervals, the team reflects on how to become more effective, then tunes and adjusts its behavior accordingly.

These agile principles provide practical guidance for development teams.

Another way of organizing the 12 principles is to consider them in the following four distinct groups:

- Customer satisfaction
- Quality
- Teamwork
- Product development

The following sections discuss the principles according to these groups.

Agile principles of customer satisfaction

Agile approaches focus on customer satisfaction, which makes sense. After all, the customer is the reason for developing the product in the first place.

While all 12 principles support the goal of satisfying customers, principles 1, 2, 3, and 4 stand out:

1. Our highest priority is to satisfy the customer through early and continuous delivery of valuable software.
2. Welcome changing requirements, even late in development. Agile processes harness change for the customer's competitive advantage.
3. Deliver working software frequently, from a couple of weeks to a couple of months, with a preference to the shorter timescale.
4. Business people and developers must work together daily throughout the project.

You may define the customer of a product in a number of ways:

- The customer is the person or group paying for the product.
- In some organizations, the customer may be a client, external to the organization.
- In other organizations, the customer may be a stakeholder or a group of stakeholders in the organization.
- The person who ends up using the product is also a customer. For clarity and to be consistent with the original 12 agile principles, that person is called the *user*.

How do you enable these principles? Consider the following:

- Agile teams include a *product owner*, a person who is responsible for translating what the customer wants into product requirements.
- The product owner prioritizes product features in order of business value or risk and communicates priorities to the development team. The development team delivers the most valuable features on the list in short cycles of development, known as *iterations*, or *sprints*.
- The product owner has deep and ongoing involvement throughout each day to clarify priorities and requirements, make decisions, provide feedback, and quickly answer the many questions that pop up during product development.

» Frequent delivery of working product features allows the product owner and the customer to have a full sense of how the product is developing.

» As the development team continues to deliver complete, working, potentially shippable functionality every one to eight weeks or less, the value of the total product grows incrementally, as do its functional capabilities.

» The customer accumulates value for his or her investment regularly by receiving new, ready-to-use functionality throughout development, rather than waiting until the end for the first, and maybe only, delivery of releasable product features.

Table 1-3 lists some customer satisfaction issues that commonly arise during product development. Use Table 1-3 and gather some examples of customer dissatisfaction that you've encountered. Do you think becoming more agile would make a difference? Why or why not?

TABLE 1-3 **Customer Dissatisfaction and How Agile Might Help**

Examples of Customer Dissatisfaction with Product Development	How Agile Approaches Can Increase Customer Satisfaction
The product requirements were misunderstood by the development team.	Product owners work closely with the customer to define and refine product requirements and provide clarity to the development team. Agile teams demonstrate and deliver working functionality at regular intervals. If a product doesn't work the way the customer thinks it should work, the customer can provide feedback at the end of the sprint, not at the end of development, when the feedback would be too late.
The product wasn't delivered when the customer needed it.	Working in sprints allows agile teams to deliver high-priority functionality early and often.
The customer can't request changes without additional cost and time.	Agile processes are built for change. Development teams can accommodate new requirements, requirement updates, and shifting priorities with each sprint — offsetting the cost of these changes by removing the lowest-priority requirements — functionality that likely will never or rarely get used.

TIP

Agile strategies for customer satisfaction include the following:

» Producing, in each iteration, the highest-priority features first

» Ideally, locating the product owner and the other members of the team in the same place to eliminate communication barriers

Applying the Agile Manifesto and Principles

- Breaking requirements into groups of features that can be delivered in one to eight weeks or less
- Keeping written requirements simple, forcing more robust and effective face-to-face communication
- Getting the product owner's acceptance as soon as functionality is completed
- Revisiting the feature list regularly to ensure that the most valuable requirements continue to have the highest priority

Agile principles of quality

An agile team commits to producing quality in every product increment it creates — from development through documentation to integration and test results — every day. Each team member contributes his or her best work all the time. Although all 12 principles support the goal of quality delivery, principles 1, 3, 4, 6–9, and 12 stand out:

1. Our highest priority is to satisfy the customer through early and continuous delivery of valuable software.
3. Deliver working software frequently, from a couple of weeks to a couple of months, with a preference to the shorter timescale.
4. Business people and developers must work together daily throughout the project.
6. The most efficient and effective method of conveying information to and within a development team is face-to-face conversation.
7. Working software is the primary measure of progress.
8. Agile processes promote sustainable development. The sponsors, developers, and users should be able to maintain a constant pace indefinitely.
9. Continuous attention to technical excellence and good design enhances agility.
12. At regular intervals, the team reflects on how to become more effective, then tunes and adjusts its behavior accordingly.

These principles, in practice on a day-to-day basis, can be described as follows:

- The development team members must have full ownership of technical quality and be empowered to solve problems. They carry the responsibility for determining how to create the product, deciding the technical work needed to create it, and organizing product development. People not doing the work don't tell them how to do it.

- With software development, an agile approach requires architectures that make coding and testing the product modular, flexible, and extensible. The design should address today's problems and make inevitable changes as simple as possible.
- A set of designs on paper can never tell you that something will work because everything works on paper. When the product quality is such that it can be demonstrated and ultimately shipped in short intervals, everyone knows that the product works — at the end of every sprint.
- As the development team completes features, the team shows the product owner the product functionality to get validation that it meets the acceptance criteria. The product owner's reviews should happen throughout the iteration, ideally the same day that the development of the requirement was completed. Feedback from the product owner is often necessary even during the development of a feature.
- At the end of every iteration (lasting two weeks or less for most agile teams), working functionality is demonstrated to the customer. Progress is clear and easy to measure.
- Testing is an integral, ongoing part of development and happens throughout the day, not at the end of the iteration. As much as possible, testing is automated.
- With software development, ensuring new code is tested and integrates with previous versions occurs in small increments, possibly several times a day (or thousands of times a day in some organizations, such as Google, Amazon, and Facebook). This process, called *continuous integration (CI),* helps ensure that the entire solution continues to work when new code is added to the existing code base.
- With software development, examples of technical excellence include establishing coding standards, using service-oriented architecture, implementing automated testing, and building for future change.

REMEMBER

Agile principles apply to more than software products. Technical excellence is crucial whether you're developing marketing campaigns, publishing books, involved in manufacturing, or engaged in research and development. All disciplines have a set of technical practices that agile teams can use to build in quality all along the way.

TIP

Agile approaches provide the following strategies for quality management:

- Defining what *done* means (that is, shippable ready for market, / go to market) at the beginning of development and then using that definition as a benchmark for quality

» Testing aggressively and daily through automated means

» Building only the functionality needed when it's needed

» Reviewing the software code and streamlining (refactoring)

» Showcasing to stakeholders and customers only the functionality that has been accepted by the product owner

» Having multiple feedback points throughout the day, iteration, and product lifecycle

Agile principles of teamwork

Teamwork is critical to agile product development. Creating good products requires cooperation among all members of the team, including customers and stakeholders. Agile approaches support team-building and teamwork, and they emphasize trust in self-managing development teams. A permanent, skilled, motivated, unified, and empowered team is a successful team.

Although all 12 principles support the goal of teamwork, principles 4–6, 8, 11, and 12 stand out as supporting team empowerment, efficiency, and excellence:

4. Business people and developers must work together daily throughout the project.
5. Build projects around motivated individuals. Give them the environment and support they need, and trust them to get the job done.
6. The most efficient and effective method of conveying information to and within a development team is face-to-face conversation.
8. Agile processes promote sustainable development. The sponsors, developers, and users should be able to maintain a constant pace indefinitely.
11. The best architectures, requirements, and designs emerge from self-organizing teams.
12. At regular intervals, the team reflects on how to become more effective, then tunes and adjusts its behavior accordingly.

TIP

Agile approaches focus on sustainable development; as knowledge workers, our brains are the value we bring to product development. If only for selfish reasons, organizations should want fresh, well-rested brains working for them. Maintaining a regular work pace, rather than having periods of intense overwork, helps keep each team member's mind sharp and product quality high.

Here are some practices you can adopt to make this vision of teamwork a reality:

- Ensure that your development team members have the proper skills and motivation.
- Provide training sufficient to the task.
- Support the self-organizing development team's decisions about what to do and how to do it; don't have managers tell the team what to do.
- Hold team members responsible as a single team, not as individuals.
- Use face-to-face communication to quickly and efficiently convey information.

WARNING

Suppose that you usually communicate to Sharon by email. You take time to craft your message and then send it. The message sits in Sharon's inbox, and she eventually reads it. If Sharon has any questions, she writes another email in response and sends it. That message sits in your inbox until you eventually read it. And so forth. This type of table tennis communication is too inefficient to use in the middle of a rapid iteration. A five-minute discussion addresses the issue quickly and with less risk of misunderstanding — and with a huge cost savings.

- Have spontaneous conversations throughout the day to build knowledge, understanding, and efficiency.
- Collocate teammates in close proximity to increase clear and efficient communication. If collocation isn't possible, use video chat rather than email. Teams who rely on written communication for collaboration are slower and more prone to miscommunication errors. Written intra-team communication is a liability.
- Make sure that *lessons learned* is an ongoing feedback loop rather than an end-of-project-only occurrence. Retrospectives should be held at the end of each iteration, when reflection and adaptation can improve development team productivity immediately going forward, creating ever higher levels of efficiency. A lessons learned meeting at the end of development has minimal value because the next product created might have a different group of people and practices. To learn more about retrospectives, see Chapter 5 in Book 4.

REMEMBER

The first retrospective is as valuable (or even more valuable) as any future retrospective because, at the beginning, the team has the opportunity to make changes that can benefit the rest of the product development moving forward.

TIP

The following strategies promote effective teamwork:

- Collocate the development team so they have no physical barriers to effective and real-time communication.
- Put together a physical environment conducive for collaboration: a team room with whiteboards, colored pens, and other tactile tools for developing and conveying ideas to ensure shared understanding.
- Create an environment where team members are encouraged to speak their minds.
- Meet face-to-face whenever possible. Don't send an email if a conversation can handle the issue.
- Get clarifications throughout the day as they're needed.
- Encourage the team to solve problems rather than having managers solve problems for the team.
- Resist the temptation to shuffle team members. Allow the team to become a stable, permanent, high-performing, capability-expanding team.

REMEMBER

A long-term product perspective requires long-term, permanent teams. High-performing teams take years to build. Their understanding of the customer, their feedback from each release, the product support they provide, and the product development environment logically encourage teams to remain as stable as possible. Team members may seek new opportunities for career development outside the team, but for the most part teams should remain as constant as possible for maximum value. As each new feature is built, the team remains constant, able to support and learn from the product's adoption by the customer.

Agile principles of product development

Agility in product management encompasses three key areas:

- Making sure the development team can be productive and can sustainably increase productivity over long periods of time
- Ensuring that information about the product's progress is available to stakeholders without interrupting the flow of development activities by asking the development team for updates
- Handling requests for new features as they occur and integrating them into the product development cycle

An agile approach focuses on planning and executing the work to produce the best product that can be released. The approach is supported by communicating openly, avoiding distractions and wasteful activities, and ensuring that the progress of the product development is clear to everyone.

All 12 principles support product management, but principles 1–3 and 7–10 stand out for us:

1. Our highest priority is to satisfy the customer through early and continuous delivery of valuable software.
2. Welcome changing requirements, even late in development. Agile processes harness change for the customer's competitive advantage.
3. Deliver working software frequently, from a couple of weeks to a couple of months, with a preference to the shorter timescale.
7. Working software is the primary measure of progress.
8. Agile processes promote sustainable development. The sponsors, developers, and users should be able to maintain a constant pace indefinitely.
9. Continuous attention to technical excellence and good design enhances agility.
10. Simplicity — the art of maximizing the amount of work not done — is essential.

Following are some advantages of adopting agile product management:

- Agile teams achieve faster time-to-market and, consequently, cost savings. They start development earlier than in traditional approaches because agile approaches minimize the exhaustive upfront planning and documentation that is conventionally part of the early stages of a waterfall project.
- Agile teams are self-organizing and self-managing. The managerial effort normally put into telling developers how to do their work can be applied to removing impediments and organizational distractions that slow down the team.
- Agile development teams determine how much work they can accomplish in an iteration and commit to achieving those goals. Ownership is fundamentally different because the development team is establishing the commitment, not complying with an externally developed commitment.
- An agile approach asks, "What is the minimum we can do to achieve the goal?" instead of focusing on including all features and extra refinements that could possibly be needed. An agile approach usually means streamlining: barely

sufficient documentation, removal of unnecessary meetings, avoidance of inefficient communication (such as email), and minimizing complexity of what's under the hood (just enough to make it work).

Creating complicated documents that aren't useful for product development is a waste of effort. It's okay to document a decision, but you don't need multiple pages on the history and nuances of how the decision was made. Keep the documentation barely sufficient (that is, sufficient but just barely), and you'll have more time to focus on supporting the development team.

- By encapsulating development into short sprints that last several weeks or less, you can adhere to the goals of the current iteration while accommodating change in subsequent iterations. The length of each sprint remains the same throughout development to provide a predictable rhythm for the team long-term.
- Planning, elaborating on requirements, developing, testing, and demonstrating functionality occur within an iteration, lowering the risk of heading in the wrong direction for extended periods of time or developing something that the customer doesn't want.
- Agile practices encourage a steady pace of development that is productive and healthy. For example, in the popular agile software development set of practices called extreme programming (XP), the maximum workweek is 40 hours, and the preferred workweek is 35 hours. Agile product development is constant and sustainable, as well as more productive, especially long term.

Traditional approaches routinely feature a *death march,* in which the team puts in extremely long hours for days and even weeks at the end to meet a previously unidentified and unrealistic deadline. As the death march goes on, productivity tends to drop dramatically. More defects are introduced, and because defects need to be corrected in a way that doesn't break a different piece of functionality, correcting defects is the most expensive work that can be performed. Defects are often the result of overloading a system — specifically demanding an unsustainable pace of work. Check out a presentation on the negative effects of "Racing in Reverse" at `https://platinumedge.com/overtime`.

- Priorities, experience with the existing product, and, eventually, the speed at which development will likely occur within each sprint are clear, making for good decisions about how much can or should be accomplished in a given amount of time.

If you've worked on a traditional project before, you might have a basic understanding of project management activities. Table 1-4 lists a few project management tasks, along with how you would meet those needs with agile approaches. Use Table 1-4 to capture your thoughts about your experiences and how agile approaches look different from traditional project management.

TABLE 1-4 Contrasting Historical Project Management with Agile Product Management

Traditional Project Management Tasks	Agile Approach to Product Development Tasks
Create a fully detailed project requirement document at the beginning of the project. Try to control requirement changes throughout the project.	Create a product backlog — a simple list of requirements by priority. Quickly update the product backlog as requirements and priorities change throughout product development.
Conduct weekly status meetings with all project stakeholders and developers. Send detailed meeting notes and status reports after each meeting.	The development team meets quickly, for no longer than 15 minutes, at the start of each day to coordinate and synchronize that day's work and any roadblocks. They can update the centrally visible burndown chart in under a minute at the end of each day. Anyone, including stakeholders, can see the real-time progress on demand.
Create a detailed project schedule with all tasks at the beginning of the project. Try to keep the project tasks on schedule. Update the schedule on a regular basis.	Work within sprints and identify only specific tasks for the active sprint.
Assign tasks to the development team.	Support the development team by removing impediments and distractions. Development teams define and pull (as opposed to push) their own tasks.

TIP

Successful product development is facilitated by the following agile approaches:

- Supporting the development team with real-time answers to their questions, shielding them from competing priorities, and empowering them to develop solutions and determine how much work to take on in each iteration
- Producing barely sufficient documents
- Streamlining status reporting so that information is pushed out by the development team in seconds rather than pulled out by a project manager over a longer period of time

- Minimizing nondevelopment tasks
- Setting expectations that change is normal and beneficial, not something to be feared or evaded
- Adopting a just-in-time requirements refinement to minimize change disruption and wasted effort
- Collaborating with the development team to create realistic schedules, targets, and goals
- Protecting the team from organizational disruptions that could undermine product goals by introducing work that is not relevant to the product objectives
- Understanding that an appropriate balance between work and life is a component of efficient development
- Viewing the product as a long-term investment requiring permanent teams pursuing value over specifications

Adding the Platinum Principles

Through in-the-trenches experience working with teams transitioning to agile product development — and field testing in large, medium, and small organizations worldwide —three additional principles of agile product development were developed. They're called the Platinum Principles:

- Resist formality.
- Think and act as a team.
- Visualize rather than write.

You can explore each principle in more detail in the following sections.

Resisting formality

Even the most agile teams can drift toward excessive formalization. For example, it isn't uncommon to find team members waiting until a scheduled meeting to discuss simple issues that could be solved in seconds. These meetings often have an agenda and meeting minutes and require a certain level of demobilization and remobilization just to attend. In an agile approach, this level of formalization isn't required.

REMEMBER

You should always question formalization and unnecessary, showy displays. For example, is there an easier way to get what you need? How does the current activity support the development of a quality product as quickly as possible? Answering these questions helps you focus on productive work and avoid unnecessary tasks.

In an agile system, discussions and the physical work environment are open and free-flowing; documentation is kept to the lowest level of quantity and complexity such that it contributes value to the product, not hampers it; and flashy displays, such as well-decorated presentations, are avoided. Professional, frank communications are best for the team, and the entire organizational environment has to make that openness available and comfortable.

TIP

Strategies for success in resisting formality include the following:

- Reducing organizational hierarchy wherever possible by eliminating titles in the team
- Avoiding aesthetic investments such as elaborate slide presentations or extensive meeting minute forms, especially when demonstrating shippable functionality at the end of a sprint
- Educating stakeholders who request complicated displays about the high costs and low returns of such displays

Thinking and acting as a team

Team members should focus on how the team as a whole can be most productive. This focus can mean letting go of individual niches and performance metrics. In an agile environment, the entire team should be aligned in its commitment to the goal, its ownership of the scope of work, and its acknowledgment of the time available to achieve that commitment.

TIP

Following are some strategies for thinking and acting as a team:

- Develop in pairs and switch partners often. Both pair programming (both partners are knowledgeable in the area) and shadowing (only one partner is knowledgeable in the area) raise product quality.

» Replace individual work titles with a uniform product developer title. Development activities include all tasks necessary to take requirements through to functionality, including design, implementation (for example, coding), testing, and documentation — not just writing code or turning a screwdriver.

» Report at the team level only, as opposed to creating special management reports that subdivide the team.

» Replace individual performance metrics with team performance metrics.

Visualizing rather than writing

An agile team should use visualization as much as possible, whether through simple diagrams or computerized modeling tools. Images are much more powerful than words. When you use a diagram or mockup instead of a document, your customer can relate better to the concept and the content.

Your ability to define the features of a system increases exponentially when you step up your interaction with the proposed solution: A graphical representation is almost always better than a textual one, and experiencing functionality hands-on is best.

TIP

Even a sketch on a piece of paper can be a more effective communication tool than a formal text-based document. A picture is worth a thousand words. A textual description is the weakest form of communication if you're trying to ensure common understanding — especially when the description is delivered by email with the request to "let me know if you have any questions."

TIP

Examples of strategies for visualization include the following:

» Stocking the work environment with plenty of whiteboards, poster paper, pens, and paper so that drawing tools are readily available

» Using models instead of text to communicate concepts

» Reporting status through charts, graphs, and dashboards, such as those in Figure 1-2

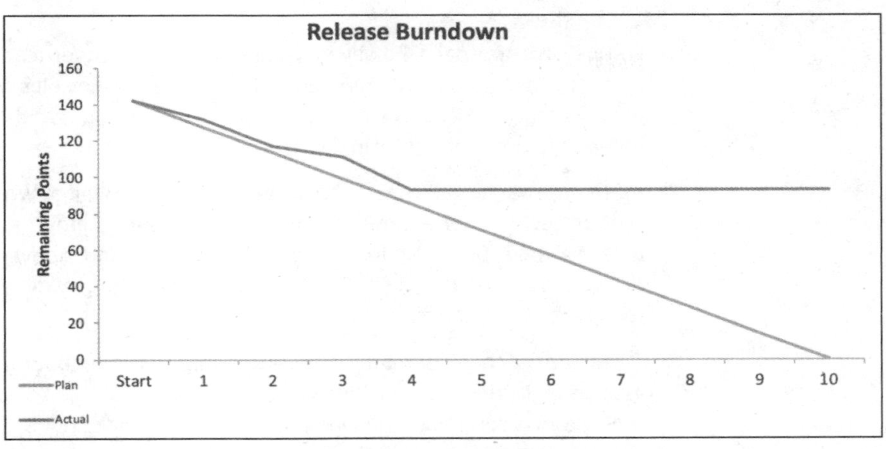

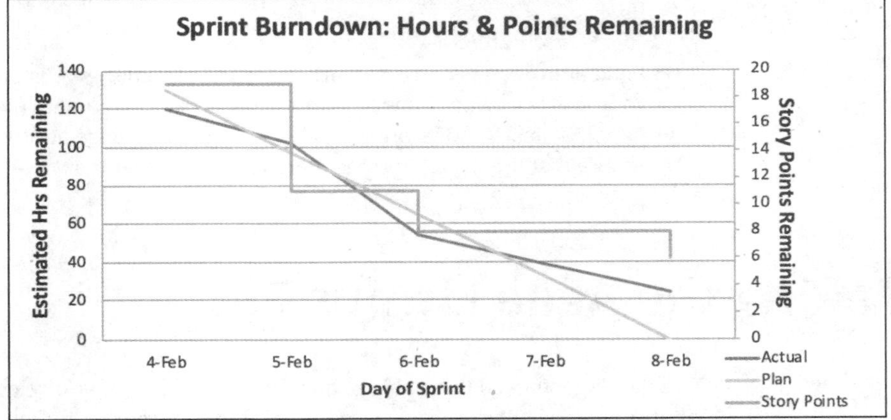

FIGURE 1-2: Charts and graphs for providing transparency.

© John Wiley & Sons, Inc.

Seeing Changes as a Result of Agile Values

The publication of the Agile Manifesto and the 12 Agile Principles legitimized and focused the agile movement in the following ways:

- **Agile approaches changed attitudes toward product management processes.** In trying to improve processes, methodologists in the past worked to develop a universal process that could be used under all conditions, assuming that more process and greater formality would yield improved results. This approach, however, required more time, overhead, and cost and often diminished quality. The manifesto and the 12 principles acknowledged that too much process is a problem, not a solution, and that the right process in the right amount differs in each situation.

- **Agile approaches changed attitudes toward knowledge workers.** IT groups began to remember that development team members aren't disposable resources but individuals whose skills, talents, and innovation make a difference to every product. The same product created by different team members will be a different product.
- **Agile approaches changed the relationship between business and IT groups.** Agile product development addressed the problems associated with the historical separation between business and IT by bringing these contributors together on the same team, at equal levels of involvement and with shared goals.
- **Agile approaches corrected attitudes toward change.** Historical approaches viewed change as a problem to be avoided or minimized. The Agile Manifesto and its principles helped identify change as an opportunity to ensure that the most informed ideas were implemented.

Taking the Agile Litmus Test

To be agile, you need to be able to ask, "Is this agile?" If you're ever in doubt about whether a particular process, practice, tool, or approach adheres to the Agile Manifesto or the 12 principles, refer to the following list of questions:

1. Does what we're doing at this moment support the early and continuous delivery of valuable software?
2. Does our process welcome change and take advantage of change?
3. Does our process lead to and support the delivery of working functionality?
4. Are the developers and the product owner working together daily? Are customers and business stakeholders working closely with the team?
5. Does our environment give the team the support it needs to get the job done?
6. Are we communicating in person face-to-face rather than over the phone or through email?
7. Are we measuring progress by the amount of working functionality produced?

8. Can we maintain our current pace of development indefinitely?
9. Do we support technical excellence and good design that allows for future changes?
10. Are we maximizing the amount of work not done — namely, doing as little as necessary to fulfill the product goal for our customer?
11. Is this development team self-organizing and self-managing? Does it have the freedom to succeed?
12. Are we reflecting at regular intervals and adjusting our behavior accordingly?

TIP

If you answered "yes" to all these questions, congratulations; you're likely becoming more agile. If you answered "no" to any of these questions, what can you do to change that answer to "yes"? You can come back to this exercise at any time and use the agile litmus test for yourself, as well as with your team and the wider organization.

» Establishing the product vision

» Creating features and a product roadmap

Chapter 2

Defining the Product Vision and Product Roadmap

It's time to dispel a common myth. If you've heard that agile product development doesn't include planning, dismiss that thought right now. You will plan not only the overall product but also every release, every sprint, and every day. Planning is fundamental to agile product development success.

If you're a project manager, you probably do the bulk of your planning at the beginning of a project. You may have heard the phrase "Plan the work, then work the plan," which sums up non-agile project management approaches.

Agile product development, in contrast, involves planning up front and throughout the entire product lifecycle. By planning at the last responsible moment, right before an activity starts, you know the most about that activity. This type of planning, called *just-in-time planning* or a *situationally informed strategy,* is a key to success. Agile teams plan as much as, if not more than, traditional project teams. However, agile planning is more evenly distributed throughout the product's life, as you can see in Figure 2-1, and is done by the entire team that will be working on the product.

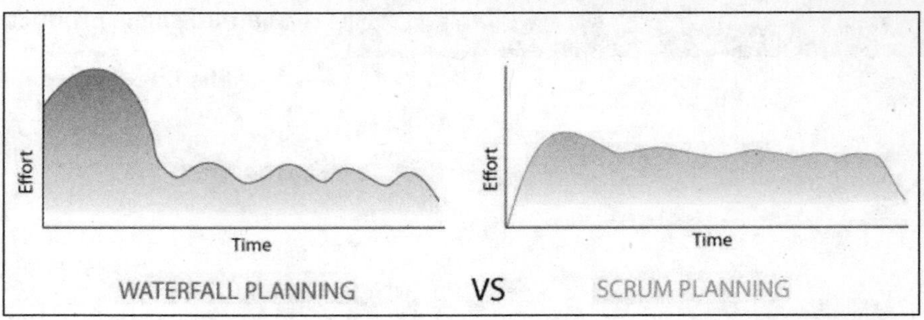

FIGURE 2-1: Traditional planning versus agile planning.

© John Wiley & Sons, Inc.

TECHNICAL STUFF

Helmuth von Moltke, a nineteenth-century German field marshal and military strategist, once said, "No plan survives contact with the enemy." That is, in the heat of a battle — much like in the thick of developing a product feature — plans always change. Just-in-time planning allows you to accommodate real-world changes non-disruptively and to be well-informed as you plan specific tasks.

This chapter describes how just-in-time planning works with agile product development. You also go through the first two steps of planning: creating the product vision and the product roadmap.

Agile Planning

Planning happens at a number of points. A great way to look at planning activities is with the Roadmap to Value. Figure 2-2 shows the roadmap as a whole.

REMEMBER

The Roadmap to Value has seven stages:

- In stage 1, the product owner identifies the *product vision.* The product vision is your product's destination or end goal. The product vision includes the outer boundary of what your product will be, how the product is different than the competition, how the product will support your company or organization's strategy, who will use the product, and why people will use the product. The product vision should be revisisted at least once a year.
- In stage 2, the product owner creates a *product roadmap.* The product roadmap is a high-level view of the product requirements, with a general time frame for when you will develop those requirements. It also gives context to the vision by showing the tangible features that will be produced during development. Identifying product requirements and then prioritizing and roughly estimating the effort for those requirements allow you to establish requirement themes and identify requirement gaps. The product owner, with support from the development team, should revise the product roadmap at least biannually.

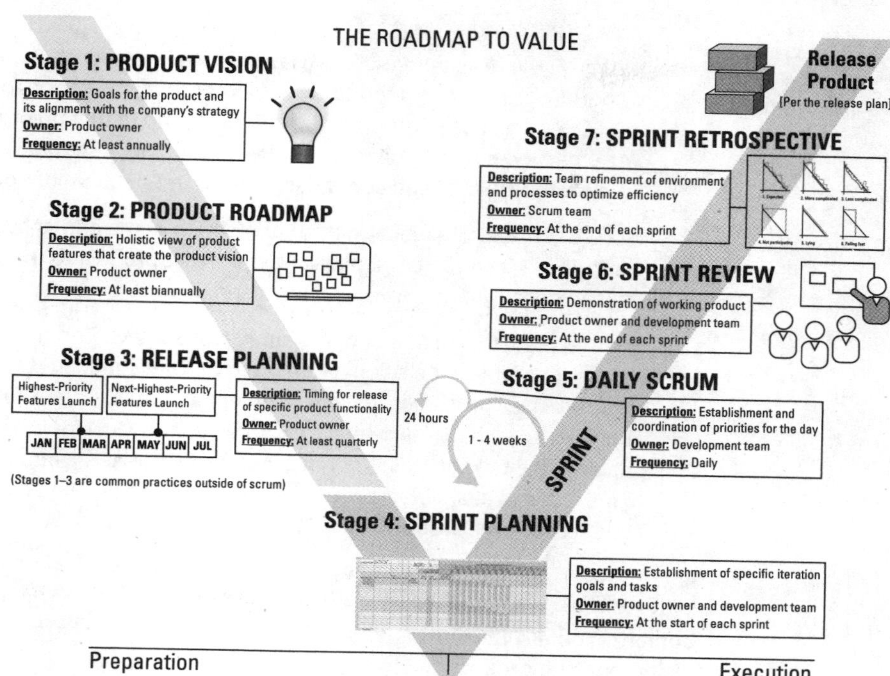

© John Wiley & Sons, Inc.

FIGURE 2-2: Stages of agile planning and execution with the Roadmap to Value.

- In stage 3, the product owner creates a release plan. The *release plan* identifies a high-level timetable for the release of working functionality to the customer. The release serves as a mid-term boundary against which the scrum team can mobilize. Many releases may be required to accomplish the product vision and the highest-priority features should appear first. You create a release plan at the beginning of each release, which according to Principle 3 should be "frequently, from a couple of weeks to a couple of months, with a preference to the shorter timescale." Read more about release planning in Chapter 3 of Book 4.
- In stage 4, the product owner, the development team, and the scrum master will plan iterations, also called sprints, and start creating the product functionality in those sprints. *Sprint planning* sessions take place at the start of each sprint. During sprint planning, the scrum team determines a sprint goal, which establishes the immediate boundary of work that the team forecasts to accomplish during the sprint, with requirements that support the goal and can be completed in the sprint. The scrum team also outlines how to complete those requirements. Read more about sprint planning in Chapter 3 of Book 4.

- In stage 5, the development team has *daily scrum* meetings during each sprint to coordinate the day's priorities for accomplishing the sprint goal. In the daily scrum meeting, based on what was completed up to that point, you coordinate what you will work on today and any roadblocks, so that you can address issues immediately. Read about daily scrums in Chapter 4 of Book 4.
- In stage 6, the scrum team holds a *sprint review* at the end of every sprint. In the sprint review, you demonstrate the working product to the product stakeholders. Find out how to conduct sprint reviews in Chapter 5 of Book 4.
- In stage 7, the scrum team holds a *sprint retrospective.* The sprint retrospective is a meeting where the scrum team discusses the completed sprint with regard to their processes and environment and makes plans for process improvements in the next sprint. Like the sprint review for inspecting and adapting the product, a sprint retrospective is held at the end of every sprint to inspect and adapt your processes and environment. Find out how to conduct sprint retrospectives in Chapter 5 of Book 4.

Each stage of the Roadmap to Value is repeatable and contains planning activities. Agile planning, like agile development, is iterative and barely sufficient.

Progressive elaboration

During each stage of product development, you plan only as much as you need to plan. In the early stages of your work, you plan widely and holistically to create a broad outline of how the product will shape up over time. In later stages, you narrow your planning and add more details to ensure success in the immediate development effort. This process is called a *progressive elaboration of requirements.*

Planning broadly at first and in detail later, when necessary, prevents you from wasting time on planning lower-priority product requirements that may never be implemented. This model also lets you add high-value requirements during product development without disrupting the flow.

The more just-in-time your detailed planning is, the more effective your planning becomes.

Standish Group studies show that customers rarely or never use as much as 80 percent of the features in an application. In the first few development cycles of an agile product development effort, you complete features that have the highest priority and that people will use. Typically, you release those groups of features as early as possible to gain market share through first-mover advantage; receive customer feedback for viability; monetize functionality early to optimize return on investment (ROI); and avoid internal and external obsolescence.

Inspect and adapt

Just-in-time planning brings into play two fundamental tenets of agile techniques: Inspect and adapt. At each stage of development, you need to look at the product and the process (inspect) and make changes as necessary (adapt).

Agile planning is a rhythmic cycle of inspecting and adapting. Consider the following:

- Each day during the sprint, the product owner provides feedback to help improve the product as the development team creates the product.
- At the end of each sprint, in the sprint review, stakeholders provide feedback to further improve the product.
- At the end of each sprint in the sprint retrospective, the scrum team discusses the lessons they learned during the past sprint to improve the development process.
- After a release, the customers can provide feedback for improvement. Feedback might be direct, when a customer contacts the company about the product, or indirect, when potential customers either do or don't purchase the product.

Together, inspect and adapt are fantastic tools for delivering the right product in the most efficient manner.

REMEMBER

At the beginning of development, you know the least about the product you're creating, so trying to plan fine details at that time just doesn't work. Being agile means you do the detailed planning when you need it, and immediately develop the specific requirements you defined with that planning. Remember the Agile Manifesto value: "Responding to change over following a plan." (See Chapter 1 in Book 4 for more about the manifesto.)

After you know a little more about how agile planning works, it's time to complete the first step: defining the product vision. Find out more in the next section.

Defining the Product Vision

The first stage in the Roadmap to Value is defining your product vision. The *product vision statement* is an elevator pitch, or a quick summary, to communicate how your product supports the company's or organization's strategies. The vision statement must articulate the end state for the product.

The product might be a commercial product for release to the marketplace or an internal solution that will support your organization's day-to-day functions. For example, say your company is XYZ Bank and your product is a mobile banking application. What company strategies does a mobile banking application support? How does the application support the company's strategies? Your vision statement clearly and concisely links the product to your business strategy.

Figure 2-3 shows how the vision statement — stage 1 of the Roadmap to Value — fits with the rest of the stages and activities in product development.

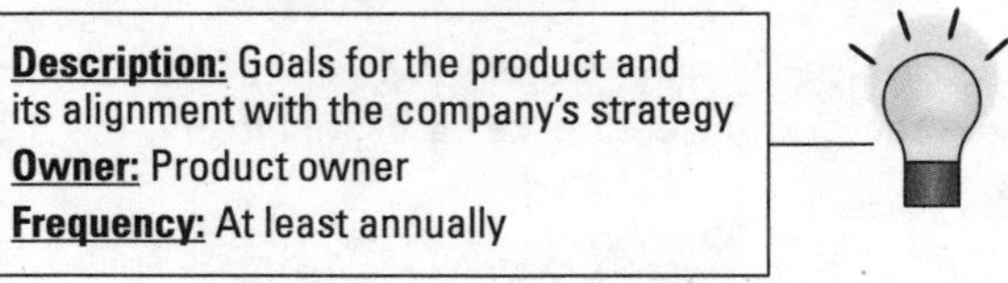

A common agile practice
Stage 1: PRODUCT VISION
Description: Goals for the product and its alignment with the company's strategy
Owner: Product owner
Frequency: At least annually

FIGURE 2-3: The product vision statement as part of the Roadmap to Value.

© John Wiley & Sons, Inc.

The product owner is responsible for knowing about the product, its goals, and its requirements throughout development. For those reasons, the product owner creates the vision statement, although other people may have input. After the vision statement is complete, it becomes a guiding light, the "what we are trying to achieve" statement that the product owner, development team, scrum master, and stakeholders refer to throughout their work.

REMEMBER

When creating a product vision statement, follow these four steps:

1. **Develop the product objective.**
2. **Create a draft vision statement.**
3. **Validate the vision statement with product stakeholders and revise it based on feedback.**
4. **Finalize the product vision statement.**

The look of a vision statement follows no hard-and-fast rules. However, anyone involved, from the development team to the CEO, should be able to understand the statement. The vision statement should be internally focused, clear, nontechnical, emotionally connecting, and as brief as possible. The vision statement should also be explicit and avoid marketing jargon.

Step 1: Developing the product objective

To write your vision statement, you must understand and be able to communicate the product's objective. You need to identify the following:

- **Key product goals:** How will the product benefit provide value to the company that is creating it? The goals may include benefits for a specific department in your company, such as customer service or the marketing department, as well as the company as a whole. What specific company strategies does the product support?
- **Customer:** Who will use the product? This question might have more than one answer.
- **Need:** Why does the customer need the product? What features are critical to the customer? What problem will the product solve?
- **Competition:** How does the product compare with similar products?
- **Primary differentiation:** What makes this product different from the status quo or the competition or both?

Step 2: Creating a draft vision statement

After you have a good grasp of the product's objective, create a first draft of your vision statement.

TIP

You can find many templates for a product vision statement. For an excellent guide to defining the overall product vision, see *Crossing the Chasm* by Geoffrey Moore (published by HarperCollins), which focuses on how to bridge the gap (chasm) between early adopters of new technologies and the majority who follow.

The adoption of any new product is a gamble. Will users like the product? Will the market take to the product? Will there be an adequate return on investment for developing the product? An effectively written product vision statement can start you on the path to quickly learning the answers to these questions.

TECHNICAL STUFF

Return on investment, or *ROI*, is the benefit or value a company gets from paying for something. ROI can be quantitative, such as the additional money ABC Products makes from selling widgets online after investing in a new website. ROI can also be something intangible, such as better customer satisfaction for XYZ Bank customers who use the bank's new mobile banking application.

By creating your vision statement, you help convey your product's quality, maintenance needs, and longevity.

Moore's product vision approach is pragmatic. Figure 2-4 shows a template based on Moore's approach to more explicitly connect the product to the company's strategies. If you use this template for your product vision statement, it will stand the test of time as your product goes from early adoption to mainstream usage.

Vision Statement for Product

For ______ (target customer) ______
who ______ (needs) ______
the ______ (product name) ______
is a ______ (product category) ______
that ______ (product benefit, reason to buy) ______
Unlike ______ (competitors) ______
our product ______ (differentiation/value proposition) ______

© John Wiley & Sons, Inc.

FIGURE 2-4: Expansion of Moore's template for a vision statement.

TIP

One way to make your product vision statement more compelling is to write it in the present tense, as if the product already exists. Using present tense helps readers imagine the product in use.

Using the expansion of Moore's template, a vision statement for a mobile banking application might look like the following:

> **For** XYZ Bank customers
>
> **who** want access to banking capability while on the go,
>
> **the** MyXYZ
>
> **is a** mobile application
>
> **that** allows secure, on-demand banking, 24 hours a day.
>
> **Unlike** online banking from your home or office computer,
>
> **our product** allows users immediate access,
>
> **which supports our strategy to** provide quick, convenient banking services, anytime, anywhere. (Platinum Edge addition)

As you can see, a vision statement identifies a future state for the product when the product reaches completion. The vision focuses on the conditions that should exist when the product is complete.

WARNING

Avoid generalizations in your vision statement such as "make customers happy" or "sell more products." You want the vision statement to help you make scope decisions throughout product development. Also watch out for too much technological specificity, such as "using release 9.x of Java, create a program with four modules that . . ." At this early stage, defining specific technologies might limit you later.

Here are a few extracts from vision statements that should ring warning bells:

- Secure additional customers for the MyXYZ application.
- Satisfy our customers by December.
- Eliminate all defects and improve quality.
- Create a new application in Java.
- Beat the Widget Company to market by six months.

Step 3: Validating and revising the vision statement

REMEMBER

After you draft your vision statement, review it against the following quality checklist:

- Is this vision statement clear, focused, and written for an internal audience?
- Does the statement provide a compelling description of how the product meets customer needs?
- Does the vision describe the best possible outcome?
- Is the business objective specific enough that the goal is achievable?
- Does the statement deliver value that is consistent with corporate strategies and goals?
- Is the vision statement compelling?
- Is the vision concise?

These yes-or-no questions will help you determine whether your vision statement is thorough. If any answers are no, revise the vision statement.

When all answers are yes, move on to reviewing the statement with others, including the following:

- **Product stakeholders:** The stakeholders will be able to identify that the vision statement includes everything the product should accomplish.
- **Your development team:** The people who will be creating the product must also understand and have ownership of what the product needs to accomplish. Many product owners create the product vision with the development team, aligning purpose and motivation (Principle 5).
- **Scrum master:** A strong understanding of the product will help the scrum master proactively remove roadblocks, enabling the team to accomplish the product vision.
- **Agile mentor:** Share the vision statement with your agile mentor, if you have one. The agile mentor is independent of the organization and can provide an external perspective, qualities that can make for a great objective voice.

See whether others think the vision statement is clear and delivers the message you want to convey. Review and revise the vision statement until the stakeholders, development team, and scrum master fully understand the statement.

Step 4: Finalizing the vision statement

TIP

After you finish revising the vision statement, make sure the development team, scrum master, and stakeholders have the final copy. You might even put a copy on the wall in the scrum team's work area, where you can see it every day. You will refer to the vision statement throughout the life of the product.

If your product development will be more than a year long, you may want to revisit the vision statement. Review the product vision statement at least once a year to make sure the product reflects the marketplace and supports any changes in the company's needs. Because the vision statement is the long-term boundary of the product, product development investment should end when the vision is achieved and expansion of the vision is no longer viable.

REMEMBER

The product owner owns the product vision statement and is responsible for its preparation and communication across and outside the organization. The product vision sets expectations for stakeholders and helps the development team stay focused on the goal.

Congratulations. You've just completed the initial definition of strategy and desired value outcome in your agile product development. Now it's time to create a product roadmap.

Creating a Product Roadmap

The product roadmap, stage 2 in the Roadmap to Value (see Figure 2-5), is an overall view of the product's requirements and a valuable tool for planning and organizing the journey of product development. Use the product roadmap to categorize requirements, prioritize them, identify gaps and dependencies, and determine a sequence for releasing to the customer.

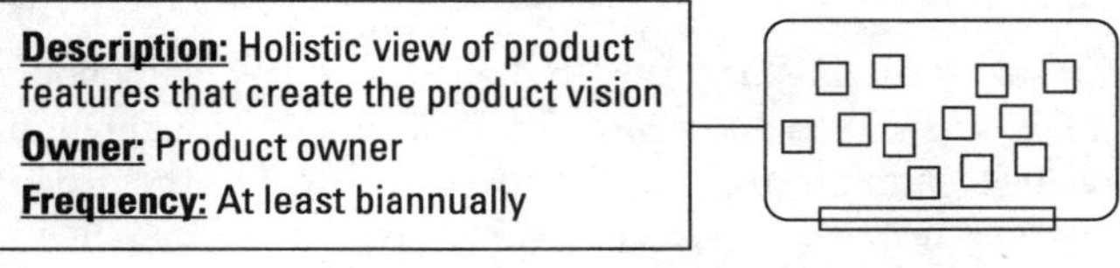

A common agile practice
Stage 2: PRODUCT ROADMAP
Description: Holistic view of product features that create the product vision
Owner: Product owner
Frequency: At least biannually
© John Wiley & Sons, Inc.

FIGURE 2-5: The product roadmap as part of the Roadmap to Value.

As with the product vision statement, the product owner creates the product roadmap with help from the development team and stakeholders. The development team often participates to a greater degree than it did during the creation of the vision statement.

Keep in mind that you will refine requirements and effort estimates throughout development. In the product roadmap phase, it's okay for your requirements detail, estimates, and timeframes to be at a very high level.

REMEMBER

To create your product roadmap, you do the following:

1. **Identify stakeholders.**
2. **List product requirements and visualize them.**
3. **Arrange the product requirements based on value, risk, and dependencies.**
4. **Estimate the development effort at a high level and prioritize the product's requirements.**
5. **Determine high-level time frames for releasing groups of functionality to the customer.**

Because priorities can change, plan to update your product roadmap at least twice a year.

TIP

Your product roadmap can be as simple as sticky notes arranged on a whiteboard, which makes updates as easy as moving a sticky note from one section of the whiteboard to another.

You use the product roadmap to plan releases — stage 3 in the Roadmap to Value. *Releases* are groups of usable product functionality that you release to customers to gather real-world feedback and to generate return on investment.

The following sections detail the steps to create a product roadmap.

Step 1: Identifying product stakeholders

When initially establishing the product vision, it's likely you will have identified only a few key stakeholders who are available to provide high-level feedback. At the product roadmap stage, you put more context to the product vision and identify how you achieve the vision, which gives more insight into who will have a stake in your product.

This is the time to engage with existing and newly identified stakeholders to gather feedback on the functionality you want to implement to achieve the vision. The product roadmap is your first cut at a high-level product backlog, discussed later in this chapter. With this first round of detail identified, you'll want to engage more than just the scrum team, the product sponsor, and obvious users. Consider including the following people:

- **Marketing department:** Your customers need to know about your product, and that's what the marketing department provides. They need to understand your plans and may have input into the order in which you release functionality to the market, based on their experience and research.
- **Customer service department:** Once your product is in the market, how will it be supported? Specific roadmap items might identify the person you'll need to prepare for support. For instance, a product owner may not see much value in plugging in a live online chat feature, but a customer service manager may see it differently because his or her representatives can handle simultaneously only one phone call but as many as six chat sessions. Plus, your customer service representatives actually talk to your end users on a daily basis and probably have many insights you should consider.
- **Sales department:** Make sure that the sales team sees the product so that they start selling the same thing you're building. Like the marketing department; the sales department will have first-hand knowledge about what your customers are looking for.

- **Legal department:** Especially if you're in a highly regulated industry, review your roadmap with legal counsel as early as possible to make sure you haven't missed anything that could put your product at risk if discovered later.
- **Additional customers:** While identifying features on your roadmap, you may discover additional people who will find value in what you will create. Give them a chance to review your roadmap to validate your assumptions.

Step 2: Establishing product requirements

The second step in creating a product roadmap is to identify, or define, the different requirements for your product.

When you first create your product roadmap, you typically start with large, high-level requirements. The requirements on your product roadmap will most likely be at two different levels: themes and features.

- *Themes* are logical groups of features and requirements at their highest levels.
- *Features* are parts of the product at a very high level and describe a new capability the customer will have once the feature is complete.

TIP

When you start creating requirements at the theme and feature level, it can help to write those requirements on index cards or big sticky notes. Using a physical card that you can move from one category to another and back again can make organizing and prioritizing those requirements very easy.

While you create the product roadmap, the features you identify start to make up your *product backlog* — the full list of what is in scope for a product, regardless of level of detail. Once you have identified your first product features, you have your product backlog started.

Step 3: Arranging product features

After you identify your product features, you work with the stakeholders to group them into *themes* — common, logical groups of features. A stakeholder meeting works well for grouping features, just like it works for creating requirements. You can group features by usage flow, technical similarity, or business need.

Visualizing themes and features on your roadmap allow you to assign business value and risks associated with each feature relative to others. The product owner, along with the development team and stakeholders, can also identify dependencies between features, locate any gaps, and prioritize the order in which each feature should be developed based on each of these factors.

Here are questions to consider when grouping and ordering your requirements:

- How would customers use our product?
- If we offered this requirement, what else would customers need to do? What else might they want to do?
- Can the development team identify technical affinities or dependencies?

Use the answers to these questions to identify your themes. Then group the features by these themes. For example, in the mobile banking application, the themes might be

- Account information
- Transactions
- Customer service functions
- Integration with other accounts

Figure 2-6 shows features grouped by themes.

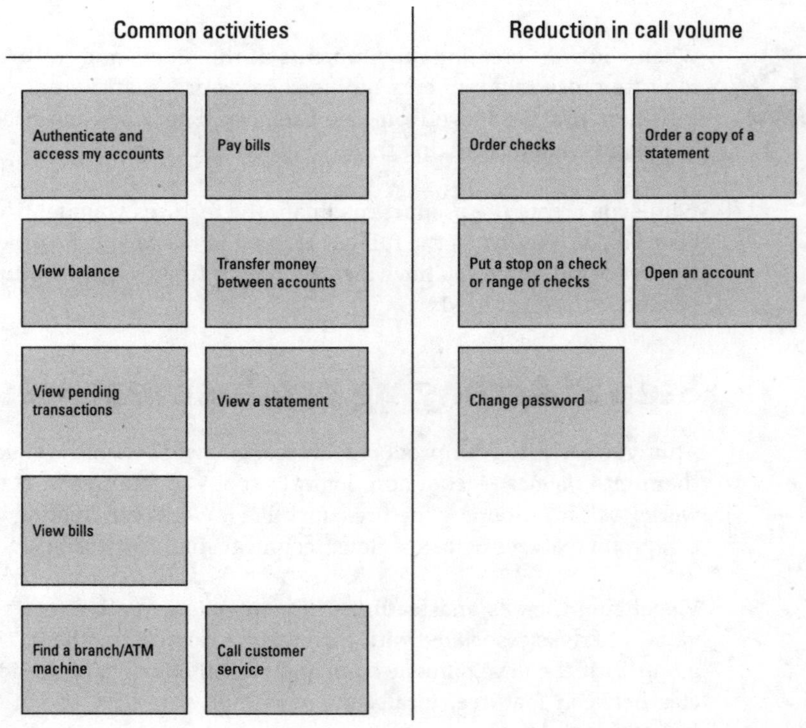

FIGURE 2-6: Features grouped by themes.

© John Wiley & Sons, Inc.

Step 4: Estimating efforts and ordering requirements

REMEMBER

You've identified your product requirements and arranged those requirements into logical groups. Next, you estimate and prioritize the requirements. Here are a few terms you need to be familiar with:

- *Effort* is the ease or difficulty of creating functionality from a particular requirement.
- An *estimate,* as a noun, can be the number or description you use to express the estimated effort of a requirement.
- *Estimating* a requirement, as a verb, means to come up with an approximate idea of how easy or hard (how much effort) that requirement will be to create.
- *Ordering,* or *prioritizing,* a requirement means to determine that requirement's value and risk in relation to other requirements, and in what order you will implement them.
- *Value* means how beneficial a product requirement might be to the customer and therefore the organization creating that product.
- *Risk* refers to the negative effect a requirement can have due to customer uncertainty or on product development.

TIP

You can estimate and prioritize requirements of any estimate size at any level, from themes and features down to single user stories.

Prioritizing requirements is really about ordering them. You can find various methods — many of them complicated — for determining the priority of product backlog items. You can keep things simple by creating an ordered to-do list of product backlog items based on business value, risk, and effort, listed in the order in which you will implement them. Forcing an order requires making a priority decision for every requirement relative to every other requirement. A scrum team works on one thing at a time, so it's important to format your product roadmap accordingly.

To estimate and assign effort values to your requirements, you work with two different groups of people:

- The development team determines the effort to implement the functionality for each requirement. Only the people who will do the work should provide effort estimates. The development team also provides critical feedback to the product owner for understanding how technical risks effect the ordering of the product backlog.
- The product owner, with support from the stakeholders, determines the value and risk of the requirement to the customer and the business.

Estimating effort

To order requirements, the development team must first estimate the effort for each requirement relative to all other requirements.

Chapter 3 of Book 4 shows you relative estimation techniques that agile teams use to accurately estimate effort. Traditional estimation methods aim for precision by using absolute time estimates at every level of the project schedule, whether the team is working on the work items today or two years from now. This practice gives traditional teams a false sense of precision and isn't accurate in reality (as thousands of failed projects prove). How could you possibly know what each team member will be working on six months from now, and how long it will take to do that work, when you are just starting to learn about the product at the beginning?

Relative estimating is a self-correcting mechanism that allows agile teams to be more accurate because it's much easier to be right when comparing one requirement against another and determining whether one is bigger than another, and by roughly how much. Agile teams value accuracy over precision.

To order your requirements, you also want to know any dependencies. *Dependencies* mean that one requirement is a predecessor for another requirement. For example, if you have an application that requires users to set up a user profile, they'll need to be authenticated by a username and password. The requirement for creating the username and password would be dependent upon setting up a profile because you generally need a username and password to establish a user profile.

Assessing business value and risk

Together with stakeholders, the product owner identifies the highest business value items (either high potential ROI or other perceived value to the end customer), as well as those items with high negative effect if unresolved.

Similar to effort estimates, values or risks can be assigned to each product roadmap item. For example, you might assign value using monetary ROI amounts or, for an internally used product, assign value or risk by using high, medium, or low.

REMEMBER

Effort, business value, and risk estimates inform the product owner's prioritization decisions for each requirement. The highest value and risk items should be at the top of the product roadmap. High-risk items should be explored and implemented first to avoid rear-loading the risk. If a high-risk item will cause the product or its development to fail (an issue that cannot be resolved), agile teams learn about it early. If something is going to fail, you want to fail early, fail cheap, and move on to a new opportunity that has value. In that sense, failure is a form of success for an agile team.

After you have your value, risk, and effort estimates, you can determine the relative priority, or order, of each requirement.

- A requirement with high value or high risk (or both) and low effort will have a high relative priority. The product owner might order this item at the top of the roadmap.
- A requirement with low value or low risk (or both) and high effort will have a lower relative priority. This item will likely end up toward the bottom of the roadmap or, better yet, be removed. If anything on your roadmap does not support the fulfillment of your product vision, you may want to ask whether it is truly needed. Remember Principle 10 from Chapter 1 of Book 4: "Simplicity — the art of maximizing the amount of work not done — is essential."

WARNING

Relative priority is only a tool to help the product owner make decisions and prioritize requirements. It isn't a mathematical universal that you must follow. Make sure your tools help rather than hinder.

Prioritizing requirements

To determine the overall priority for your requirements, answer the following questions:

- What is the relative priority of the requirement?
- What are the prerequisites for any requirement?
- What set of requirements belong together and will constitute a solid set of functionalities you can release to the customer?

Using the answers to these questions, you can place the highest-priority requirements first in the product roadmap. When you've finished prioritizing your requirements, you'll have something that looks like Figure 2-7.

Your prioritized list of requirements is called a *product backlog*. Your product backlog is an important agile document, or *artifact*. You use this backlog throughout your entire product development.

With a product backlog in hand, you can start adding target releases to your product roadmap.

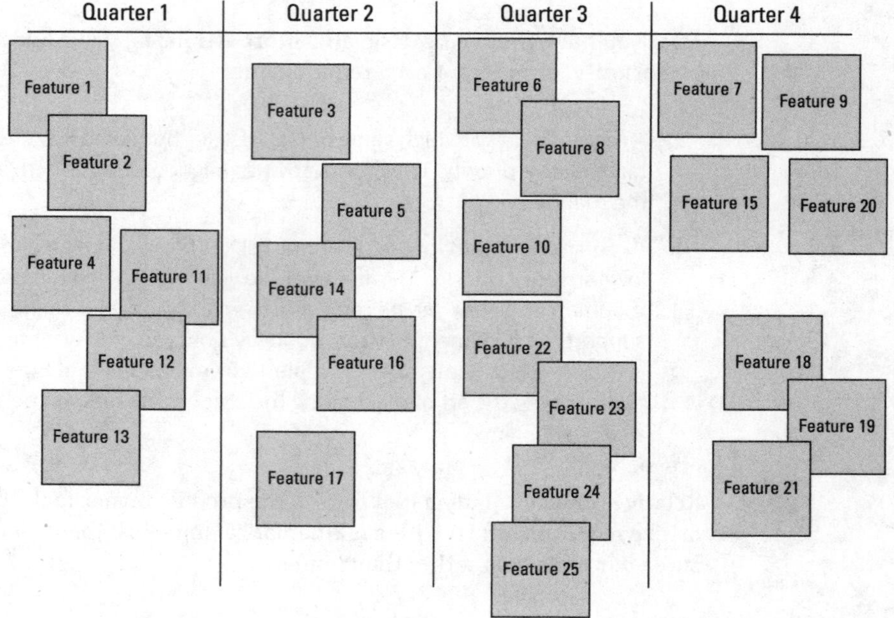

FIGURE 2-7: Product roadmap with ordered requirements.

© John Wiley & Sons, Inc.

Step 5: Determining high-level time frames

When you create your product roadmap, your time frames for releasing product requirements are at a very high level. For the initial roadmap, choose a logical time increment for your product development, such as a certain number of days, weeks, months, quarters (three-month periods), or even larger increments. Using both the requirement and the priority, you can add requirements to each increment of time.

REMEMBER

Creating a product roadmap might seem like a lot of work, but you can have a product vision, product roadmap, and release plan for your first release, and be ready to start your sprint, in as little as two to three days! To begin developing the product, you need only enough requirements for your first sprint. Having bought yourself some time, you can determine the rest as the team learns more from reality through progressive elaboration.

Saving your work

TIP

Up until now, you could do all your roadmap planning with whiteboards and sticky notes. After your first full draft is complete, however, save the product roadmap, especially if you need to share the roadmap with remote stakeholders or development team members. You could take a photo of your sticky notes and whiteboard, or you could type the information into a document and save it electronically.

Whatever format you choose, ensure that the roadmap can be easily changed and transparently accessed.

You update the product roadmap throughout development, as priorities change. For now, the contents of the first release should be clear — and that's all you need to worry about to start executing and delivering value.

Completing the Product Backlog

The product roadmap contains high-level features and some tentative release timelines. The requirements on your product roadmap are the first version of your *product backlog.*

The product backlog is the list of all requirements associated with the product. The product owner is responsible for creating and maintaining the product backlog by updating (adding, changing, removing) and prioritizing requirements. The scrum team uses the prioritized product backlog throughout development to plan its work each release and each sprint.

Figure 2-8 shows a sample product backlog. At a minimum, when creating your product backlog, be sure to do the following:

- Include a description of your requirement.
- Order the requirements based on priority.
- Add the effort estimate.

PRODUCT BACKLOG

Order	ID	Item	Type	Status	Estimate
1	121	As an Administrator, I want to link accounts to profiles, so that customers can access new accounts.	Requirement	Not Started	5
2	113	Update requirements traceability matrix.	Overhead	Not Started	2
3	403	Test automation training for Michael.	Improvement	Not Started	3
4	97	Refactor Login Class.	Maintenance	Not Started	8
5	68	As a Site Visitor, I want to find locations, so that I can use bank services.	Requirement	Not Started	8

© John Wiley & Sons, Inc.

FIGURE 2-8: Product backlog items sample.

You can also include the type of backlog item as well as the status. Teams will work mainly on developing features as described in the words of the user (user stories). But there may be a need for other types of product backlog items, such as overhead items (things the team determines are needed but don't contribute to the functionality), maintenance items (design improvements that need to be done to the product or system but don't directly increase value to the customer), or improvement items (action items for process improvements identified in the sprint retrospective). You can see examples of each of these in Figure 2-8. The product owner prioritizes all product backlog items through the lens of the customer and stakeholders.

REMEMBER

Chapter 1 of Book 4 explains how documents for agile product development should be barely sufficient, with only information that is absolutely necessary to create the product. If you keep your product backlog format simple and barely sufficient, you'll save time updating it throughout product development.

The scrum team refers to the product backlog as the main source for requirements. If a requirement exists, it's in the product backlog.

The user stories in your product backlog will change throughout development in several ways. For example, as the team completes user stories, you mark those stories as complete in the backlog. You also record any new user stories. Some user stories will be updated with new or clarified information, broken down into smaller user stories, or refined in other ways. Additionally, you update the priority and effort scores of existing user stories as needed.

The total number of story points in the product backlog — all user story points added together — is your current *product backlog estimate.* This estimate changes daily as user stories are completed and new user stories are added.

REMEMBER

Keep your product backlog up to date so that you always have accurate cost and schedule estimates. A current product backlog also gives you the flexibility to prioritize newly identified product requirements — a key agile benefit — against existing features.

After you have a product backlog, you can begin planning releases and sprints, which are described in Chapter 3 of Book 4.

» **Creating a product backlog, release plan, and sprint backlog**

» **Getting the product ready to ship and preparing the rest of the organization for the release**

» **Understanding spring backlogs and planning meetings**

Chapter 3

Planning Releases and Sprints

After you create a product roadmap for your product (see Chapter 2 in Book 4), it's time to start elaborating on your product details. In this chapter, you discover how to break down your requirements to a more granular level, refine your product backlog, create a release plan, and build a sprint backlog for execution. This chapter also discusses how to prepare the rest of the organization for the release, including operational support and ensuring that the marketplace will be ready for your release.

First, you see how to break down the larger requirements from your product roadmap into smaller, more manageable requirements called *user stories.*

Refining Requirements and Estimates

You start agile development with very large requirements. As the work progresses and you get closer to developing those requirements, you will break them down into smaller parts — small enough to begin developing. See Chapter 2 in Book 4 for more about this process, which is known as *decomposition.*

One clear, effective pattern for defining product requirements is the user story. In this section, you find out how to create a user story, prioritize user stories, and estimate user story effort.

What is a user story?

The *user story* is a simple description of a product value requirement in terms of what that requirement must accomplish for whom. It's called a *story* because the simplest way people tell stories is by talking to each other. User stories are most effective when they're told by speaking to each other face to face. The written pattern described in this section can be used to help with that conversation.

Traditional software requirements usually read something like this: "The system shall [insert technical description]." This requirement addresses only the technical nature of what will be done; the overall business objective is unclear. Because the development team has the context to engage more deeply through the user story pattern, their work becomes more personal and real. They come to know the value of each requirement to the user (or the customer or the business) and deliver what the customer wants faster and with higher quality.

REMEMBER

Your user story will have, at a minimum, the following parts:

Title (recognizable name for the user story)

As a (type of user)

I want to (take this action)

so that (I get this benefit)

The user story tells the "who," "what," and "why" for the desired functionality. The user story should also be supported by a list of validation steps *(acceptance criteria)* to take so you can confirm whether the working requirement for the user story is correct. Acceptance criteria follows this pattern:

When I (take this action), (this happens)

User stories may also include the following:

- **A user story ID:** A unique identifying number to differentiate this user story from other user stories in the product backlog tracking system.

- **The user story value and effort estimate:** *Value* is how beneficial a user story might be to the organization creating that product. *Effort* is the ease or difficulty in creating that user story. You find out how to score a user story's business value, risk, and effort in Chapter 2 of Book 4.
- **The name of the person who thought of the user story:** Anyone can create a user story.

TIP

Although agile product development approaches encourage low-tech tools, the scrum team should also find out what works best for themselves in each situation. A lot of electronic user story tools are available, some of which are free. Some are simple and are only for user stories. Others are complex and will integrate with other product documents. We love the simplicity of index cards, but use what works best for your scrum team and your product.

Figure 3-1 shows a typical user story card, front and back. The front has the main description of the user story. The back shows how you will confirm that the requirement works correctly, after the development team has created the functionality.

Title Transfer money between accounts

As Carol,

I want to transfer funds between accounts

so that each account has the correct amount of funds

Value | Jennifer Author | Estimate

When I do this:	This happens:
When I view my account balances,	I see an option to transfer funds.
When I select the transfer option,	I choose between which accounts I want to transfer funds.
When I select the "transfer from" option,	I see a list of my available accounts and balances.
When I select the "transfer to" option,	I see a list of my available accounts and balances.

© John Wiley & Sons, Inc.

FIGURE 3-1: Card-based user story example.

TIP

The three Cs formula for user story creation — card, conversation, and confirmation — illustrates how the user story pattern enables agile teams to create customer value. By limiting user stories to fit on a 3x5 index *card*, you encourage a *conversation* for achieving a shared understanding of the job to be done for the customer (rather than excessive documentation that implies nothing is left to discuss). If the conversation is supported by the answers to the quiz upfront (acceptance criteria that is a *confirmation* that the actions the user will take meet the intended needs), you're probably on the right track.

The product owner gathers the user stories and manages them (that is, determines the priority and initiates the decomposition discussions). It is not the sole responsibility of the product owner to write user stories. The development team and other stakeholders are also involved in creating and decomposing user stories to ensure clarity and shared understanding across the scrum team.

TIP

Note that user stories aren't the only way to describe product requirements. You could simply make a list of requirements without any given structure. However, because user stories include a lot of useful information in a simple, compact format, they're very effective in conveying exactly what a requirement needs to do for the customer.

The big benefit of the user story pattern is realized when the development team starts to create and test requirements. The development team members know exactly for whom they are creating the requirement, what the requirement should do, and how to double-check that the requirement satisfies its intention. Using the user's voice is something everyone can understand and relate to — not so much with technical jargon.

Note: This book includes user stories as examples of requirements for software product development. Keep in mind that anything described that you can do with user stories, you can do also with more generically expressed requirements and other product types.

Steps to create a user story

When creating a user story, follow these steps:

1. **Identify the stakeholders.**
2. **Identify who will use the product.**
3. **Working with the stakeholders, write down, in a user story format, what the product will need to do.**

Find out how to follow these three steps in the following sections.

REMEMBER

Being agile and adaptive requires iterating. Don't spend a ton of time trying to identify every single requirement your product might have. You can always add items to your product backlog later. The best changes often come at the end, when you know the most about the product and the end-customers.

Identifying product stakeholders

You probably have a good idea about who your stakeholders are — anyone involved with, affected by, or who can affect the product and its creation. Stakeholders provide valuable feedback about every product increment you deliver each sprint.

REMEMBER

You also will work with stakeholders when you create the product vision and product roadmap; see Chapter 2 in Book 4 for more details.

Make sure the stakeholders are available to help you gather and write product backlog items. Stakeholders of a sample mobile banking application might include the following:

- People who interact with customers on a regular basis, such as customer service representatives or bank branch personnel.
- Business experts for the different areas where your product's customers interact. For example, XYZ Bank might have one manager in charge of checking accounts, another manager in charge of savings accounts, and a third manager in charge of online bill payment services. If you're creating a mobile banking application, all these people would be stakeholders.
- Users of your product.
- Experts of the type of product you're creating. For example, a developer who has created mobile applications, a marketing manager who knows how to create mobile campaigns, and a user experience specialist who specializes in mobile interfaces all might be helpful on the sample XYZ Bank mobile banking product.
- Technical stakeholders. These are people who work with the systems that might need to interact with your product.

Identifying users

Agile product development is customer focused. Building on the personas you've defined, your understanding of their needs, and the problems to be solved helps the team more clearly understand the product requirements. Knowing who your end users are and how they will interact with your product drives how you define and implement each item on your product roadmap.

With your product roadmap visualized (see Chapter 2 in Book 4), you can identify each type of user. For the mobile banking application, you would have individual and business bankers. The individual category would include youth, young adults, students, and single, married, retired, and wealthy users. Businesses of all sizes might be represented. Employee users would include tellers, branch managers, account managers, and fund managers. Each type of user will interact with your application in different ways and for different reasons. Knowing who these people are enables you to better define the purpose and desired benefits of each of their interactions.

TIP

You can define users using *personas*, or a written description about a type of user represented by a hypothetical person. For instance, "Ellen is a 65-year-old retired engineer who is spending her retirement traveling the world. Her net worth is $1,000,000, and she has residual income from several investment real estate properties."

Ellen represents 30 percent of XYZ Bank's customers, and a good portion of the product roadmap includes features that someone like Ellen will use. Instead of repeating all the details about Ellen every time the scrum team discusses these features, they can simply refer to the type of user as Ellen. The product owner might identify several personas, as needed, and will even print the descriptions with a stock photo of what Ellen might look like and post them on the wall in the team's work area to refer to throughout development.

REMEMBER

Know who your users are, so you can develop features they'll actually use.

Suppose that you're the product owner for the XYZ Bank's mobile banking product. You're responsible for the department that will bring the product to market, preferably in the next six months. You have the following ideas about the application's users:

- The customers (the end users of the application) probably want quick access to up-to-date information about their balances and recent transactions.
- Maybe the customers are about to buy a large-ticket item, and they want to make sure they can charge it.
- Maybe the customers' ATM cards were just refused, but they have no idea why, and they want to check recent transactions for possible fraudulent activities.
- Maybe the customers just realized that they forgot to pay their credit card bill and will have penalty charges if they don't pay the card today.

Who are your personas for this application? Here are a few examples:

- **Persona #1:** Jason is a young, tech-savvy executive who travels a lot. When he has a spare moment, he wants to handle personal business quickly. He carefully invests his money in high-interest portfolios. He keeps his available cash low.
- **Persona #2:** Carol is a small-business owner who stages properties when clients are trying to sell their home. She shops at consignment centers and often finds furnishings she wants to buy for her clients.
- **Persona #3:** Nick is a student who lives on student loans and a part-time job. He knows he can be flaky with money because he's flaky with everything else. He just lost his checkbook.

TIP

Your product stakeholders can help you create personas. Find people who are experts on the day-to-day business for your product. Those stakeholders will know a lot about your potential customers.

Determining product requirements and creating user stories

After you have identified your different users, you can start to determine product requirements and create user stories for the personas. A good way to create user stories is to bring your stakeholders together for a product discovery workshop.

Have the stakeholders write down as many requirements as they can think of, using the user story format. One user story for the product and personas from the previous sections might be as follows:

- Front side of card:
  - **Title** See bank account balance
  - **As** Jason,
  - **I want to** see my checking account balance on my smartphone
  - **so that** I can decide whether I have enough money in my account to make a transaction
- Back side of card:
  - **When I** sign into the XYZ Bank mobile application, my checking account balance appears.
  - **When I** sign into the XYZ Bank mobile application after making a purchase or a deposit, my checking account balance reflects that purchase or deposit.

You can see sample user stories in card format in Figure 3-2.

REMEMBER

Be sure to continuously add and prioritize new user stories to your product backlog. Keeping your product backlog up-to-date will help you have the highest-value user stories when it is time to plan your sprint.

You will create new user stories throughout product development. You'll also take existing large requirements and decompose them until they're manageable enough to work on during a sprint.

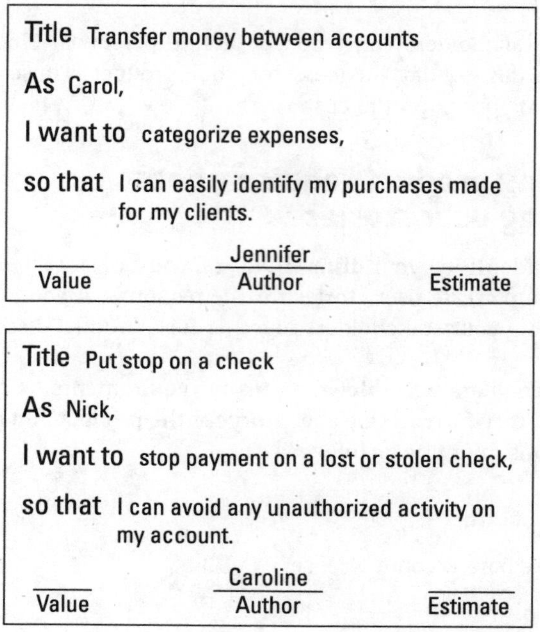

Title Transfer money between accounts

As Carol,

I want to categorize expenses,

so that I can easily identify my purchases made for my clients.

Value | Jennifer
Author | Estimate

Title Put stop on a check

As Nick,

I want to stop payment on a lost or stolen check,

so that I can avoid any unauthorized activity on my account.

Value | Caroline
Author | Estimate

FIGURE 3-2: Sample user stories.

© John Wiley & Sons, Inc.

Breaking down requirements

You refine requirements many times throughout development. For example:

- When you create the product roadmap (see Chapter 2 in Book 4), you create *features* (capabilities your customers will have after you develop the features), as well as *themes* (logical groups of features). Although features are intentionally large, features at the product roadmap level should be no larger than 144 story points on the Fibonnaci scale (see the later section "Estimation poker" to find out more about Fibonacci sizing.) Both features and themes are considered very large by a development team.
- When you plan releases, you break down the features into more concise user stories. User stories at the release plan level can be either *epics,* very large user stories with multiple actions, or individual user stories, which contain a single action. For our clients, user stories at the release plan level should be no larger than 34 story points. You find out more about releases later in this chapter.
- When you plan sprints, you break down requirements even further. User stories are broken down to eight points or fewer. See Figure 3-3 for a helpful requirement decomposition guide.

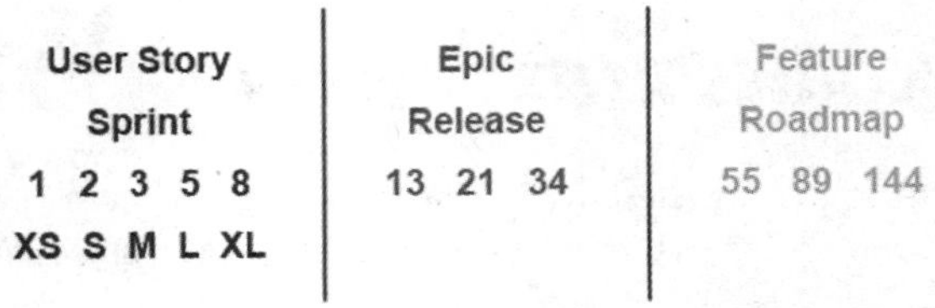

User Story	Epic	Feature
Sprint	Release	Roadmap
1 2 3 5 8	13 21 34	55 89 144
XS S M L XL		

© John Wiley & Sons, Inc.

FIGURE 3-3: User story decomposition guidelines.

To decompose requirements, you'll want to think about how to break down the requirement into individual actions. Table 3-1 shows a requirement from the XYZ Bank application introduced in Chapter 2 of Book 4 that is decomposed from the theme level down to the user story level.

Planning Releases and Sprints

TABLE 3-1 Decomposing a Requirement

Requirement Level	Requirement
Theme	See bank account data on a mobile device.
Features	See account balances. See a list of recent withdrawals or purchases. See a list of recent deposits. See my upcoming automatic bill payments. See my account alerts.
Epic user stories — decomposed from "see account balances"	See checking account balance. See savings account balance. See loan balance. See investment account balance. See retirement account balance.
User stories — decomposed from "see checking account balance"	See a list of my accounts once securely logged in. Select and view my checking account. See account balance changes after withdrawals. See account balance changes after purchases. See day's end account balance. See available account balance. Change account view.

USER STORIES AND THE INVEST APPROACH

You may be asking, just how decomposed does a user story have to be? Bill Wake, in his blog at XP123.com, describes the INVEST approach to ensure quality in user stories.

Using the INVEST approach, user stories should be

- **Independent:** To the extent possible, a user story should need no other user stories to implement the feature that the story describes.
- **Negotiable:** Not overly detailed. The user story has room for discussion and an expansion of details.
- **Valuable:** The user story demonstrates product value to the customer. It describes features, not technical tasks to implement it. The user story is in the user's language and is easy to explain. The people using the product or system can understand the user story.
- **Estimable:** The story is descriptive, accurate, and concise, so the developers can generally estimate the work necessary to create the functionality in the user story.
- **Small:** It is easier to plan and accurately estimate small user stories. A good rule of thumb is that the development team can complete 6–10 user stories in a sprint.
- **Testable:** You can easily validate the user story, and the results are definitive.

Estimation poker

As you refine your requirements, you need to refine your estimates of the work required to complete your user stories as well. It's time to have some fun!

One of the most popular ways of estimating user stories is by playing *estimation poker*, sometimes called *planning poker*, a game to determine user story size and to build consensus among the development team members.

REMEMBER

The scrum master can help coordinate estimation, and the product owner can provide information about features, but the development team is responsible for estimating the level of effort required for the user stories. After all, the development team has to do the work to create the features that those stories describe.

To play estimation poker, you need a deck of cards like the one in Figure 3-4. You can get a digital version online at `www.platinumedge.com/estimationpoker`, or you can make your own with index cards and markers. The numbers on the cards are from the Fibonacci sequence, which follows this progression:

1, 2, 3, 5, 8, 13, 21, 34, 55, 89, 144, and so on

If you start with the numbers 1 and 2, each subsequent number in the Fibonacci sequence is derived by taking the sum of the previous two numbers.

FIGURE 3-4: A deck of estimation poker cards.

© John Wiley & Sons, Inc.

Planning Releases and Sprints

Each user story receives an estimate relative to other user stories. For instance, a user story that is a 5 requires more effort than a 3, a 2, and a 1. It is about 5 times as much effort as a 1, more than double the effort of a 2, and roughly the amount of effort as a 3 and a 2 combined. It is not as much effort as an 8, but is just over half the effort of an 8.

As user stories and epic user stories increase in size, the difference between Fibonacci numbers gets bigger. Acknowledging these increasing gaps in precision for larger requirements is why the Fibonacci sequence works so well for relative estimation.

To play estimation poker, follow these steps:

1. **Provide each member of the development team with a deck of estimation poker cards.**
2. **From the list of user stories presented by the product owner, the team agrees on one user story that would be a 5.**

   This user story is the *anchor user story* for the team. The scrum master helps the development team reach consensus by using a fist of five or thumbs up/thumbs down, with discussion until everyone agrees on a user story that represents an estimate of 5.

TIP

The fist of five looks like rock-paper-scissors. On the count of three, each person holds up a number of fingers, reflecting the degree of comfort with the idea in question. Five means "I love the idea," four means "I think it's a good idea," three means "I can support the idea," two means "I have reservations, so let's discuss," and one means "I am opposed to the idea." If some people have three, four, or five fingers up, and some have only one or two, discuss the idea. Find out why the people who support the idea think it will work, and what reservations the people who oppose the idea have. You want to get all group members showing at least three fingers — they don't need to love the idea, but they need to support it.

TIP

You can also quickly get an idea of consensus on a decision by asking for a simple thumb up (support), thumb down (don't support), or thumb to the side (undecided). It's quicker than a fist of five, and is great for answering yes-or-no questions.

3. **The product owner reads a high-priority user story to the players.**

4. **Each player selects a card representing his or her estimate of the effort involved in the user story and lays the card facedown on the table.**

   You don't want the players to see each other's cards until all cards have been played. This limits how much one player can influence others to vote a certain way. The players should compare the user story to other user stories they have estimated. (The first time through, the players compare the user story to only the anchor story.)

5. **All players turn over their cards simultaneously.**

6. **If the players have different story points:**

   a. It's time for discussion.

      Discussion is the value-add of estimation poker, which enables team alignment and consensus. The players with the highest and lowest scores talk about their assumptions and why they think the estimate for the user story should be higher or lower, respectively. The players compare the effort for the user story against the anchor story. The product owner provides more clarification about the story, as necessary.

   b. Once everyone agrees on assumptions and has any necessary clarifications, the players reevaluate their estimates and place their new selected cards on the table.

   c. If the story points are different, the players repeat the process, usually up to three times.

   d. If the players can't agree on the estimated effort, the scrum master helps the development team determine a score that all the players can support (he or she may use a fist of five or thumbs up/thumbs down) or determine that the user story requires more detail or needs to be further broken down.

7. **The players repeat Steps 3 through 6 for each user story.**

REMEMBER

Consider each part of the definition of *done* — developed, integrated, tested (including test automation), and documented — when you create estimates.

You can play estimation poker at any point — but definitely play during the product roadmap development and as you progressively break down user stories for inclusion in releases and sprints. With practice, the development team will get into a planning rhythm and become more adept at quickly estimating.

TIP

On average, development teams may spend about 10 percent of their time each sprint decomposing and refining product backlog items, including estimating and reestimating. Make your estimation poker games fun! Bring in snacks, take breaks as needed, use humor, and keep the mood light.

Affinity estimating

Estimation poker can be effective, but what if you have many user stories? Playing estimation poker for, say, 500 user stories could take a long time. You need a way to estimate your entire product roadmap, but one that allows you to focus on only the user stories you must discuss to gain consensus.

When you have a large number of user stories, many of them are probably similar and would require a similar amount of effort to complete. One way to determine the right stories for discussion is to use affinity estimating. In *affinity estimating*, you quickly categorize your user stories and then apply estimates to these categories of stories.

TIP

When estimating by affinity, write your user stories on index cards or sticky notes. These types of user story cards work well when quickly categorizing stories.

Affinity estimating can be a fast and furious activity — the development team may choose to have the scrum master help facilitate affinity estimating sessions. To estimate by affinity, follow these steps:

1. **Taking no more than 60 seconds for each category, the development team agrees on a single user story in each of the following categories:**
   - Extra-small user story
   - Small user story
   - Medium user story
   - Large user story
   - Extra-large user story
   - Epic user story that is too large to come into the sprint
   - Needs clarification before estimating
2. **Taking no more than 60 seconds per user story, the development team puts all remaining stories into the categories listed in Step 1.**

   If you're using index cards or sticky notes for your user stories, you can physically place those cards into categories on a table or a whiteboard, respectively. If you divide the user stories among the development team members, having each development team member categorize a group of stories, this step can go quickly!

3. **Taking another 30 minutes, maximum, for each 100 user stories, the development team reviews and adjusts the placement of the user stories.**

   The entire development team must agree on the placement of the user stories into size categories.

4. **The product owner reviews the categorization.**
5. **When the product owner's expected estimate and the team's actual estimate differ by more than one story size, they discuss that user story.**

   The development team may or may not decide to adjust the story size.

REMEMBER

   Note that after the product owner and the development team discuss clarifications, the development team has the final say on the user story size.

6. **The development team plays estimation poker on the user stories in both the epic and the needs clarification categories.**

   The number of user stories in these categories should be minimal.

User stories in the same size category will have the same user story score. You can play a round of estimation poker to double-check a few, but you won't need to spend time in unnecessary discussion for every user story.

Story sizes are like T-shirt sizes and should correspond to Fibonacci scale numbers, as shown in Figure 3-5.

SIZE	POINTS
Extra small (XS)	1
Small (S)	2
Medium (M)	3
Large (L)	5
Extra large (XL)	8

FIGURE 3-5: Story sizes as T-shirt sizes and their Fibonacci numbers.

© John Wiley & Sons, Inc.

TIP

You can use the estimating and prioritizing techniques in this chapter for requirements at any level, from themes and features down to single user stories.

That's it. In a few hours, your entire product backlog was estimated. In addition, your scrum team has a shared understanding of what the requirements mean, having discussed them face to face rather than relying on interpretations of extensive documentation.

Release Planning

A *release* is a group of usable product features that you deploy to the market. A release does not need to include all the functionality outlined in the product roadmap but should include at least the *minimal marketable features,* the smallest group of product features that you can effectively deploy and promote in the marketplace. Your early releases will include highest priority (high value, or high risk, or both) items and exclude lower-priority requirements you identified during the product roadmap stage.

When planning a release, you establish the next set of minimal marketable features and identify an imminent product launch date around which the team can mobilize. As when creating the vision statement and the product roadmap, the product owner is responsible for creating the release goal and establishing the release date. However, the development team's estimates, with the scrum master's facilitation, contribute to the process.

Release planning is stage 3 in the Roadmap to Value (refer to Chapter 2 in Book 4 to see the roadmap as a whole). Figure 3-6 shows how release planning fits into product development.

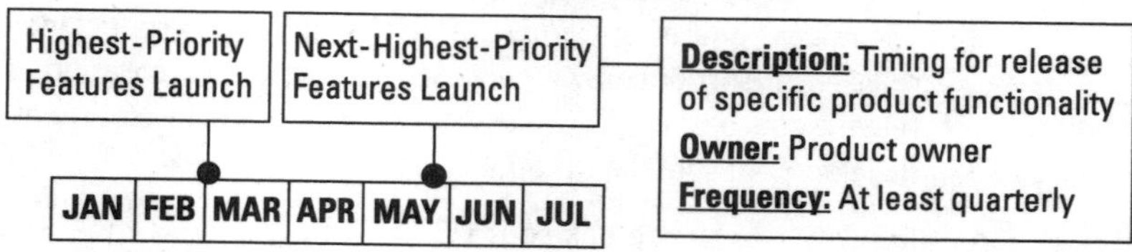

FIGURE 3-6: Release planning as part of the Roadmap to Value.

© John Wiley & Sons, Inc.

Release planning involves completing two key activities:

- **Revising the product backlog:** Chapter 2 in Book 4 tells you that the product backlog is a comprehensive list of all the user stories you currently know for your product, whether or not they belong in the current release. Keep in mind that your list of user stories will usually probably change throughout development.
- **Creating the release plan:** This activity consists of defining the release goal, release target date, and prioritization of product backlog items that support the release goal. Whereas the product vision provides the long-range goal of the product, the release plan provides a midrange goal that the team can accomplish.

Don't create a new, separate backlog during release planning. The task is unnecessary and reduces the product owner's flexibility. Prioritizing the existing product backlog based on the release goal is sufficient and enables the product owner to have the latest information when he or she commits to the scope during sprint planning.

The product backlog and release plan are some of the most important information radiators between the product owner and the development team. (See Chapter 4 in Book 4 for more on information radiators.) In Chapter 2 of Book 4, you find out how to complete a product backlog. How to create a release plan is described next.

The release plan contains a release schedule for a specific set of features. The product owner creates a release plan at the start of each release. To create a release plan, follow these steps:

1. **Establish the release goal.**

   The release goal is an overall business goal for the product features in your release. The product owner and development team collaborate to create a release goal based on business priorities and the development team's development speed and capabilities.

2. **Identify a target release date.**

   Some scrum teams determine release dates based on the completion of functionality; others may have hard dates, such as March 31 or September 1. The first case has a fixed scope and flexible date; the second case has a fixed date and a flexible scope.

WARNING

If a fixed date and fixed scope are determined for the release, adjustments may need to be made to the number of teams to accomplish the release goal according to schedule. The development team, not the product owner, estimates the effort required to implement product backlog items. Imposing a fixed scope and timeline without adjusting quality or resources (in this case, talent resources) will not be successful.

3. **Review the product backlog and the product roadmap to determine the highest-priority user stories that support your release goal (the minimum marketable features).**

   These user stories will make up your first release.

TIP

   Try to achieve a release goal with about 80 percent of the user stories, using the final 20 percent to add robust features that will meet the release goal while adding to the product's "wow" factor. This approach provides appropriate flexibility and slack for the scrum team to deliver value without having to complete every single task.

4. **Refine the user stories in your release goal.**

   During release planning, dependencies, gaps, or new details are often identified that affect estimates and prioritization. This is the time to make sure the portion of the product backlog supporting your release goal is sized. (Refer to Figure 3-3.) Make sure that items supporting the current release goal have been decomposed and are sized appropriately for the release. The development team helps the product owner by updating estimates for any added or revised user stories, and commits to the release goal with the product owner.

REMEMBER

   Release planning is the initial opportunity to identify and break down dependencies before they become impediments. Dependencies are anti-patterns to becoming agile. Teams should work to become highly aligned and highly autonomous. Dependencies are an indication that your team does not have the capability to do whatever they are dependent on.

5. **Estimate the number of sprints needed, based on the scrum team's velocity.**

TECHNICAL STUFF

   Scrum teams use velocity as an input to plan how much work they can take on in a release and sprint. *Velocity* is the sum of all user story points completed within a sprint. So, if a scrum team completed six user stories during its first sprint with sizes 8, 5, 5, 3, 2, and 1, their velocity for the first sprint is 24. The scrum team would plan its second sprint keeping in mind that it completed 24 story points during the first sprint.

   After multiple sprints, scrum teams can use their running average velocity as an input to determine how much work they can take on in a sprint, as well as to extrapolate their release schedule by dividing the total number of story points in the release by their average velocity. Find out more about scrum in Book 5.

Be aware that some teams add a *release sprint* to a release to conduct activities unrelated to product development but necessary to release the product to customers. If you need a release sprint, be sure to factor that into the date you choose.

REMEMBER

Delaying crucial development tasks such as testing until the end of development rearloads risk. Agile techniques frontload risk to avoid the surprises and defects that result from delayed testing. If a scrum team requires a release sprint, it probably means the broader organization can't support being truly shippable with each sprint, which is an impediment to becoming agile. The goal for agile teams is to have every type of work or activity required to release functionality to the market as part of the sprint-level definition of done. Scrum masters should work together to remove organizational impediments preventing teams from being able to release at scale according to their sprint-level definition of done.

In some traditional or project-focused organizations, some tasks, such as security testing or load testing a software product, can't be completed within a sprint because the task's environment takes time to set up and request. Although release sprints allow scrum teams to plan for these types of activities, doing so is an anti-pattern, or the opposite of being agile. In these examples, the scrum master would work with the organizational leaders who manage the security or load testing environments to find ways to enable scrum teams to accomplish security or lead testing during the sprint.

Each planned release shifts from what was a tentative plan (high-level product roadmap items) to a more concrete goal ready to execute in the sprint(s) of the release. Figure 3-7 represents a typical release plan.

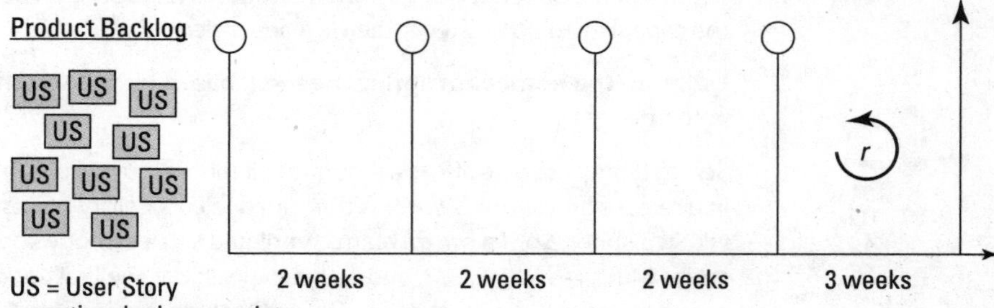

FIGURE 3-7: Sample release plan.

TIP

Bear in mind the pen-pencil rule: You can commit to (write in pen) the plan for the first release, but anything beyond the first release is tentative (written in pencil). In other words, use just-in-time planning for each release. After all, things change, so why bother getting microscopic too early?

Preparing for Release

In release planning, you also need to prepare your organization for the product release. This section discusses how to prepare for supporting the new functionality in the marketplace and how to get stakeholders in your company or organization ready for product deployment.

Preparing the product for deployment

In each sprint, a valuable working product increment is created in support of the release goal. With a definition of done that means your increment each sprint is shippable, there's not much more you need to do to prepare the product for technical deployment. Every sprint, you're ready to release if there is enough value accumulated for the customer.

TECHNICAL STUFF

With software product development, releasing to production is done through continuous integration (CI) and continuous deployment (CD), which are extreme programming (XP) practices used with software product development. The product code is checked in and moved to quality assurance (QA) and then to the production (live) environments as quickly and seamlessly as possible. Advancements in technology enable teams to automate a pipeline for building, integrating, testing, and fixing without delay. Combining a CI/CD pipeline with a robust automated testing harness raises the bar of your product development agility. Teams developing non-software products should use techniques that automate testing and integration of new functionality to the existing product as much as possible.

TECHNICAL STUFF

In information technology (IT), usually involving software development, *development operations (DevOps)* is the integration of software development and IT operations (which includes functions such as systems administration and server maintenance). Taking a DevOps approach enables everyone involved (user experience, testing, infrastructure, database, coding, design) to work together, to eliminate handoffs, and to streamline collaboration for reduced deployment cycle times. Multiple teams working on the same product will not be successful without a reliable CI/CD pipeline.

TIP

Not all agile product development efforts use release planning. Some scrum teams release functionality for customer use with every sprint or even every day. The development team, product, organization, customers, stakeholders, and product's technological complexity can all help determine your approach to product releases. Helpful for this discussion are Principles 1 and 3, respectively: "satisfy the customer through early and continuous delivery" and "deliver. . .frequently, from a couple of weeks to a couple of months, with a preference to the shorter timescale." (For details, see Chapter 1 in Book 4.)

Prepare for operational support

After your product is released to the customer, someone will have to support it, a responsibility that involves responding to customer inquiries, maintaining the system in a production environment, and enhancing existing functionality to fill minor gaps. Although new development work and operational support work are both important, they involve different approaches and cadences.

Separating new development and support work ensures that new development teams can focus on continuing to bring innovative solutions to customers at a faster rate than if the team frequently switches between the two types of work.

Consider a model that separates new development and maintenance work, as illustrated in Figure 3-8.

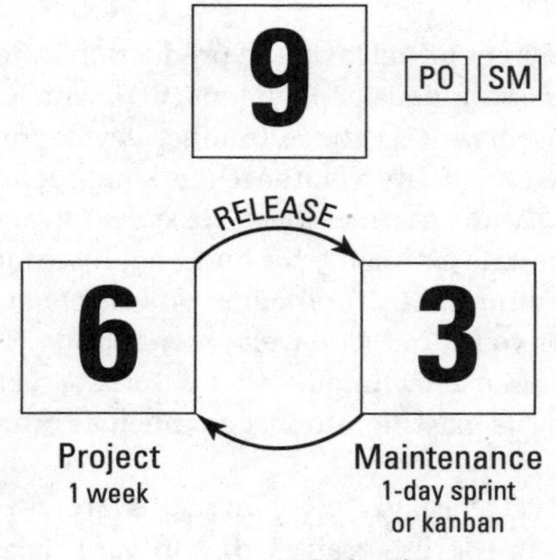

FIGURE 3-8: Operational support scrum team model.

© John Wiley & Sons, Inc.

For a scrum team of nine developers, for instance, you would divide the development team into two teams, one with six developers, and the other with three. (These numbers are flexible.) The team of six does new development work from the product backlog in one-week to two-week sprints, as described in Book 4. The work that the team commits to during the sprint planning meeting will be the only work they do.

The team of three are your firefighters and do maintenance and support work in one-day sprints or by using kanban. (You learn about one-day sprints in Chapter 4 of Book 4.) Single-day sprints allow the scrum team to triage all incoming requests from the previous day, plan the highest-priority items, implement those items as a team, and review the results at the end of the day (or even earlier) for go or no-go approval before pushing the changes to production. For continuity, the product owner and scrum master are the same for each team.

REMEMBER

Although the newly modified product development team is smaller than before, there are still enough developers to keep new development efforts moving forward, uninterrupted by maintenance work. By the time you begin releasing functionality to the market, your scrum team will be working well together and the developers will have increased their versatility by being able to complete more types of tasks than when the project first started.

Teams should rotate team members between the two activities at sprint boundaries (every three to five sprints, for example) to give everyone an opportunity to learn from both types of work. If support is excessive, the product owner may want to reevaluate the product backlog to see if there are ways to reduce the weight of support and its distraction. Support distractions cause the team to focus on tactical resolutions rather than strategic value creation. Team stability and acceleration will improve.

When preparing for release, establishing expectations upfront regarding how the functionality will be supported in production allows the scrum team to develop the product in a way that enables the team to effectively support the product after it's deployed. Establishing expectations also increases ownership across the scrum team and heightens the team's awareness and dedication to long-term success.

TIP

Product owners who maintain a strong working relationship with help desks or those providing customer support benefit greatly by understanding how their products are used by real users. Help desk reporting can be valuable for evaluating product backlog candidates or upcoming priorities. Help desks benefit by knowing that the scrum team is working to address any escalated incidents. The product owner involves these groups in release planning to ensure that all are prepared for operational support well in advance of release.

Preparing the organization

A product release often affects a number of departments in a company or an organization. To get the organization ready for the new functionality to be released next, the product owner coordinates with the rest of the organization regarding what to expect and what will be needed from them during release planning. When product owners do this effectively, there shouldn't be surprises at release time.

Release planning addresses not only the activities for the development team to release but also the activities to be performed by the rest of the organization. These might include the following:

- **Marketing:** Do marketing campaigns related to the new product need to launch at the same time as the product?

- **Sales:** Do specific customers need to know about the product? Will the new product cause an increase in sales?
- **Logistics:** Is the product a physical item that includes packaging or shipping?
- **Product support:** Does the customer service group have the information it needs to answer questions about the new product? Will this group have enough people on hand in case customer questions increase when the product launches?
- **Legal:** Does the product meet legal standards, including pricing, licensing, and correct verbiage, for release to the public?

The departments that need to be ready for the release and the specific tasks these groups need to complete will vary from organization to organization. A key to release success, however, is that the product owner and scrum master involve the right people and ensure that those people clearly understand what they need to do to be ready for the functionality release.

During release planning, you also need to include one more group: the customer. The next section discusses getting the marketplace ready for your product.

Preparing the marketplace

The product owner is responsible for working with other departments to ensure that the marketplace — existing customers and potential customers — is ready for what's coming. The marketing or sales teams may lead this effort; team members look to the product owner to keep them informed as to the release date and the features that will be part of the release.

Some software products are for only internal employee use. Certain things you're reading in this section might seem like overkill for an internal application — that is, an application released only within your company. However, many of these steps are still good guidelines for promoting internal applications. Preparing customers, whether internal or external, for new products is a key part of product success.

To help prepare customers for the product release, the product owner may want to work with different teams to ensure the following:

- **Marketing support:** Whether you're dealing with a new product or new features for an existing product, the marketing department should leverage the excitement of the new product functionality to help promote the product and the organization.

- **Customer testing:** If possible, work with your customers to get real-world feedback about the product from a subset of end users. (Some people use focus groups.) Your marketing team can also use this feedback to translate into testimonials for promoting the product right away.
- **Marketing materials:** An organization's marketing group also prepares the promotional and advertising plans, as well as packaging for physical media. Media materials, such as press releases and information for analysts, need to be ready, as do marketing and sales materials.
- **Support channels:** Ensure that customers understand the available support channels in case they have questions about the product.

Review the items on your release backlog from the customer's standpoint. Think of the personas you used when creating your user stories. Do those personas need to know something about the product? Update your launch checklist with items that would be valuable to customers represented by your personas.

Finally, you're there — release day. Whatever role you played along the way, this is the day you worked hard to achieve. It's time to celebrate!

Sprint Planning

With agile product development, a *sprint* is a consistent iteration of time in which the development team creates a specific group of product capabilities from start to finish. At the end of each sprint, the functionality that the development team has created should be working, ready to demonstrate, and potentially shippable to the customer.

REMEMBER

Sprints should be the same length. Keeping the sprint lengths consistent helps the development team measure its performance and plan better at each new sprint.

Sprints generally last one to four weeks. One month is the longest amount of time any sprint should last; longer iterations make changes riskier, defeating the purpose of being agile. It's rare to see sprints lasting longer than two weeks, and more often you see sprints lasting a week. One-week sprints are a natural cycle with the Monday-to-Friday business week, which structurally prevents weekend work. When priorities change on a daily basis, some scrum teams work in one-day sprints, as discussed in Chapter 4 of Book 4.

Market and customer needs are changing more and more quickly, and the amount of time you can afford between opportunities to gather customer feedback only gets shorter. Your sprint shouldn't be longer than your stakeholders can consistently go without changes in priority regarding what the scrum team should be working on in the sprint. Sprint duration is a function of the business's need for change.

Each sprint includes the following:

- Sprint planning at the beginning of the sprint
- Daily scrum meetings
- Development work — the bulk of the sprint
- A sprint review and a sprint retrospective at the end of the sprint

Discover more about daily scrums, development work, sprint reviews, and sprint retrospectives in Chapters 4 and 5 of Book 4.

Sprint planning is stage 4 in the Roadmap to Value, as you can see in Figure 3-9. The entire scrum team — the product owner, scrum master, and development team — works together to plan sprints.

Stage 4: SPRINT PLANNING

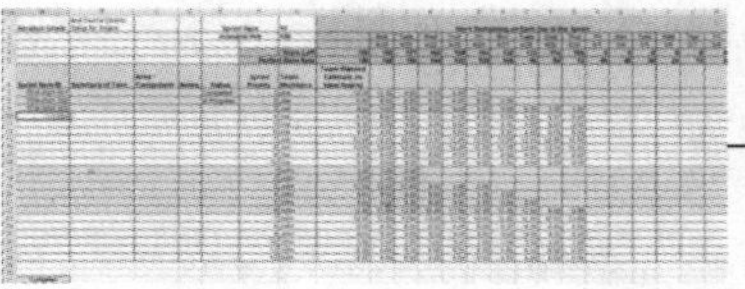

Description: Establishment of specific iteration goals and tasks

Owner: Product owner and development team

Frequency: At the start of each sprint

© John Wiley & Sons, Inc.

FIGURE 3-9: Sprint planning as part of the Roadmap to Value.

The sprint backlog

The *sprint backlog* is a list of user stories associated with the current sprint and related tasks. When planning your sprint, you do the following:

- Establish the goal for your sprint.
- Choose the product backlog items (user stories) that support your goal.
- Break user stories into specific development tasks.
- Create a sprint backlog. The *sprint backlog* consists of the following:
  - The list of user stories in the sprint in order of priority (value).
  - The relative effort estimate for each user story.

- The tasks necessary to develop each user story.
- The effort, in hours, to complete each task (if needed). At the task level, if you estimate the number of hours each task will take to complete, use hours instead of using story points. Because your sprint has a specific short length, and thus a known number of available working hours, you can use the time each task takes to determine whether the tasks will fit into the team's capacity of the sprint. Each task should take one day or less for the development team to complete.

TIP

Some mature development teams may not need to estimate their tasks as they get more consistent at breaking down their user stories into executable tasks. Estimating tasks is helpful for newer development teams to ensure that they understand their capacity and plan each sprint appropriately.

- A burndown chart, which shows the status of the work in progress for the sprint.

Tasks should take a day or less to complete for two reasons:

» The first reason involves basic psychology: People are motivated to get to the finish line. If you have a task that you know you can complete quickly, you're more likely to finish it on time, just to check it off your to-do list.

WARNING

» The second reason is that one-day tasks provide good red flags that development targets might be veering off course. If a development team member reports that he or she is working on the same task for more than one or two days, that team member probably has a roadblock and the scrum master should investigate what might be keeping the team member from finishing work. (For more on managing roadblocks, see Chapter 4 in Book 4.)

The development team collaborates to create and maintain the sprint backlog, but only the development team can modify the sprint backlog. The sprint backlog should reflect an up-to-the-day snapshot of the sprint's progress. Figure 3-10 shows a sample sprint backlog at the end of the sprint planning meeting. You can use this example, find other samples, or even use a whiteboard.

The sprint planning meeting

On the first day of each sprint, often a Monday morning, the scrum team holds the sprint planning meeting.

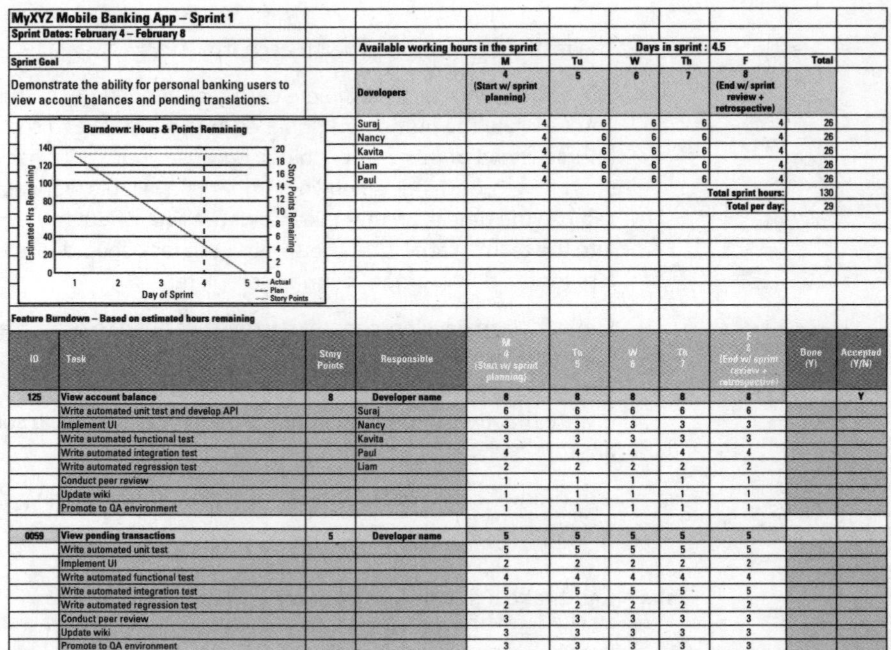

MyXYZ Mobile Banking App – Sprint 1

Sprint Dates: February 4 – February 8

Sprint Goal

Demonstrate the ability for personal banking users to view account balances and pending translations.

Available working hours in the sprint — **Days in sprint : 4.5**

Developers	M 4 (Start w/ sprint planning)	Tu 5	W 6	Th 7	F 8 (End w/ sprint review + retrospective)	Total
Suraj	4	6	6	6	4	26
Nancy	4	6	6	6	4	26
Kavita	4	6	6	6	4	26
Liam	4	6	6	6	4	26
Paul	4	6	6	6	4	26
					Total sprint hours:	130
					Total per day:	29

Feature Burndown – Based on estimated hours remaining

ID	Task	Story Points	Responsible	M 4 (Start w/ sprint planning)	Tu 5	W 6	Th 7	F 8 (End w/ sprint review + retrospective)	Done (Y)	Accepted (Y/N)
125	**View account balance**	**8**	**Developer name**	**8**	**8**	**8**	**8**	**8**		**Y**
	Write automated unit test and develop API		Suraj	6	6	6	6	6		
	Implement UI		Nancy	3	3	3	3	3		
	Write automated functional test		Kavita	3	3	3	3	3		
	Write automated integration test		Paul	4	4	4	4	4		
	Write automated regression test		Liam	2	2	2	2	2		
	Conduct peer review			1	1	1	1	1		
	Update wiki			1	1	1	1	1		
	Promote to QA environment			1	1	1	1	1		
0059	**View pending transactions**	**5**	**Developer name**	**5**	**5**	**5**	**5**	**5**		
	Write automated unit test			5	5	5	5	5		
	Implement UI			2	2	2	2	2		
	Write automated functional test			4	4	4	4	4		
	Write automated integration test			5	5	5	5	5		
	Write automated regression test			2	2	2	2	2		
	Conduct peer review			3	3	3	3	3		
	Update wiki			3	3	3	3	3		
	Promote to QA environment			3	3	3	3	3		

FIGURE 3-10: Sprint backlog example.

© John Wiley & Sons, Inc.

REMEMBER

For a successful sprint planning meeting, make sure everyone involved in the session (the product owner, the development team, the scrum master, and anyone else the scrum team requests) is dedicated to the effort for the entire meeting.

Base the length of your sprint planning meeting on the length of your sprints. Sprint planning should take no longer than two hours per week of the sprint, or no longer than a full day for a one-month sprint. This timebox helps ensure that the meeting stays focused and on track. Figure 3-11 is a good quick reference for your sprint planning meeting lengths.

If my sprint is this long…	My sprint planning meeting should last no longer than…
One week	Two hours
Two weeks	Four hours
Three weeks	Six hours
Four weeks	Eight hours

FIGURE 3-11: Ratio of sprint planning meeting to sprint length.

© John Wiley & Sons, Inc.

TIP

With agile product development, the practice of limiting the time of your meetings is sometimes called *timeboxing*. Keeping your meetings timeboxed provides focus and ensures that the development team has the time it needs to create the product.

You'll split your sprint planning meetings into two parts: one to set a sprint goal (the "why") and choose user stories for the sprint (the "what"), and another to break down your user stories into individual tasks (the "how" and "how much"). The details on each part are discussed next.

Part 1: Setting goals and choosing user stories

In the first part of your sprint planning meeting, the product owner and development team, with support from the scrum master, decide what to do during the sprint by doing the following:

1. **Discuss and set a sprint goal.**
2. **Select the user stories from the product backlog that support the sprint goal, further refine them for understanding, and revisit their relative estimates.**
3. **If needed, create user stories to fill gaps to achieve the sprint goal.**
4. **Determine what the team can commit to in the current sprint.**

TIP

Consistently refining the product backlog ensures that the scrum team plans items into each sprint with which they're already familiar. This refinement is also critical for ensuring that sprint planning stays within the timebox and results in a clear plan to deliver potentially shippable functionality at the end of each sprint. Scrum teams, on average, spend about 10 percent of their sprint in product backlog refinement for future sprints.

At the beginning of your sprint planning meeting, the product owner should propose a sprint goal that identifies a problem to solve for the customer and then together with the development team discuss and agree on the sprint goal. The sprint goal should be an overall description of the working customer functionality that the team will demonstrate and possibly release at the end of the sprint. The goal is supported by the highest-priority user stories in the product backlog. A sample sprint goal for the mobile banking application (refer to Chapter 2 in Book 4) might be as follows:

> Demonstrate the ability of a mobile banking customer to log in and view account balances and pending and prior transactions.

Using the sprint goal, you determine the user stories that belong in the sprint and refine the estimates for those user stories, as needed. For the mobile banking application sprint goal example, the group of user stories for the sprint might include the following:

- Log in and access my accounts.
- View account balances.
- View pending transactions.
- View prior transactions.

All these would be high-priority user stories in the product backlog that support the sprint goal.

Don't forget to bring at least one improvement item agreed to during a previous sprint retrospective.

The second part of reviewing user stories is confirming that the effort estimates for each user story have been reviewed and adjusted, if needed, and reflect the development team's current knowledge of the user story. Adjust the estimate if necessary. With the product owner in the meeting, resolve any outstanding questions. At the beginning of the sprint, the scrum team has the most up-to-date knowledge about the system and the customer's needs, so make sure the development team and product owner have one more chance to clarify and size the user stories going into the sprint.

Finally, after you know which user stories support the sprint goal, the development team should agree and confirm that it can complete the goal planned for the sprint. If any of the user stories you discussed earlier don't fit in the current sprint, remove them from the sprint and add them back into the product backlog.

Always plan and work on one sprint at a time. An easy trap to fall into is to place user stories into specific future sprints. For example, when you're still planning sprint 1, don't decide that user story X should go into sprint 2 or 3. Instead, keep the ordered list of user stories up to date in the product backlog and focus on always developing the next highest-priority stories. Commit to planning only for the current sprint. What you learn in sprint 1 may fundamentally change how you go about sprint 2 or 10 or 100.

After you have a sprint goal, user stories for the sprint, and a commitment to the goal, move on to the second part of sprint planning.

TIP

Because a sprint planning meeting for sprints longer than one week might last a few hours, you might want to take a break between the two parts of the meeting.

Part 2: Breaking down user stories into tasks for the sprint backlog

In the second part of the sprint planning meeting, the scrum team does the following:

1. **The development team creates the sprint backlog tasks associated with each user story. Make sure that tasks encompass each part of the definition of done: developed, integrated, tested (including test automation), and documented.**
2. **The development team double-checks that it can complete the tasks in the time available in the sprint.**
3. **Each development team member should choose his or her first task to accomplish before leaving the meeting.**

TIP

Development team members should each work on only one task on one user story at a time to enable *swarming* — the practice of the entire development team working on one user story until completion. Swarming can be an efficient way to complete work in a short amount of time. In this way, scrum teams avoid getting to the end of the sprint with all user stories started but few finished.

At the beginning of part two of the meeting, break the user stories into individual tasks and allocate a number of hours to each task. The development team's target should be completing a task in a day or less. For example, a user story for the XYZ Bank mobile application might be as follows:

> Log in and access my accounts.

The team decomposes this user story into tasks, such as the following:

- Write the unit test.
- Write the user acceptance test.
- Create an authentication screen for a username and password, with a Submit button.
- Create an error screen for the user to reenter credentials.
- Create a screen (once logged in) displaying a list of accounts.

- Using authentication code from the online banking application, rewrite code for an iPhone/iPad/Android application. (This task could potentially be three different tasks.)
- Create calls to the database to verify the username and password.
- Re-factor code for mobile devices.
- Write the integration test.
- Promote the product increment to QA.
- Update the regression test automation suite.
- Run the security test.
- Update the wiki documentation.

After you know the number of hours that each task will take, do a final check to make sure that the number of hours available to the development team reasonably matches the total of the tasks' estimates. If the tasks exceed the hours available, one or more user stories will have to come out of the sprint. Discuss with the product owner what tasks or user stories are the best to remove.

If extra time is available within the sprint, the development team might be able to include another user story. Just be careful about over-committing at the beginning of a sprint, especially during the first few sprints.

After you know which tasks will be part of the sprint, choose what you will work on first. Each development team member should select his or her initial task to accomplish for the sprint. Team members should focus on one task at a time.

TIP

As the development team members think about what they can complete in a sprint, use the following guidelines to ensure that they don't take on more work than they can handle while they're figuring out new roles and techniques:

- **Sprint 1:** 25 percent of what the development team thinks it can accomplish. Include overhead for learning the new process and starting product development.
- **Sprint 2:** Assuming the scrum team was able to complete sprint 1 successfully, 50 percent of what the development team thinks it can accomplish.
- **Sprint 3:** Assuming success in sprint 2, 75 percent of what the development team thinks it can accomplish.
- **Sprint 4 and forward:** Assuming success in sprint 3, 90 percent. The development team will have developed a rhythm and velocity, gained insight into agile principles and the product, and will be working at close to full pace.

TIP

Avoid planning 100 percent of capacity for a sprint. Scrum teams should build in slack in their sprint to account for unknowns that inevitably come up. Instead of padding estimates, simply be wise and don't commit every available hour, assuming everything will go as planned. Teams that finish early accelerate faster.

The scrum team should constantly evaluate the sprint backlog against the development team's progress on the tasks. At the end of the sprint, the scrum team can also assess estimation skills and capacity for work during the sprint retrospective (see Chapter 5 in Book 4). This evaluation is especially important for the first sprint.

TIP

For the sprint, how many total working hours are available? In a one-week sprint or a 40-hour week, you could wisely assume that 4.5 working days are available to develop user stories. Why 4.5 days? About one-fourth of day one is taken up with sprint planning, and about one-fourth of day five is taken up with the sprint review (when the stakeholders review the completed work) and the sprint retrospective (when the scrum team identifies team improvements for future sprints). That leaves 4.5 days of development. If you assume each full-time team member has 30 hours per week (6 productive hours per day) to focus on the sprint goal, the number of working hours available is

Number of team members × 6 hours × 4.5 days

After sprint planning is finished, the development team can immediately start working on the tasks to create the product!

The scrum master should make sure the product vision and roadmap, product backlog, definition of done, and sprint backlog are in a prominent place and accessible to everyone during sprint planning as well as in the area in which they work. In this way, stakeholders can view the product information and progress on demand without interrupting the development team. For details, see Chapter 4 in Book 4.

» Tracking daily progress

» Looking at team members' daily roles

» Developing and testing every day

» Ending the day

Chapter 4 Working throughout the Day

It's Tuesday, 9 a.m. Yesterday, you completed sprint planning, and the development team started work. For the rest of the sprint, you'll be working *cyclically*, where each day follows the same pattern.

In this chapter, you find out how to use agile principles daily throughout each sprint. You see the work that you will do every day as part of a scrum team: planning and coordinating your day, tracking progress, creating and verifying usable functionality, inspecting and adapting, and identifying and dealing with impediments to your work. You see how the different scrum team members work together each day during the sprint to ensure transparency as they help create the product.

Planning Your Day: The Daily Scrum

With agile product development, you make plans throughout the entire development effort — and on a daily basis. Agile development teams start each workday with a *daily scrum* meeting to evaluate their progress and adapt their plan for the day based on what was accomplished previously. They will identify and coordinate the resolution of impediments (roadblocks requiring scrum master involvement), note completed items, and synchronize and plan what each team member will do during the day to achieve the sprint goal.

The daily scrum is stage 5 on the Roadmap to Value. You can see how the sprint and the daily scrum fit into product development in Figure 4-1. Note how they both repeat.

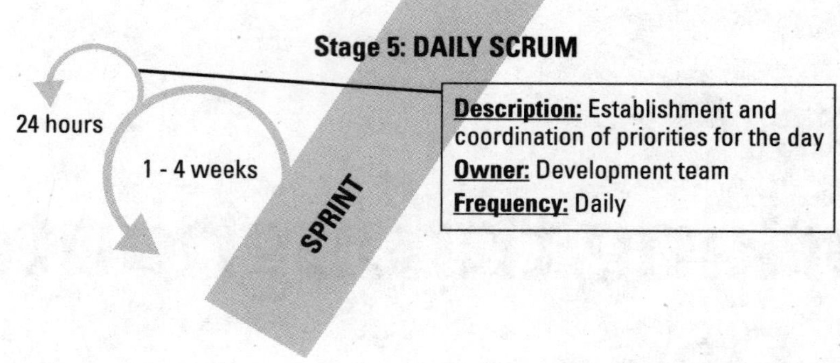

FIGURE 4-1: The sprint and the daily scrum in the Roadmap to Value.

© John Wiley & Sons, Inc.

Covering important topics

In the daily scrum meeting, each development team member addresses the following four topics, which facilitate team coordination:

- **What was completed yesterday** to help accomplish the sprint goal?

  WARNING

  Avoid using the daily scrum as a status report by having each developer give an accounting of what they did the day before or by moving completed items around on the task board. Developers should update their task as soon as they complete it, or at the very least at the end of the day, so that when the scrum team comes together for their daily scrum the next day, the status is already reflected. In other words, don't spend time on what was accomplished yesterday unless it effects how to go about the work to be done today.

- **What will be done today** to help accomplish the sprint goal?
- **What impediments** are in the way of accomplishing the sprint goal?
- **This is how I feel.** (The fourth topic helps the scrum master better understand team health daily rather than once per sprint.)

TIP

Other names you might hear for the daily scrum meeting are the *daily huddle* or the *daily standup* meeting. Daily scrum, daily huddle, and daily standup all refer to the same thing. Daily scrum is how scrum refers to it.

The scrum master also addresses these three statements regarding the team's impediments:

- Impediments resolved yesterday
- Impediments that need to be resolved today (and order of priority)
- Impediments that need to be escalated

What does the product owner do during the daily scrum? Listen. The product owner listens to see whether there is anything he or she can do to help the team accomplish their work more effectively. The product owner may provide clarification as needed, and might say something if he or she hears something that indicates that the development team is working on something outside the sprint goal. An engaged, decisive product owner makes life easier for a development team.

Ensuring an effective meeting

One of the rules of scrum is that the daily scrum meeting should last 15 minutes or less. Longer meetings eat into the development team's day. Standing encourages shorter meetings (which is why the meeting is referred to also as the daily standup). You can also use props to keep daily scrum meetings quick.

TIP

Consider starting meetings by tossing an item, such as a squeaky burger-shaped dog toy — keep it clean! — to a random development team member. Each person addresses the four topics and then passes the squeaky toy to someone else. If people are long-winded, change the prop to a 500-page ream of copy paper, which weighs about five pounds. Each person can talk for as long as he or she can hold the ream out to one side. Either meetings will quickly become shorter, or development team members will quickly build up their arm strength — it'll probably be the former.

REMEMBER

To keep daily scrums brief and effective, the scrum team can follow several guidelines:

- **Anyone may attend a daily scrum, but only the development team, the scrum master, and the product owner may talk.** The daily scrum is the scrum team's opportunity to coordinate daily activities, not take on additional requirements or changes from stakeholders. Stakeholders can discuss questions with the scrum master or product owner afterward, but stakeholders should not distract the development team from the focus of the sprint.

- **The focus is on immediate priorities.** The scrum team should review only completed tasks, tasks to be done, and roadblocks.
- **Daily scrum meetings are for coordination, not problem-solving.** The development team and the scrum master are responsible for having relevant discussions of the tasks they're working on and removing roadblocks during the day.

  To keep meetings from drifting into problem-solving sessions, scrum teams can

  - Create a list on a whiteboard to keep track of issues that need immediate attention, and then address those issues directly after the meeting with only those team members who need to be involved.
  - Hold a meeting, called an *after-party,* to solve problems after the daily scrum is finished. Some scrum teams schedule time for an after-party every day; others meet only as needed.
- **The daily scrum is for peer-to-peer coordination.** It is not used for an individual to report status to one person, such as the scrum master or product owner. Status is reported at the end of each day in the sprint backlog, and should take developers about one minute.
- **Such a short meeting must start on time.** It's not unusual for the scrum team to have a working agreement for ensuring that meetings start and end on time. Creative punishments for tardiness include doing pushups or adding penalty money into a team celebration fund. Whatever punishment is used, the scrum team agrees on it together; the method is not dictated to them by someone outside the team, such as a manager.
- **The scrum team may request that daily scrum attendees stand up — rather than sit down — during the meeting.** Standing up makes people eager to finish the meeting and get on with the day's work.

Daily scrum meetings are effective for keeping the development team focused on the right tasks for any given day. Because the development team members are accountable for their work in front of their peers, they are less likely to stray from their daily commitments. Daily scrum meetings also help ensure that the scrum master and development team can deal with roadblocks immediately. These meetings are so useful that even organizations that are not using any other agile techniques sometimes adopt daily scrums.

TIP

Think about holding daily scrum meetings 30 minutes after the development team's normal start time to allow for traffic jams, emails, coffee, and other rituals when starting the day. Having a later daily scrum meeting also allows the development team time to review defect reports from automated testing tools that were run the night or weekend before.

The daily scrum is for discussing progress and planning each upcoming day. As you see next, you also track progress — not just discuss it — every day.

Tracking Progress

You also need to track the progress of your sprint daily. This section discusses ways to keep track of the tasks in your sprint.

Two tools for tracking progress are the sprint backlog and a task board. Both the sprint backlog and the task board enable the scrum team to show the sprint's progress to anyone at any given time.

REMEMBER

The Agile Manifesto values individuals and interactions over processes and tools. Make sure your tools support, rather than hinder, your scrum team. Modify or even replace tools if needed. Read more about the Agile Manifesto in Chapter 1 of Book 4.

The sprint backlog

During sprint planning, you concentrate on adding user stories and tasks to the sprint backlog. During the sprint itself, you update the sprint backlog daily, tracking progress of the development team's tasks for each working day. Figure 4-2 shows the sprint backlog for this book's sample application, the XYZ Bank's mobile banking application, as it would appear after day 4 of the first sprint. (Chapter 3 in Book 4 discusses details of the sprint backlog.)

TIP

You can create a sprint backlog using a spreadsheet and charting program such as Microsoft Excel. Make the sprint backlog available to the entire team every day. That way, anyone who needs to know the sprint status can find it instantly.

Near the top left of Figure 4-2, note the *sprint burndown chart*, which shows the progress that the development team is making. You can see that the development team members have completed tasks close to the even burn rate of their available hours, and the product owner has accepted several user stories as complete.

You can include burndown charts on your sprint backlog and on your product backlog. (This chapter concentrates on the sprint backlog.) Figure 4-3 shows the burndown chart in detail.

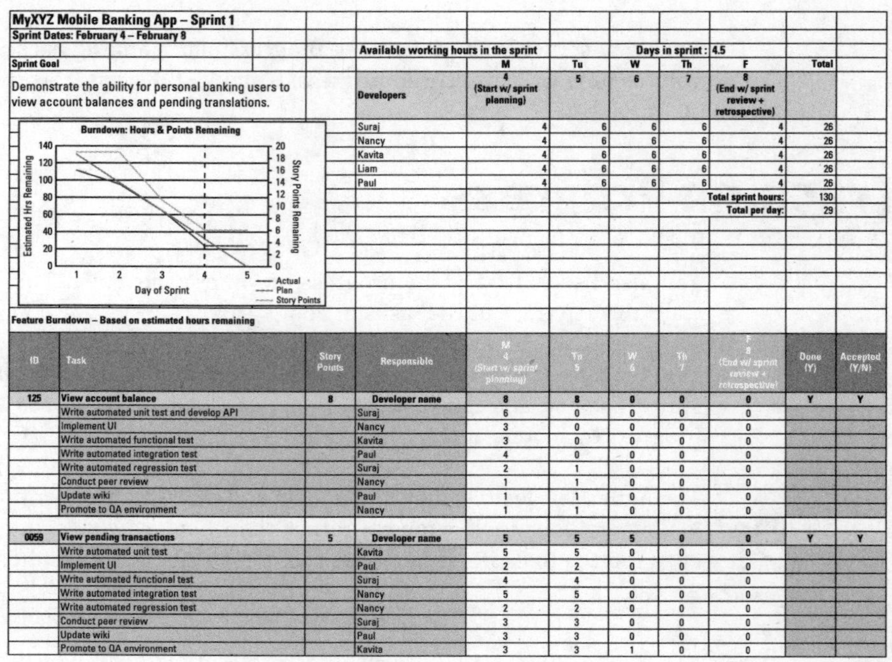

MyXYZ Mobile Banking App – Sprint 1

Sprint Dates: February 4 – February 8

Sprint Goal

Demonstrate the ability for personal banking users to view account balances and pending translations.

Available working hours in the sprint — **Days in sprint : 4.5**

Developers	M 4 (Start w/ sprint planning)	Tu 5	W 6	Th 7	F 8 (End w/ sprint review + retrospective)	Total
Suraj	4	6	6	6	4	26
Nancy	4	6	6	6	4	26
Kavita	4	6	6	6	4	26
Liam	4	6	6	6	4	26
Paul	4	6	6	6	4	26
					Total sprint hours:	130
					Total per day:	29

Feature Burndown – Based on estimated hours remaining

ID	Task	Story Points	Responsible	M 4 (Start w/ sprint planning)	Tu 5	W 6	Th 7	F 8 (End w/ sprint review + retrospective)	Done (Y)	Accepted (Y/N)
125	**View account balance**	**8**	**Developer name**	**8**	**8**	**0**	**0**	**0**	**Y**	**Y**
	Write automated unit test and develop API		Suraj	6	0	0	0	0		
	Implement UI		Nancy	3	0	0	0	0		
	Write automated functional test		Kavita	3	0	0	0	0		
	Write automated integration test		Paul	4	0	0	0	0		
	Write automated regression test		Suraj	2	1	0	0	0		
	Conduct peer review		Nancy	1	1	0	0	0		
	Update wiki		Paul	1	1	0	0	0		
	Promote to QA environment		Nancy	1	1	0	0	0		
0059	**View pending transactions**	**5**	**Developer name**	**5**	**5**	**5**	**0**	**0**	**Y**	**Y**
	Write automated unit test		Kavita	5	5	0	0	0		
	Implement UI		Paul	2	2	0	0	0		
	Write automated functional test		Suraj	4	4	0	0	0		
	Write automated integration test		Nancy	5	5	0	0	0		
	Write automated regression test		Nancy	2	2	0	0	0		
	Conduct peer review		Suraj	3	3	0	0	0		
	Update wiki		Paul	3	3	0	0	0		
	Promote to QA environment		Kavita	3	3	1	0	0		

FIGURE 4-2: Sample sprint backlog.

© John Wiley & Sons, Inc.

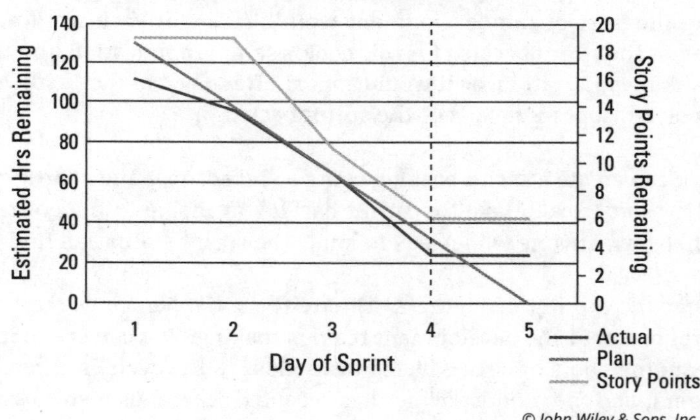

FIGURE 4-3: A burndown chart.

© John Wiley & Sons, Inc.

A burndown chart is a powerful tool for visualizing progress and the work remaining. The chart shows the following:

- The outstanding work (in hours) on the first vertical axis
- Time, in days along the horizontal axis

Some sprint burndown charts, like the one in Figure 4-3, also show the outstanding story points on a second vertical axis that is plotted against the same horizontal time axis as hours of work remaining.

REMEMBER

A burndown chart enables anyone to see the status of the sprint at a glance. Progress is clear. By comparing the realistic number of hours available to the work remaining, you can find out daily whether the effort is going as planned, is in better shape than expected, or is in trouble. This information helps you determine whether the development team is likely to accomplish the sprint goal and helps you make informed decisions early in the sprint.

Figure 4-4 shows samples of burndown charts for sprints in different situations. Looking at these charts, you can tell how the work is progressing:

- **Expected:** This chart shows a normal sprint pattern. The remaining work hours rise and fall as the development team completes tasks, ferrets out details, and identifies tactical work it may not have initially considered. Although work occasionally increases, it is manageable, and the team mobilizes to complete all user stories by the end of the sprint.
- **More complicated:** In this sprint, the work increased beyond the point at which the development team felt it could accomplish everything. The team identified this issue early, worked with the product owner to remove some user stories, and still achieved the sprint goal. The key to scope changes within a sprint is that they are always initiated by the development team — no one else.

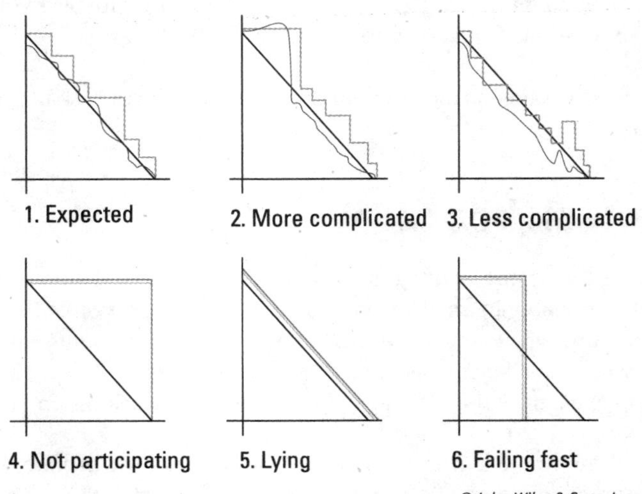

FIGURE 4-4: Profiles of burndown charts.

» **Less complicated:** In this sprint, the development team completed some critical user stories faster than anticipated and worked with the product owner to identify additional user stories it could add to the sprint.

» **Not participating:** A straight line in a burndown means that the team didn't update the burndown or made zero progress that day. Either case is a red flag for future problems.

WARNING

Just like on a heartbeat graph, a horizontal straight line on a sprint burndown chart is never a good thing.

» **Lying (or conforming):** This burndown pattern is common for a new agile development team that might be accustomed to reporting the hours that management expects, instead of the time the work really takes, and consequently tends to adjust the team's work estimates to the exact number of remaining hours. This pattern often reflects a fear-based environment, where the managers lead by intimidation.

» **Failing fast:** One of the strongest benefits of this simple visualization of progress is the immediate proof of progress or lack thereof. This pattern shows an example of a team that wasn't participating or progressing. Halfway through the sprint, the product owner decided to cut losses by killing the sprint and starting a new sprint with a new sprint goal. Only product owners can end a sprint early.

TIP

The sprint backlog helps you track progress throughout each sprint. You can also refer to earlier sprint backlogs to compare progress from sprint to sprint. You make changes to your process in each sprint (read more about the concept of inspect and adapt in Chapter 5 of Book 4). Constantly inspect your work and adapt to make it better. Hold on to those old sprint backlogs.

Another way to keep track of your sprint is by using a task board. Read on to find out how to create and use one.

The task board

Although the sprint backlog is a great way to track and show development progress, it's probably in an electronic format, so it might not be immediately accessible to anyone who wants to see it. Some scrum development teams use a task board along with their sprint backlog. A *task board* provides a quick, easy view of the items in the sprint that the development team is working on and has completed.

You can't deny the status a task board shows. Like the product roadmap, the task board can be made up of sticky notes on a whiteboard. The task board will have at least the following four columns, from left to right:

- **To Do:** The user stories and tasks that remain to be accomplished are in the far left column.
- **In Progress:** User stories and tasks that the development team is currently working on are in the In Progress column. Only one user story should be in this column. Having more user stories in progress is an alert that development team members are not working cross-functionally and, instead, are hoarding desired tasks (not swarming). You risk having multiple user stories partially done instead of more user stories completely done by the end of the sprint.
- **Accept:** After the development team completes a user story, it moves it to the Accept column. User stories in the Accept column are ready for the product owner to review and either provide feedback or accept.
- **Done:** When the product owner has reviewed a user story and verifies that the user story is complete, the product owner can move that user story to the Done column.

REMEMBER

Limit your work in progress! Select only one task at a time. Leave other tasks available in the To Do column. Ideally, a development team will work on only one user story at a time and swarm on the tasks of that user story to complete it quickly. High-performing teams and organizations do one item well before moving onto the next item.

Because the task board is tactile — people physically move a user story card through its completion — it can engage the development team more than an electronic document ever could. The task board encourages thought and action just by existing in the scrum team's work area, where everyone can see the board.

TIP

Allowing only the product owner to move user stories to the Done column prevents misunderstandings about user story status.

Figure 4-5 shows a typical task board. As you can see, the task board is a strong visual representation of the work in progress.

TECHNICAL STUFF

The task board is a lot like a kanban board. *Kanban* is a Japanese term that means *visual signal.* Toyota created these boards as part of its lean manufacturing process.

In Figure 4-5, the task board shows four user stories, each separated by a horizontal line called *swim lanes.* The first user story is done. All tasks are completed, and the product owner has accepted the work done. For the second user story, the development work is completed but is waiting for acceptance by the product owner. The third user story is in progress, and the fourth user story has not yet been started. At a glance, the status of each user story is clear not only to the scrum team, making tactical coordination faster and easier, but also to interested stakeholders.

RELEASE GOAL: SPRINT GOAL:

RELEASE DATE: SPRINT REVIEW:

US = User Story

Task = Task

TO DO	IN PROGRESS	ACCEPT	DONE
			US Task Task Task Task Task Task Task Task Task Task Task Task
		US	Task Task Task Task Task Task Task Task Task Task Task Task
Task Task Task Task Task Task Task Task	US Task Task Task Task Task		
US Task Task Task Task Task Task Task Task			

FIGURE 4-5: Sample task board.

© John Wiley & Sons, Inc.

Agile product development day-to-day work involves more than just planning and tracking progress. In the next section, you see what most of your day's work will include, whether you're a member of the development team, a product owner, or a scrum master.

REMEMBER

The product owner owns the product backlog. The development team owns the sprint backlog. Ownership means keeping the backlog updated, clarified, and transparent.

Understanding Agile Roles in the Sprint

Each member of a scrum team has specific daily roles and responsibilities during the sprint. The day's focus for the development team is producing valuable shippable functionality. For the product owner, the focus is on preparing the product backlog for future sprints while supporting the development team's execution of the sprint backlog with real-time clarifications. The scrum master is the agile coach and maximizes the development team's productivity by removing roadblocks and protecting the development team from external distractions.

Following are descriptions of the responsibilities of each member of the product team during the sprint. In the later section "Creating Shippable Functionality," you see how the product owner and development team work together to create the product.

Keys for daily product owner success

A successful product owner focuses on ensuring that the development team has everything they need to keep the development speed (velocity) high. The product owner works to understand the problems and needs of customers by meeting with them frequently. Product owners shield the development team from competing priorities, allowing them to focus on the sprint goal. By sitting with the rest of the scrum team, the product owner can provide instant feedback as work is completed, enabling the development team to turn requirements into valuable working functionality.

The product owner has the following responsibilities during a typical day in a sprint:

- **Proactive contributions:**
  - Look forward to the next sprint and elaborate user stories in readiness for the next backlog refinement or sprint planning meeting.
  - Add new user stories to the product backlog as necessary and ensure that new user stories support the product vision, release goal, and sprint goal.
  - Collaborate with other product owners or stakeholders to align on release or sprint goals. Maintain the product backlog as necessary.
  - Review the product budget to stay abreast of product expenses and revenues.
  - Review product performance information and trends in the marketplace.
  - With the scrum master, watch for opportunities to proactively remove impediments that could impede development if not addressed early, such as product questions arising during sprint planning or legal wording.
- **Reactive contributions:**
  - Provide immediate clarification and decisions about requirements to keep the development team developing.

Working throughout the Day

- Remove business impediments brought by other members of the scrum team, such as unplanned requests from other teams or stakeholders. Shield the team from business distractions.
- Review completed user story functionality and provide feedback to the development team.

Keys for daily development team member success

Successful development team members have pride in their work. They build high-quality, enduring products. They engineer their work for change, realizing refactoring is necessary and expected as more is learned. They sit next to their teammates and perform tasks, even unfamiliar tasks, to expand their capabilities and contributions to their team. They excel in their particular discipline and look to expand their capability each day.

If you're a member of the development team, you

- **Proactive contributions**
  - Select the tasks of highest need and complete them as quickly as possible.
  - Collaborate with other development team members to design the approach to a specific user story, seek help when you need it, and provide help when another development team member needs it.
  - Collaborate with other scrum development teams to technically align on release or sprint goals.
  - Continually improve regression test automation, CI/CD pipelines, and unit testing. (CI stands for continuous integration, and CD stands for continuous deployment. Find out more in the later section "Developing.")
  - Evaluate opportunities to improve the product architecture and development processes.
  - Alert the scrum master to any roadblocks you can't effectively remove on your own.
- **Reactive contributions**
  - Request clarification from the product owner when you're unclear about a user story.
  - Conduct peer reviews on one another's work.
  - Take on tasks beyond your normal role as the sprint demands.

- Fully develop functionality as agreed to in the definition of done (described in the later section "Creating Shippable Functionality").
- Report daily on the amount of work remaining for your tasks in the sprint backlog.

Keys for daily scrum master success

Successful scrum masters are both coaches and facilitators. They coach the team to improved performance and facilitate team interactions to help the team reach decisions quickly. They inspire, lead, challenge, and serve. Because they also sit with the team, each day they look for opportunities to serve their team members by removing impediments, by coaching the broader organization to better work with the team, and by making sure the organization's environment enables success. After low-hanging-fruit team improvements are made, a scrum master's job only gets harder as he or she works to remove more difficult organizational impediments affecting the team. The scrum master is the process owner in the scrum framework.

If you're a scrum master, you do the following during a typical day:

- **Proactive contributions:**
  - Uphold agile values and practices by coaching the product owner, development team, and organization when necessary.
  - Remove roadblocks and organizational issues, both tactically for immediate problems and strategically for potential long-term issues. Scrum masters question the status quo of organizational constraints that strategically impede scrum teams from becoming higher functioning.
  - Build relationships to foster close cooperation with people working with the scrum team. Build clout and champion agility throughout the organization.

TIP

Nonverbal communication says a lot. Scrum masters can benefit from understanding body language to identify unspoken tensions in the scrum team.

  - Prepare for upcoming facilitation opportunities, such as researching retrospective models to help the team maximize their retrospective discussion and acquiring supplies to facilitate affinity estimation.
  - Shield the development team from external distractions.
  - Collaborate with other scrum masters and stakeholders to resolve or escalate impediments.
- **Reactive contribution:**
  - Facilitate consensus building in the scrum team, as needed.

Here is some advice for scrum masters: "Never lunch alone. Always be building relationships." You never know when you'll need to rely on relationships to remove an obstacle.

Keys for daily stakeholder success

As members of the product team, successful stakeholders know how to work with the product owner to ensure product success. They counsel, collaborate, and listen. They give feedback and support. In flat, agile organizations, stakeholders empower, coach, and serve the scrum team rather than direct their activities from the outside or top-down. Each day, they participate in team discussions when asked but otherwise reserve their feedback for sprint review discussions.

If you're a product stakeholder, you do the following during a typical day:

- **Proactive contributions:**
  - Counsel with the product owner on customer needs and backlog priorities.
  - Look for opportunities to remove team impediments. Continually ask how you can help.
- **Reactive contributions:**
  - Participate in sprint reviews and provide feedback. Be available to attend any other discussion requested by the team.
  - Look at team burndowns or task boards. Look for opportunities to help the team become successful.
  - Practice Principle 5, "Give the team the environment and support they need, then trust them to get the job done." (See Chapter 1 in Book 4 for more information.)

Keys for daily agile mentor success

For teams new to agile techniques, agile mentors are critical sounding boards for the team. They challenge the team's thinking, helping to create healthy tension. Similar to scrum masters, they coach, challenge, and serve. They teach them to find answers themselves (rather than just give them the answers). The team understands that they'll get honesty and candor from the agile mentor. Agile mentors work to become redundant, transitioning their experience and expertise to the scrum master. Agile mentors participate daily in whatever way the team needs them.

Strategically, agile mentors engage with the organization's leaders to help maximize the value created by the teams. The scrum team's maximum pace is determined by the environment in which they're working. Agile mentors help leaders improve the environment according to agile values and principles.

If you're an agile mentor, you do the following during a typical day:

- **Proactive contributions:**
  - Counsel with the scrum master, primarily to help them build expertise, clout, and capability to effectively coach, trailblaze, and facilitate.
  - Provide agility mentoring to developers and the product owner in the form of in-the-moment course corrections as they strive to learn and improve their roles.
  - Coach stakeholders and other organizational leaders on how they can best support the scrum team to deliver valuable and potentially shippable functionality for the customer at every sprint.
- **Reactive contributions:**
  - Observe scrum team events as well as informal interactions and provide feedback and guidance.
  - Attend any discussion requested by the team.
  - Inspect team burndowns or task boards. Provide feedback on opportunities to help the team become successful.

Creating Shippable Functionality

The objective of the day-to-day work of a sprint is to create shippable functionality for the product in a form that can be delivered to a customer or user.

Within the context of a single sprint, a *product increment* or *shippable functionality* means that a work product has been developed, integrated, tested, and documented according to the definition of done and is deemed ready to release. The development team may or may not release the increment at the end of the sprint because release timing depends on the release plan. The release plan may require multiple sprints before the product contains the set of minimum marketable features necessary to justify a market release.

It helps to think about shippable functionality in terms of user stories. A user story starts out as a written requirement on a card. As the development team creates functionality, each user story becomes an action a user can take. Shippable functionality equals completed user stories.

To create shippable functionality, the development team and the product owner are involved in three major activities:

- Elaborating
- Developing
- Verifying

During the sprint, any or all of these activities can be happening at any given time. As you review them in detail, note that they don't always occur in a linear way.

Elaborating

With agile product development, *elaboration* is the process of determining the details of a product feature. Whenever the development team tackles a new user story, elaboration ensures that any unanswered questions about a user story are answered so that the process of development can proceed.

The product owner works with the development team to elaborate user stories, but the development team should have the final say on design decisions. The product owner should be available for consultation if the development team needs further clarification on requirements throughout the day.

Collaborative design is a major factor for successful products. Keep in mind these agile principles from Chapter 1 in Book 4: "The best architectures, requirements, and designs emerge from self-organizing teams," and "Business people and developers must work together daily throughout a project." Watch out for development team members who have a tendency to try to work alone on elaborating user stories. If a member of the development team separates himself or herself from the team, perhaps part of the scrum master's job should be coaching that person on upholding agile values and practices.

Developing

During product development, most of the activity naturally falls to the development team. The product owner continues to work with the development team on an as-needed basis to provide clarification and to approve developed functionality.

TIP

The development team should have immediate access to the product owner. Ideally, the product owner sits with the development team when he or she is not interacting with customers and stakeholders.

The scrum master should also sit with the development team. He or she focuses on protecting the development team from outside disruptions and removing impediments that the development team encounters.

To sustain agile practices during development, be sure to implement the following development practices from extreme programming:

- **Pair up development team members to complete tasks.** Doing so enhances the quality of the work and encourages the sharing of skills.
- **Follow the development team's agreed-upon design standards.** If you can't follow them for whatever reason, revisit these standards and improve them.
- **Start development by setting up automated tests.** You can find more about automated testing later in this chapter.
- **Avoid coding new features that are outside the sprint goal.** If new, nice-to-have features become apparent during development, add them to the product backlog.
- **Integrate changes that were coded during the day, one set at a time.** Test for 100 percent correctness. Integrate changes at least once a day; some teams integrate many times a day.
- **Undertake code reviews to ensure that the code follows development standards.** Identify areas that need revising. Add the revisions as tasks in the sprint backlog.
- **Create technical documentation as you work.** Don't wait until the end of the sprint or, worse, the end of the sprint prior to a release.

TECHNICAL STUFF

Continuous integration is the term used in software development for integrating and comprehensively testing with every code build. Continuous integration helps identify problems before they become crises. Continuous integration (CI) paired with continuous deployment (CD) is known as CI/CD. Together, teams are able to release early and often. Read more about CI/CD in Chapter 3 of Book 4.

Verifying

Verifying the work done in a sprint has three parts: automated testing, peer review, and product owner review.

REMEMBER

It is exponentially cheaper to prevent a defect than it is to rip it out of a deployed system.

Automated testing

Automated testing means using a computer program to do the majority of your testing for you. With automated testing, the development team can quickly develop and test the product, which is a big benefit for improved team agility.

Often, agile teams develop during the day, with regression test automation and security vulnerability scanning run on a nightly or weekly cycle. After the cycle completes, the team can review the defect report that the testing program generated, report on any problems during the daily scrum, and correct those issues immediately during the day.

Software automated testing can include the following:

- **Unit testing:** Testing source code in its smallest parts — the component level
- **System testing:** Testing the code with the rest of the system
- **Integration testing:** Verifying that new functionality created in the development environment still works when integrated with the existing functionality
- **Regression testing:** Testing the product increment with previous product increments to ensure that previous functionality continues to work
- **Vulnerability or penetration testing:** Security testing to evaluate the product's exposure to internal and external threats.
- **User acceptance testing:** Validating that the new functionality satisfies the acceptance criteria
- **Static testing:** Verifying that the product's code meets standards based on rules and best practices that the development team has agreed upon

Peer review and team development techniques

Peer review and pair programming are techniques teams use to build product increments. *Peer review* simply means that development team members review one another's work. *Pair programming* means that two people work together, with one person driving (the pilot) and one observing from behind (the navigator). Both practices improve product quality, build or expand team member capability, and reduce single-point-of-failure exposure.

A newer trend gaining momentum is mob programming. *Mob programming* is an approach for product development in which the entire team works on the same thing, at the same time, in the same space, and at the same computer. The entire team continuously collaborates at a single computer to deliver a single work item at a time. Customers are often invited to participate with the team as well. Mob programming extends the benefits of pair programming from two people to the entire team.

Benefits of mob programming include a broader technical understanding of the product, a faster resolution of communication and decision-making problems, preventing the need to do more than is barely sufficient, reduced technical debt, reduced thrashing of the team and team members, and reduced work in progress.

However the team chooses to review each other's work, collocation helps make the review easy and informal — you can turn to the person next to you and ask him or her to take a quick look at what you just completed. Self-managing teams should decide what works best for them.

Product owner review

When a user story has been developed and tested, the development team moves the stories to the Accept column on the task board discussed earlier in this chapter. The product owner then reviews the functionality and verifies that it meets the goals of the user story, per the user story's acceptance criteria. The product owner verifies (accepts or rejects) user stories throughout each day as the development team completes them.

As discussed in Chapter 3 of Book 4, the back side of each user story card has verification steps. These steps allow the product owner to review and confirm that the code works and supports the user story. Figure 4-6 shows a sample user story card's verification steps.

When I do this:	This happens:
When I go to the accounts page :	I am able to see my active account balance.
When I select transfer funds :	I am able to select "Transfer to Account" and amount.
When I submit transfer requests :	I get an account confirmation funds were transferred.

FIGURE 4-6: User story verification.

© John Wiley & Sons, Inc.

Finally, the product owner should run through some checks to verify that the user story in question meets the definition of done. When a user story meets its acceptance criteria as well as the definition of done, the product owner updates the task board by moving the user story from the Accept column to the Done column.

While the product owner and the development team are working together to create shippable functionality for the product, the scrum master helps the scrum team to identify and clear roadblocks that appear along the way, as you find out in the next section.

Identifying roadblocks

A major part of the scrum master's role is managing and helping resolve roadblocks that the scrum team identifies. Roadblocks are anything that thwarts a team member from working to full capacity.

REMEMBER

Although the daily scrum is a good place for the development team to identify roadblocks, the development team may come to the scrum master with issues anytime throughout the day.

Examples of roadblocks include the following:

- Local, tactical issues, such as
  - A manager trying to pull away a team member to work on a "priority" sales report.
  - The development team needing additional hardware, software, or access to facilitate progress.
  - A development team member who doesn't understand a user story and says the product owner isn't available to help.
- Organizational impediments, such as
  - An overall resistance to agile techniques, especially when the company established and maintained prior processes at significant cost.
  - Managers who might not be in touch with the work on the ground. Technologies, development practices, and project management practices are always progressing.
  - External departments that may not be familiar with scrum needs and the pace of development when using agile techniques.
  - An organization that enforces policies that don't make sense for agile teams. Centralized tools, budget restrictions, and standardized processes that don't align with agile processes can all cause issues for agile teams.

REMEMBER

The most important trait a scrum master can have is organizational clout or influence. Organizational clout gives the scrum master the ability to have difficult conversations and make the small and large changes necessary for the scrum team to be successful.

Beyond the primary focus of creating shippable functionality, other things happen during the day. Many of these tasks fall to the scrum master. Table 4-1 shows potential roadblocks and the action that the scrum master can take to remove the impediments.

TABLE 4-1 Common Roadblocks and Solutions

Roadblock	Action
The development team needs simulation software for a range of mobile devices so that it can test the user interface and functionality.	Do some research to estimate the cost of the software, prepare a summary with the product owner, and have a discussion about funding. Process the purchase through procurement, and deliver the software to the development team.
Management wants to borrow a development team member to write a couple of reports. All your development team members are fully occupied.	Tell the requesting manager that the person is not available and probably will not be for the duration of the sprint. Recommend that the requester discuss the need with the product owner so he or she can prioritize it against the rest of the product backlog. As you're likely a problem solver, you may want to suggest alternative ways in which the manager could get what he or she needs.
A development team member can't move forward on a user story because he or she does not fully understand the story. The product owner is out of the office for the day on a personal emergency.	Work with the development team member to determine whether any work can happen around this user story while waiting for an answer. Help locate another person (stakeholder, customer, or subject matter expert) who could answer the question. Failing that, ask the development team to review upcoming tasks (not related to this stopped one) and move things around to keep progressing.
A user story has grown in complexity and now appears to be too large for the sprint length.	Have the development team work with the product owner to break the decompose user story down so that some demonstrable value can be completed in the current sprint and the rest can be put back into the product backlog. The goal is to ensure that the sprint ends with completed user stories, even smaller ones, rather than incomplete user stories.

Implementing Information Radiators

Each day, the team uses information radiators to broadcast important information to not only themselves but also to stakeholders. An *information radiator* is a poster, task board, list, or any artifact that can be viewed on-demand. Information radiators such as a sprint backlog or a task board reduce questions such as "What's the status of a story?" or "Is the team on track to meet the sprint goal?" Most information radiators are posted in the team's physical workspace or, if the team is collaborating with other teams, in a common collaboration or meeting area. If teams are using digital collaboration tools, these information radiators are clearly made transparent through obvious links and easy access.

TIP

Low-fidelity tactile information radiators are in your face and can't be ignored, even unintentionally. They are referenced more frequently than digital tools, which you have to click or search to find. One way that a scrum master creates an environment for team success is by ensuring transparency of useful artifacts through information radiators.

Information radiators that teams find helpful include the following:

- **Product vision statement and product roadmap:** Provides constant visibility and clarity on the strategic product direction. See Chapter 2 in Book 4.
- **Product canvas:** Visualizes personas, needs, objectives, and other considerations established at the beginning of product development, and can be updated as the scrum team learns more about the customer and marketplace.
- **Product backlog:** Helps scrum team members and stakeholders visualize product capability and what priorities are coming up next. See Chapter 2 in Book 4.
- **Sprint backlog:** Displays the scope of the sprint and the status of each task.
- **Task board:** Displays the status of each user story in the sprint. See an example of a task board earlier in this chapter.
- **Team working agreement:** Reminds the team of the behaviors they agree to uphold as they work together. The agreement can be updated during sprint retrospectives and other team discussions.
- **Release and sprint burndown charts with goals:** Visualizes daily the progress and trends of each iteration towards goals. See Chapter 3 in Book 4.
- **Definition of done:** Reminds the team what shippability means and the work each user story requires. Updated during retrospectives and as the team's abilities evolve. See Chapters 1, 3, and 5 in Book 4.
- **Personas:** Reminds the team through visualization of who their customers are as the team performs their work.
- **Agile Manifesto, Agile Principles, and scrum values:** Reminds the team of the guiding values and principles they are trying to enable, and are referred to frequently by scrum masters and agile mentors as they coach the team throughout the day. See Chapter 1 in Book 4.

Wrapping Up at the End of the Day

At the end of each day, the development team reports on the progress of tasks by updating the sprint backlog with which tasks were completed and how much work, in hours, remains to be done on new tasks started. Depending on the tool that the scrum team uses for tracking progress, the sprint backlog data may automatically update the sprint burndown chart as well.

TIP

Update the sprint backlog with the amount of work remaining — not the amount of time already spent — on open tasks. The important point is how much time and effort remains, which informs the team as to whether the scrum team is on track to meet its sprint goal. If possible, avoid spending time tracking how many hours were spent working on tasks, which is less necessary with self-correcting agile models. Also, it should take a development team less than one minute to update enterprise status reporting. If it's taking longer than that, you have the wrong tool.

The product owner should also update the task board at least at the end of the day, and move any user stories that have passed review to the Done column.

The scrum master should review the sprint backlog or task board for any risks or impediments before the next day's daily scrum.

The scrum team follows this daily cycle until the end of the sprint, when it will be time to step back, inspect, and adapt at the sprint review and the sprint retrospective meetings.

» Reviewing the sprint and improving processes

Chapter 5 Showcasing Work, Inspecting, and Adapting

At the end of each sprint, the scrum team gets a chance to put the results of its hard work on display in the sprint review. The sprint review is where the product owner and the development team demonstrate to the stakeholders the sprint's completed and to market functionality. In the sprint retrospective, the scrum team (the product owner, development team, and scrum master) review how the sprint went and determine possible improvement opportunities for the next sprint. Underpinning both events is the agile concept of inspect and adapt, which Chapter 2 in Book 4 explains.

In this chapter, you discover how to conduct a sprint review and a sprint retrospective.

The Sprint Review

The *sprint review* is a meeting to review and demonstrate the shippable and valuable functionality that the development team completed during the sprint, and for the product owner to gather feedback and update the product backlog accordingly. The sprint review is open to anyone interested in reviewing the sprint's accomplishments. This means all stakeholders get a chance to see progress on the product and provide feedback.

The sprint review is stage 6 in the Roadmap to Value. Figure 5-1 shows how the sprint review fits into agile product development.

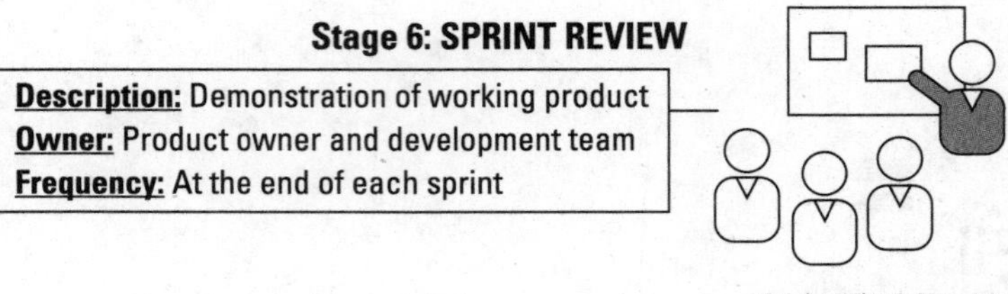

Stage 6: SPRINT REVIEW
Description: Demonstration of working product
Owner: Product owner and development team
Frequency: At the end of each sprint

FIGURE 5-1: The sprint review in the Roadmap to Value.

© John Wiley & Sons, Inc.

The following sections show you what you need to do to prepare for a sprint review, how to run a sprint review meeting, and the importance of collecting feedback.

Preparing to demonstrate

Preparation for the sprint review meeting should not take more than a few minutes at most. Even though the sprint review might sound formal, for agile teams, the essence of showcasing is informality. The meeting needs to be prepared and organized but doesn't require flashy materials. Instead, the sprint review focuses on demonstrating what the development team has done.

WARNING

If your sprint review is overly showy, ask yourself whether you're covering up for not spending enough time developing. Get back to working on value — creating a working and shippable product. Pageantry is the enemy of agility.

The preparation for the sprint review meeting involves the product owner and the development team, facilitated by the scrum master as needed. The product owner knows exactly what the development team completed in the sprint because he or she was working alongside them to accept or reject the items completed as valuable and shippable. The development team needs to be ready to demonstrate completed, shippable functionality.

The time needed to prepare for sprint review should be minimal — usually no more than 20 minutes — just enough to make sure everyone knows who is doing what and when, so the demonstration goes smoothly.

REMEMBER

Work not delivered has no business value. Within the context of a single sprint, *shippable functionality* means that the development team has satisfied their definition of done for each requirement, and the product owner has verified that the work product meets all acceptance criteria and could be released, or *shipped*, to the market if the value and timing are right for the marketplace. The actual release may be at a later time, per the communicated release plan. Find out more about shippable functionality in Chapter 4 of Book 4.

For the development team to demonstrate the functionality in the sprint review, it must be complete according to the definition of done. In other words, the product increment is fully

- » Developed
- » Tested
- » Integrated
- » Documented

As user stories are moved to a status of done throughout the sprint, the product owner and development team should check that the product meets these standards as well as the user stories' acceptance criteria. This continuous validation throughout the sprint reduces end-of-sprint risks and helps the scrum team spend as little time as possible preparing for the sprint review.

Knowing the completed user stories and being ready to demonstrate those stories' functionality prepare you to confidently start the sprint review meeting.

The sprint review meeting

Sprint review meetings have three activities: Demonstrate and showcase the scrum team's finished work, allow stakeholders to provide feedback on that work, and make product adaptations based on reality and stakeholder feedback. Figure 5-2 shows the different loops of feedback a scrum team receives about a product.

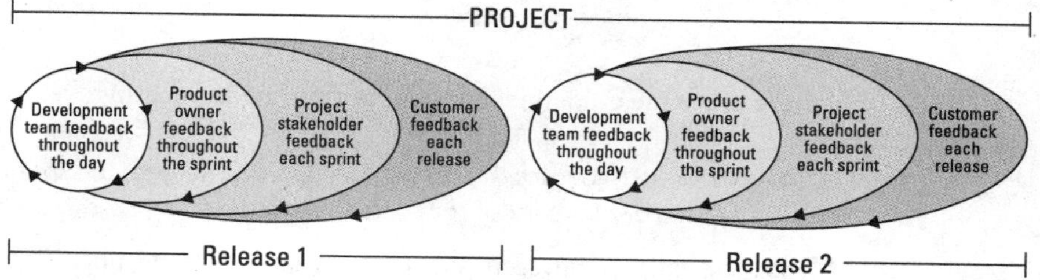

FIGURE 5-2: Agile project feedback loops.

This cycle of feedback repeats throughout the project as follows:

- Each day, development team members work together in a collaborative environment that encourages feedback through peer reviews and informal communication.
- Throughout each sprint, as soon as the development team completes each requirement, the product owner provides feedback by reviewing the working functionality for acceptance. The development team then immediately incorporates that feedback, if any, to satisfy the user story's acceptance criteria. When the story is complete, the product owner gives final acceptance of the functionality created for the user story, according to the user story's acceptance criteria.
- At the end of each sprint, project stakeholders provide feedback about completed functionality in the sprint review meeting.
- With each release, end-customers provide feedback about new working functionality.

The sprint review usually takes place later in the day on the last day of the sprint, often a Friday for a sprint that starts on a Monday. One of the rules of scrum is to spend no more than four hours in sprint review for a one-month sprint, so you usually spend no more than one hour in a sprint review meeting for every week of the sprint, as shown in Figure 5-3.

If my sprint is this long...	My sprint review meeting should last no more than...
One week	One hour
Two weeks	Two hours
Three weeks	Three hours
Four weeks	Four hours

FIGURE 5-3: Ratio of sprint review meeting to sprint length.

© John Wiley & Sons, Inc.

Here are some guidelines for your sprint review meeting:

- No slides! Show actual working functionality. Refer to the sprint backlog if you need to display a list of completed user stories.
- The entire scrum team should participate in the meeting.

- Anyone who is interested in the product may attend. The product stakeholders, the summer interns, and the CEO could all theoretically be in a sprint review. Customers may also be invited whenever available.
- The product owner introduces the release goal, the sprint goal, and the new capabilities.
- The development team demonstrates what it *completed* during the sprint. Typically, the development team showcases new features or architecture. When negative or critical feedback is given, resist the temptation to become defensive because it will discourage stakeholder feedback.

TIP

- The demonstration should be on equipment and environments as close as possible to the planned production environment. For example, if you're creating a mobile application, present the features on a smartphone — perhaps hooked up to a monitor — rather than from a simulator on a laptop.
- The stakeholders can ask questions and provide feedback on the demonstrated product increment.

WARNING

- Do not use non-disclosed rigged functionality, such as hard-coded values and other programming shortcuts that make the application look more mature than it currently is. Rigged functionality creates more work for the scrum team in future sprints, catching up to what the stakeholders think already exists. Build trust by setting accurate expectations.
- Sprint reviews are excellent opportunities to reflect with transparency on the remaining budget to help the product owner evaluate the value of the remaining backlog.

TIP

The formula AC+OC>V is helpful here for deciding when to stop or shift development. When the actual cost (AC) plus the opportunity cost (OC) of the future development is greater than the value (V), stop or shift development. Sprint reviews are great opportunities for concluding with stakeholders that future investment in the feature or product development should end.

- The product owner can lead a discussion about what is coming next based on the features just presented and new items added to the product backlog during the current sprint.

REMEMBER

By the time you get to the sprint review, the product owner has already seen the functionality for each of the user stories that will be presented and has agreed that they are complete. If the product owner does not accept a user story that the development team worked on, the story doesn't get demonstrated in the sprint review. As the product is iteratively built sprint after sprint, the sprint review is critical for ensuring alignment with the stakeholders and the product vision. Every sprint, the team should be obsessed with solving customer problems.

The sprint review meeting is valuable for the development team because they can show their work to stakeholders and customers and get their efforts acknowledged. The meeting contributes to development team morale, keeping the team motivated to accomplishing the product vision, solving customer problems, and achieving the desired business outcomes. Stakeholder confidence and trust in the development team increases as they hear them use business language during the product demonstration. (Another benefit of having stable teams is that they retain hard-earned knowledge about the customer and the business.)

TIP

Inspection is a valuable tool. The largest number of world records are broken at the Olympics. Why? Because millions of people from all over the world are watching. Sprint reviews provide a similar, albeit much smaller, stage for scrum teams. Accountability is higher because of the frequently exposed transparency of their work.

Collecting feedback in the sprint review meeting

Gather sprint review feedback informally. The product owner or scrum master can take notes on behalf of the development team, as team members often will be engaged in the presentation and resulting conversation. Capturing feedback publicly on a whiteboard, for example, validates that the feedback was given and received as intended. The transparency also prevents duplicates.

Because the sprint goal was selected based on the team's assumptions about what the customer wanted, the sprint review offers the team the opportunity to validate their assumptions with stakeholders and, even better, customers.

Keep in mind the example project used throughout Book 4: a mobile application for XYZ Bank. Stakeholders responding to functionality they saw for the XYZ Bank mobile application might have comments such as the following:

- From a person in sales or marketing: "You might want to consider letting the customers save their preferences, based on the results you showed. It will make for a more personalized experience going forward."
- From a functional director or manager: "Given what I've seen, you might be able to leverage some of the code modules that were developed for the ABC project last year. They needed to do similar data manipulation."
- From someone who works with the quality or user experience professionals in the company: "I noticed your logins were pretty straightforward. Will the application be able to handle special characters?"

New user stories may come out of the sprint review. These stories could be new features or changes to existing functionality. Both are welcome.

TIP

In the first few sprint reviews, the scrum master may need to remind stakeholders about agile principles and practices. Some people hear the word *demonstration* and immediately expect fancy slides and printouts. The scrum master can shield the scrum team by managing these expectations and helping stakeholders uphold agile values and practices.

The product owner needs to add any new user stories to the product backlog and order those stories by priority value. The product owner also adds back to the product backlog any stories scheduled for the current sprint but not completed, and reorders those items based on the most recent priorities.

The product owner needs to complete updates to the product backlog in time for the next sprint planning meeting.

When the sprint review is over, it's time for the sprint retrospective. You may want to take a brief break between the sprint review and the sprint retrospective so that scrum team members can come to the retrospective discussion fresh and relaxed. Having just completed the sprint review, the scrum team will come into the retrospective ready to inspect its processes and will have ideas for adaptation.

The Sprint Retrospective

The *sprint retrospective* is a meeting in which the product owner, development team, and scrum master discuss how the sprint went and what they can do to improve the next sprint. The scrum team should conduct this meeting in a self-directed way. If managers or supervisors attend sprint retrospectives, scrum team members will avoid being open with each other, which limits the effectiveness of the team's ability to inspect and adapt in a self-organizing way.

The team might invite others with whom they regularly interact (such as stakeholders) to participate in the sprint retrospective, but these invitations are generally an exception.

The sprint retrospective is stage 7 in the Roadmap to Value. Figure 5-4 shows how the sprint retrospective fits into agile product development.

Stage 7: SPRINT RETROSPECTIVE

Description: Team refinement of environment and processes to optimize efficiency
Owner: Scrum team
Frequency: At the end of each sprint

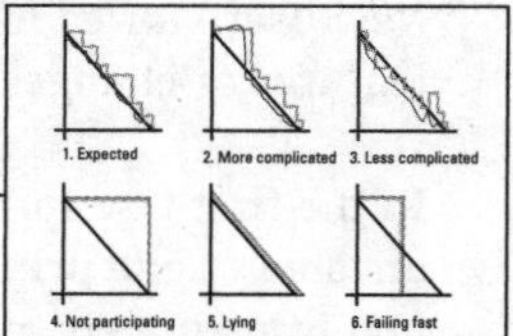

© John Wiley & Sons, Inc.

FIGURE 5-4: The sprint retrospective in the Roadmap to Value.

The goal of the sprint retrospective is to continuously improve your processes, environment, collaboration, skillsets, practices, and tools. Improving and customizing how people work together according to the needs of your scrum team increases scrum team morale, improves effectiveness in achieving desired outcomes, and increases *velocity* — work output.

However, what works for one team won't necessarily work for another team. Managers outside the scrum team should not dictate how all scrum teams should overcome their challenges and should instead allow them to find the best solutions for themselves.

Your sprint retrospective results may be unique for your scrum team. For example, members of one scrum team decided that they would like to come to work early and leave early, so they could spend summer afternoons with their families. Another team at the same organization felt that they did better work late at night and decided to come to the office in the afternoon and work into the evenings. The result for both teams was increased morale, effectiveness, and velocity.

Use the information you learn in the retrospective to review and revise your work processes and make your next sprint better.

REMEMBER

Agile approaches — particularly scrum — quickly reveal problems in projects. Scrum doesn't fix problems; it simply exposes them and provides a framework for inspecting and adapting exposed issues. Data from the sprint backlog shows exactly where the development team has been slowed down. The development team talks and collaborates. These tools and practices help reveal inefficiencies and allow the scrum team to refine practices to improve, sprint after sprint. Pay attention to what gets exposed. Don't ignore it and don't work around it.

In the following sections, you find out how to plan for a retrospective, how to run a sprint retrospective meeting, and how to use the results of each sprint retrospective to improve future sprints.

Planning for retrospectives

For the first sprint retrospective, everyone on the scrum team should think about a few key things and be ready to discuss them. What went well during the sprint and what should we keep doing more of? What would we change, and how?

TIP

Everyone on the scrum team may want to make a few notes beforehand or even take notes throughout the sprint. The scrum team could keep the roadblocks from the sprint's daily scrum meetings in mind. For the second sprint retrospective forward, you can also start to compare the current sprint with prior sprints, and track progress on the improvement efforts from sprint to sprint. Chapter 4 in Book 4 mentions saving sprint backlogs from prior sprints; this is one instance where they might come in handy.

If the scrum team has honestly and thoroughly thought about what went right and what could be better, they'll go into the sprint retrospective ready to have a useful and actionable conversation.

The retrospective meeting

The retrospective meeting is an action-oriented meeting. The scrum team immediately applies what it learned in the retrospective to the next sprint.

REMEMBER

The sprint retrospective meeting is an action-oriented meeting, not a justification meeting. If you are hearing *because* . . ., the conversation is moving away from action and toward rationale.

One of the rules of scrum is to spend no more than three hours in sprint retrospective for a one-month sprint. So you usually spend no more than 45 minutes in a sprint retrospective meeting for every week of the sprint. Figure 5-5 shows a quick reference of this timetable.

If my sprint is this long...	My sprint retrospective meeting should last no more than...
One week	45 minutes
Two weeks	1.5 hours
Three weeks	2.25 hours
Four weeks	3 hours

© John Wiley & Sons, Inc.

FIGURE 5-5: Ratio of sprint retrospective meeting to sprint length.

REMEMBER

The sprint retrospective should cover three primary questions:

- What went well during the sprint?
- What would we like to change?
- How can we implement that change?

The following areas are examples of topics for inspection:

- **Results:** Compare the amount of work planned with what the development team completed. Review the sprint or release burndown charts and what they tell the team about how they're working.
- **People:** Discuss team composition and alignment.
- **Relationships:** Talk about communication, collaboration, and how the team works together.
- **Processes:** Go over support, development, and peer review processes.
- **Tools:** How are the different tools working for the scrum team? Think about the artifacts, electronic tools, communication tools, and technical tools.
- **Productivity:** How can the team improve productivity and get the most work done in the next sprint while maintaining a sustainable pace? Remember Principle 8, "Agile processes promote sustainable development." Perhaps there are opportunities to "maximize the amount of work not done" (Principle 10) or to work smarter? (See Chapter 1 in Book 4 for more on agile principles.)

TIP

If the team works in one-week sprints, they'll have nearly 52 opportunities each year to hold a retrospective. To maintain engagement in each retrospective, many retrospective formats exist, and it's helpful for the team to have variety and to have these discussions in a structured format. Esther Derby and Diana Larsen, authors of *Agile Retrospectives: Making Good Teams Great* (Pragmatic Bookshelf, 2006), offer a great framework for sprint retrospectives that keep the team focused on discussions that will lead to real improvement:

1. **Set the stage.**

   Establishing the goals and scope for the retrospective upfront will help keep your scrum team focused on providing the right kind of feedback later in the meeting. As you progress into later sprints, you may want to have retrospectives that focus on one or two specific areas for improvement.

2. **Gather data.**

   Discuss the facts about what went well in the last sprint and what needed improvement. Create an overall picture of the sprint; consider using a white board to write down the input from meeting attendees.

3. **Generate insights.**

   Take a look at the data gathered and come up with ideas about how to make improvements for the next sprint.

4. **Decide what to do.**

   Determine — as a team — which ideas you want to put into place. Decide on specific actions you can take to make the ideas reality.

5. **Close the retrospective.**

   Reiterate your plan of action for the next sprint. Thank people for contributing. Also find ways to make the next retrospective better!

For some scrum teams, it might be difficult to open up at first. The scrum master may need to ask specific questions to start discussions. Participating in retrospectives takes practice. What matters is to encourage the scrum team to take responsibility for the sprint — to truly embrace being self-managing.

In other scrum teams, a lot of debate and discussion ensues during the retrospective. The scrum master facilitates these discussions to guide them towards the desired outcome and keeps the meeting within its allotted time.

TIP

Any action item coming out of a sprint retrospective should be added to the product backlog. All work the scrum team will do to achieve the product vision, such as features, technical debt, overhead, and improvements, should be added and prioritized in the product backlog. Scrum teams should agree to include at least one improvement item from a previous retrospective in each sprint to continuously improve how they go about the work of delivering potentially shippable functionality every sprint.

Be sure to use the results from your sprint retrospectives to inspect and adapt every sprint throughout your product development, not just when it is convenient.

Inspecting and adapting

The sprint retrospective is one of the best opportunities you have to put the ideas of inspect and adapt into action. You came up with challenges and solutions during the retrospective — don't leave those solutions behind after the meeting. Make the improvements part of your work every day.

TIP

You could record your recommendations for improvement informally. Some scrum teams post the actions identified during the retrospective meeting in the team area to ensure visibility and action on the items listed. Don't forget to add action items to the product backlog as a reminder to implement them during an upcoming sprint.

In subsequent sprint retrospective meetings, it's important to review the evaluations of the prior sprint and make sure you put the suggested improvements into place. High-performing teams have learned how to convert retrospectives into velocity acceleration.

5

A Popular Agile Approach: Running a Scrum Project

Contents at a Glance

» Structuring the product owner role

» Creating your product vision

» Implementing the scrum master role

» Following common practices

Chapter 1
The First Steps of Scrum

Scrum is simple in concept yet often difficult in application. Changing 70 years' worth of product development paradigm is challenging. Still, achieving 30 to 40 percent time-to-market increase and 30 to 70 percent cost savings are realistic. Jeff Sutherland, a co-creator of scrum, has documented 1,000 percent performance improvements by using scrum. Given that potential, it's worthwhile to get out of your comfort zone and start dealing with the organizational dysfunctions that are holding you back.

If the number-one trend in IT is converting to scrum and associated agile engineering approaches (such as eXtreme Programming), it's possible for your organization to make the transition. Many companies are making it and making it well. (It's important, though, to review the suitability factors when considering an agile approach to your project.) The process takes an open mind — something that's good for all of us. By the end of this chapter, you'll be up and running with your project and ready to take the next scrum steps.

Getting Your Scrum On

REMEMBER

Two factors come into play as you convert to scrum:

» **The nature of the project:** Any project for which you want early, empirical evidence of performance and quality can and should be done with a scrum framework.

» **The social culture within which the project resides:** Social culture is complex because people are complex. Changing processes can be easy; changing people isn't. Every person and every group of people has idiosyncrasies. As entertaining as these idiosyncrasies are at a barbecue, they can be a hurdle to overcome in teaching new project management techniques.

It's important that the organization, as well as senior leaders, are supportive of a change of project methodology. It's natural for people to resist change, and people resist to different degrees and in different ways. When people understand how the changes will benefit them directly, however, the conversion is faster and easier.

Billion-dollar companies benefit from scrum, as do everyday folks. For example, one man used scrum to plan, day by day, a recent vacation. He and his wife agreed that because scrum allowed the right combination of structure with freedom, the vacation was the best they'd ever had.

Show me the money

Consider Net Present Value 101: A dollar today is more valuable than a dollar six months from now. The biggest problem in organizations isn't the efficiency of the tactical execution teams; it's poor portfolio management. Executives fail to show the leadership necessary to make the tough prioritization calls, which results in too many projects being pushed down to a lower level of management that lacks the power to fight back.

This dysfunction is masked by stretching people across multiple projects so that each business unit gets something. Getting everything done takes considerably longer, but the managers of each project are placated by binders of documents telling them how great their products are going to be when they eventually get them. This thrashing between projects comes at a real cost.

Scrum is the opposite. You focus, you produce deliverable tangible results, and then you increment forward. The product backlog (described in detail in Chapter 2 of Book 5) forces you to be effective before worrying about efficiency. Your organization may be a billion-dollar company or a mom-and-pop store struggling to get a great idea to market. Maybe you're one of a gazillion employees, and you've been given this one project to prove yourself. In each case, disciplined prioritization, increased efficiency, and incremental tested progress can help you survive.

Because of the prioritization within scrum, you're working on the highest-value features first. You're not perfecting a third-tier widget instead of a high-value feature. You're going for the meat every time. As a result, what you produce during each sprint is what's most important, practical, and immediately desirable.

In every release, you have something that the marketplace values. That's scrum. That's showing you the money.

REMEMBER

When your back is against the wall, everyone reverts to agile techniques, whether realizing it or not. (Check out Book 4 for an introduction to these techniques.) If your company had 60 days' worth of cash left on hand, nobody would worry about whether a status report has the right cover sheet. Bureaucracy is the luxury of the financially bloated, and it's a luxury that can change overnight in today's economy.

REMEMBER

It's better to do all of something than a little bit of everything. If you wait for everything to be ready, chances are that nothing will get done. Instead, take those tangible steps of progress that you achieve through scrum, get them out to market, get feedback, and let the revenue flow in. Here's an example: A client agreed to put a product out to market with only one way for the customer to purchase it. Instead of making sure that every credit card on Earth was tied in, that PayPal was set up, and that personal checks could be processed with speed, the client decided to chance raising early funds with only one credit card payment option. The result? Between October and January, he brought in more than $1 million in sales. Now the site can process multiple credit cards, PayPal, and several other payment options — each of which was rolled out one sprint at a time *after* the product was actively generating revenue.

Fortunately, scrum is built around delivering tested, usable results early and implementing feedback often. You don't wait to see results. You see them after every sprint. Try this approach for yourself. Ask yourself or your customer, "If we had only one month to deliver value to the marketplace, what would we build, and how?" See how taking this incremental approach brings value to the forefront?

I want it now

Ever heard that? Three-year-old preschoolers aren't the only people who say it; bosses and colleagues also demand "I want it now," or you may even hear that inner voice within your own head saying it. Scrum makes it more possible to see immediate results. Scrum projects regularly see less than a 30–40 percent time-to-market. But how?

The answer is simple: Start development early and thereby end development early. You're creating shippable products from the start. You don't wait for months or years for results that may have passed their technological sell-by date. You quickly plan, create, inspect, adapt, ship, and benefit. In this process, you churn out value early and continuously.

WARNING

In science as in business, the rule isn't survival of the fittest but survival of the fastest. Whoever could crawl into safety fastest missed being snatched up by the predator. In business, innovations are released to market at exponentially increasing speeds. Brands are created and killed overnight. You simply can't afford to be late.

That's not the only reason why you want to experience increased speed to market. As you create your product backlog (the project to-do list), you order and prioritize the items. In prioritization, you take two things into consideration:

- Items with the highest value
- Items with the highest risk

Both factors get to the top of the list. These types of projects are also called *high-uncertainty projects* because they have high rates of change, uncertainty, and risk.

I'm not sure what I want

Most people don't know what they want, at least not until they interact with it. The majority of people, companies, and organizations realize what they want only when they interact with the product or service directly. The gap is the difference between waterfall (seeing it in documents) and scrum (using it).

In your Roadmap to Value, you begin with a vision of what you want your product to be. This vision acts as a beacon for your team, the way that any established destination acts as a beacon. The roadmap allows for the natural progression of decision-making, from large fuzzy generalities down to small specific operationalization of that goal. The vision provides the outer boundary of what can change. If resulting product deviates from the vision, it's a different project.

Scrum enables you to build out a successful business no matter what that business is. For example,

- Developing a website where people can order organic, allergy-specific restaurant food for home delivery
- Constructing an Alzheimer's patient residence with individual-specific, on-site monitoring; alerts; and security
- Selling Grandma's doughnut recipe that you're convinced will lead to the next Krispy Kreme

How these ideas would pan out in reality is yet to be determined. The good news is that you develop the most effective path of progress through the scrum framework. The process of tangible creation, inspection, feedback and adaptation gives you the tools to create the product that's needed.

Is that bug a problem?

Each item that the development team completes is tested and integrated to ensure that it works. The product owner is responsible for either accepting or rejecting each requirement as it's completed. In other words, if something doesn't work, it doesn't make it out of the sprint.

Issues can come up with enterprise integration, load limits, and so on after a product makes it into production, of course. But the feedback cycle is so strong during development that as soon as a defect or process inefficiency is spotted, it can be corrected. The problem is fixed in that sprint or placed back in the product backlog to be prioritized against future work.

Your company's culture

When people see the success and value of scrum, using it becomes easier. Employees discover that scrum improves communication and collaboration, creates *esprit de corps*, has a natural life cycle, develops an honest and transparent environment, and increases ownership and empowerment, all of which affects company culture in a hugely positive way.

The level of resistance to change varies from company culture to culture. The solution, as with so many things, is tangible success. (You'll find no defense against demonstrated success!) Find what the key people need — increased profits, higher product quality, faster delivery, or improved talent retention — and show them how the scrum model delivers.

In any group of people, you'll find the influencers — the ones with clout who can get change rolling. Maybe you're an influencer, or maybe someone else is. Get that person on board (which may mean going to higher management), and your job will be easier.

The Power in the Product Owner

Involvement begets commitment. You want to build a team that can move the gears of change. The key to moving the gears of change is the product owner.

The product owner's primary job is to take care of the business side of the project. This person is responsible for maximizing product value by delivering return on investment (ROI) to the organization. The product owner is one person, not a committee, and is a full-time, dedicated member of the scrum team. This person doesn't own the product but takes ownership of the business-side duties, representing the stakeholders and customers.

REMEMBER

Some of the primary responsibilities of the product owner are as follows:

- Setting the goals and vision for the product, including writing the vision statement
- Creating and maintaining the product roadmap, which is a broad view of the scope of the product and the initial product backlog
- Making in-the-moment priority and trade-off decisions
- Ensuring visibility of the product backlog
- Optimizing the work done by the development team
- Taking full ownership of and responsibility for the product backlog
- Accepting proposed requirements and ordering them by priority in the product backlog
- Setting release and sprint goals
- Determining which product backlog items go into the next sprint
- Handling business aspects of the project, including ROI and business risk, and interfacing with business stakeholders and customers
- Socialize the vision and the roadmap
- Being available throughout the day to work directly with development team members, thereby increasing efficiency through clear and immediate communication
- Accepting or rejecting work results throughout the sprint, ideally the day they are completed

It's shocking that organizations that plan to pour millions of dollars into a project say they don't have the resources for a dedicated product owner to ensure that the business and technical priorities align and that the product created is the product needed. Yet many of these organizations have a project manager to direct the project. Because the project manager role doesn't exist in scrum (relevant duties are part of the three scrum roles: the product owner, the development team, and the scrum master), the money for product owners can be taken from there.

Product owners clarify, prioritize, and set an environment for focus. They work with stakeholders, customers, and their team to define the product direction. They rank the work to be performed based on its business value. They ensure that the scrum team is effective. The product owner determines what requirements are pursued and when work shifts to those requirements — that is, what and when but not how or how much. How and how much is the responsibility of the development team.

Imagine that your passion is building something. In scrum, you'd be a member of the development team. For you, the product owner is a gift. This person excels in portfolio management because he or she is empowered to make decisions, clarify, prioritize, and fight to ensure that team members focus on one project at a time. Because of effective product owners, development team members are freed (and often self- regulating) from distractions and can spend more of their attention on getting their jobs done.

Both the product owner and the scrum master work to create the best environment possible for the development team to do the highest-quality work it can. The product owner handles and deflects business concerns and noise, and the scrum master ensures that other organizational interruptions don't affect the development team.

The abstraction layer created by the product owner and scrum master doesn't mean less business noise. It means that for the most part, the development team doesn't have to deal with the noise.

On the other hand, development team members can contact stakeholders or other team or nonteam people directly when they need clarification on something they're working on. This model of filtering prioritization but not clarification is like the membrane of a cell that's designed to let certain fluids travel in one direction but not the other.

The result is that the development team is protected from outside interferences but not hindered in their quest for knowledge. These boundaries are important and integral to the successful functioning of the development team.

Why Product Owners Love Scrum

Product owners love scrum for the following reasons:

- Development and business are aligned and held accountable as a single unit, rather than being at odds as in historical methodologies.
- Schedules and costs are empirically forecasted, and product owners have daily clarity on progress.
- After every sprint, product owners know that they'll have the highest-priority items fully functioning and shippable.

- Customer feedback is early and continuous.
- The earliest possible tangible measurement on ROI is available — that is, after every sprint (or before or during the sprint).
- Systematic support is provided for changing business needs, giving the product owner continuing flexibility to adapt to market realities.
- Product and process waste are reduced through emphasis on prioritized product development, not process artifact development (usually, documents).

REMEMBER

The product owner's number-one characteristic should be *decisiveness.* This person makes tough, pragmatic, and uncomfortable decisions every hour of every day. She needs to be able to create an environment of trust and pivot when changes are needed. The product owner must begin by doing what she thinks is right and then change based on empirical evidence. To be effective, a product owner must be empowered to make tactical decisions without escalating to upper management or senior leaders.

THE PRODUCT OWNER AGENT OPTION

In today's world, it's not always possible to have an on-site product owner. You may be headquartered in California yet running projects out of a facility in India. A controversial but workable solution is the *product owner agent* role. This role is an on-site person who is responsible for day-to-day communication and decision-making. The agent is the physical representation of the product owner, speaking and acting on behalf of the product owner, who isn't on-site.

Product owner agents aren't scrum. Although product owner agents aren't recommended as a matter of course, they've been used with success in certain situations while an organization matures. The goal is to make the role of the agent temporary, like an apprenticeship, while the person proves his ability to be a true product owner.

With the product owner agent, you're able to provide the quick clarifications and decision-making that scrum requires. Much as a real estate broker takes final responsibility for any real estate agent's decisions and actions, however, the headquartered product owner is responsible for the agent's decisions. The liability remains singular.

Rather than having one foot in each place and getting marginal results, embed a product owner on-site. The up-front cost may seem to be high, but if you consider the increased speed and quality of the result, your true project costs are lowered.

A scrum product owner's role is much different from a traditional project manager's role. Imagine telling a golfer to hit the ball 400 yards and straight into the hole and also telling him that he'll be hit with his own club if he doesn't succeed. The traditional IT world works that way. With scrum, the golfer hits the ball, assesses the results, receives feedback, and adapts to achieve the goal in the best possible way given where he is, not where he should be.

The Company Goal and Strategy: Stage 1

Vision statements aren't part of the scrum model, but vision statements are useful and widely adopted. Companies, not-for-profit organizations, and individuals often use vision statements.

TIP

Create a vision statement so that your goal is right in front of you. You want a crisp, concise, clear elevator pitch that can be conveyed during the ground-to-fourth-floor ride. It doesn't take long to create this invaluable artifact. Vision statements are so useful that they are Stage 1 in the Roadmap to Value (see Figure 1-1). Think of your vision statement as a destination with a beacon. You may have 100 ways to get to the destination, and it doesn't matter which way you take; the point is to end there. With this beacon of a statement, you always know where you're headed because you have the goal in sight. From this stable, strategic destination, you have limitless tactical flexibility.

A common agile practice.

Stage 1: VISION

Description: The goals for the product and its alignment with the company's strategy
Owner: Product owner
Frequency: At least annually

© John Wiley & Sons, Inc.

FIGURE 1-1: The vision statement is Stage 1 of the Roadmap to Value.

A vision statement is

- Internally focused, with no marketing fluff
- Fine-tuned to the goals of the marketplace and customer needs
- Strategic in nature, showing what rather than how

- Reviewed annually (for multiyear projects)
- Owned by the product owner

REMEMBER

Your vision statement must be communicated throughout the organization or group of people you're working with. Whether the team is designing a new model of sports car or planning a wedding, everyone needs to clearly understand the goal, which sets expectations and the tone of the project.

Structuring your vision

In his excellent book *Crossing the Chasm* (Collins Business Essentials), Geoffrey Moore recommends an effective method for creating your vision statement. You can use this model with first-rate results.

TIP

The entire statement should be no longer than two or three sentences. Moore recommends this model:

- For <*target customer*>
- who <*statement of the need*>
- the <*product name*>
- is a <*product category*>
- that <*product key benefit, compelling reason to buy*>
- Unlike <*primary competitive alternative*>
  - our product <*final statement of product differentiation*>

A recommendation is to add this conclusion:

- which supports our strategy to <*company strategy*>

Here are examples of what this format looks like in real life:

- Tankless water heater
  - *For* home owners *who* desire continuous hot water flow and better conservation of energy, *the* Acme Tankless Water Heater *is a* demand, point-of-use, or instantaneous water heater *that* efficiently heats water as you use it. *Unlike* tank-type water heaters, *our product* provides continuous flow at consistent temperatures with lower operating costs at 94 percent efficiency, *which supports our strategy to* provide for tomorrow's generation by reducing the waste of natural resources today.

» Hawaiian vacation

- *For* my spouse and me, *who* are stressed out of our minds, *the* Hawaii or Bust 2020 vacation *is a* spontaneous, last-minute getaway *that* will remove us from our hectic lives long enough to provide new experiences. *Unlike* family vacations or structured itineraries, *our product* provides complete flexibility without expectations, *which supports our strategy to* make the most of each moment together.

REMEMBER

The vision statement itself is functional, but the addition of business strategy is emotional. Bring purpose to your project in the form of a company strategy that makes people's lives better. It's never your company strategy to make money; it's to do something of such value that it can be monetized.

Finding the crosshair

TIP

The vision statement is created and owned by the product owner and is integral to the business side of the project. One mind, however, is just that: one mind. The product owner may own this statement, but she'll surely have better luck creating and refining it by using collective intelligence. To this end, the product owner can choose to receive input from development team members, the scrum master, external or internal stakeholders, and even users themselves. What to do with input is the product owner's choice and the product owner's responsibility.

When product owners are open to input from others, the product owner may become aware of nuances, features, and market angles that one person alone wouldn't think of. The product owner may be wise to take feedback and then carefully filter it through her own understanding of the project.

The Scrum Master

In *The New One Minute Manager* (William Morrow), Ken Blanchard and Spencer Johnson describe how some of the most effective managers who were studied lacked the technical skills that their employees had. Oddly enough, they also had a lot of time on their hands. If they couldn't do the job themselves, what were these managers good at?

The managers were able to clear the path so that their employees could get the work done, which is the role of the scrum master. Whereas product owner is a directing role, scrum master is an enabling role. The scrum master is responsible for the environment for success.

Scrum master traits

The scrum master's most important trait, after deep expertise in scrum, is clout. Diplomacy, communication skills, and ability to manage up are all good qualities, but the scrum master also needs to have the respect and clout to get difficult situations resolved. Where clout comes from — expertise, longevity, charisma, association — doesn't matter, because it works in the scrum master role.

As a servant leader, the scrum master teaches, encourages, removes tactical impediments, and most importantly, removes strategic impediments so that the tactical ones don't reappear. As with every other role, the scrum master is best full-time and solely dedicated to the scrum master job, especially with new teams, projects, and organizations.

TIP

If the product owner is the quarterback calling the plays and the development team is the running back gaining the yards, the scrum master is a blocker who clears the path. Yet they're all peers with a common goal.

WARNING

Developers who double as scrum masters and scrum masters thrashed across multiple teams throw off a team's ability to extrapolate past performance to future capability. This situation introduces availability variation and delivers inferior protection to a development team, which rarely makes sense quantitatively because a minor improvement in a scrum team's velocity (see Chapter 3 in Book 5) often has a huge effect on the bottom line.

Like every other role, the scrum master should be a full-time role, and the person who holds it should be solely dedicated to that job, especially for new teams, projects, and organizations.

REMEMBER

An ideal development team is three to nine people, so one scrum master improves the performance of up to nine people. Even a minor reduction in performance has a ninefold effect.

In addition to coaching the team on how to play scrum, the scrum master facilitates the events: sprint planning meetings, daily scrums, sprint reviews, and sprint retrospectives.

A scrum team is a bunch of intelligent, engaged people with a high degree of ownership in the work that they're doing. Put these folks in a meeting together, and the creative energy may cause them to explode — or at least go off on a lot of tangents. The scrum master's role is to focus this energy.

The scrum master's influence extends to everyone involved, including stakeholders and product owners. The scrum master is a coach to everyone because everyone needs ongoing education and smooth facilitation in scrum.

WARNING

If you're making decisions as a scrum master, you're not doing the right job. A development team will never become self-organizing if it's not making its own decisions. Scrum masters extract themselves from day-to-day decisions and create a conducive collaboration environment while shielding the team from interference.

As the scrum master shields the development team from external interference, the velocity of the team increases dramatically. Think about how well you work when the door's shut, the phone's off, and everybody's away or asleep versus when you're fielding constant interruptions from colleagues, family members, and even the dog.

Even when outside interference is kept to a minimum, because social density is higher in scrum, it's not unusual for conflict to also be higher. The pressure to get products working in short sprint windows can be wearing, so the scrum master's job entails managing conflict to the right level. Task conflict (being willing to fight for what you think is right) is healthy. Personal conflict (challenging someone personally) is not.

Scrum master as servant leader

The concept of *servant leader* dates to around 500 BCE and was developed by Lao Tzu, who is thought to be the author of the *Tao Te Ching*. Yet this concept is mentioned in every major religion and is popular in modern-day corporate leadership models. That's staying power.

The servant leader puts others first so that they can do their jobs. The leader enables people rather than presenting the solution on a silver plate. If someone says, "I'm hungry," the servant leader doesn't hand him a fish. Rather, the leader asks, "How can I help you so that you're not hungry today, tomorrow, or next year?" The scrum master helps each person build skills and find the solution that works best for that person, whether the answer lies inside or outside the project.

As a servant leader, a scrum master coaches, encourages, removes tactical impediments, and removes strategic impediments so that tactical impediments don't reappear.

Why scrum masters love scrum

Scrum masters love scrum for many reasons, including these:

- They can focus on having quantifiable impact rather than administrative responsibilities. Rising velocity has a direct tie to additional value that the scrum team can deliver.

- They coach people rather than serve as check-the-box managers.
- They get to enable people rather than direct them.
- They ask questions rather than give answers.
- They're involved with fewer meetings, and those meetings are shorter.
- They facilitate building empowered, motivated teams that think for themselves and act with authority.
- Performance accountability isn't outsourced to them (as in "Hey, Joe, what's the status of the tasks Nancy is working on?"). Instead, accountability is sourced directly to the person who's doing the work.

TIP

A good scrum master motto is "Never lunch alone." Always create and develop relationships. Influence is your currency, so make sure that you create an environment in which you can easily pick up the phone or walk to a person's desk and get results.

Common Roles Outside Scrum

Product owner and scrum master are scrum roles created by the founders of scrum and these roles integral to any scrum project. Another role is development team member (see Chapter 3 in Book 5). But like all good things, project management is evolving and growing. Scrum remains a solid framework and foundation. Some common and proven practices can add value.

The following two roles aren't scrum, but they add enormous value and clarity when approached properly. Consider adding these roles to your project; they may add value to your scrum endeavor.

Stakeholders

Stakeholders (introduced in Chapter 2 of Book 1) are people who affect or are affected by your project. Internal stakeholders are within your company or organization; they could be from the legal, sales, marketing, management, procurement, or any other division of your company. External stakeholders could be investors or users.

REMEMBER

Although scrum prescribes only scrum team members, the role of stakeholder explicitly interfaces with scrum teams; you can acknowledge this role explicitly so that you can manage it explicitly. The product owner is the business interface for the scrum team, so stakeholders should work with the development team *through* the product owner. Stakeholders may communicate directly with the development team during sprint reviews or when a development team member contacts them directly for clarification, but stakeholders generally work through the product owner.

Two roles deal with stakeholders:

- If the stakeholders are on the business side (such as customers, sales teams, or marketing), the product owner is responsible.
- If the stakeholders are on the nonbusiness side (such as vendors or contractors), the scrum master is responsible.

The key to interacting successfully with stakeholders is to recognize and leverage stakeholders' influence while shielding the development team from any interference.

Scrum mentors

Scrum is a simple framework in concept but complex in practice. The same can be said of golf. Theoretically, you use a stick to whack a motionless white ball into a hole, using the fewest strokes possible. Yet in practice, golf isn't easy. Like scrum, it's a game of nuance. Small factors make an enormous difference in performance.

The mentor, sometimes called a scrum coach, will work alongside the team to help them develop maturity in practicing scrum. The benefit of using a mentor is that mentors are outside of the normal politics and focus on getting the product out the door. They can step back and see objectively watch how the team works. They can not only identify old habits, but also put the brakes on homemade modifications to scrum that are simply ways to let an old dog do its old tricks.

You'll have the greatest ease and success with scrum if you stick to it in its truest form. A scrum mentor's job is to help team members keep good form. Like athletic coaches, they stand aside; see old, unproductive habits; and help you form new habits that make you successful.

» Turning your project into actionable-size chunks

» Managing your master to-do list

» Following common practices to expand the backlog

Chapter 2 Planning Your Project

William of Ockham, a fourteenth-century logician and Franciscan friar, was quoted as saying, "Entities should not be multiplied unnecessarily." In simpler, modern-day terms, this statement is known as Occam's Razor. (When you have two competing theories that make the same predictions, the simpler one is better.)

In other words, Keep It Simple, Smarty. You can apply this mantra again and again when managing your project with scrum.

In this chapter, you see that keeping things simple applies to a technique used to enhance scrum projects — called the product roadmap — as well as to decompose your product's features into the smallest requirements possible.

This book points out common practices that scrum trainers and coaches use successfully. Although they're optional, consider giving them a try. They might make your project transition and completion more successful.

The Product Roadmap: Stage 2

In the seven Roadmap to Value stages, you begin with the end in mind by creating your vision statement (a common agile practice that works well; see Chapter 1 in Book 5). The next step is creating a map to help you achieve that vision (see Figure 2-1).

A common agile practice outside of scrum

Stage 2: PRODUCT ROADMAP

Description: Holistic view of product features that create the product vision.
Owner: Product owner
Frequency: At least biannually

© John Wiley & Sons, Inc.

FIGURE 2-1: The product roadmap is Stage 2 in the Roadmap to Value.

Although neither the vision statement nor the product roadmap is a formal aspect of scrum, both elements are common within the agile industry.

REMEMBER

Creating a product roadmap is a common-sense way to set off on the journey and align an entire group. If you were to go on a voyage with a crew and passengers, you'd want to know your destination and most likely your route before you leave the safety of the harbor. The same holds true with almost any project. Following are the general steps in creating a roadmap:

1. Decide where you want to go (develop the vision).
2. Figure out how to get there (design the product roadmap).
3. Socialize the vision (communicate the plan).

The product roadmap can change, but it gives you something tangible to start with, thereby increasing efficiency. By socializing the roadmap as an artifact of planning or replanning, you can make sure that influencers and stakeholders understand the direction and path. Adjustments to the plan are less costly, and a shared vision contributes to team unification.

Take the long view

The product roadmap is a holistic, high-level view of the features necessary to achieve the product goal that you outlined in your vision statement. Natural project affinities are established ("If we do this, we should logically do that"), and gaps in features are made readily visible ("Hey, where is . . .?").

The product roadmap is the initial product backlog (your master to-do list), the user-centric requirements that the team maintains for product development, and as the likelihood of product backlog items being developed increases, items are increasingly broken down (progressive elaboration). The product backlog expands to include items that are

* Small (imminently developable; often referred to as user stories)
* Midsize (midrange developable; often referred to as epics)
* Conceptual (clear but lacking details; often referred to as features)

TIP

See the nearby sidebar "Roadmap and backlog terminology" for more information about features, epics, and user stories.

REMEMBER

The product roadmap isn't fixed in stone and fully paved; it's a living, fluid artifact. You can review and update these roadmaps at least twice a year, although this frequency varies depending on the individual project.

Although the vision statement is fully owned by the product owner, the development team needs to be part of the roadmap-building process. Members of the development team are the technological experts who will be doing the work, and they must provide technical constraints and effort estimates. If the development team hasn't been chosen yet, include the functional managers after you create the initial product roadmap. These managers can help identify the skills that will be necessary and get the development team assembled as quickly as possible so that the team can provide high-level effort estimates.

The business stakeholders, the product owner, the development team, and the scrum master can create the vision statement and the product roadmap on Day 1. The actual development begins on Day 2.

Use simple tools

When creating your product roadmap, use the simplest tools possible. Consider a whiteboard and sticky notes. Each product feature fits onto a sticky note. This method is simplicity in true working form.

Human brains weren't created in the digital age. Studies have proved that electronics have a dulling effect. In fact, it takes less brain-wave function to watch TV than it does to watch paint dry. Yet using a simple system like sticky notes is physically and mentally engaging, and using it fosters an environment of change and creativity.

TIP

To create a product roadmap, you can simply place sticky notes with major requirements on a wall and talk through ideas and issues. For one large project (worth almost half a billion dollars), a roadmap was put together in less than three hours. Start with the highest priority items. As you talk through the vision, stickies are simple to move as the roadmap begins to take shape.

ROADMAP AND BACKLOG TERMINOLOGY

The following terms relating to product roadmaps and product backlogs have been developed by scrum experts over the years. They aren't scrum but are part of a collection of common practices that many people use in the field:

- **Themes:** *Themes* are logical groups of the features that you create in your product roadmap. If a feature is a new capability that a customer will have, a theme is the logical grouping of these features. The functionality that enables a customer to purchase items from a website is an example of a theme. Your product roadmap usually identifies and/or groups features as part of a theme.
- **Features:** *Features* are capabilities that your customers will have that they didn't have before. The functionality that enables a customer to purchase items online via a mobile phone is a feature. Your product roadmap usually consists of feature-level requirements.
- **Epics:** *Epics,* which are a series of actions related to a feature, are the next stage in breaking features into actionable requirements. The functionality that enables a customer to purchase an item via a mobile phone from a shopping cart by using a credit card is an epic. An epic is smaller than a feature (purchasing an item online) but bigger than the credit card integrations that enable an item to be purchased.

  Note: Don't allow requirements larger than epics into a release plan because they aren't specific enough to plan.
- **User stories:** *User stories* are the smallest forms of requirements that can stand on their own. A user story consists of one action of value or one integration of value. Purchasing an item via a mobile phone from a shopping cart by using a Visa card is a user story. Purchasing an item by using a MasterCard is a different integration and a different user story. User stories are small enough to add to sprints and begin developing.
- **Tasks:** *Tasks* are the steps needed to implement a user story. During sprint planning (see Chapter 4 in Book 5), a user story is broken into tasks.

The bottom line: *Requirements* are things that users do; *tasks* are what the development team does to make the requirement work.

Create your product roadmap

You can use seven easy, common-sense steps to build your product roadmap. Perform these steps on Day 1 of your project; they should take no longer than a few hours. For smaller projects, you'll get the job done over morning coffee. The product owner completes the steps with the rest of the project team (the entire scrum team and the business stakeholders).

Using sticky notes, several colors of flags, and a whiteboard, follow these steps to build your product roadmap:

1. **Write down one product requirement per sticky note.**

   Think of as many product requirements as you can.

2. **If appropriate and synergistic, arrange some requirements in related categories or groups.**
3. **Prioritize the requirements on the roadmap.**

   At the macro level, the highest-priority items are on the left side, and the lowest-priority items are on the right side. At the micro level, the highest-priority requirements are at the top, and the lowest-priority items are at the bottom. The highest-priority items are top-left, and the lowest-priority items are bottom-right.

4. **Identify business dependencies (noted by colored flags on the sticky note).**
5. **Have the development team identify technical dependencies (noted by flags of a different color).**
6. **Have the development team provide order-of-magnitude estimates for the sticky notes.**
7. **Adjust ordering based on dependencies and estimates as appropriate.**

TIP

Note the items that prompt the most discussion or concern from the team; these items may be the riskiest or require further breakdown. For estimation methods that your development team can use, check out Chapter 3 in Book 5.

Set your time frame

The nature of your product determines the quantity and timing of your product releases. Consider a minimum of once per quarter, but the pace of innovation is increasing product releases. Some companies push to production every day. The most successful social media and Internet firms push twice a day or more.

Ideally, you want to release tested, approved product after every sprint or, better, several times during a sprint (continuous delivery). Some companies create high-level product releases (for framing the requirements, not for timeline commitment) so that they can see how those releases align with other product releases, budgetary cycles, holiday cycles, and so on.

Figure 2-2 shows an example of quarterly product releases (common with publicly traded companies). The first release reflects initial release planning and has a level of commitment assigned to it. Everything after that shows how outside influences may affect the project.

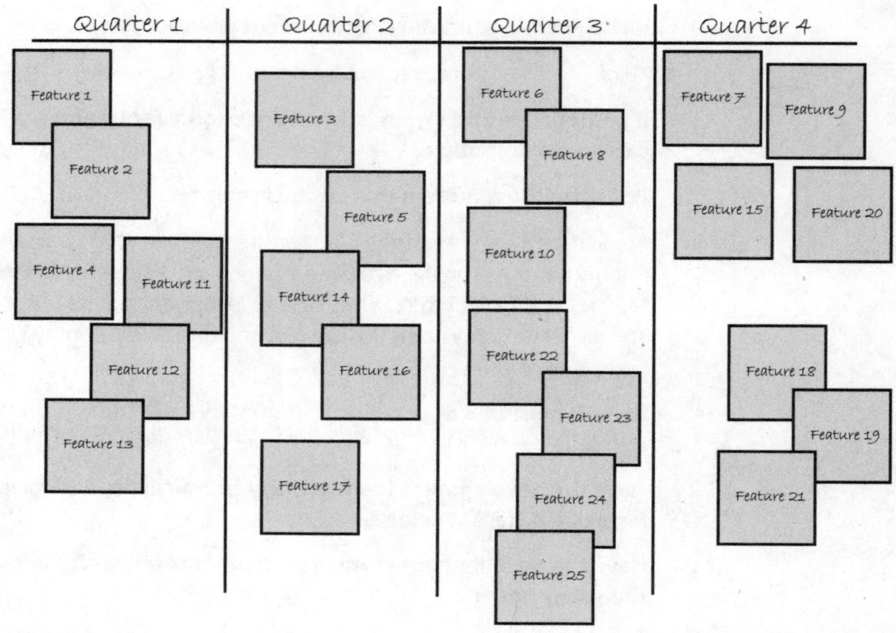

FIGURE 2-2: An example product roadmap broken down by quarters.

© John Wiley & Sons, Inc.

If your time frame is shorter or isn't relevant to your project, consider what your project's time frame is and break it into the initial logical groups, going no further out than necessary (usually, no more than a year). Follow these steps:

1. **Create the initial groups' worth of features, starting with the highest-priority requirements and moving down.**
2. **Assume at each product release that you will deliver tested, approved, shippable results.**
3. **Above each release, write its conceptual theme.**
4. **Adjust as necessary.**

TIP

The product roadmap and product backlog are excellent for scope control. In traditional project management models, every new idea has to be justified. With scrum, if an idea brings you closer to the project vision, add it to the list. The idea's level of prioritization determines whether it gets completed. Sometimes, only the highest-priority items get done; at other times, every requirement gets done, depending on the budget and the organizational drag on the scrum team.

Breaking Down Requirements

It won't take you long to notice that one product requirement can be decomposed into several pieces. Chances are that those pieces can be broken down further, and those pieces, you may be willing to bet, can be peeled apart too. This section explains how to manage this decomposition process.

Prioritization of requirements

With the product roadmap, you begin with the largest pieces of your project. This roadmap truly provides an eagle's-eye view and is based on what makes sense according to business value and/or risk elimination. These pieces (requirements) are prioritized by the product owner, who decides what is most important to get to that customer first and which requirements logically belong together.

As requirements are prioritized and aligned, they become part of the product backlog. In scrum, you work on the smallest set of highest-value items necessary to generate value, not just anything scoped for the project, which is why scrum projects release functionality faster.

Take two things into consideration as you prioritize: business value and risk. Business value is easy. If a thing has high value, it has high priority. You want to take on the highest-risk requirements first, for four reasons:

- At the beginning, you have the simplest system to work with. You want to take on your highest-risk developments within the simplest system.
- You have the greatest amount of money at the beginning. If you're going to take on something that involves high risk, you should do so with the greatest resources at your disposal.
- Because you have the greatest amount of money, you can fund the development team for the longest time. If you're going to take on a high-risk item, do so with the benefit of the longest runway possible.

» If you're going to fail, fail early and cheap. If a fundamental flaw exists, you want to know as early as possible. The highest-risk requirements are where the land mines are lurking.

Working with the highest-priority value requirements to completion isn't just convenient, but also saves money and is why scrum projects can come in at a 30–70 percent cost savings. If your project runs out of money 80 percent of the way through, you can say without a doubt that you have 80 percent of the highest-priority items completed, functioning, and accepted. The remaining 20 percent? If they were such a low priority, many times you can live without them anyway.

The product roadmap creates your first cut of dependencies. For example, you don't need to worry about having functionality to submit application functionality until you have a website to house that functionality. Critical dependencies are revealed early and help the product owner prioritize the product backlog. Teams begin working on the highest-priority items on Day 2, not Day 120.

REMEMBER

A requirement must earn the right of your investment. Only the highest-priority (value) items deserve your effort to break them into digestible requirements. Everything else can wait. This way, you're always working on only the most important things. Don't waste your time trying to boil the ocean. Learning and adapting is valuable even while building requirements.

Levels of decomposition

In decomposing your requirements into smaller pieces, you want to capture as little detail as possible. In fact, you should become expert in doing the bare minimum, progressively elaborating requirements as the likelihood of bringing them into a sprint grows. Gone are the days of spending endless hours working on defining and refining requirements that never see the light of day. Figure 2-3 depicts the layers of requirement decomposition.

Seven steps of requirement building

Seven steps are involved in building the scope of each requirement. At the end of the seven steps, you know that each requirement works, can be integrated, and has been approved by the product owner. You're tangibly building products to showcase to stakeholders from whom you can garner feedback. This feedback is then used to refine and create new requirements that make the product better reflect stakeholder needs, and the cycle is run again. You incrementally improve the product based on reality.

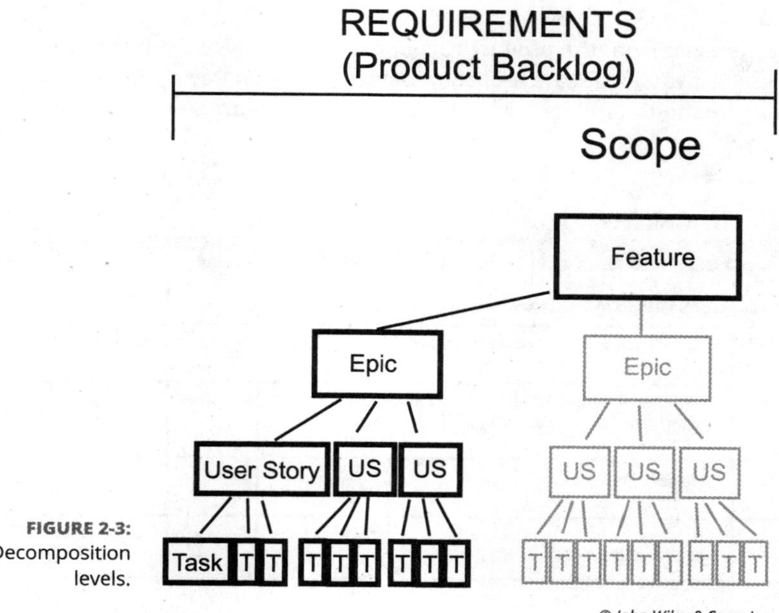

FIGURE 2-3: Decomposition levels.

© John Wiley & Sons, Inc.

The seven steps for building each requirement are

1. Requirement elaboration
2. Design
3. Development
4. Comprehensive testing
5. Integration
6. Documentation
7. Approval

Your Product Backlog

The product backlog is a true scrum artifact and the master to-do list for the entire project. It's also the user-centric requirements that the team maintains for product development. All scrum projects have product backlogs, which are owned and maintained by the product owner and the team.

The requirements from the product roadmap initially create the product backlog, and the highest value ones are broken into user stories on Day 1. (You find out how in the later section "Product backlog refinement.") Figure 2-4 depicts a sample product backlog.

PRODUCT BACKLOG

Order	ID	Item	Type	Status	Estimate
1	121	As an Administrator, I want to link accounts to profiles, so that customers can access new accounts.	Requirement	Not Started	5
2	113	Update requirements traceability matrix	Overhead	Not Started	2
3	403	As a Customer, I want to transfer money between my active accounts, so that I can adjust each account's balance.	Improvement	Not Started	3
4	97	Refactor Login Class	Maintenance	Not Started	8
5	68	As a Site Visitor, I want to find locations, so that I can use bank services.	Requirement	Not Started	8

© John Wiley & Sons, Inc.

FIGURE 2-4: The product backlog is your project's ordered to-do list.

Each item in the product backlog has the following elements:

REMEMBER

- Specific order number (priority slot in the product backlog)

  Although product backlog items may be similar in priority, they can't be worked on at the same time.
- Description
- Estimate of the effort required to complete
- ID number (optional)
- Status (optional)
- Value to the business or product
- Type of item (optional), which could be a requirement, overhead, maintenance, or improvement (see the later section "The dynamic to-do list")

REMEMBER

Highest value requirements get broken into the smallest actionable requirements possible in the product backlog. A small requirement, however, isn't automatically a high-priority item. Many small requirements have low priority and never see production.

REMEMBER

Anyone can write a product feature or requirement. An idea or concern can be sparked by a business stakeholder, a member of the development team, the scrum master, the product owner, and even the company barista. Ideas are expected from everyone. Only the product owner has the power to accept or reject a requirement into the product backlog, based on whether it supports the vision for the product. The product owner is the full owner of this artifact. If accepted, they will then number, refine, prioritize, and order that new requirement.

The dynamic to-do list

The product backlog never goes away while the project is active. If you have a project, you have a product backlog, which is always changing. As larger requirements are broken into smaller requirements, the backlog changes. As client feedback is received, the backlog changes. As your competitors bring new offerings to market, the backlog changes.

The product owner not only prioritizes items in the product backlog but also orders them in a logical sequence. This way, the next sprint can be quickly and efficiently organized from these ordered items.

All changes made in the product backlog are made by the product owner with input from the product team. At any point, if anyone (product owner, developer, stakeholder) identifies a new requirement or design idea, it's given to the product owner to be prioritized along with everything else.

REMEMBER

In traditional project management frameworks, change is viewed as a reflection of poor planning. If something had to be changed, it was because someone messed up. In scrum, change is a sign of growth. As you discover your product more deeply, you will identify changes that need to be made. In scrum, if you're not changing, your product s not evolving, and that's a problem. It's a lack of change that is a sign of failure. Every day you need to learn something and that causes change. With scrum, change is no longer something you crawl under your desk and hide from. Change is good. Change is life. Change is scrum.

Product backlog refinement

Product backlog refinement is how the scrum team advances its understanding of the items in the product backlog and prepares them for upcoming sprints. Product backlog refinement is a continuous process of breaking down and preparing feedback and responses to change for future development. This process is owned by the product owner and performed with the help of development team members, who ask clarifying questions and provide estimates based on the best information available at that time. The scrum team as a whole spends up to 10 percent of its active sprint time in this process. The scrum master usually facilitates product backlog refinement activities to keep the group focused and on task.

The target outcomes of product backlog refinement are

- **Clarity:** All developers and the product owner reach a clear consensus on the scope of the product backlog items being discussed.
- **Acceptance criteria:** All requirements (backlog items) include sufficient acceptance criteria. Acceptance criteria is a term frequently used in scrum practices. It refers to a section on the back of the story card or in project software to communicate to everyone what "done" means for each story. It may include testing criteria and specific examples of how the feature is expected to function when the work is complete.
- **Risks identified and mitigated to the best extent possible:** Other known risks should be documented and accepted by the team as necessary.
- **Sizing:** Requirements are estimated and broken down sufficiently to be accomplished within a sprint.

Backlog refinement should be a regular occurrence, but scrum doesn't prescribe how formal or frequent refinement discussions should be; neither does it prescribe an agenda. Here are suggestions that have worked well:

- **Format:** The product owner presents one requirement to the team at a time. For each requirement, team members ask questions, challenge assumptions, explore implementation strategies, and use a whiteboard for drawing and clarification until they have consensus on the details and scope of the requirement. Then the development team uses estimation poker or affinity estimating (see Chapter 3 in Book 5) to assign a relative estimation.

  For a requirement that moves up in priority, the estimation indicates when the requirement is small enough to fit into a sprint.
- **Time:** Scrum teams on average spend about 10 percent of a sprint in refining the backlog in preparation for the next sprint.
- **Frequency:** Backlog refinement is a progressive activity. Requirements get refined gradually, just in time, with those closer to delivery being made ready for sprints. Teams may prefer conducting backlog refinement on one of these schedules:

- Daily, at the end of each day

  This schedule also acts as a demobilization exercise for development team members to transition into going home for the day.
- Daily, at some other agreed-on time
- Once per sprint during a regularly scheduled block of time
- Once per week during a regularly scheduled block of time
- Multiple times per week during a regularly scheduled block of time
- As needed, determined, and scheduled by the team in each sprint

» **Activities:** Backlog refinement activities may consist of the following types of activities:

- Entire team discussions, including whiteboarding, modeling, question-and-answer sessions, and design discussions
- Research of items identified during team discussions
- Interviews of subject-matter experts or stakeholders to gain insights for determining scope and suggested solutions to requirements
- Estimation poker or affinity estimation sessions

As the team discusses and refines the next-highest-priority requirement candidates, use as many of the following questions and guidelines as needed to guide the team through the refinement process. Not all these items apply to every team and/or requirement.

» Breaking down large requirements

- Does the user story satisfy the INVEST criteria (see the nearby sidebar "INVEST" for details)?
- Can the requirement be completed within one sprint or part of one sprint?
- Is the user story a single action of value or a series of actions?
- Is the scope barely sufficient?
- Has the product owner added technical tasks or other technical details that should be left to the development team to determine?
- Has the scrum team's definition of *done* (see Chapter 3 in Book 5) been considered before determining that the story is sufficiently broken down?
- Is more research required before the team can estimate?

- Clarifying and refining where needed
  - Does the development team understand the business intent and/or value of the requirement?
  - Have development team members tried paraphrasing the requirement to make sure that everyone is on the same page?
  - Is the desired deliverable clear?
  - Does an implementation approach make sense from both technical and business perspectives?
  - Is the team considering all the work needed to fully complete and deliver the story?
  - Does the team know the tasks that will be required?
  - Will the team be able to deliver a fully done increment of the product at the end of this sprint?
- Ensuring adequate acceptance criteria
  - If needed, have personas been identified (see the later section "Product Backlog Common Practices")?
  - Are the acceptance criteria complete and adequate?
  - Have test-oriented development team members stated that the criteria are sufficient?
- Addressing potential issues and risks
  - Can the story stand alone, or are there dependencies?
  - What conflicts may arise during implementation?
  - What technical debt might this requirement introduce?
- Assigning high-level estimates
  - Has the scrum team decided on a consistent estimation method (see Chapter 3 in Book 5)?
  - Has the team agreed on how to reach consensus?
  - Have estimations revealed that any of the requirements are still too big?

If estimations bring up additional points that need clarification, use these guidelines to further refine them before reestimating.

INVEST

Bill Wake, an early influencer in the eXtreme Programming (XP) movement, the INVEST mnemonic for user stories. INVEST is an acronym for qualities that you want to look for in your user stories:

- **Independent** (to the best degree possible): The story doesn't need other stories to implement it or for the user to interact with it.
- **Negotiable:** The product owner and the development team must discuss and expand on the story's nuances and details. The value of a user story is in the conversation, not the card.
- **Valuable:** The story shows product value to the customer, not the technical steps (tasks) that the developer uses to enable the story.
- **Estimable:** The story is refined enough for developers to estimate the amount of effort required to create the functionality.
- **Small:** Smaller stories are easier to estimate. A rule of thumb is to bring six to ten user stories into each sprint, so a story should be able to be finished by one or two people during the sprint.
- **Testable:** The story needs to be testable so that the development team knows that the story has been done correctly. "It needs to be fast" or "It needs to be intuitive" isn't testable. "I need to get a response from the application in less than a second" or "I need to complete the action in three clicks or less" is testable.

REMEMBER

You need to watch a few factors in this process:

- Only development team members estimate requirements because they're the ones doing the work.
- The product owner provides immediate clarifications to developers' questions by being actively involved in the refinement discussions.
- The frequency and duration of refinement activities will vary from team to team, from project to project, and even from sprint to sprint.

Other possible backlog items

When you're building your product backlog, you're encouraged to identify a type of backlog item (refer to Figure 2-4 earlier in this chapter).

Here are four types to clarify the nature of the item to be completed. All these items can be done (or not done) at the product owner's discretion:

- **Requirement:** Basic business requirements make up the bulk of a product backlog. A requirement explains why a feature is being built and what needs to be done.
- **Maintenance:** Design improvements for the code, such as fundamentally rethinking a login class that can't be tactically tweaked anymore. Maintenance items reduce the technical debt of the project.
- **Improvements:** Based on results from the sprint retrospective, what can be done differently in the process, such as expand automated testing skills.
- **Overhead:** Companies often have overhead items that they like to see, such as a requirement traceability matrix, and most companies don't add the matrix into the equation. They assume that it's free, but it costs time and money. You should make that cost obvious.

Product Backlog Common Practices

Agile techniques are practiced by thousands of companies and organizations throughout the world. As a natural result, common agile practices abound. You should incorporate some of these practices into your work and discard others. No set of universal best practices exists.

User stories

User stories are used to gather customer requirements. *User story* is a common term for requirements small enough to be brought into a sprint and broken into tasks. User stories are one action of value that a user will achieve, such as "As a shopper, I want to be able to scan a product bar code with my phone so that I can compare and find the lowest price of the same product at multiple stores."

Multiple user stories go into every sprint, and each are highest value at that time. On average, you may have six to ten user stories per sprint. Therefore, at the end of each sprint, if the development team concentrates on completing one requirement at a time (a process called *swarming*, described in Chapter 5 of Book 5), you always have something to show for your work.

You can use 3x5 index cards to write user stories. Even with these small cards, in a Card ⇨ Conversation ⇨ Confirmation model, you get rich requirement clarity before development starts. User stories aren't the only way to describe what needs to be done, but they can be incredibly effective. Figure 2-5 shows example index-card user stories.

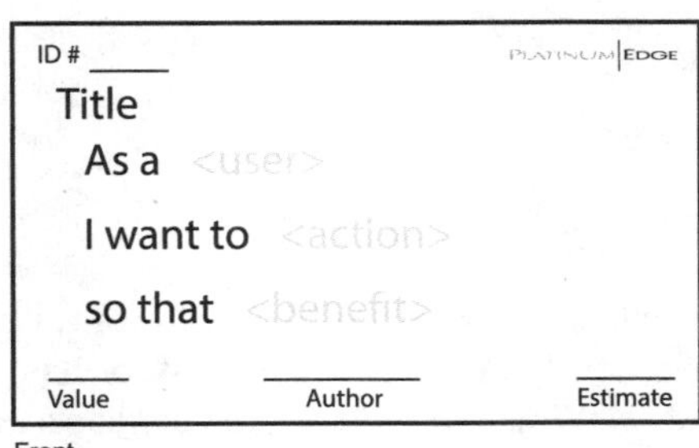

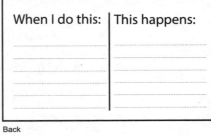

FIGURE 2-5: A format for writing user stories.

© John Wiley & Sons, Inc.

TIP

Don't use technical jargon in your user stories. You're writing them with the user in mind. Keep them direct, customer-focused, and simple.

In the Card ⇨ Conversation ⇨ Confirmation model, the product owner uses the 3x5 card as a reminder of the requirement — a reminder that a conversation must take place to refine and clarify it. This model enables the immensely valuable activity of conversing with development team members and answering their questions, supported by an explicit description of what success looks like on the back of the card.

Sometimes, it's easiest to work with *personas:* fictional characters who are amalgams of the target qualities of your clients. A persona might be a 35-year-old single male, professionally employed, who lives in Portland, Oregon, and is looking for his future significant other. Use a persona to ensure that your project meets your target customer's needs.

A user story description is simple yet focused, clearly describing the user, the action, and the benefit. On each card, enter the following lines:

- An ID number that's the same as in the product backlog and that's assigned by the product owner when she accepts an item into the product backlog

TIP

Keep your product ID numbers simple. You don't need to be able to track every item back to its more generic origin; you just need to give it a numerical name, like 123, not like 10.8.A.14. You minimize the amount of work you do by ridding your project of time-wasters so that you can focus on the important things.

- A shorthand title
- A description of the user
- What the user wants to accomplish
- The reason the user wants to accomplish the task

Critical to the user story is what's written on the flip side of the card — the acceptance criteria. This is how you know that the user story has been successfully implemented. It's phrased as "When I do this. . . this happens." Figure 2-6 shows an example of a completed card.

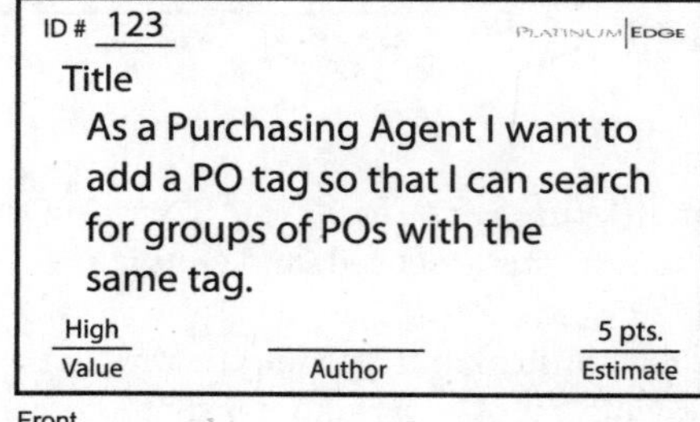

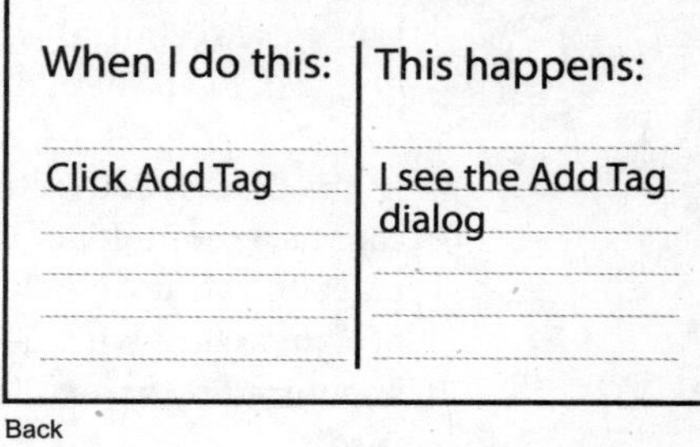

FIGURE 2-6: A completed index card.

© John Wiley & Sons, Inc.

TIP

Each user story is written in the first-person point of view ("When *I* do this, *I* get this"). First person puts the author in the shoes of the user or customer.

The person who writes the user story gives it to the product owner to share with the development team. Often, the stakeholder also participates in the conversation phase, sitting down with the product owner and development team to go over every card. This act of direct communication is vital to a thorough understanding of the tasks necessary to achieve the result desired. As a result, communication is clearer and mistakes are fewer, and project quality and delivery speed increase.

Further refinement

Development team effort determines whether a requirement needs to be broken down further to progress to the product roadmap, into the release plan, or into the sprint (see Chapter 4 in Book 5 for details). Especially at the beginning, as you find out how to apply user stories within your scrum framework, you may find that the ones you write are too big to fit into a sprint.

Although most user stories have multiple steps, some are bigger than practical and can (and should) be broken into more granular requirements. This process is part of the discovery process and part of the benefit of using user stories.

You may find additional requirements that need to be placed in the product backlog during the user-story elaboration discussion. Excellent! These discoveries help you gain deeper understanding of what the customer and/or user need.

- Excelling at backlog estimation
- Defining done
- Benefiting from estimation techniques

Chapter 3
The Talent and the Timing

The development team sits at the core of scrum projects. The primary focus of the product owner and the scrum master revolves around making sure that the environment is as ideal as possible for the development team to reach maximum productivity. In this chapter, you find out how a development team is organized and therefore able to best contribute to the scrum team.

After you have your team roles, vision, and roadmap in place, the next step is to begin to estimate the amount of work for each requirement. The development team begins by estimating the effort involved in high-level requirements. Here, you create a starting point for future reference. You establish the numerator (product backlog total)/denominator (average velocity) relationship that gives you the estimated number of sprints necessary to complete all, or a target portion of, items in the product backlog. This chapter shows you how these high-level estimates can be achieved quickly and accurately.

The Development Team

In Hollywood, actors and singers are referred to as "the talent." They're the ones who get on stage and do the job. Everyone else facilitates this process, because when the talent is successful, everyone is successful. Think of the development team as the talent. Retaining that talent as one of the byproducts of a good scrum implementation.

The development team is the talent responsible for creating and developing the actual product. They drive the how and the how much. In other words, they determine how they will develop the requirements and how many they can do in any one sprint. They are dedicated to one project at a time, cross-functional, self-organizing, and self-managing.

REMEMBER

The development team is intentionally size-limited to around six members, plus or minus three. Optimal development team size is small enough to remain nimble and large enough to complete significant work within a sprint. This size allows for a self-sufficient and self-organizing group with a diversity of skills, yet it's not too big and unwieldy. Keep in mind that for each new member, the lines of communication increase geometrically. With more than nine development team members, you can't have a self-organizing team. Under a waterfall model, this issue is masked with a project manager, who is responsible for coordinating all the communication. Scrum doesn't have the overhead cost of too many lines of communication or a project manager.

Although six people, plus or minus three, is a manageable and efficient size, the key factor is self-encapsulation. Is the team able to elaborate the requirements, design them, develop them, test them, integrate them, document them, and have them approved? Have single points of failure been eliminated (that is, at least two people can do any one skill)? Is the total size no more than nine people? If all three answers are yes, you have a good-size, cross-functional development team. Whereas a product owner must be decisive and a scrum master must have clout, a development team member must be versatile, intellectually curious, and predisposed to sharing. No prima donnas are allowed. Development team members' fires are lit with building and creating.

The uniqueness of scrum development teams

In many ways, the scrum development team is the opposite of a traditional team. In scrum, development team members are going to develop cross-functional skills. They're part of the goal-setting process, and, as a team, they have complete control of how they do their development. Additionally, credit is taken as a team.

Dedicated teams and cross-functionality

As mentioned previously, development team members are dedicated to one project at a time. Not making your development team switch back and forth between projects, which is known as *thrashing*. You want them to focus each day on the current sprint's goal. Whether functional management chooses the team members or someone else does, a diversity of skills is sought after so the team has all the skills they need to be successful (they're self-encapsulated). This leads us to the next point: cross-functionality.

REMEMBER

People don't necessarily start out being cross-functional; they grow into this state. Start with a team of diverse talents and then organically build that team toward being individually cross-functional. Ideally, you want every developer to be able to do everything. This isn't always possible, but you at least want every developer to be able to do more than one thing and for every skill to have more than one person. Becoming cross-functional is a process, but it prevents bottlenecks in work delivery.

Whatever your business or organization, the facts remain: People go on vacation; they get sick; they take on new roles and jobs. One day, they're there next to you, and the next day, they might be somewhere else. In traditional projects, when a key development team member goes on vacation, the project goes on vacation. You're forced into delays as you wait for that person to return or (in the case of attrition) until you recruit and mobilize another person.

In scrum, you strive for cross-functionality in your development team. In this way, you eliminate that single point of failure. If one development team member comes down with the flu or is deeply involved in another task, someone else can take his place and get the job done. Cross-functionality also has these benefits:

- It allows for diverse input on development for optimal solutions.
- It enables pair development (which is described later in this section) to ensure higher quality.
- It's one of the best ways to increase your primary skill. Learning an associative skill exposes you to other ways of thinking about your primary skill.
- It allows people to work on various things and keeps the work interesting.
- It can produce high-quality work delivered in the shortest amount of time without external dependencies.

TIP

Several ways exist to create cross-functional individuals from cross-functional teams:

- **Don't use titles.** Encourage an equal playing field. Doing so stimulates junior developers to get up to speed faster, and senior-level skills increase because senior people don't want to be outdone by young, hungry talent. A lack of titles also emphasizes skills over a fixed hierarchy, thereby encouraging skill development. Informal status still exists, but now it's based on skills.
- **Do use pair programming.** Commonly used in software development practices such as Extreme Programming, pair programming can be used by a development team to develop any type of product. Two developers work together on the same piece of functionality. Developer A is tactically developing (cutting code, for example), while Developer B is free to think strategically about the functionality (scalability, extensibility, risks, and so on). They switch these roles throughout the day. Because these developers are working so tightly together, they can quickly catch errors. Developers stay more on task and make fewer errors as they're pair programming, and the result is an overall shorter timeline.
- **Do use shadowing.** Again, two developers are working together, but in this case, only one does the work while the other watches and learns.

  Shadowing also increases product quality. Note that visibility and performance are correlated: Increase visibility, and you generally increase performance. The working developer doesn't want to take a lazy shortcut in front of the learning one, and the learning one will ask those smart "dumb questions." Explaining something improves your own knowledge of it, and vocalizing something uses a different part of your brain and improves functioning. Finally, ownership is reinforced if you're teaching and explaining.

Self-organizing and self-managing

The key word is *ownership.* Self-organizing and self-managing teams develop ownership in what they do. With a scrum development team, whole team ownership is part of what creates such efficiency and success.

Think of this example: How can you be assured that a professional sports team will give 100 percent? The answer is that the team gives 100 percent because they would lose if they didn't. The visibility and acknowledgment of their hard work increases drive.

REMEMBER

Visibility and performance are directly correlated. Increase performance by increasing visibility.

One technique sometimes used is to have two (or more) development teams. Synchronize their sprints so that the sprint reviews happen at the same time on the same day. Then invite an executive to come to both sprint reviews randomly for a few minutes and have her ask at least one question before leaving. Each development team knows that its performance will have executive visibility, and all teams want to look good. Historically, they may not have been given credit for the work they did. Now they can produce a product that they can be proud of. They're on stage, getting all the credit. This is hugely motivating and increases drive and buy-in.

Ownership and, therefore, accountability are increased in a scrum development team in the following ways:

- The development team is directly accountable for the deliverables that they create. This isn't always easy on them because visibility brings intrinsic pressure to perform, but this visibility also creates ownership.
- Cross-functionality creates ownership because there isn't any "my job" versus "your job." Everything is our job.
- Because the whole scrum team is held accountable, individual performance is increased. Everyone wins as a team, and everyone contributes to the success of every sprint.
- The development team actively participates in creating the sprint goals and demonstrating the working functionality during the sprint review.
- The development team is responsible for tactical status reporting every single day. In less than one minute of administration per day (see the burndown charts in Chapter 4 of Book 5), the organization gets a level of tactical status reporting that it's never had before.

WARNING

Development teams perform best when they're stable. Feed them projects and give them what they need to do their best possible work. Every time you switch members on your team, it takes time to stabilize again. Protect your development team to nurture good dynamics.

Cognitive consistency theory describes humans' tendency to seek out information, beliefs, and stimuli that are consistent with current beliefs and attitudes. In scrum, if development team members have a voice, and if they have buy-in and control, they strive harder to achieve their work-related goals. They try to find consistency between the ownership that they created and their future output.

Co-locating or the nearest thing

Many people have forgotten what it's like to work with a co-located team and to experience the increased production involved. Most people appreciate the concept but may not understand the underlying principles. Here are a few benefits of a co-located team:

- Increased speed and effectiveness of face-to-face communication, especially through kinetics, voice tonality, facial expressions, and so on.

  The value of face-to-face communication shouldn't be underestimated. Albert Mehrabian, PhD, and professor emeritus of psychology at the University of California-Los Angeles, proved the following:

  - 55 percent of meaning is conveyed through body language and facial expressions.
  - 38 percent of meaning is *paralinguistic* (conveyed by the way we speak).
  - 7 percent of meaning is conveyed in the actual words spoken.

  These statistics alone are a whopping case for co-locating your development team.

- Ease of using simple tools for planning and communicating, such as whiteboards and sticky notes.
- Ease in immediate clarification of questions.
- Understanding what other members are working on.
- Ease in supporting other team members in their tasks.
- Cost savings due to decreased lag times and fewer misunderstandings that lead to defects or wasted work.

When co-located, your product owner and development team have access to each other all day every day. All sort of banality is exchanged, and it's tempting to think that this might be wasteful. However, it's during these exchanges when the really good work gets done. Little things aren't actually little; they're differentiators, and they're the things that matter. Quality needs input, and input needs access. When access is high, great things are possible.

Sometimes, outsourcing is the only viable solution for your company or organization. If this is the case, do it with both feet. Co-locate the entire scrum team. Your development team needs an available product owner, so send one to the outsourcing location to work directly with the remote scrum team. Or develop a local product owner, even if he has to start as a product owner agent (see Chapter 1 in Book 5). The increase in quality and efficiency far outweighs the cost of the product owner.

Getting the Edge on Backlog Estimation

In the product roadmap stage, the development team does a high-level estimate of the amount of work entailed in the project. The practical value of this estimation process doesn't come into play until the sprints start (see Chapter 4 in Book 5), but this initial estimation sets a mark from which future estimates may be calculated. The development team does the estimating because only the people who do the work should be estimating the effort of the work. The backlog is the list of work presented in story form for the team. The stories are developed in iterations.

REMEMBER

These backlog estimation techniques aren't requirements of scrum. They're common practices that scrum practitioners have found useful in the field.

The product roadmap is the start of the product backlog. What's on your roadmap is what you will begin developing. So how do you take all those items on your product backlog and with any degree of accuracy estimate the work involved? A few common practices are used depending on the situation. Before you look at these estimating techniques individually, it's important to understand what you're trying to achieve.

Your Definition of Done

If you ask the members of a scrum team what they expect to see when a requirement is done, you get as many answers as there are team members. So before starting a project, scrum teams define what done means with a definition of done. Until you have consensus on this definition, estimations will be based on bad data.

As described in Chapter 2 of Book 5, for each requirement within a sprint, you complete the following stages of development:

- Requirement elaboration
- Design
- Development
- Comprehensive testing
- Integration
- Documentation
- Approval

This definition of done needs to be specific, refined, and focused on what it means to do these things to completion to achieve the level of quality that you're striving for in your project. Consider which environment the product or service needs to work within and at what level of integration to be considered done. "Works in the development environment," for example, is probably a bad, loose definition of done.

Consider these four factors in your definition of done:

- **Developed:** The product has been fully developed by the development team.
- **Tested:** The development team fully tested the product to make sure that it functions in the required environment without any glitches.
- **Integrated:** The product has been fully integrated within the product as a whole and any related systems.
- **Documented:** The development team created whatever documentation is needed. Just remember that the goal with all things agile is "barely sufficient."

TIP

When you've come up with your definition of done, write it out on a white poster board and tape it on the wall. You'll always have it right in front of the development team and product owner. You can call it *in-your-face documentation*. No cover sheet, no table of contents — simply the lowest-fidelity way that communicates and makes the information the most visible.

In your definition of done, consider not only the development but also the depth of testing and documentation that you might need. You might consider which tests must pass the following:

- Unit
- Functional/system
- Performance/load
- Security
- User acceptance

Also consider what documentation you need:

- Technical
- User
- Maintenance

Each of these testing and documentation points may differ between the sprint level and the release level, though the sprint-level definition of done should include everything necessary to release. You also may have organizationally specific items that you want to include. It's your choice. The point is to have a clear definition of done that's defined by the scrum team for all to work by.

REMEMBER

A *release* occurs when a set of marketable features is released outside the scrum team. This could happen several times during a sprint, at the end of each sprint, or after a series of sprints. These requirements may be released into the market and to the users, or they may go to internal or external stakeholders for real-world use and feedback.

TIP

A regular sprint entails completing the development, testing, documentation, and approval of items in the sprint backlog. However, before you do a product release, other activities may be needed (such as performance and load testing) that the development team wouldn't have access to in a regular sprint. Therefore, sometimes scrum teams have a release sprint just before the release itself to allow these additional tests to be addressed. The key is at the end of every sprint, the requirements must work and be demonstrable. You can test and tune for scale in the release sprint, but the requirements must work every sprint.

Common Practices for Estimating

Estimating the effort involved in developing product backlog requirements is an ongoing process. (Chapter 2 in Book 5 discusses product backlog refinement.) For example, you could do estimations for 30 minutes at 5 every evening before team members go home. This way, at the end of the week, you've covered lots of ground and will be ready for each sprint start. Some teams don't like to develop on Friday afternoon and do product backlog refinement then.

Teams are likely to refine their estimates at three levels as part of the process of breaking the requirements down for sprint-level execution. Depending on your product, you may include more. Your estimate refinement usually goes in this order:

1. Product roadmap
2. Release planning
3. Sprint planning

REMEMBER

The development team is responsible for estimating the effort required to fully build the requirements. The scrum master can facilitate the process, and the product owner can provide clarification, but the decision is made by developers doing the actual work.

TIP

You should use relative estimating in lieu of precise (absolute) estimating, because in many situations, it's much more feasible. If you're asked to look out the window and say how tall the neighboring building is, how precise would be your reply? Very — it's 950 feet. How accurate would be your reply? Not very. Why? Because you honestly have no idea; you gave it a wild guess. But if you're asked to look at two nearby buildings and say which one is taller, barring some vision problem, it's guaranteed that you'll give the right answer. Using *relative* sizing is an effective way to overcome the difficulty we humans have in making absolute estimates.

Fibonacci numbers and story points

The Fibonacci sequence is an excellent sizing technique for relative estimating. With Fibonacci, if something is bigger, you get an idea of how much bigger it is. The last two numbers in the sequence are added to create the next number. Fibonacci numbers look like this:

> 1, 2, 3, 5, 8, 13, 21, 34, 55, 89, 144, and so on

As the numbering progresses, the distance between the numbers increases. This technique is used to acknowledge the lesser degree of accuracy in predicting larger chunks of work.

REMEMBER

A *story point* is the Fibonacci number assigned to an individual requirement (that is, a user story).

Initial high-level requirements are estimated at the product roadmap level:

- The development team understands that requirements with Fibonacci number estimates from 1 through 8 can be brought into a sprint. This level of refinement usually results in a user story.
- Requirements with estimates numbered from 13 through 34 are those that you would let into a release but need to be broken down further before you would let them into a sprint. At this level of refinement, these requirements are called epics.
- Requirements from 55 through 144 are too big for a release but are estimable at the order-of-magnitude product roadmap level. These requirements typically reflect features.

» Requirements larger than 144 need to be broken down before the development team can give any semblance of an accurate estimate, so don't estimate beyond 144. These may represent broader themes.

Whatever the Fibonacci number, only the highest-priority cards get broken down into sprint-level sizes (which shouldn't be more than an 8). So, if you have a high-priority requirement with a 21 Fibonacci number assigned to it, it needs to be broken into smaller requirements before it can come into a sprint.

With the sizes established, you can apply a few techniques to estimate requirements:

» When you have shorter lists of requirements, you begin with *estimation poker.*

» When you have hundreds of requirements, you begin with *affinity estimation* (discussed later in this chapter).

In the estimation process with smaller projects, the development team begin as follows. The team sits down with their stack of requirements written on 3x5 cards. Then they pick a requirement that they can all agree has an effort level of 5. This creates a reference point.

They then pick another card and, based on the first one being a 5, ask themselves what number the next one would be. If it's greater than a 5, is it an 8, a 13, or a 21? This process continues until a few representational sizes have been established.

Estimation poker

A popular way to estimate requirements is to use a variation of poker. You need a deck of estimation poker cards like the one shown in Figure 3-1. (You can find them at `https://platinumedge.com/store/estimation-poker-cards`). You can also download a poker estimation app for iPhone and/or Android by searching for *Platinum Edge Estimation Poker* in your device's app store or make your own deck with index cards and a marker.

FIGURE 3-1: Estimation poker cards for estimating the amount of effort required in each requirement.

© John Wiley & Sons, Inc.

The Talent and the Timing

Because only the development team decides how much it will take to develop a requirement, only the development team plays estimation poker. The scrum master facilitates, and the product owner reads the requirements and provides requirement details, but neither of those two gives estimates. It goes like this:

1. The product owner reads a targeted requirement to the development team, including acceptance criteria.
2. The development team asks any questions and gets any clarifications they need.
3. Each member of the development team picks from his deck a card with his estimate of the difficulty of the requirement.

REMEMBER

   The estimate is to accomplish the complete definition of done, not just to write code.

   Members don't show anyone else their cards because you don't want others being influenced.

4. After everyone has picked a number, the team members simultaneously show their cards.
   - If everyone has the same estimate, nothing is left to discuss. Assign the requirement that estimate and move on to the next requirement.
   - If differences exist in estimates, those with the highest and lowest estimates are asked to explain. Further clarification from the product owner is given as needed.
5. With increased knowledge, everyone picks a new number for that requirement by repeating Steps 3 and 4.

You can normally do up to three rounds of estimation poker for each requirement to get the core assumptions on the table and clarified, and at that point, you usually have the estimates in a tighter cluster of numbers.

If all developers agree on a single number after three rounds, you're ready to move on to the next requirement. But you won't always have all developers in agreement on a single number after three rounds. At this point, you can go on to a consensus-building technique called fist of five.

Fist of five

A fast and efficient method of reaching consensus, fist of five can be used on its own or as an addendum to estimation poker. The purpose of fist of five is to quickly find an estimate that all team members can support (see Figure 3-2).

5 = LOVE IT!
4 = Good idea.
3 = Yeah, I can support it.
2 = I have reservations, let's discuss further.
1 = Opposed. Do not move forward.

FIGURE 3-2: Fist of five is an efficient way of finding consensus in many situations.

© John Wiley & Sons, Inc.

Perhaps when you tried estimation poker, some team members have given a requirement a 5, and others have given it an 8.

It begins with the scrum master holding up the requirement card in question and saying, for example, "How comfortable would you be with this as an 8?" Each development team member holds up the number of fingers associated with their level of comfort. If everyone is holding up three, four, or five fingers, it's settled.

If some developers are holding up one or two fingers, as in estimation poker, the outliers would be asked to explain, and further information would be garnered if necessary. Fist of five would be performed again. Continue with this process until all team members can give the number at least a 3 (which is, "I don't love it, but I can support it").

With fist of five completed and requirements estimated, you're ready to move to release or sprint planning. They're covered in Chapter 4 of Book 5.

Affinity estimating

Estimation poker and fist of five are effective methods of establishing consensus in small projects. But what if you have several hundred requirements on the product backlog? It could take days to complete. This is where affinity estimating comes into play.

Instead of beginning with Fibonacci numbers, you begin with a more familiar concept: T-shirt sizes (XS, S, M, L, and XL).

With affinity estimating, you first create several areas marked with each size and then place each requirement in one of the size categories. It goes like this:

1. **Identify small tables to sort the cards.**

   Label a table Clarify, and label other small tables for each of these size categories:

   - Extra-small
   - Small
   - Medium
   - Large
   - Extra-large
   - Epic (too large to fit into the sprint, given that six to ten requirements are the target for each sprint; more on this is in Chapter 4 of Book 5)

2. **For each size category, give your development team 60 seconds to pick a requirement from the overall stack of requirements and place it on the corresponding table.**

   This establishes the *representational anchor* for each size.

3. **Each member of the development team grabs a stack of requirements.**

4. **Each member places each card on the table that they feel reflects its size based on the representational anchor for that size.**

   As you can see, these are like T-shirt sizes. Each "size" will eventually correspond to a Fibonacci number:

   - Extra-small equals 1.
   - Small equals 2.
   - Medium equals 3.
   - Large equals 5.
   - Extra-large equals 8.

   Anything larger than an 8 needs to be broken down further before it can come into a sprint.

TIP

Don't let team members linger too long on their stack of requirements. Establish a timebox for them to work within, for example, 20 minutes for 20 cards. *Timebox* is a term that refers to the allotted time for an event or activity. If your sprints last two weeks, the timebox is two weeks.

Figure 3-3 shows what the relationship between size piles and Fibonacci numbers looks like.

5. Have the development team members play something called *gallery* until all members agree on the sizes for each requirement. In gallery, the team members flip through all the cards on all the tables and provide feedback on only the cards that don't appear to be on the right table.

   If one team member wants to move a story from small to medium, for example, check that the original person who placed it there doesn't disagree. If the person disagrees, place that card on a separate Clarify table. Don't get into extensive discussions just yet.

6. Invite the product owner to review for major disagreements:

   - If the product owner sees a requirement on the medium table that she thought would be a small, don't waste any time discussing it. The development team ultimately gets to say the size of the requirement, and a one-size difference isn't worth the time to discuss.
   - If you have greater than one table of difference between where development team members think a card should be placed and where the product owner thought it would be placed, put that card on the Clarify table. The development team may not have understood the product owner's explanation of the requirement.

7. For cards on the Clarify table, play estimation poker (discussed earlier in this chapter).

SIZE	POINTS
XtraSmall (XS)	1 pt
Small (S)	2 pts
Medium (M)	3 pts
Large (L)	5 pts
XtraLarge (XL)	8 pts

© John Wiley & Sons, Inc.

FIGURE 3-3: Affinity estimating uses T-shirt sizes for story sizes and gives each one a corresponding Fibonacci number.

Within a relatively short amount of time, you've been able to reliably estimate the effort on hundreds of separate requirements. You're ready to plan your first release and/or your first sprint.

Velocity

After you have Fibonacci numbers assigned to your requirements, you have story points to work from.

Chapter 4 in Book 5 shows how to plan both releases and sprints. To plan your first sprint, among those requirements that are between 1 and 8 story points, a scrum team determines a modest number of combined story points to work on. Then, at the end of the sprint, a scrum team looks at the requirements that were done to completion and adds their story points. The result might be 15, 25, or 35 story points. This is the development team's velocity for the first sprint and starting input for a team determining how much it can accomplish in the next sprint.

Velocity is the combined number of story points that your development team completed in an individual sprint. It's a postsprint fact used for extrapolation, not a presprint goal.

To accurately determine velocity, you need more than one sprint to find an average. Velocity follows the law of large numbers; the more data points you have, the better. At minimum, you need three data points to establish an optimistic, pessimistic, and most likely extrapolation of how many requirements will be done during the project. After you have these, you can tell stakeholders optimistic, pessimistic, and most likely estimates for how many of the highest-priority requirements on the product backlog can be completed within a project. Giving stakeholders this type of estimation range provides the level of detail they're looking for while allowing some flexibility for the development team as they're still getting into a development rhythm.

In the first few sprints of a project, the team's velocity will usually vary greatly. It becomes more stable as the team gets into a development rhythm. Of course, changes in team members or sprint duration will introduce variability into the team's velocity.

Velocity isn't a goal; it's a fact used for extrapolation. Higher numbers are not automatically better than lower numbers.

When story points are used, you'll find that some teams are pessimistic in their estimates. Their numbers always come in high. Other teams are optimistic. Their story point total comes in low.

Consider that an optimistic team's velocity is 15 and the estimates for the release total 150 points. It would take them ten sprints to complete the release.

If a pessimistic team's velocity were 30 and the estimates for the release total 300 points, it would take them ten sprints as well.

REMEMBER

Optimistic or pessimistic doesn't really matter. Teams will generally be consistent one way or the other and therefore balance out in the end. This is the reason you always value a team's velocity against itself, not against other teams. In fact, don't even tell anyone what a team's velocity is. Consider it an extrapolation system, not a performance system.

When you have a clear method of estimating the effort required to complete each requirement, and you have an average velocity established for the development team, you're able to accurately predict the quantity of product that can be created within fixed cost and time constraints. You're harnessing your variables.

Successful scrum teams need to share ownership of outcomes and value authentic transparency between the team and its stakeholders. Progress is visible to everyone.

IN THIS CHAPTER

» Developing the roadmap into release plans

» Applying the scrum sprint cycle

» Planning your sprints for maximum effectiveness

» Using the sprint backlog

Chapter 4
Release and Sprint Planning

So far you have a product, a product owner, and a development team. Release and sprint planning is really where the rubber hits the road. As mentioned before, with scrum, you'll do more planning than ever before, but it's focused, continuous, value-based, results-oriented, and packaged such that you'll wonder how you ever managed projects without it.

In this chapter, you find out how to plan the release of project features in a logical and organized way. The purpose of release planning is to mobilize the wider project team around a specific set of functionality that the organization wants to release to the marketplace. This is when such departments or stakeholders as the marketing department, field support, and customer service get mobilized and prepared to support functionality that end customers are going to be using in the real world.

You also go through the scrum event of sprints. Scrum at its core is the sprint cycle. You find out how to use this valuable process and get the best possible results.

REMEMBER

A *sprint* is a fixed timebox iteration within which development is done to produce a working, potentially shippable product. A typical sprint might be one or two weeks in duration but could be as little as a day and as much as a month.

This chapter discusses how prioritizing releases and sprints accelerates time to market and maximizes return on investment (ROI) and explains that by having feedback loops, you create the product that your clients want, with the features they'll actually use.

Release Plan Basics: Stage 3

The Roadmap to Value begins with the bird's-eye basics: your vision statement. This allows you to establish your destination and define the end of the project. The second stage, the product roadmap, provides a holistic view of the features that support the vision. As you narrow your focus and generate more detail, you come into release planning, which is Stage 3 in your Roadmap to Value (see Figure 4-1). The release planning concept is scrum. However, the release plan artifact is a common practice that many scrum aficionados use with success.

Stage 3: RELEASE PLANNING

Highest-Priority Features Launch
Next Highest-Priority Features Launch
JAN | FEB | MAR | APR | MAY | JUN | JUL
Description: Release timing for specific product functionality
Owner: Product owner
Frequency: At least quarterly

(Stages 1 - 3 are common practices outside of scrum)

© John Wiley & Sons, Inc.

FIGURE 4-1: Stage 3 of the Roadmap to Value is the release plan.

A *release plan* is a high-level timetable for releasing a set of product requirements. So, you're working down, segmentally, from the big-picture roadmap to the midlevel release plan. (Later in this chapter, you discover the next-smaller size, which is the actual sprint.) The release plan provides a focal point around which the project team can mobilize.

REMEMBER

Do the minimum amount possible that still creates a working product. When planning a set of features to release to the market, always ask yourself, "What is the minimum set of features that delivers value to my customer?" This is what is commonly referred to as the *minimum viable product* (MVP).

You should release product to the market as often as you have something of value to offer your customers — the minimum viable product. Your product releases could also come on a regular schedule (for example, four times a year, at the end of each quarter). But with the advances in technology and the need to be quick to market, releases now may be monthly, weekly, or even multiple times a day in some cases.

TIP

Consider the pen-and-pencil rule. You can use a pen to commit to the plan for the first release, but anything beyond this plan is written in pencil. It's just-in-time planning for each release. (You are learning while delivering value.)

A project may have multiple releases. For each release, you start with the goal, which is supported by the next-highest-priority features and requirements. You'll see that this is a pattern you follow at each stage of the Roadmap to Value. Each release has a release goal, and you commit to only one release at a time. Figure 4-2 depicts a typical release plan with an optional release sprint.

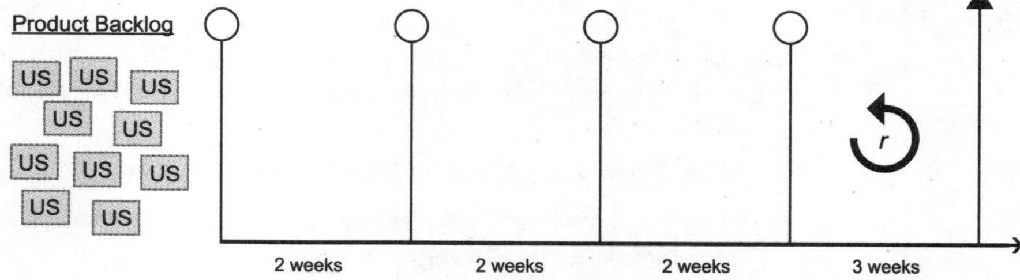

FIGURE 4-2: A typical release plan with the release goal and date and an optional release sprint.

The number of sprints within each release can vary depending on the release goal and what's required to complete the requirements to achieve that goal. An option is to use release trains, in which each release has a set time schedule. Releases are set so that everyone knows when to expect them.

At each scheduled release, the product owner decides which of the completed functionalities will be released on that date. This way, organizations and customers know to expect new features on a set schedule. Scrum teams can predictably organize their release plans to cadence.

Scrum is an empirical approach. Each step of the way, you inspect your results and adapt immediately to the changing needs of your customers. These fundamentals enable you to achieve significant cost and time savings while delivering value and what the client wants. You may have a bird's-eye view of four releases for your project, but you plan in detail only one release at a time. What you learn in the first release may change what you do in the second release.

WARNING

Your organization may be afraid to release software incrementally. You may find it difficult to release completed work before the entire backlog is complete. Sometimes that hesitancy derives from a sense that once the product is released you can't improve it or add to it. Overcome these antipatterns to support more effective and frequent releases.

Prioritize, prioritize, prioritize

You've heard this before, and you'll hear it throughout this book. Identifying the highest-priority (or highest-value) requirements, according to business value and risk, and working with only those requirements are key common practices within the agile community.

Think of each release as the next, incremental MVP of your product. When planning each release, ask these questions to identify the highest-priority features:

- What makes a requirement important for this release?
- What is the minimum number of features providing business value to the customer do we need to bring to market?
- Which requirements present the greatest risk and should be addressed sooner than later?

A famous Standish Group study from 2001 showed on a representational software development project that only 20 percent of the features were used always or often by the customers. Interestingly, 64 percent of features were never or rarely used. With scrum's emphasis on prioritization, only those most important and useful features are developed first. What if your project runs out of funding and you're only 80 percent done? Based on what the Standish study found, you might not have needed the remaining 20 percent anyway.

The following four key reasons are why you want as small a set of features per release as possible:

- First-mover advantage of speed to market and increased market share
- Accelerated customer feedback cycle
- Maximized ROI (a dollar today is literally worth more than a dollar will be worth six months from now)
- Reduced internal risk from such factors as organizational change and budget poaching

The product owner fully owns the release plan and is the one who prioritizes the requirements in the product backlog and sets the release goal (as shown in the following section). While the product owner decides what the priorities are and when to release completed shippable functionality, she consults stakeholders and the development team to make her decisions. Figure 4-3 applies the 80/20 rule to the value versus effort idea. It's isn't a magic formula, but a helpful way to understand and explain value.

The Pareto Principle (80/20 rule) and the Law of Diminishing Returns

	Imagine a current unstarted project and let's apply the 80/20 rule a few times.	**Delivered Business Value**	**Expended Effort**	**Value Leverage**
Low hanging fruit	80 percent of business value delivered with 20 percent of the effort (a good value by delivering the highest value and best defined stories first).	**80%**	**20%**	4:1
Hard or risky but needed	Now taking 80% of the remaining part (20) of business value leaves us with 16% and taking 20% of the remaining effort (80).	**16%**	**16%**	1:1
Whoops we feel stuck	We've delivered 96% of the business value so far with only 36% of the effort! Let's do it one more time. 80% of 4% = 3.2 value and 20% of remaining 64% effort = yields 12.8 effort.	**3.2%**	**12.8%**	1:4
	We still have over 50% of the estimated effort remaining to gain hardly business delivered value.	**99.2%**	**48.8%**	

This illustration isn't intended to be an exact project estimation but rather to demonstrate something scrum professionals experience across projects. If the roadmap to value is followed you will do the most valued stories first.

- More than half of software features don't get used (see the Standish study).
- **Law of diminishing returns** refers to a point at which the level of benefits gained is less than the amount of effort (time, money) expended.

© John Wiley & Sons, Inc.

FIGURE 4-3: Applying the Pareto Principle (80/20 rule) to scrum.

Release goals

Each release plan has an overall business goal called a *release goal.* This goal is created by the product owner and ties directly to the product end goal, which is the product's vision statement. The release goal establishes the midterm boundary around specific functionality that will be released to customers to use in the real world.

Having an explicit release goal expedites the prioritization process: If a requirement doesn't align with the goal, you don't have to worry about that requirement in this release. Any given requirement should earn the right of your investment. Leave it tucked away in the product backlog until it can support a priority goal. Figure 4-4 shows a matrix to help you determine the priority stories.

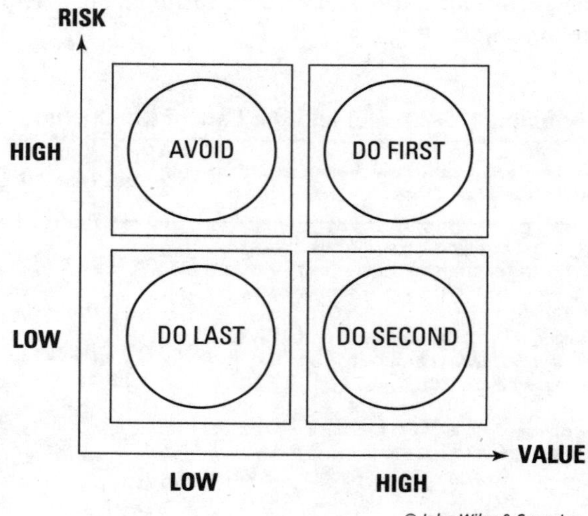

FIGURE 4-4: Backlog priority matrix.

© John Wiley & Sons, Inc.

TIP

Think of the three layers of goal setting as a prioritization filter system. The vision statement is the highest boundary. If a feature doesn't fit the overall vision, it doesn't belong in this project. Don't even put that requirement on the product backlog. The requester needs to go get funding for that idea separately. Don't allow features to be stowaways on your project.

Next comes the release goal. This is the midterm boundary. If a requirement doesn't fit this goal, it stays in the product backlog. Finally, the shortest-term boundary is the sprint goal.

REMEMBER

Goals drive the product backlog and the release plan, not the other way around. Every feature and requirement must be thought of in terms of whether it fits the goal. This is *purpose-driven development.* Goals drive what makes the product backlog. Goals drive what gets included in a release. And goals drive what gets included in each sprint.

Release sprints

Sometimes, releasing product features into the marketplace requires completing certain jobs that can't fit within a normal developmental sprint. Ideally, all activities required to release a product to the market are done within a normal sprint. But if the way an organization is set up doesn't allow it, a release sprint may be used to accomplish such purposes as

- Verifying scaling (for example, load or performance testing)
- Broader testing activities (for example, focus groups or validating that developed functionality works with live data)

Although it's preferable not to have release sprints, simply phrased, a release sprint is for all that other stuff that needs doing to get the product to market.

The release sprint is commonly used at the end of the normal series of sprints within a release. The length of a release sprint may be different from the development sprints in the release. The release sprint length depends on the types of activities and the amount of work required to release the completed product increments from each sprint. The scrum team determines all these factors during release planning.

REMEMBER

During a release sprint, no actual development of requirements is done. All development tasks (such as testing, technical documentation, quality assurance, and peer review) are completed during each sprint to satisfy the team's definition of done, which in turn ensures potentially shippable product at the end of each sprint. But before the product can go out to the market, other things (such as focus groups or load and performance testing) may need to be done.

Because the release sprint length and activities are often different from the development sprints, no concept of velocity exists for a release sprint. Development teams estimate to the best of their knowledge the effort and complexity of the tasks for the release sprint. They should all agree and feel comfortable with the release sprint length after it is decided.

WARNING

The release sprint is a form of antipattern in organizations that can't do scaled testing and organizational support tasks within the sprint. If you don't need it, don't do it.

Including examples already given, uses for release sprints may include the following:

- Conducting focus groups (keep in mind that this isn't to identify new features but to validate what you've done and identify release issues)
- Scaling tests
- Tweaking performance based on scaling test results
- Integrating the product within enterprise wide systems
- Creating documentation such as user manuals
- Finalizing any regulatory requirements

Release plan in practice

To see how a release plan works in the real world, follow these steps:

1. **Develop a release goal.**

   This goal is the target for everything else. The product owner ensures that the goal aligns with the product vision and works with the scrum team to make sure that the entire team feels comfortable with the goal.

2. **Identify the target release date.**

   This date may be influenced by factors outside the control of the scrum team.

3. **Identify the highest-priority (highest-value) requirements (MVP) on the product backlog that support the release goal.**

   Priority is a function of value and risk. Tackle the highest value/highest risk items first. Refer to Figure 4-4 for a value matrix.

4. **Refine the requirements estimates as needed.**

   Sometimes, issues and/or synergies are discovered when the development team looks at the smaller package of requirements that go into a release plan. The requirements themselves will also be more detailed and broken down (no larger than 34; see Chapter 3 in Book 5) than when the development team originally estimated at the product roadmap level.

5. **Identify the team's velocity.**

   If the team is stable and has been working on the same project, established velocity from previous sprints is a great starting point. If the team hasn't established velocity, start modestly until you have run a few sprints and velocity can be ascertained.

6. **Plan a release sprint (if needed).**

   Determine as a scrum team whether you'll need one and, if so, how long it will be.

7. **Finalize the release scope.**

   Based on velocity, total estimates of requirements and number of sprints within the release timebox, how much functionality can you include? Which is more flexible — the date or the amount of functionality? What adjustments need to be made to the release date or scope of requirements to release as much as you can within your timebox?

   Suppose that your velocity is 20, the release timebox is 5 sprints, and the total estimated points for the release is 110. This puts you ten points over what's available in the release. The product owner has a decision to make. Are the requirements that make up the bottom ten points in the release valuable enough to include, or can the release go on without them? Or does the release need to be extended one sprint, and will that be acceptable to the stakeholders and customers?

TIP

One option in release planning is to use the *release train* model. Rather than have releases of varying duration, in this scenario, each release is exactly the same length — six weeks, for example. At the end of each six-week cycle, the completed functionality from each of the sprints is packaged and released. This way, a development rhythm is created, and everyone in the organization can anticipate his workload and schedule moving forward.

Use any of the estimation and consensus-building techniques discussed in Chapter 3 of Book 5 to refine the product backlog items in the release, if requirements still need to be refined and estimated (see the preceding Step 4). If your releases consist of many product backlog items, use affinity estimating (the T-shirt sizing technique discussed in Chapter 3 of Book 5) for release planning.

REMEMBER

As with all scrum documentation, the simplest tools possible are preferred. The entire release plan can be mapped out with your trusty whiteboard and sticky notes. This allows for ease in change and immediate access. As well, it just plain saves time.

Sprinting to Your Goals

Finally, the heart of scrum! Sprints, and their built-in inspect and adapt model, are integral scrum features. It is through the sprint process that you can achieve the three agile pillars of improvement — transparency, inspection, and adaptation.

By breaking your project into tangible pieces and then using the empirical model of scrum to assess your progress, you can pivot constantly moving forward. This allows you the nimbleness and ease of adaptation so sorely missing in waterfall.

Each scrum team member has the same purpose in the sprints: maximizing effectiveness in delivering potentially shippable product.

Defining sprints

Sprints are the essence of scrum. They're a consistent timebox for product development by the development team. Each sprint includes the following:

- Sprint planning, including goal setting
- Daily scrums
- Development time, including regular review by the product owner
- Sprint review
- Sprint retrospective

The consistent timebox of sprints allows the development team to establish a development rhythm. It also enables scrum teams to extrapolate into the future based on empirical data such as velocity. As soon as one sprint is finished, another begins. A flow of consistent iterative feedback loops is created and thereby creates an ideal environment for production and continuous improvement.

TIP

Imagine that you're a runner. You're consistently training for the 100-yard dash and have become incredibly proficient at it, but suddenly your coach asks you to run a marathon. If you attempt the marathon at your 100-yard-dash pace, you won't finish the marathon. You need to modify your training to adjust for a marathon pace, which will require coaching, schedule, and diet changes over time. All the muscle memory and the type of endurance that your body has developed will need to be relearned to run a different length of race.

Planning sprint length

Because sprint goals don't change during a sprint, the answer to the question "How long should a sprint be?" depends on your project and how long your organization can go without making changes. That is the outer edge. You have no reason to discuss going beyond that in duration. For example, if your organization struggles to go a week without needing changes, don't even entertain the idea of a two-week sprint. You won't be able to maintain the integrity of the stability of the sprint, and stability is a huge driver of performance in scrum. Instead, discuss how much shorter you can make the sprint.

Also, sprint lengths don't change after they begin and ideally don't change throughout a project unless they're being made shorter. If a scrum team changes sprint length during a project, it comes at a significant cost: Their earlier velocity is no longer relevant. Performance is not a straight mathematical line that can be sliced, diced, and reassembled. Just because a scrum team doubles their sprint from one to two weeks doesn't mean that they will automatically accomplish double their historical two-week velocity.

Shorter sprints decrease the amount of time between feedback received from stakeholders, enabling scrum teams to inspect and adapt earlier and more often. Longer sprints have a diminishing return because less of a sense of urgency exists due to the multiple days still available to the team. Weekends and longer sprint meetings can also have a negative effect on efficiency.

The capacity of a development team during a one-week sprint may be higher or lower than half the historical two-week velocity. You don't have any idea until you run a few sprints, and you don't know for sure until you run a lot of sprints.

WARNING

Whereas the cost of changing sprint lengths throughout a project is significant, the cost of changing a sprint goal during a sprint is probably worse. If a sprint goal becomes irrelevant (for example, because of changes of company direction or changes in the market) before the end of a sprint, a product owner may decide to cancel the sprint. But be aware that canceling wastes valuable development resources and is quite traumatic to the scrum team and the organization. Also, the shorter the feedback loop (that is, length of sprint), the less likely a product owner would be to cancel a sprint.

One things we know from science is that you can't turn off your mind. It's always working. If you can give your development team a small number of problems to solve, and tell them that they'll face those problems tomorrow, they'll think about them consciously at work. Whether they want to or not, they'll also think about them unconsciously when they're away from work. This is the reason why the stability of sprints is so important. After a sprint starts, the developers must have confidence that the scope is stable so that their minds can be fully focused on what needs to be done for this sprint, whether they're at work or away from it. Have you ever had an epiphany while brushing your teeth? That's the dynamic discussed here. But you need two elements: a limited number of problems and confidence that you'll face those problems tomorrow. If every day a developer could be working on Project A, Project C, or Project who-knows-what, this won't happen. A developer will mentally engage only when he gets to the office and discovers what's ahead of him in reality. One reason why agile projects are so innovative is that they have this stability and, thus, more of the developer's mind share.

TIP

The one-week sprint length is a nice rhythm. It gives the development team clear time off, avoids weekend cheating to get more work done than is within the team's capacity, yet is long enough for real progress to be made every week. This shorter feedback cycle also allows scrum teams to inspect and adapt more frequently. For these reasons, scrum teams should always be looking for ways to responsibly shorten their sprint length.

The key is to run sprints that enable your development team to realistically create tangible, tested, and approved product every single sprint. After each sprint, you will have something real to show to stakeholders.

Following the sprint life cycle

Each sprint has the same process: sprint planning, daily scrums, a sprint review, and a sprint retrospective. Sprints are developmental cycles that repeat until your project is complete. Requirements (often in the form of user stories) are developed, tested, integrated, and approved within each sprint. The process continues sprint after sprint. Figure 4-5 depicts a one-week sprint life cycle.

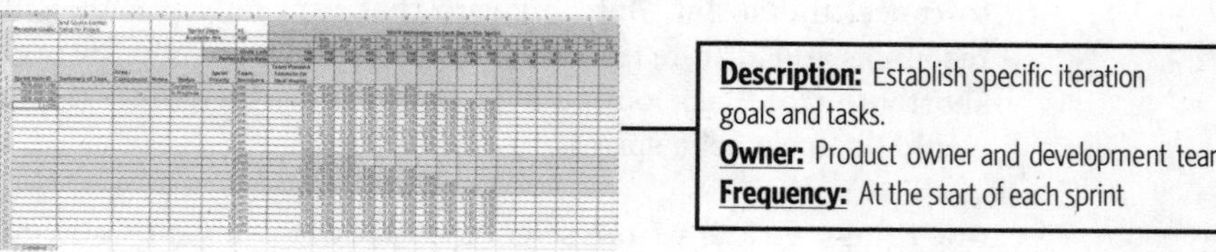

Stage 4: SPRINT PLANNING
Description: Establish specific iteration goals and tasks.
Owner: Product owner and development team
Frequency: At the start of each sprint

FIGURE 4-5: The one-week sprint life cycle.

© John Wiley & Sons, Inc.

TIP

When scrum teams are distributed offshore with team members in faraway time zones (such as the United States and India), arrangements need to be made for all team members to attend each of the sprint meetings. To account for time-zone differences, the domestic team members might join the meeting Sunday night while it's Monday morning for the offshore team members. At the end of the sprint, the domestic team members finish the sprint Friday morning and take the rest of the day off while the offshore team is joining the sprint review and retrospective Friday night. Rotating each sprint might be appreciated on each end so that each team member doesn't always have to work on Sunday nights or Friday nights.

The key is that after each sprint, the scrum team learns new things. Change happens; it's inevitable. Responding and adapting to it should be considered progress, not failure.

Change is easy in scrum because at the end of every cycle, what was created was done to completion. When you go into your next sprint and work on items from the product backlog, it doesn't matter whether those items have been on the product backlog for four months, four weeks, or four minutes. Old or new, each product backlog item gets prioritized not by the order in which it was received, but by the order in which it will deliver the highest value to the customer.

TIP

The Monday-to-Friday work week is a natural, biorhythmic time frame. Teams need a weekend break, which fits naturally with life patterns. So, avoid off-kilter sprint patterns of Wednesday to Tuesday or the like.

Planning Your Sprints: Stage 4

The planning of sprints is Stage 4 in the Roadmap to Value. All the work to be accomplished during that specific sprint is planned here. Each sprint planning session is timeboxed to no more than two hours for each week of the sprint. If you have a one-week sprint timebox, you have a maximum of two hours to plan your sprint, for example.

Sprint goals

A goal is created for each sprint. The product owner initiates the goal discussion, identifying the business value objective that needs to be met. After the team is clear on the goal, the product owner chooses the requirements from the product backlog that best support the goal. As with the release goal, the sprint goal drives the requirements developed, not the other way around.

The sprint goal itself must support the release goal, which supports the vision statement. This goal decomposition and alignment are essential for ensuring that you're doing purpose-driven development.

The development team is critical in creating the sprint goal. Because they're the ones doing the actual work, while the product owner establishes the direction, or the what, the development team establishes the how and how much.

If your development team has an established average velocity, it may be used as input in determining the amount of work they will take on during the sprint.

The development team can also use velocity for stretching, testing its limits, or backing off if they're struggling to achieve the goals set. If they've been achieving 34 story points comfortably, they might push it to 38 or 40. If they've been struggling to achieve 25, they might lower it to 23 while the scrum team figures out organizational drag that can be removed.

Both phases of sprint planning occur in the single sprint planning meeting at the beginning of the sprint. Phase I is where the product owner, with input from the development team and facilitated by the scrum master, determines what needs to be accomplished (the goal). In Phase II, the development team determines how to achieve the sprint goal and develops the actual sprint backlog of supporting tasks.

WARNING

The sprint planning meeting may not always go smoothly, especially at first. You may slip down rabbit holes, discover tangents, and unearth different estimations of what's possible. This is where a strong and deft facilitator is needed in the form of the scrum master. It's their job to make sure that the session stays on track and the heat stays on low.

Phase I

At the start of Phase I, the sprint goal is created, and the development team must fully understand it, because it will provide the boundaries and direction for the work they will do throughout the sprint. The product owner then selects a portion of the product backlog that supports the goal. This won't necessarily be the final sprint backlog, but is the forecasted functionality that if finished in the sprint, would satisfy the sprint goal. It's what the development team will work from to achieve the sprint goal and determine the actual sprint backlog.

Phase I gives the development team and product owner another opportunity to clarify any existing requirements or identify new ones that are needed to achieve the sprint goal. This would also be the time to give the final size estimation on any clarified requirements and size any new requirements for the sprint. Remember the yardstick: If any requirements are sized higher than an 8, they're too big for a sprint (see Chapter 3 in Book 5).

TIP

Consider bringing six to ten product backlog items into each sprint. This is usually the right balance of being able to deliver a product increment with substantial functionality as well as litmus that each individual item is sufficiently broken down.

TIP

The only requirements discussed in sprint planning should be those estimated between 1 and 8 on the Fibonacci scale. This isn't a scrum rule, but it aligns with the affinity estimating model (see Chapter 3 in Book 5) and has been an effective way for many teams to keep focused on properly refined requirements that can be completed within a sprint. For more on Fibonacci numbers, see Chapter 3 in Book 5.

Phase II

When the goal and the supporting requirements have been determined by the scrum team, the development team breaks down those requirements into individual tasks — how they will turn product backlog items into the product increment. The tasks for each requirement should explicitly satisfy the team's definition of done. For instance, if the definition of done includes integration with system A, at least one task for the requirement should be "integration test with system A."

TIP

Ideally, each task should be able to be completed in one day. This gives the development team a tangible, realistic time target as they break requirements down into tasks. It also sets a benchmark from which the team can be alerted to any development problems. If a task is taking multiple days to develop, an issue might need to be addressed with the task or the developer.

Development teams may choose to estimate the tasks for each requirement in hours if the organization wants that level of visibility. But many teams simply use velocity and complete/not complete of product backlog items to adequately visualize sprint risk.

The development team is forced to be the most detailed here, which helps to sharpen the mind. They can really dig down and look at what needs to be done.

By the end of sprint planning, the development team should be clear on how the chosen sprint backlog items support the sprint goal and how the work to complete those backlog items will be done. This does not mean that all (or any) of the tasks on the sprint backlog get assigned at this time. Rather, each day the development team self-organizes by having each developer pull a task and work on it to completion. (You find more on pull versus push in "Working the sprint backlog" later in this chapter.)

Your Sprint Backlog

The sprint backlog is created in the sprint planning session and is the ordered list of requirements and tasks necessary to achieve the sprint goal.

A sprint backlog might contain the following information:

- The sprint goal and dates
- A prioritized list of the requirements (for example, user stories) to be developed in the sprint
- The estimated effort (that is, story points) required to develop each requirement
- The tasks required to develop each requirement
- The hours estimated to complete each task (if needed)
- A burndown chart to show the status of the work developed in the sprint

The burndown chart benefit

Burndown charts are ways to visually represent progress achieved within the sprint. They depict the amount of work accomplished versus the amount left to go. Figure 4-6 shows an example:

- The vertical axis represents the work left to be done.
- The horizontal axis depicts the time still available in the sprint.

Your sprints will show a diagonal line from the top-left corner to the bottom-right corner, which represents what an even and consistent burn would look like, though really you won't have a perfectly even burndown.

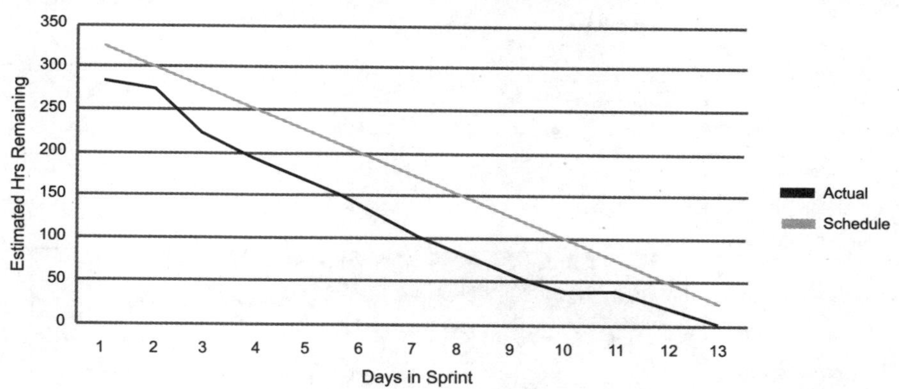

FIGURE 4-6: Sprint burndown chart.

Some burndown charts also have a line showing the outstanding story points. This allows you to quickly and easily see the status of your sprint from both time and relative estimation perspectives.

You can create your own burndown chart with Microsoft Excel or download the one that's included within the sprint backlog template, which you can download from this page: `https://platinumedge.com/blog/anatomy-sprint-backlog`.

The burndown chart is generated from the sprint backlog. The sprint backlog should be updated every day, and only the development team can do this. At the end of each day, each developer updates their task (whether on a 3x5 card, on a spreadsheet, or in an electronic tool) by entering the number of *remaining* hours (*not* the number of completed hours) that are left to complete the task. That's it. One number. It takes seconds and the results are invaluable. See Figure 4-7 for a sample sprint backlog.

The sprint burndown chart is an information radiator that shows anyone who wants to know the status of the sprint. Burndown charts get generated automatically as development team members update the amount of time left on their one active task at the end of each day.

The burndown chart shows the amount of time remaining for the sum of all the requirements on the sprint backlog. Compared with the trend line, it provides a daily level of status detail for a scrum team that you can't get with traditional project management techniques.

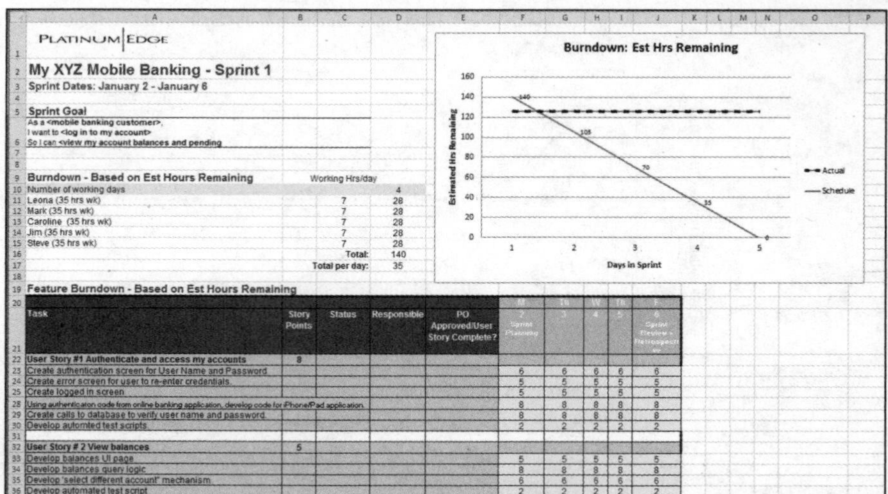

PLATINUM | EDGE

My XYZ Mobile Banking - Sprint 1

Sprint Dates: January 2 - January 6

Sprint Goal

As a <mobile banking customer>,
I want to <log in to my account>
So I can <view my account balances and pending

Burndown - Based on Est Hours Remaining

	Working Hrs/day	
Number of working days		4
Leona (35 hrs wk)	7	28
Mark (35 hrs wk)	7	28
Caroline (35 hrs wk)	7	28
Jim (35 hrs wk)	7	28
Steve (35 hrs wk)	7	28
	Total:	140
	Total per day:	35

Feature Burndown - Based on Est Hours Remaining

Task	Story Points	Status	Responsible	PO Approved/User Story Complete?	M 2 Sprint Planning	Tu 3	W 4	Th 5	F 6 Sprint Review + Retrospective
User Story #1 Authenticate and access my accounts	8								
Create authentication screen for User Name and Password					6	6	6	6	6
Create error screen for user to re-enter credentials.					5	5	5	5	5
Create logged in screen					5	5	5	5	5
Using authenticaton code from online banking application, develop code for iPhone/iPad application.					8	8	8	8	8
Create calls to database to verify user name and password.					8	8	8	8	8
Develop automted test scripts.					2	2	2	2	2
User Story # 2 View balances	5								
Develop balances UI page					5	5	5	5	5
Develop balances query logic					8	8	8	8	8
Develop 'select different account" mechanism					6	6	6	6	6
Develop automated test script					2	2	2	2	2

FIGURE 4-7: A sprint backlog is a key scrum artifact.

© John Wiley & Sons, Inc.

Setting backlog capacity

How much capacity is in a day? If you're looking at the number of hours per day that a development team member is able to devote to her main job — developing! — allow for less than eight. Every organization has a certain amount of overhead. For most organizations, somewhere between five and seven hours is a normal effective workday.

How much capacity is really in a sprint? In a one-week sprint, scrum teams will spend up to two hours in sprint planning, up to one hour in sprint review, and up to 45 minutes in a sprint retrospective. That's about four hours in sprint meetings. (Do you have to use all four hours? No. Can you go over the limit for any given meeting? No.)

That accounts for four of the five scrum events (assume that a maximum 15-minute daily scrum won't affect development time), but don't forget product backlog refinement. Development teams will on average spend 10 percent of their time each sprint in product backlog refinement activities. This translates to about three to four hours in a one-week sprint.

So, for a one-week sprint, each developer spends between seven and eight hours in sprint events, which takes care of one full workday for an efficient organization and about a day and a half for a less efficient organization.

TIP

Is there any buffer in scrum? Sure. Consider that a development team has 165 hours available to them for a sprint. They shouldn't take on 164 hours under the false assumption that everything is going to go exactly according to plan. The buffer varies from team to team, but you should make it transparent.

So capacity for one developer for a one-week sprint would be 18 to 27 hours, depending on the organization's established effective workday. Take this into consideration when identifying a development team's capacity during sprint planning. This is assuming that no paid holidays, vacations, or other time off is planned that will keep developers from developing.

Who said scrum is rudderless? You can't get much more disciplined than this.

What an incredible impact having a dedicated and effective scrum master means to a development team's capacity. By removing the organizational drag (impediments) that keep effective workdays from increasing from five to seven hours, the impact can add up to an additional nine work hours in a one-week sprint per developer. For a development team of seven, that's a potential 63-hour efficiency increase. Scrum masters add value.

What happens if at the end of sprint planning, the development team finds that the number of estimated hours for their tasks from the sprint backlog is more than their capacity? Do they hunker down and work overtime? No, the product owner has a decision to make: which sprint backlog items will be moved back to the product backlog to get the number of hours below the development team's capacity. Sustained overtime leads to poor team morale, poorer quality, and long-term productivity loses.

The value of the iterative planning process is easily visible within sprint planning. By the time the work to be done is outlined and broken down to the task level, you will have done so in a way that minimizes time waste and maximizes business value and ROI. This is because the Roadmap to Value, from the vision statement all the way down to the sprint level, has enabled continuous prioritization and progressive elaboration of only the most important product backlog items.

Working the sprint backlog

Development teams can get distracted and go off target by making some common mistakes. Follow these practices to counter those mistakes when working with the sprint backlog:

- Make sure that requirements are broken down into tasks that accurately and completely reflect your definition of done (see Chapter 3 in Book 5).

The product owner should not accept a requirement until it completely satisfies the sprint definition of done.

- The entire development team ideally works on only one requirement at a time and completes that requirement before starting another. This is called *swarming.*

  Swarming can be accomplished by such activities as

  - Each team member working on individual tasks related to the same requirement
  - Pairing two people on one task to ensure quality
  - Team members shadowing each other to increase cross-functionality

  As development teams swarm around one requirement at a time, this ensures cross-functionality and ensures that every sprint will have something tangible accomplished at its end.

- Each requirement must be fully developed, tested, integrated, and accepted by the product owner before the team moves on to the next requirement.
- Don't assign multiple tasks to individual development team members.

  Each day, the development team coordinates priorities and decides who will do what. A developer should be working on only one task at a time until that task is completely done. This is called a *pull mechanism.*

WARNING

Don't fall back into the traditional method of a manager assigning tasks out to team members. Traditional project management follows the push model of assigning tasks to individuals when they're identified. Each individual manages and focuses solely on the tasks in his personal queue. This queue builds up over time, and attempts are made to redistribute task load across team members to avoid over- or underloading. The trouble with push systems is that it's difficult to know the status of things unless everything is either unstarted or all the way complete. This also tends to contribute to team members operating as silos rather than cross-functional teams.

TIP

Swarming on requirements stems from the lean concept of work in progress (WIP) limits. When a development team has a lot of work in progress, it delays taking the actions necessary to finalize that work and rear-loads issue correction. Your WIP limit should ideally be only one requirement at a time for the development team and only one task at a time per developer. The development team usually finds that their tasks get completed sooner than if they had started them all at the same time. Having only one requirement open at a time is also an effective way of exposing process bottlenecks, which can then be addressed and fixed for faster throughput.

Prioritizing sprints

Each sprint has its own life cycle, as shown in Figure 4-5 earlier in this chapter. Within each sprint, each requirement has its own prioritization and life cycle, too. Each requirement and task are developed, tested, integrated, and approved before the team moves on to the next-highest-priority item. See Figure 4-8 for a representation.

The sprint backlog items are prioritized from highest to lowest and developed in that order. The development team works on only one requirement at a time. When that requirement is finished, the team moves on to the next-highest-priority one rather than picking one lower on the list that might be easier or more interesting.

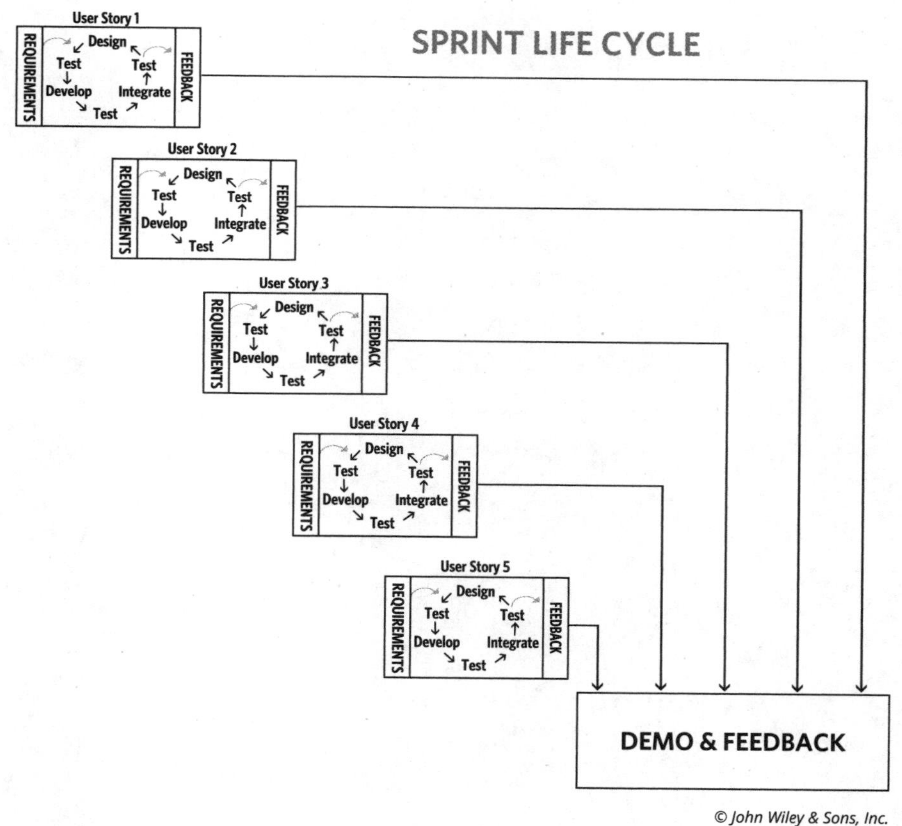

FIGURE 4-8: Prioritization within a sprint.

Release and Sprint Planning

» Swarming to get to done

» Running effective sprint reviews

» Finding the key elements of the sprint retrospective

Chapter 5
Getting the Most Out of Sprints

Sprints are the essence of scrum, so it's worth spending an entire chapter on them. You have the gist already: Sprints are fixed timeboxes designed so that your development team can create a development rhythm. They also nurture the inspect-and-adapt premise.

But that's not all that sprints do. This chapter introduces the daily scrum — an invaluable 15 minutes every day that will focus and organize your short-term goals like never before. Facilitated by the scrum master, the daily scrum keeps your project on track as the scrum team deals with impediments and coordinates the day's priorities.

This chapter also exposes you to the sprint review and sprint retrospective. These two meetings take the concepts of inspection and adaptation to new levels. Stakeholders review the product developed and give the product owner immediate feedback; the scrum team itself assesses how the sprint went and incorporates any improvements into the process.

The Daily Scrum: Stage 5

The daily scrum is one of the five scrum events and Stage 5 on the Roadmap to Value (see Figure 5-1).

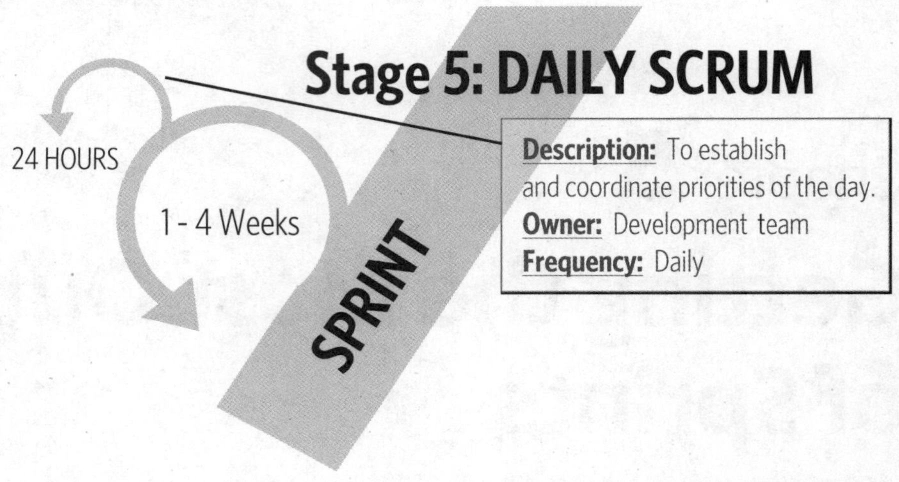

FIGURE 5-1: The daily scrum is an integral aspect of the sprint and Stage 5 in the Roadmap to Value.

© John Wiley & Sons, Inc.

REMEMBER

Planning is huge in scrum. You don't set a goal, forget it, and then gather together six months later to see what happened. You inspect and adapt every single day, and even throughout the day.

Because a development team swarms each day to attack a single requirement, coordination is key. The removal of impediments is also crucial for developers who work closely together to deliver potentially shippable increments within short periods. The daily scrum is how the development team coordinates.

REMEMBER

If you manage your projects by weeks (that is, with weekly project manager status reports that may not get reviewed promptly), you slip by weeks. In scrum, you may still slip but only by a day, because scrum teams manage by day through the sprint backlog, the daily scrum, and daily and direct interaction. You look more closely at this comparison in Chapter 6 of Book 5.

Defining the daily scrum

As its name implies, a daily scrum takes place during each sprint. The timebox is 15 minutes maximum, no matter what the overall length of the sprint is. Meetings in scrum, like artifacts, are barely sufficient. Anything longer than 15 minutes would eat into valuable developing time. Besides, 15 minutes is plenty of time to accomplish everything necessary.

The purpose of the daily scrum is to coordinate the day's sprint activities and identify impediments keeping the development team from accomplishing its sprint goal. Every member of the development team participates, so everyone is dialed into what the entire team is working on. If an impediment comes up during the daily scrum, it's dealt with following the daily scrum. The event is a coordination meeting, not a problem- or complaint-solving meeting.

The scrum master either removes impediments or facilitates their removal. Some impediments may need to be removed by the product owner or require discussion between a team member and someone outside the team.

Participants in the daily scrum are the development team members and the scrum master. The scrum master ensures that the meeting takes place, and the development team directs it. The product owner should attend (and must attend if specifically asked to do so by the development team). The product owner may provide clarifications on prioritization as needed, and anyone else who's involved and interested can listen in but can't say anything. This way, they can enjoy the daily transparency and be involved in the daily process, but they can't hinder or derail it.

The daily scrum is how a development team self-organizes and self-manages. Each day, the team decides who will do what and who will help whom. Work isn't dictated by a project manager or some other nondeveloper.

If a daily scrum starts to feel like a status-report meeting or development team members start addressing one person (such as an informal team lead or the scrum master), the meeting has missed the point. A daily scrum should be peer to peer.

The key takeaway from a daily scrum is clarity about what it means to be successful that day. Then the team swarms if necessary to do the highest-priority work. (Find out more about swarming later in this chapter.) The team finds value in this ceremony only if team members achieve relevant clarity and purpose about the day's goals. Daily scrums offer an opportunity to inspect and adapt in the moment.

Scrum meetings ask the same questions daily: What was accomplished yesterday? What are you working on today? Do you need any help? A common misconception about the daily scrum is that it's a time for the development team to report to the product owner or a time for product owners to introduce new requirements or update a sprint goal. Don't let the daily scrum become a business-status-reporting meeting; it's a coordination meeting to enable high performance.

Scheduling a daily scrum

Because a daily scrum lasts only 15 minutes, everyone needs to be on time and ready. You'll find a direct correlation between how late a meeting starts and how loose the focus is after the meeting starts. You may have different ways of encouraging punctuality, such as the following:

- **Start your daily scrum half an hour after the normal workday begins.** This schedule gives your development team members time to get coffee, answer emails, discuss the previous evening's antics, and cover anything else in their morning rituals.
- **Penalize members for being late in a friendly, spirited way.** Have team members pay a certain amount into a celebration fund for each minute they're late or have them sing their college song at full tilt. Get creative and make the penalty uncomfortable enough to stop tardiness.

A scrum team in Portland implemented a "$20 or 20 pushups with multiplier" incentive. The first time he was late, a team member paid $20 or did 20 pushups. The next time he was late, he paid $40 or did 40 pushups, and so on. This penalty was invented by the team members, not imposed on them. It worked for them and was successfully prevented tardiness.

A key disruptor of the daily scrum is distraction. Some teams have a regular habit of each member focusing on his or her own laptop screen. Some members even attend via phone while driving to the office. Listen for indicators such as "Can you say that again? I missed it." No electronics should be the rule during the daily scrum.

Conducting a daily scrum

Imagine a scrum team gathering around its sprint backlog or task board at the beginning of the day. Each person can see at a glance the progress made the day before; then each person proactively chooses a new task for the current day. Team members coordinate where help is needed to accomplish a task before the day ends; then they go straight to work.

Each team member should make three statements about how he or she is helping the team achieve its sprint goal:

» Yesterday, I accomplished . . .
» Today, I'm going to focus on . . .
» The things impeding me are . . .

Scrum masters should participate beyond facilitation by addressing the impediments that are identified and/or in progress. The scrum master might say after the team members have spoken:

» Yesterday, I removed this impediment.
» Today, I can remove this impediment.
» The impediments I can't remove are . . . , and I'll see whether so-and-so can help me.

As discussed in Chapter 4 of Book 5, tasks should be broken down so that they can be accomplished in a day or less. Even then, when developers are left to themselves for days on end without coordinating and swarming as a team, they can get bogged down in unnecessary details or problems that could be easily resolved with help.

Daily scrums synchronize a team, and everyone goes to work helping each other do what it takes to get to done. Together they completely own the outcome. Come the next day, the team members are excited to talk about their progress.

Making daily scrums more effective

The following tactics can keep your daily scrum meetings quick and effective:

» Diligently start on time. See the earlier section "Scheduling a daily scrum" for some tips on enforcing punctuality.
» Conduct the meeting standing up. Studies have shown that meetings conducted standing up are 34 percent shorter than those conducted sitting down. No one has a chance to slump in a chair and relax; it's as though everyone is already on the move.
» Focus the meeting on coordination, not problem-solving. Impediments get removed after the daily scrum.

TIP

When impediments are uncovered in the daily scrum, the scrum master can deal with them by hosting an after party immediately following the daily scrum. This event involves only those who need to be involved and is for addressing any issues that came up during the daily scrum.

A backlog of these "team topics" can also be kept so that the topics can be addressed by the team during the after party when appropriate or during the team retrospective. Not all topics raised during the daily standup need to be addressed that day, but they should be recorded in the backlog.

- The scrum master is the meeting facilitator and, as necessary, keeps the meeting on time and on track, and makes sure that only development team members participate. The scrum master's touch should be as light as possible.
- Cover only immediate issues and priorities in relation to that day in support of the sprint goal.
- Gather around the task board to ensure context and focus.
- Don't assign a set speaking order because when people know the order, they tend to check out until it's their turn. In some cases, they don't even show up until just before their turn.

TIP

You can toss a squeaky dog toy to a random member of the development team when that person should speak. If anyone takes too long, you can switch to a timer ball with an alarm. An alternative is to toss a ream of paper (which weighs 5 pounds) and let the person talk for as long as he can hold the paper out to his side. These tactics keep the daily scrum fast, forward-moving, and fun.

- Don't allow vague statements or rely on team members' memories of what's in the sprint backlog (see the next section, "The Team Task Board").

The Team Task Board

A *task board* is one way to display the sprint backlog. Although it's common for scrum teams to manage their sprint backlog in digital format, all you really need are some wall or whiteboard space, 3x5 cards, sticky notes, and tape. Figure 5-2 shows a sample task board.

The task board, like the product roadmap, increases engagement and flexibility because it's tangible.

A physical task board is excellent because it's a quick, effective way to show the status of an entire sprint. Keeping the task board within sight of the development team and product owner ensures that everyone instantly knows what's done, what's not done, and everything in between.

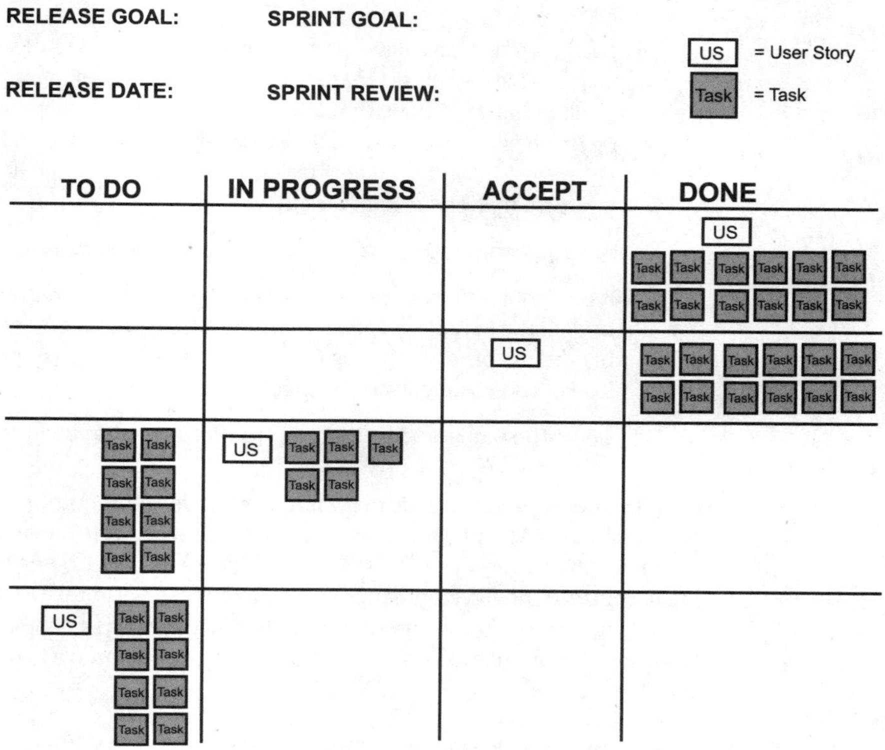

FIGURE 5-2: A team task board.

© John Wiley & Sons, Inc.

Use these basic elements:

- **»** Top
  - The specific sprint goal
  - The overall release goal

  Release and sprint dates can also be included.
- **»** Columns (from left to right)
  - *To Do:* Requirements and tasks in the sprint that have yet to be developed

    Developers pull from the top of this list to start a new task. If two developers want to take the same task, they can pair up on it, one developer can shadow the other, or they can decide who can best handle it.
  - *In Progress:* The product backlog items and tasks that the development team is working on

Each task may have different colored dots or stickers to designate ownership or to identify tasks that are blocked by an impediment. Work-in-progress limits, if used, should be displayed in this column. After developers complete a task, they look here to see who they can help. Otherwise, they pull the next task from the To Do column and verify with the team that it's the right task to work on.

- *Accept:* Requirements that are awaiting acceptance by the product owner

  If the requirement is rejected, and enough time is left in the sprint, it goes back to the In Progress column. Otherwise, the requirement gets moved back to the product backlog for consideration in a future sprint (see the later section "Handling unfinished requirements").

- *Done*: The requirements that the product owner has accepted as complete

Only the development team members can move the requirements from To Do to In Progress to Accept, and only the product owner can move them from Accept to Done. After a requirement is accepted by the product owner and moved to the Done column, the development team moves tasks with it. Otherwise, if a requirement gets rejected, the development team moves tasks back to In Progress to rework them or creates new tasks to address the reason why the requirement was rejected.

REMEMBER

Requirements in the Accept column shouldn't be allowed to pile up. Ideally, when a card is placed in Accept, it should either be placed in Done or rejected for further development the same day. If a delay occurs, the product owner needs to be coached to not letting stories accumulate as they wait to be accepted. You have no reason for delay if the product owner is a dedicated scrum team member who is available at any time for clarification, the requirements have been detailed to a single action or integration, and the requirements have passed the definition of done. It's critical for the development team members to know when their work is done and can swarm the next requirement.

Swarming

Chapter 4 in Book 5 introduces the concept of swarming in the context of the sprint backlog. *Swarming* is all development team members working on only one requirement at a time during the sprint. Although this principle isn't specific to scrum, it's such an effective way for teams to execute their sprint backlog that it warrants discussion here.

One of the main benefits of scrum is that development teams start and finish requirements to satisfy their definition of done to produce a potentially shippable product increment within a relatively short timebox. The team revises the process based on lessons learned and repeat that cycle again and again. The goal is to finish, not just start, as many requirements as possible.

Swarming enables teams to enjoy the following benefits:

- Maximizing chances for success, with the skills and abilities of the entire team focused on a single requirement
- Completing the cycle of planning, designing, developing, and testing to completion for each requirement
- Resolving issues and impediments today
- Dramatically decreasing the introduction of defects into a product through pairing and single-tasking (versus multitasking)
- Eliminating single points of failure in knowledge, processes, and skill sets
- Finishing the most important requirements completely and first

When team members see all their fellow developers working on a task, and there are no other tasks left for the same requirement (the user story), it's perfectly natural for them to consider it more productive to start a new requirement than to help other developers on the requirement in progress. This tendency can get out of hand, however, to the point where teams find themselves with multiple requirements started but none of them finished. By shadowing, pairing, researching, or helping in whatever way gets the task to done, development teams avoid this risk.

This process ensures that in every sprint, *something* gets completely developed and is available to show stakeholders. Every sprint produces shippable results. The development team's efforts are focused, teamwork is enhanced, and the iterative process of scrum is put into play.

REMEMBER

Stay focused. Stop starting and start finishing.

Dealing with rejection

If a requirement placed in the Accept column is rejected by the product owner, the developers have two options:

- **Finish their current tasks and then swarm the rejected requirement:** This option might be better if plenty of time is left in the sprint to complete both the current tasks and the rejected requirement.

- **Abandon their current tasks to swarm the rejected requirement:** This option might be better if not enough time remains in the sprint to finish both the current tasks and the rejected requirement.

The product owner decides the priority when faced with this decision. Variables other than time left in the sprint may influence the product owner's decision. As the team inspects its learning and adapts throughout a sprint, the rejected story may become less valuable to achieving the sprint goal than the next requirement in progress, so even though time is left in the sprint to do both, the risk of not finishing the in-progress requirement may be higher than the risk of not finishing the rejected requirement.

In any case, attention to priority and close daily coordination with the product owner throughout the sprint keep the entire scrum team (including the product owner) on focus and on task.

REMEMBER

Scrum teams should always push themselves. If development teams accomplish 100 percent of their sprint backlog every time, they may not be pushing themselves to their limit. A high percentage of sprint backlog completion should be the goal, but you shouldn't expect scrum teams to hit 100 percent every time. Scrum masters, like aeronautical engineers, help the scrum team find ways to reduce drag to become more effective and accomplish more in each sprint. As long as teams finish what they start each sprint and increase velocity, they realize the continuous-improvement benefit of scrum.

Handling unfinished requirements

Even high-functioning development teams that estimate well, swarm, and stick to a work-in-progress (WIP) limit of one throughout each sprint may end up with incomplete or unstarted requirements left on the sprint backlog at the end of a sprint. This result may be okay if team members swarmed on the higher-priority requirements to completion and have working product increments that can be shipped.

But what does the team do with those remaining requirements?

If a requirement isn't started, or was started and not completed, the product owner puts it back in the product backlog in its entirety (keeping all notes, tasks, and documentation intact, of course) and then reprioritizes it against the rest of the product backlog. The product owner may potentially pull the requirement into a future sprint according to its new priority.

Based on what was completed during the sprint, the unstarted or unfinished requirement may no longer be necessary, or it may not have as high a value as it had before. What was done may be enough; it may be time to move on to a different feature.

Whatever effort was made on the requirement, because it wasn't finished, it isn't included in the team's velocity for that sprint. If the requirement does make it into a future sprint, it needs to be refined, clarified, and reestimated based on the remaining work to be done. You can't bank or cache story points.

An exception may occur when, after working on an unfinished requirement, you find that you can split it. You finish one part of the requirement during the sprint; the other part goes back into the product backlog to be reestimated and reprioritized.

The lesson in all this is swarm to get to Done during the sprint.

The Sprint Review: Stage 6

The next stop on the Roadmap to Value is Stage 6, the sprint review (see Figure 5-3). This scrum event is integral to the inspect-and-adapt process of scrum and takes place at the end of each sprint.

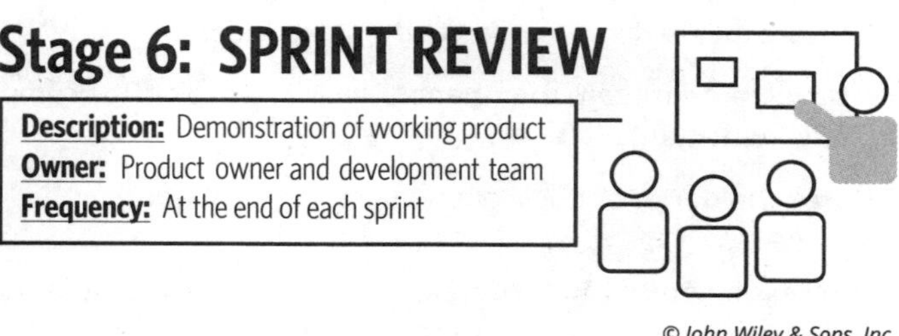

Stage 6: SPRINT REVIEW
Description: Demonstration of working product
Owner: Product owner and development team
Frequency: At the end of each sprint
© John Wiley & Sons, Inc.

FIGURE 5-3: The sprint review is a scrum event and Stage 6 of the Roadmap to Value.

The purpose of the sprint review is for the product owner to get organizational feedback on whether the product is moving in the right direction. This review is also a great opportunity for the development team to stand up and show off what it's accomplished. Team members get full credit for what they've achieved and what they haven't.

This meeting at the end of every sprint ensures that the stakeholders are up to date on what was accomplished in the sprint and have a forum for delivering feedback directly to the product owner, with the development team listening in. Also, stakeholders have working, shippable product in their hands.

The sprint review process

The sprint review, which is timeboxed to one hour per week of sprint, takes place at the end of the last day of the sprint. Allow for this time expenditure during the sprint-planning session.

The participants in the sprint review are the entire scrum team and the stakeholders, in these roles:

- **Scrum master:** Facilitates the meeting, ensuring that it stays in focus and on time.
- **Product owner:** Briefly reviews the sprint goal and how well the scrum team met the goal, fills in the stakeholders on what items from the backlog have been completed, and summarizes what's left to go in the release.

REMEMBER

The sprint review isn't the time for the product owner to provide feedback on the completed functionality. This event is for the product owner to receive feedback from stakeholders on the direction in which they're taking the product. The product owner accepts or rejects each requirement as it's completed, not at the end of the sprint, and approves the requirements before they're demonstrated to the stakeholders.

- **Development team members:** Display and explain the completed requirements.
- **Stakeholders:** Ask questions and provide feedback.

The process begins with the development team preparing for the review. Consider the following guidelines for sprint-review preparation:

- The development team prepares a sprint review for the minimal amount of time (no more than 20 minutes) to showcase completed requirements.
- No formal slides should be used in a sprint review. Rather, the development team should spend its time developing the product instead of preparing a presentation.

- Only the requirements that have been deemed done (according to the definition of done) and approved by the product owner are demonstrated.
- The development team showcases the shippable (to market) functionality of the requirement — that is, how it works in the real world.

WARNING

If you spend your time showing stakeholders what could or should have been done, you're giving a rigged demonstration and haven't done anyone any favors. Stakeholders never expect less; they always expect more. By making it look as though your product increment works when it really doesn't, you increase your workload for the coming sprint, because you'll have to make work what you showed should work, as well all the new work you'll plan for. Demonstrate only working product increments.

Stakeholder feedback

Critical to the success of the sprint review is stakeholder feedback. A constant cycle of communication keeps the project on track and produces what stakeholders want. Although stakeholders can't tell development team members how to develop requirements, they can give feedback to the product owner about the requirements and features they want developed and about how well the implementations serve customers' needs.

The feedback loop is a lean principle of continuous improvement. It also serves another purpose: The feedback loop keeps the development team involved and, therefore, emotionally engaged in the project.

Feedback is a common theme throughout scrum. Figure 5-4 shows how many layers of feedback are involved in the scrum framework. Each time feedback is received, it gets cycled back into the product backlog and sprint-planning sessions — truly inspection and adaptation.

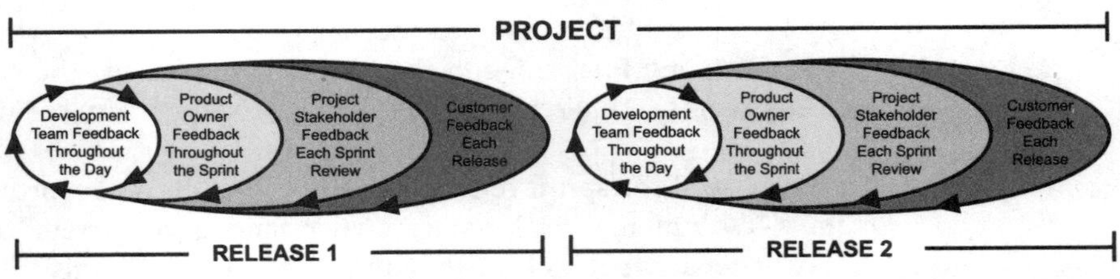

FIGURE 5-4: Multiple layers of feedback exist in a typical scrum project.

© John Wiley & Sons, Inc.

Product increments

The product increment is the final of the three scrum artifacts. (Chapter 2 in Book 5 discusses the product backlog, and Chapter 4 in Book 5 discusses the sprint backlog.)

Within a single sprint, the product increment is working product deemed done by the product owner and now ready to go to market. It's *potentially* ready to go to market because the product owner may not decide that the product is ready until later. But it's ready to ship as soon as the product owner is ready.

A product increment has been

- Developed
- Tested
- Integrated
- Documented

During the sprint-review meeting, this product increment is demonstrated to stakeholders. The inspect-and-adapt sprint life cycle continues as feedback is taken and translated into requirements. Then these requirements may be enhanced during product-backlog refinement; they may rise in priority for consideration in future sprints and eventually become new product increments.

The sprint review is about improving the value of the product. The sprint retrospective is how scrum teams can make this continuous improvement happen for their team and process.

The Sprint Retrospective: Stage 7

The seventh and final stage in the Roadmap to Value is the sprint retrospective (see Figure 5-5). This scrum event takes place after every sprint.

The purpose of the sprint retrospective is to provide an opportunity for the scrum team — scrum master, product owner, and development team members — to assess what went well in the sprint that was just finished and what can be improved. The process is inspection and adaptation one more time, with a focus on the people, processes, and tools that the scrum team uses.

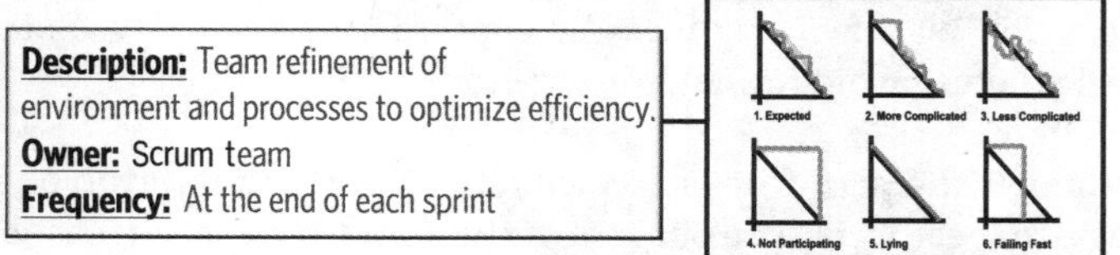

Stage 7: SPRINT RETROSPECTIVE
Description: Team refinement of environment and processes to optimize efficiency.
Owner: Scrum team
Frequency: At the end of each sprint
1. Expected
2. More Complicated
3. Less Complicated
4. Not Participating
5. Lying
6. Failing Fast

FIGURE 5-5: The sprint retrospective, the seventh and final stage in the Roadmap to Value.

© John Wiley & Sons, Inc.

The outcome of the retrospective should be plans of action to continuously improve scrum, people, processes, and tools in every sprint. Although the scrum framework is simple — three roles, three artifacts, and five events — and doesn't require tweaking, each scrum team has quirks and nuances because of their product, organization, and development methods. Through the process of inspection and adaptation, you can aim those individualities toward the project goals.

Because the sprint retrospective asks for input and feedback from all scrum team members, it increases ownership through engagement and a sense of purpose. Team spirit is enhanced, which in turn leads to an increase in productivity and velocity, which is self-management.

REMEMBER

It's critical in sprint retrospectives to create a trusting environment. Each person's view is listened to and respected, and nothing is taken personally. Trust is the key to keeping the retrospective from being a labyrinth of euphemisms or politics. The scrum master plays a pivotal role in creating an environment of trust.

WARNING

The sprint retrospective may unveil problems within the team. An adept scrum master can facilitate the event so that these issues are dealt with in an equitable, low-intensity environment. A sprint retrospective isn't for venting, but for actionable plans for improvement. Be on the lookout for passive-aggressive speech and personal agendas.

The sprint retrospective process

The sprint retrospective takes place at the end of every sprint, after the sprint review and before the next sprint's planning session. For each week of the sprint, 45 minutes is timeboxed for this event, so a two-week sprint has a timeboxed retrospective of 90 minutes.

The entire scrum team participates, and at the team's discretion, other people may be invited (such as customers and stakeholders) if the team believes that these people have valuable insights about needed improvements.

TIP

In preparation for the retrospective, everyone should consider how the sprint went and jot down any ideas or concerns. As always, use simple tools such as sticky notes; avoid formal presentations.

Although the scrum master facilitates the meeting, everyone participates at a peer-to-peer level. The purpose of the sprint retrospective is to inspect the sprint that just ended to

» Identify what went well in the sprint with the processes, tools, and team dynamics.

» Discuss and discover opportunities for improvement.

» Define an action plan for implementing the improvement(s).

During the retrospective, be sure to emphasize and give equal air time to what went well. It's important to focus on the positive and to identify what's working well so that you can keep doing it. Rejoice as a team in successes. Especially during initial scrum implementation, it's important to recognize the wins — big and small.

TIP

An effective way to keep things positive and avoid isolating people during a retrospective is the sandwich technique. Start with positive, work through negative, and end with more positive.

A retrospective discussion is action-oriented and doesn't focus on justifications. When you hear the word *because*, that's a good indication that the discussion has turned to justifying why someone did something a certain way. Keep moving forward by saying something like "This is what I experienced, and this is what might work better going forward." Don't say "I did it this way because . . ."

The Derby and Larsen process

TIP

Esther Derby and Diana Larsen wrote an excellent book called *Agile Team Retrospectives: Making Good Teams Great* (published by Pragmatic Bookshelf). Check it out for more tips and techniques on sprint retrospectives and other agile practices.

In *Agile Team Retrospectives*, Derby and Larsen point out that there is more to finding out what went well and what improvements need to be made than simply asking the same three questions at the end of every sprint. Retrospective facilitation takes preparation and strategy to get maximum participation, candor, and useful data from team members. The Derby and Larsen model for structuring a retrospective consists of answering these questions:

- What do you think went well?
- What would you like to change?
- How should we implement that change?

To maximize retrospective effectiveness, consider the Derby and Larsen process:

1. **Set the stage.**

   You want to establish ground rules for productive communication and clarify expectations and purpose from the beginning. Prepare the team for open and honest discussion.

2. **Gather data.**

   Making decisions based on superficial, bad, or incomplete data can do more harm than good. You want to uncover important topics, jog memories, and correlate experiences that need to be addressed. You want to know not only what people think, but also how they feel about it.

3. **Generate insights.**

   Many teams gather data but do nothing with it. Just as the best designs come from self-organizing teams, the best insights come from teams that take time to explore what the data means.

4. **Decide what to do.**

   Only through action can change and adaptation take place. Action requires a plan. Deciding what to do shifts the team's focus to moving forward — to the next sprint.

5. **Close the retrospective.**

   Closing provides the opportunity to scrum the retrospective through activities that evaluate the effectiveness of the retrospective experience and identify ways to improve it. It also encourages expressing appreciation.

TIP

Each aspect of the retrospective can be facilitated by a number of activities that are engaging and provoke individual thought and group discussion. Try doing an Internet search for *Triple Nickels*, *Five Whys*, *SMART Goals*, *Temperature Reading*, *Team Radar*, and *Mad Sad Glad*, which are all good activities to use during a retrospective.

TIP

To stimulate discussion in retrospectives, organize activities around specific questions such as the following:

- What is keeping us from increasing our velocity from 36 to 38?
- Does everyone have the tools needed to do the job?

- Do any impediments keep repeating?
- Is our daily scrum effective in identifying impediments and coordinating daily priorities?
- Is our team lacking certain skills, and if so, how can we gain them?

Some scrum teams need to be coaxed and prodded to get engaged. They may be hesitant at first to say what they truly feel. Others may want to talk at once and are bursting with ideas and input. A perceptive, proactive scrum master adapts to work with either type of group, or anything in between, to achieve the best results.

TIP

Find only one action to take each sprint. At the beginning, it may be tempting to address all issues the team discusses. Instead, find an action that is both high-impact and easy to implement. Pick the low-hanging fruit.

TIP

The results from the retrospective should be put into the product backlog as improvement items. The scrum team should agree that at least one improvement action goes into every sprint. Bring at least one priority retrospective item into the next sprint, perhaps from the latest retrospective. After all, why wait? The purpose is to inspect and adapt, so don't delay the adaptation part!

Inspection and adaptation

Scrum is about planning the right things at the right time. It's about responding to changing markets and lessons learned. It's about continually learning and assessing, minimizing risk, and maximizing value at every step — each point of work.

REMEMBER

The inspecting and adapting perspective provided in the official Scrum Guide (`http://scrumguides.org`) is a good way to wrap up this chapter. The italics have been added for emphasis:

> Inspections are most beneficial when diligently performed by skilled inspectors *at the point of work.*

The scrum guide goes on to state that adjustments are made as soon as possible. Adjustments occur as soon as an inspector realizes that the work has moved outside the limits and will cause an unacceptable product.

» **Understanding the feedback loop**

» **Maintaining transparency**

» **Dealing with antipatterns and external forces**

» **Correcting the course and testing in the feedback loop**

» **Establishing a culture of innovation**

Chapter 6

Inspect and Adapt: How to Correct Your Course

Often during product development, you find your product in a different place from what you expected. This chapter explores how scrum facilitates continuous learning and improvement. It also looks at how you can work in the presence of uncertainty instead of hoping that you can plan it away. After all, being agile is being able to learn and adjust as you go — being flexible enough to build the best product with the right features and with the best quality.

The Need for Certainty

Management's need for certainty of outcomes may well drive the downward spiral or decay of many projects and great ideas. They could refuse to accept the basic reality of uncertainty, settling for the relative safety of the known at the expense of the better. The power of the empirical approach is being okay with uncertainty until you've learned the information you need to have more certainty about the outcome of your project or goal. For example, six months from now, it will be difficult to know for certain if a needed component being built by another team will be finished on time if the other team won't begin development for three months from now. But two weeks before its expected delivery you can have a much clearer expectation of its readiness.

REMEMBER

Empirical means to learn or verify by means of observation. So, scrum is considered an empirical approach because each step of the way, you inspect your results and adapt immediately to a better outcome.

Figure 6-1 depicts the forecasting tool known as the Cone of Uncertainty. The basic principle is that outcomes are hard to predict across a span of time, but as you arrive closer to your goal, certainty increases.

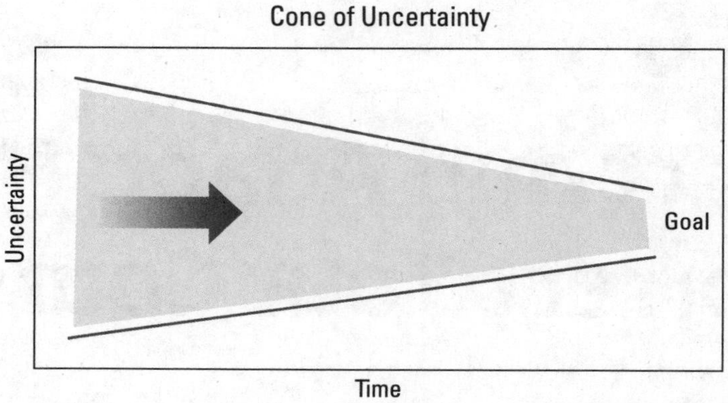

Cone of Uncertainty

Uncertainty

Goal

Time

FIGURE 6-1: The Cone of Uncertainty.

© John Wiley & Sons, Inc.

Weather forecasters use the Cone of Uncertainty to depict the path of hurricanes over the course of several days. The empirical approach embraces the reality of some uncertainty and provides a framework for managing the associated risks by continually improving and adapting.

The Feedback Loop

In economics, a *feedback loop* is defined as the outcome or results of one process or one cycle used to inform the next. This feedback loop is what feeds the data to the empirical inspection process. Figure 6-2 looks at the feedback process of scrum teams.

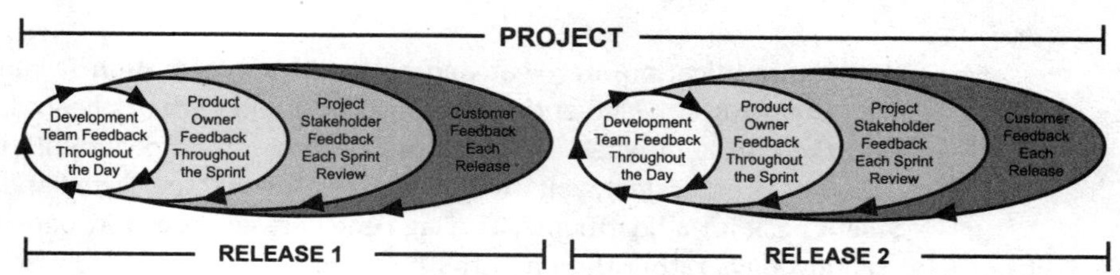

FIGURE 6-2: The feedback process.

© John Wiley & Sons, Inc.

The idea behind a feedback loop is that you can continually improve from the information learned from experience if you have a way to apply the lessons learned to future situations. An inherent part of the scrum process is recognizing that the knowledge and experience gained during each sprint need to be reintroduced in later sprints to inform the evolving plan. At the outset of a project, product roadmap and sprint plans are always made with the best information available at the time. The plans are accepted by the whole team and socialized throughout stakeholders. Rigid adherence to an exhaustive initial plan can ignore lessons learned during the process and stifle innovations from within the team. Instead, scrum uses customer and team feedback to continuously improve the plan.

You may wonder why you should plan at all if you know that an initial plan is likely to be flawed. You establish a plan as the first step in your learning process. Much as a flight crew files a flight plan based on the expected conditions so that crew members and air traffic controllers know what to expect, product roadmaps lay out the scrum team's preflight expectations. After a flight crew takes off, the members evaluate actual conditions such as weather, winds, and scheduling to adjust the flight plan as needed. Likewise, in scrum, you provide feedback throughout every day, and as you learn more information, you adapt your ideas and plan.

TIP

Feedback loops can be positive (resulting from successes) or negative (resulting from failures). Success can breed success, but failure can inform success if you learn from it. This concept is why you should ask both what worked well and what can be improved during each sprint retrospective. It's important to continue to support scrum successes and look for changes that can have a positive effect.

Transparency

Transparency is pervasive in modern society. In everything from open-source software to open collaboration on ideas, transparency is a broadly interpreted term. In scrum, transparency is a basic pillar of improvement. When channels of communication are clear and accessible, information is radiated throughout an organization. The entire organization knows what's been done, what's being worked on, and what's left to work on and any impediments blocking the way. Right from the start, you produce real results that are tested and then approved or sent back for adjustments. The lag time between the start date and usable results is now days rather than months.

Transparency isn't just about quickly seeing results. Everyone needs to look through the same lens. A framework (such as scrum) is shared, along with an agreed-on definition of *done*. Both observers and participants can see what's being accomplished and interpret the results in a common language.

It's important not to miss the critical value of transparency within the inspect-and-adapt process. Without a transparent culture, decisions are made with inaccurate data. Far too often we see organizations value fake good news over truth and end up making decisions based on bad information.

REMEMBER

Following are some basic principles of employing transparency in your projects:

- Just the facts. Display what is fully true to stakeholders specifically by only showing as complete work that is fully done according to your definition of done.
- Be open and clear about the plan, design, process, and progress.
- Make all information easily accessible to everyone.
- Post the roadmap, the release plan, and the definition of done on the wall where everyone involved can see them.
- Encourage an environment of factual measurements and outcomes.
- Have potentially awkward conversations early.

WARNING

It's common to want to avoid having honest and awkward conversations, but avoiding uncomfortable situations can cause problems. (In fact, whole books and courses have been written to teach people how to deal these situations.) You should understand the importance of knowing the hard costs associated with avoiding or delaying awkward moments. The most direct of these costs is time wasted going in the wrong direction and delaying a better course of action. Don't put off having those uncomfortable conversations; have them as soon as you realize that something needs to be addressed.

Antipatterns

The term *antipattern* has been used to describe a well-intentioned solution to a problem that instead causes unintended negative consequences. It's important for an organization that's adopting or maturing its scrum practice to allow scrum to expose antipatterns as part of the inspect-and-adapt process. It's also important not to customize scrum to match a flawed culture or practices. Instead, make changes in the culture to facilitate the success of your scrum practice.

You may be familiar with some of the following antipattern examples that occur in management and software development:

- **Analysis paralysis:** Being unable to move forward due to continual analysis and unwillingness to accept uncertainty
- **Smoke and mirrors:** Creating the illusion of further accomplishment, such as overstating quality or completeness
- **Seagull management:** Swooping in as a leader and making a bunch of noise and then flying away, hoping to have motivated everyone with a sense of urgency but instead causing fear and panic

Scrum teams and agile leaders need to look for the root causes and cultural antipatterns that block the feedback loop. Once the antipatterns are identified, they should be escalated to leadership as an impediment to the scrum process. Removing these cultural impediments needs to be a priority because they may hinder multiple scrum teams within the organization.

External Forces

A team can be affected by things outside the team that affect its ability to deliver the product. These forces act like a headwind or crosswind that forces an aircraft off course or behind schedule.

For scrum teams, these forces may be changing regulations, evolving architecture, or reprioritized features. A team may be powerless to change these realities, but scrum exposes the effects of the forces and often exposes alternative courses of action.

One common excuse for saying that scrum can't work in an environment is that external forces make it impossible for scrum to be successful. But scrum can succeed anywhere as long as there are sufficient buy-in and effort from the people involved to make it work.

In-Flight Course Correction

This section goes back to the analogy of the flight crew and the flight plan to explain the dynamics at play in planning and replanning based on empirical data. A flight crew always plans the details of an upcoming mission based on parameters assigned for that mission. The crew estimates fuel use, time in flight, and execution details based on all known and expected details. On the day of the mission, the crew members gather any updated weather reports and mission changes.

When the aircraft is airborne, members of the flight crew continuously evaluate speeds and headings and compare the plane's actual position with the flight plans. Figure 6-3 shows a planned route and a measured location in flight.

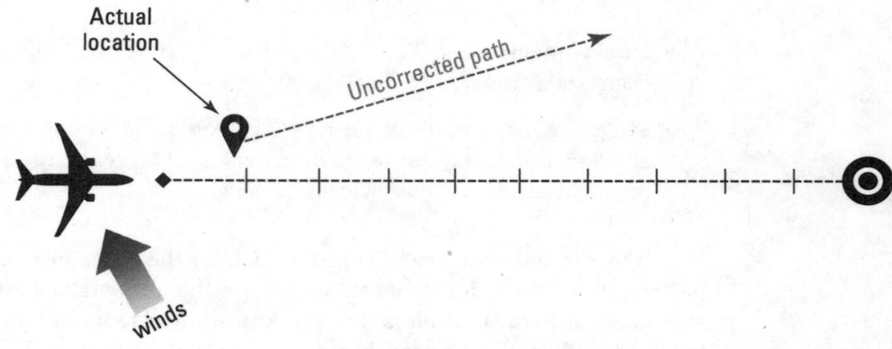

FIGURE 6-3: A flight path.

Each time crew members measure the location in flight, they evaluate why they're moving away from the plan. They look at the data to determine possible causes for the course adjustment, such as unexpected wind directions or velocities, or a difference between the planned heading and speed and the actual heading and speed. Next, they use the new information to adjust the plan to achieve the mission objectives — all this while going faster than 400 miles per hour. The flight crew repeats this inspect-and-adapt process over and over to ensure a mission's success.

In scrum, sprints (see Chapter 5 in Book 5) serve as perfect times to reevaluate and improve plans. In a transparent organization, new information is welcomed and applied to achieving product success.

WARNING

It is important to avoid the costly overhead of redundant or bureaucratic parallel processes. Some well-intentioned organizations expend more effort in measuring status and producing status slides than they do in building products, all in the hope of maintaining control or avoiding uncertainty. Creating status reports is an unnecessary parallel activity. An organization that has transformed to being agile and that has fully adopted scrum lets go of these artifacts and embraces the new way.

Testing in the Feedback Loop

In scrum, you test during every sprint, doing things such as code tests, functional tests, and tests for user feedback. Contrast that type of project with a typical waterfall project, in which testing happens only at the end of a project. Finding errors at the last minute causes either heroic and expensive fixes or pushing out the timeline. Like an aircraft whose path goes uncorrected, a product that is not validated ends up way off course.

The feedback received during testing and customer validation as the sprint progresses necessarily informs the daily priority. Corrections in the product are usually made the same day, while they're easiest and least expensive to fix and don't hold up further progress.

REMEMBER

On a scrum team, everyone is responsible for everything. It isn't up to one specialized tester to test everything for everyone else. The entire team owns the outcome, and all members care about quality.

A Culture of Innovation

Many companies, from the newest to the oldest, say that they want to be innovative. They likely see the market advantages of creative approaches. Yet the command-and-control structures that they use to manage products and processes impede the innovations they seek. Organizations' fundamental beliefs about purpose determines whether their teams work in a culture of innovation.

The scrum framework functions best in a culture of self-organization, purpose, and innovation. Product and process innovations are encouraged via the inspect-and-adapt model, and the idea of innovation is at the heart of working as a team. Using the feedback loop is a great way to encourage innovation.

Following are some ways that you can create an innovative culture:

- Empower teams to challenge conventions or constraints.
- Remove organizational barriers to creativity.

» Rethink how you motivate.
» Seek out creative lateral-thinking people.

Psychologist and philosopher Edward de Bono is credited with coining the term *lateral thinking*, which he defined as a mindset of challenging conventions and constraints. A lateral thinker can overcome his previous beliefs about limitations and conventions. A person who engages in lateral thinking doesn't ignore the existence of constraints; instead, he searches for ideas and solutions that aren't immediately obvious.

A popular modern narrative seems to be that engineers and developers are robotic, logic-based or linear thinkers. That isn't the case for most highly effective knowledge workers. They're creators with well-honed cognitive skills who can't be replaced by the complex algorithms that they create, and they thrive in a culture of innovation. As companies trend toward replacing business functions with automation, they need to make space for lateral thinkers who can go beyond perceived constraints. Without creativity, people get stuck making the same mistakes.

6

The Next Level: Enterprise Agility

Contents at a Glance

IN THIS CHAPTER

» Defining enterprise agility

» Transforming your organization with the 1-2-3 approach

Chapter 1
Taking It All In: The Big Picture

When you're getting ready to tackle a complex topic, such as enterprise agility, having a general understanding of the topic and what it entails is a great place to start. This chapter gives you that eye-in-the-sky view of enterprise agility. Here you develop a general understanding of agile and enterprise agility and the key distinction between the two. You discover how to build an agile enterprise without making the common mistake of trying merely to scale up agile frameworks to your entire organization. And you're introduced to some commonly used agile frameworks.

Defining Agile and Enterprise Agility

Because you're reading a book about enterprise agility, you're likely familiar with the topic, but readers may have different levels of understanding and different ideas about what "agile" and "enterprise agility" mean. This section defines the two terms and explain the key differences between them.

Understanding agile product delivery

According to the Agile Alliance, *agile* is "the ability to create and respond to change in order to succeed in an uncertain and turbulent environment." Instead of relying on extensive up-front planning, "solutions evolve through collaboration between self-organizing, cross-functional teams utilizing the appropriate practices for their context." (*Self-organizing* means the teams manage themselves. *Cross-functional* means each team has all the expertise and skills required to complete its work.)

Small teams (typically fewer than nine people) are empowered to collaborate and make decisions as opposed to being subject to intensive planning, rigid processes, and consulting management for direction and approval. The goal is to remove the management obstacles and excessive documentation that commonly get in the way of competent people doing their jobs.

REMEMBER

Agile frameworks originated in the context of software development, an area subject to rapid change — changes in end-user needs, technologies, and even the tools and processes used to develop software. To be effective, developers needed to be agile. They had to be able to make decisions locally instead of having to wade through the bureaucracy of traditional management matrixes. See Book 4 for a full introduction to agile project management.

The Agile Manifesto

In 2001, 17 software developers gathered at The Lodge at Snowbird ski resort in the Wasatch mountains of Utah and talked about why companies were having difficulty developing software. They represented some of the newer methods in software development — Scrum, Extreme Programming, the Crystal Methods, and continuous integration. After some discussion, they identified what was common among all these approaches: They were all lightweight compared to the complexities of the popular software development approaches at the time, including IBM's Rational Unified Process (RUP) and the manufacturing-inspired waterfall approach. They didn't want to become known as a bunch of "lightweights," so they settled on calling their approach "agile." Together they formed the Agile Alliance.

The word "agile" implied that software developers needed to be quick, nimble and flexible and able to change course quickly to take advantage of new ideas, changing customer needs, and emerging technologies. Many of the first articles and books on the topic included drawings of cheetahs.

After they settled on a name for their workgroup, a few of the members drafted the *Manifesto for Agile Software Development*. The Agile Manifesto, as it has come to be called, provides insight into the mindset agile embraces (from agilemanifesto.org):

We are uncovering better ways of developing software by doing it and helping others do it. Through this work we have come to value:

- **Individuals and interactions** over *processes and tools*
- **Working software** over *comprehensive documentation*
- **Customer collaboration** over *contract negotiation*
- **Responding to change** over *following a plan*

That is, while there is value in the italicized items on the right, we value the bolded items on the left more.

After the group came down from the mountain, they decided to continue to work together. In the weeks and months following their return, they added 12 agile principles they deemed to be consistent with the Agile Manifesto's four values and exemplary of the kinds of operating principles one could expect to observe in an agile group.

Agile principles

REMEMBER

Agile is based on the following 12 guiding principles:

- Our highest priority is to satisfy the customer through early and continuous delivery of valuable software.
- Welcome changing requirements, even late in development. Agile processes harness change for the customer's competitive advantage.
- Deliver working software frequently, from a couple of weeks to a couple of months, with a preference to the shorter timescale.
- Business people and developers must work together daily throughout the project.
- Build projects around motivated individuals. Give them the environment and support they need, and trust them to get the job done.
- The most efficient and effective method of conveying information to and within a development team is face-to-face conversation.
- Working software is the primary measure of progress.
- Agile processes promote sustainable development. The sponsors, developers, and users should be able to maintain a constant pace indefinitely.
- Continuous attention to technical excellence and good design enhances agility.
- Simplicity — the art of maximizing the amount of work not done — is essential.

- The best architectures, requirements, and designs emerge from self-organizing teams.
- At regular intervals, the team reflects on how to become more effective, then tunes and adjusts its behavior accordingly.

Agile frameworks

To facilitate their product development process, agile teams use different methodologies, referred to as "frameworks," such as the following:

- **Extreme Programming (XP):** A team of contributors, formed around a business representative called "the customer," operates according to certain basic values including simplicity, communication, feedback, courage, and respect. Through high customer involvement, close teamwork, rapid feedback loops, and continuous planning and testing, teams strive to deliver working software at frequent intervals (generally one to three weeks).
- **Kanban:** A team uses a "Kanban board" to track and visualize workflow. The board divides product development stages into columns, such as To Do, In Progress, and Done. Each work item is described on a "Kanban card" (index card or sticky note) and cards are arranged in the To Do column in order of priority. As team members are able, they pull work items from the To Do column and perform the work required. When they're done, the card is moved to the Done column. It gets more complicated, and the Kanban board can have many columns, but that's the general idea. Kanban strives to minimize work in progress (WIP), eliminate bottlenecks, and minimize waste (increase efficiency).
- **Lean Startup:** The Lean methodology follows a "Think it, build it, ship it, tweak it" approach with data driving ideas that lead to the development of code. The framework calls for a close connection with customers and frequent tests that drive a never-ending cycle of improvement.
- **Scrum:** A *product owner* provides a prioritized wish list of features, fixes, and so on, called a *product backlog.* A *development team* draws from the top of that list (a *sprint backlog*), decides how to implement those items, and estimates the amount of time it will take to complete that work in the form of a potentially shippable product (typically 30 days or fewer). The development team meets daily to assess progress and discuss issues. A *Scrum Master* functions as the servant-leader for the Scrum team — more in the capacity of facilitator than project manager. There is a clear separation of concerns as the product owner prioritizes *what* must be done next, and the development team figures out *how* to get those things done. See Book 5 for more about running a Scrum project.

Agile practices

Agile practices are specific applications of agile, as opposed to more general theories and principles. Here are just a few of the many agile practices:

- **Planning poker:** A game for estimating product backlogs. The product owner describes a product feature or function, and each player (team member) draws a card from her own deck with a value, such as 1, 2, 3, 5, 8, 20, 40, or 100 to estimate the time or work required. After all players have chosen their cards, they flip their cards over at the same time. If everyone's estimate is the same, that becomes the estimate; otherwise, players discuss the reasons for their estimates until consensus is reached or the team determines that more information is needed.
- **Product backlog:** A prioritized list of work items that must be completed to deliver a product.
- **Stand-up meetings:** Daily meetings during which everyone stands as a clear message that the meetings cannot extend past 15 minutes.
- **User story:** A description of a product feature from the user's perspective such as, "Customers can pay with credit cards, debit cards, or PayPal."
- **Work-in-progress (WIP) pull board:** Kanban uses a WIP pull board designed to limit WIP and encourage collaboration among team members. Seeing a WIP item on the board, the team can address the issue and remove the item. The notion of "pull" is key; instead of having work pushed on them, which often produces traffic jams and delays, team members pull work items from the board as they're able to do the work.

WARNING

Don't equate agile with a framework or a set of agile practices. Agile is more of a culture or shared mindset among team members that influences the way team members think about their work and impacts the way they work individually and together as a team. Having a shared understanding and appreciation of the agile concept is far more important than having shared practices. For example, mutual respect, trust, and a spirit of innovation are far more important than user stories and stand-up meetings.

Defining "enterprise agility"

Enterprise agility is agile for big products — typically one that requires many different teams throughout the organization that coordinate with many different departments and stakeholders.

While agile involves one or two teams working on a *part* of a product, enterprise agility may involve dozens or even hundreds of teams working on a *whole* enterprise solution. When you have that many teams working on a single enterprise solution, you start running into alignment issues and creating a lot of dependencies. Although you may want to remain agile, you need to start with at least a unified vision and have a system in place that enables the teams to communicate, coordinate, and collaborate efficiently and effectively to bring the vision to fruition and improve on the vision through innovation.

While agile team frameworks, including Scrum and Extreme Programming, work well on a small scale, they can lead to chaos when you attempt to scale up. To resolve this issue, the agile community has developed a number of enterprise agile frameworks — systems to help align the efforts of teams working together on a big product and reduce the number of dependencies.

Don't confuse enterprise agility with business agility. *Business agility* applies the agile mindset to the entire organization, which is sometimes referred to as "diffusion of IT-based innovations." Business agility deals with all domains, including those outside of product development, such as adaptive leadership, organizational design, human resources (HR) or personnel, and budgeting. This book's focus is on enterprise agility, *not* business agility (but a brief section on business agility is included near the end of this chapter).

However, for enterprise agility to work in your organization, everyone in the organization must adopt an agile mindset. Otherwise, the traditional management practices that are common in a culture that values predictability and failure avoidance will clash with the agile values of experimentation and innovation. You won't get the full benefit of agile if agile teams are merely doing what they're told.

Few organizations that consider themselves agile enterprises have the culture and mindset to make that claim. What typically happens is that an organization will have five or six agile teams that practice Scrum, Extreme Programming, Kanban, or Lean Startup. The teams may achieve some degree of success — the organization may produce higher-quality software and the developers may be happier — but until the agile mindset permeates the entire organization, it's not an agile enterprise and will not reap the full benefits of enterprise agility.

Checking out popular enterprise agile frameworks

Just as agile has several different frameworks for structuring the way teams function, enterprise agility has a selection of frameworks that provide direction for how teams work together on enterprise solutions. Currently, about a dozen well-established frameworks are available, and each one takes a different approach. Collectively, these methodologies form a cafeteria of ideas from which organizations can choose based on the organization's existing culture and the culture it wants to establish moving forward.

Following are some of the most popular frameworks:

- **Disciplined Agile Delivery (DAD):** A *process decision framework*, DAD encourages you to make certain choices at different points in product delivery, but doesn't prescribe any specific process to follow to make your organization agile. Instead of prescribing a process, it offers general guidance such as, "Here are the goals, and here are a few approaches for meeting each of those goals, and here's some guidance to help you choose the best approach." You're free to choose any framework and practices to mix and match, or create your own.
- **Large-Scale Scrum (LeSS):** A framework that contains many of the elements familiar in Scrum at the team level, including sprint planning, backlogs (prioritized lists of work items), sprints (the basic unit of development that results in an iteration of the product), daily sprint meetings, and a sprint retrospective (a sort of post-mortem meeting). The primary distinction between LeSS and Scrum is that with LeSS, you have several teams working in different "lanes" on different sprints, sometimes coordinating and collaborating between lanes.
- **Lean Product Delivery:** A system for reducing waste in products and processes by eliminating anything that's unnecessary, including excessive steps (in a process) and functionality (in a product) that don't bring value to a customer. The focus is on minimizing waste and maximizing value.
- **Kanban:** A system in which team members pull work items from a list of prioritized items on a Kanban board to work on them as their capacity allows. Kanban (signal) cards are used to indicate when a work item is ready for the next stage in the process. A buildup of Kanban cards in any stage of the process signals a bottleneck that must be addressed. The emphasis is on maintaining a smooth and continuous workflow.
- **Scaled Agile Framework (SAFe):** A collection of frameworks, principles, and practices that attempts to combine the best of top-down management with the best of agile. Teams work together as teams of teams (called "agile release trains," or ARTs) and as teams of teams of teams (called "solution trains") to achieve the enterprise's vision. SAFe is one of the more complex frameworks, adding numerous processes, layers, roles, and tools to solution delivery.
- **Spotify Engineering Culture:** A mashup or composite of agile frameworks and practices that's anchored by a strong culture of mutual respect, trust, and innovation. Teams (called "squads") and teams of teams (called "tribes") are encouraged to experiment freely, release products frequently, and tweak their products and processes for continuous improvement. Failure is not punished, and learning from failure is revered to encourage squads to experiment.

Practicing as much agile as your organization can tolerate

The downside of some of these enterprise agile frameworks, with the exception perhaps of DAD and the Spotify Engineering Culture, is that they try to "productize" your transformation. (To *productize* is to take a concept like agile and turn it into a pre-packaged solution.) It's like getting a suit off the rack when you really need something that's tailored to your organization.

The suit off the rack isn't really how most enterprise agile transformations are done. There won't be a day when you cross the agile finish line. Your organization will never reach an agile end state. Instead, much like a fitness program, you try to integrate these new ideas into the way you already work. It is a long process of small adjustments and continuous improvement, which is why you should think of your enterprise agile transformation as your organization accepting as much agile as it can tolerate. It's about how well your organization accommodates change.

TIP

Before you even think about where you want to be on the agile scale, look at where you are. How much change can your organization tolerate? Think of it almost like a room in which you can only put so much furniture. If your organization can tolerate only small changes, then think of the highest priority agile practices that you can try to implement.

WARNING

Don't try to go too big too soon. Many enterprise agile frameworks require that you make several big changes simultaneously. The hope is that if your organization can tolerate big changes, you can quickly reap the benefits of your transformation. However, your organization will likely snap back if you try to make too many big changes too quickly, especially if your organization has a low change tolerance. Consider a more gradual approach — starting with a few teams, reviewing the results, and then building on your success. Build the desired culture in one small corner of your organization and, if successful, it will spread, as long as you remove any obstacles.

REMEMBER

Large organizations usually have a change tolerance — how much change they can stomach without too much grumbling. If you exhaust everybody's ability to change, transformation is likely to grind to a halt. Everyone will go on working, but don't expect any more progress in the change department.

Achieving Enterprise Agility in Three Not-So-Easy Steps

The best way to implement enterprise agility in your organization is to take the following three steps:

1. **Review the top enterprise agile frameworks.**
2. **Identify your organization's existing culture.**
3. **Create a strategy for making big changes.**

This three-step process isn't really unique to enterprise agile transformations; it's pretty standard for making any large-scale organizational changes. You want to better understand the changes you're proposing, then understand the environment in which you're making the changes, and finally figure out how to apply these changes to your environment.

Step 1: Review the top enterprise agile frameworks

The first step toward an enterprise agile transformation is to understand what being agile means and get a sense of what different manifestations of agile look like. The fact is that you can achieve enterprise agility in an infinite number of different ways, just as you can use different health and fitness programs, mix-and-match programs, or develop your own program to become healthy and fit.

A great way to start is to look at the top enterprise agile frameworks described in the earlier section "Checking out popular enterprise agile frameworks": SAFe, LeSS, DAD, the Spotify Engineering Culture, Kanban, and Lean. Collectively, they provide several frameworks and include numerous agile principles and practices. Simply by exploring the different frameworks, you will start to develop a more agile mindset and begin to appreciate the full scope of enterprise agility.

As you explore the enterprise agile frameworks, try to look beyond each framework to understand the rationale behind it. If you can understand what the developers of each framework were thinking and the problems they were trying to solve, you will be well on your way to making the right decisions and choices for your organization. Remember, pulling a framework off the shelf may work fine, but be open to the possibility of tailoring it to your organization. No framework is a one-size-fits-all solution.

Step 2: Identify your organization's existing culture

One of the biggest reasons organizations fail in their transformation effort is that they don't take their existing culture into account. The problem is worst when an organization with a firmly embedded traditional management matrix tries to become more agile, because strong management tends to clash with some of agile's emphasis on self-organizing teams.

Organizations don't intentionally ignore culture. They're just so immersed in it that they no longer notice it. Culture is sort of like the air that surrounds us; we don't notice the air until a cold front sweeps in. We don't notice culture until it comes in contact with another culture, at which point cultural differences become readily apparent. You may not notice your organization's culture until you try to change it to something that's very different.

Don't make the common mistake of ignoring your existing culture, so size up your culture before attempting to transform it. Following are four common corporate culture types:

- **Collaboration culture:** Common in schools and professional training organizations, collaboration cultures are run like family businesses, with leaders acting as decision-makers, team builders, and coaches. Managers work closely together like a small group of friends, and the closer you are to the head of the organization, the more authority you have. These organizations are typically more open to change than those with a control or competence culture, so they tend to adopt an enterprise agile mindset more readily. However, in a collaboration culture, leadership may have a difficult time allowing decisions to be made at the team level.
- **Competence culture:** Those with the highest level of expertise rise to the top, become managers, and create and delegate tasks. A meritocracy. The management style is task-driven; it's all about who can do the best job at finishing the work. People in competence cultures often become highly specialized in their areas of expertise, because expertise is what is valued and rewarded. If they excel in more than one area, they're likely to be given too many tasks and become quickly overwhelmed, so they specialize. They also don't like to share their knowledge, because it places them at risk of losing some of their authority.
- **Control culture:** This culture is authoritarian with alpha managers setting the direction and beta managers following close behind. Leadership gives orders and demands compliance. Only a few individuals in the organization have decision-making powers; others must seek approval or permission, making the organization slow to respond to change. Such organizations favor order

and certainty and rely on large management systems that ensure predictable outcomes.

- **Cultivation culture:** Employee growth and development form the cornerstone of the organization. Managers seek to bring someone into the organization, hold them up, and then build them up. Charismatic individuals quickly rise to the top, and generalists commonly do well. These organizations tend to be more democratic and transition more easily to an agile mindset, but decision-making can be slow as consensus is sought among large groups of individuals.

TIP

Consider choosing a framework that's a closer match to your current culture than a match to the culture you want for your organization, so the transformation won't be too much of a stretch. Some frameworks are much more agile than others. For example, Spotify's approach gives teams a lot of autonomy, and that may strike you as the way you want your organization to be. However, Spotify's approach works for Spotify, because it's not a huge organization. Spotify has nurtured a collaborative culture from its inception, and the company redesigned its product's architecture to make it more modular, so a squad can work on one feature without having to integrate its work with a lot of other squads and tribes. If your organization has a strong control culture, making the leap to Spotify's approach may be as challenging as trying to jump across the Grand Canyon on a motorcycle.

Instead, SAFe may be the better choice because it has more practices for top-down decision-making. It allows for some agility while giving managers deep insight and control over the organization.

REMEMBER

An organization may fit into more than one category; for example, its engineers may be driven more by a competence culture, whereas marketing is run more in line with a cultivation culture.

The famous management consultant Peter Drucker once said that "Culture eats strategy for breakfast." This holds true for enterprise agility. Whatever strategies you pick for your enterprise agile transformation, they won't succeed without the support of a culture that values people, respect, trust, and innovation.

Step 3: Create a strategy for making big changes

As you think about your strategy for making big changes, look for the sweet spot between your organization's acceptable and unacceptable change, as shown in Figure 1-1. Finding that sweet spot is more art than science. Identify areas you want to change and areas where you're likely to encounter resistance. Try to understand why you may encounter resistance in certain areas. Your organization probably has gravitated toward a particular culture for good reasons, so you can decide whether and how an area needs to be changed. If a certain area is less agile for good reason, you may want to let it be.

After you've found your sweet (and not so sweet) spots, you're ready to start adopting the agile frameworks, processes, and principles you choose.

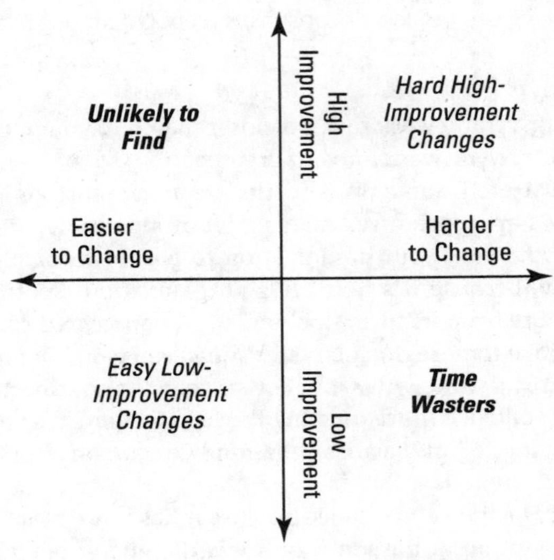

FIGURE 1-1: The change sweet spot.

Choosing a top-down or bottom-up strategy

When you're ready to start your enterprise agility adoption journey, you basically have two big-change strategies from which to choose:

- **Fearless Change:** A bottom-up approach, which can be driven by a few employees. Fearless Change tends to work better in competence, cultivation, and collaboration cultures. Fearless Change may also be effective in smaller, newer organizations that don't yet have a deeply entrenched hierarchy.
- **Kotter approach:** An eight-step, top-down process driven by a change leader, who can be a manager or an outside consultant. The Kotter approach tends to work better in control cultures — the most common culture in large organizations, which typically have a well-defined hierarchy.

See Chapter 3 in Book 6 for more about these two options.

TIP

Whichever strategy you choose, look for opportunities to make smaller, realistic changes. Instead of trying to force change on your organization all at once, win the war gradually, battle by battle. Pick the low-hanging fruit. Giving teams shared workspaces and providing agile training can get the culture ball rolling. Then, build on the momentum of your success.

Mapping out your plan

After you've thought about which approach is likely to work best, map out your plan. As you develop your change management plan, you're likely to end up with an odd combination of general and specific. You'll have specific deadlines of when to expect real improvement. Maybe you'll have a concrete objective to have all your business analysts sit with your team in a shared workspace. But then you'll have general guidelines on how to reach that objective. You may decide to have everyone in that shared workspace receive coaching on the benefits of sitting together. You could also just make it a simple matter of rearranging desks.

This combination of specific and general guidance gives your plan enough structure to be useful, but enough flexibility to allow teams to adapt. No change management plan will survive implementation; that is, your plan will change as you implement it, and that's okay. The trick is to spend just enough time planning to make your organization more agile, but not so much that you steal away time from the implementation or make your plan so restrictive that it undermines the agile mindset.

Setting the stage for business agility

A growing movement among businesses is to extend enterprise agility from product delivery to the entire organization in order to achieve *business agility*. This movement is really about "agile management" — taking agile ideas that have worked well for product development and using them to run an entire organization. Business agility is about "agilizing" every part of your organization.

The best way to think about the relationship among agile, business agility, and enterprise agility is to look at them as three levels of agile implementation (see Figure 1-2):

- **Agile (at the team level):** You have one-or-two agile teams working on a part of a larger product.
- **Business agility:** The entire organization adopts an agile mindset and a set of agile principles that guide the way everyone works independently and together.

» **Enterprise agility:** You have dozens or hundreds of agile teams working in concert on a single large product — an enterprise-level product. Some enterprise agile frameworks are simply expansions of team agile approaches; for example, SAFe is Scrum only with more Scrum teams and additional roles and structure to coordinate their work.

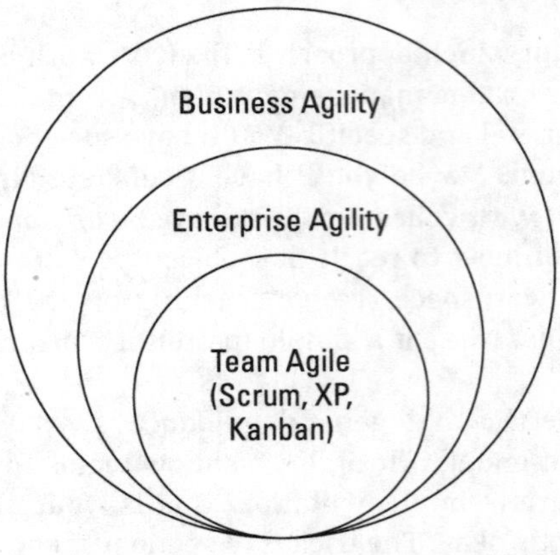

FIGURE 1-2: The three levels of agility.

© John Wiley & Sons, Inc.

In general, business agility deals with all domains, including those outside of product development, such as adaptive leadership, organizational design, and budgeting. While the more robust frameworks, including SAFe, touch on these domains, they offer little guidance to help you extend agile into these domains. It's a little like old maps that put dragons in place of uncharted territory with the caption "there be dragons here." They suggest that agility involves changes in other domains, but they don't explicitly describe the changes or offer guidance on how to make those changes.

WARNING

Resist the urge to tackle all three circles at once. Start with a few agile teams. After finding success with those teams, try enterprise agility with a larger product. As you gain success with several teams working together to deliver a whole enterprise solution, you can begin to start thinking about using agile methodologies to rework your entire organization. Don't try to rework your whole organization until you have a proven strategy for delivering enterprise-level products.

REMEMBER

Enterprise agility is *not* business agility. Enterprise agility is about delivering product. All the changes that you make to your organization in terms of frameworks, roles, processes, and practices should sit neatly within the realm of product development. Any changes you make to the overall organization or to organizational leadership will be in the realm of culture and mindset — to make management more receptive to an agile mindset and supportive of the big changes you're introducing to product delivery. Stay focused on delivering better products and not on creating a better organization. Certainly, success in product delivery may lead to an expansion of agile to the entire organization, but start with product delivery and work your way up.

You may find it strange to use practices that were designed for software development to run domains such as human resources, sales, marketing, or legal, but advocates of business agility argue that the accelerating pace of change demands that the entire organization become agile.

Practicing shuhari

Many of the agile and enterprise agile frameworks are influenced by Japanese manufacturing models developed to minimize waste and optimize workflow. Another common agile practice that comes from the Japanese is *shuhari,* a martial arts model of learning and honing one's skills:

- **Shu:** Follow the rules and learn the basics.
- **Ha:** Start to break the rules and put your own learning in context.
- **Ri:** Create your own rules and find your own way.

As you transition your organization's product delivery to enterprise agility, follow the shuhari approach. Here's how:

- **Shu:** Explore the top enterprise agility frameworks, principles, and practices to gain knowledge and wisdom of the commonly accepted approaches to enterprise agility. In other words, learn from the masters.
- **Ha:** Start thinking about how these approaches to enterprise agility would look in your organization. Think about them in the context of what's already in place and in the context of your organization's existing culture. What ideas make sense to you? Where do you think the developers may be wrong? Which ideas are likely to work well (and not so well) in your organization?
- **Ri:** Using all the knowledge and wisdom you've acquired, create your own custom framework tailored to your organization. Adopt the principles and practices that work best for your organization, mix and match, modify, and create your own.

REMEMBER

No two organizations are identical, and none of the enterprise agile frameworks is a one-size-fits-all solution. Use what works, toss what doesn't, and keep your eye on the prize — delivering value to your customers while achieving your business goals. That's what agile is all about.

» Grasping the challenges you're likely to face

» Getting to know your organization's existing culture

» Preparing for a cultural overhaul

Chapter 2

Sizing Up Your Organization

In many organizations, people think of enterprise agility as a bunch of new roles and practices. They spend most of their time transitioning people to new roles and having them adopt agile practices, such as writing user stories and conducting 15-minute stand-up meetings. Such an approach doesn't really address the biggest hurdle most organizations face.

Enterprise agility is a *radical* organizational change. It requires that the people in your organization think about their work in an entirely new way and act accordingly. They need to change ingrained behaviors and interact differently, as higher degrees of change lead to hgher degrees of collaboration. This is a much larger challenge, and it's one your organization should immediately start to tackle.

From the outset, start to think about your organization's culture and its tolerance for big changes. Almost every organization can make big changes, including yours. You just need to know how tall of a mountain you're climbing, what the obstacles are along the way, and how to avoid or overcome these obstacles. This chapter helps you identify your organization's culture to better determine if you are ready for a big change, and then provides you with a starting point for making that change.

Committing to Radical Change

Transformation means dramatic change. *Enterprise agile transformation* involves radical change in how an organization is structured and managed, how its people think and interact, how information flows, and how the organization responds to change and engages in innovation. As with most endeavors that require radical change, the most difficult challenge is to accept and embrace all that's required to make the change. Your entire organization must commit to no less than transformation.

A transformation is not a quick fix; it's a long and hard transition to get your organization where you want it to be. If you're unprepared or don't commit fully, you'll stumble through the transformation and gain only a small fraction of the potential benefit.

One of the biggest mistakes organizations make when trying to improve their enterprise agility is to underestimate the large effort required to make lasting changes. To avoid this common pitfall, prepare everyone at the very beginning for a long change process and overcommunicate the changes, as explained in Chapter 3 of Book 6. Encourage everyone in your organization to think about the transition as though he or she is packing for a long trip. If employees start out thinking that the transition will take only a few days or a couple of weeks, you're likely to experience one of the following outcomes:

- They'll short-change the transformation by declaring victory after only a few process improvements.
- They'll become overwhelmed by the change and quickly run out of steam.

Approach your enterprise agile transformation as you would a physical fitness routine. Can you imagine saying, "Of course I'm committed to better fitness, but I'm not ready to give up sweets," or "I'm ready for the change, but I don't have the time to exercise every day"? Achieving an aggressive health and fitness goal involves changing routines, working out, adjusting your diet, giving up bad habits, reducing stress, and so on. If you take only one or two of those steps, you'll get some benefit, but you won't achieve your goal.

Don't try to shoehorn agile into how your organization already operates. For example, one organization started its transformation to enterprise agility by saying, "Of course we want to be agile, but we can't combine our quality assurance team with our developers. They report to different managers." Another organization said, "Yes, we want to give agile a try, but we still need to work with scheduled milestones. That way, there's plenty of time for testing." That's not transformation. Following such an approach, the most you can hope for is a few positive agile-like changes; you won't achieve a true transformation.

Understanding What Culture Is and Why It's So Difficult to Change

Have you ever started working at an organization and been told, "This is how we do things here"? Maybe you made a mistake, and a colleague or supervisor said, "This is not how we work."

Now imagine if you responded, "Well, maybe we should change how we do things." How do you think that would be received by your coworkers? It's a safe bet most people working with you would find that attitude jarring, bordering on hostile.

That's what *culture* is — shared, deeply ingrained assumptions and beliefs that control the thoughts and behaviors of individuals in a group. Culture is at the very core of what makes a particular organization unique. The managers, business analysts, and project managers have all accepted that these practices (often referred to as *success patterns*) are the way to succeed in their organization. Fortunately, although these assumptions, beliefs, and success patterns are deeply ingrained, they're also learned, so they can be unlearned and replaced. But it's not easy.

Many organizations start by trying to scratch and claw their way through the agile practices, changing the way a few teams work. All their effort goes into implementing specific agile practices, such as standing up during meetings and creating new user stories (common agile practices described in Chapter 1 of Book 6), but these practices only scratch the surface; they don't change the thinking and behaviors required to stimulate innovation and achieve continuous competitive advantage.

Figuring out why culture is so entrenched

Former MIT professor Edgar Schein wrote a terrific book on culture called *Organizational Culture and Leadership.* He defined an organization's culture as a "pattern of shared basic *assumptions* that the group learned as it solved its problems that has worked well enough to be considered valid and is *passed on* to new members as the *correct* way to perceive, *think,* and feel in relation to those problems." One of Schein's key points is that culture is deeply ingrained, so ingrained that it controls how people perceive, think, and feel. Changing culture requires changing thought and behavior patterns, and that is no small feat.

In *Organizational Culture and Leadership*, Schein presents culture as three levels of stacked assumptions (see Figure 2-1):

- **Artifacts:** Subtle expressions of values, such as the organization's dress code, workspace, hours, posters, and even its perks, such as flextime or free coffee.
- **Espoused values:** The organization's values, as expressed in its mission statement, vision statement, and goals. These values reflect the way the organization *wants* to be perceived.
- **Underlying beliefs:** The thoughts, feelings, perceptions, and beliefs that employees share without explicitly talking about them. For example, everyone in the organization may value creativity and innovation over predictability or the organization may have an unspoken bias against women in leadership positions.

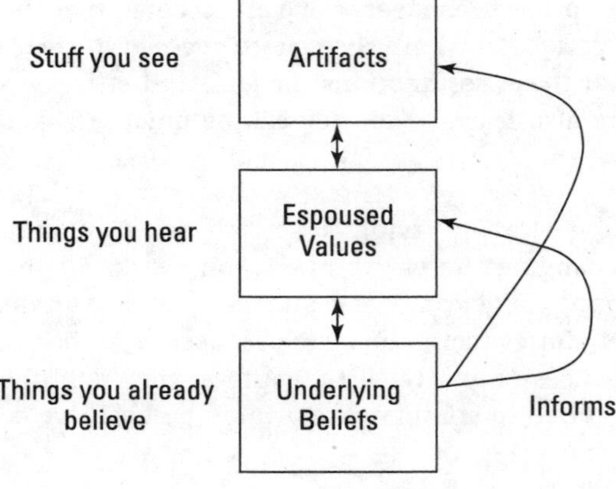

FIGURE 2-1: Three levels of assumptions about organizational culture.

© John Wiley & Sons, Inc.

You can usually sense an organization's culture when you first step into its office space. A high-tech business in Silicon Valley has a vastly different feel from that of a top law firm in Chicago. The tech business is likely to have large, shared workspaces. You'll probably see bicycles in the hallways, toys on desks, and people walking around in jeans. At the law firm, on the other hand, you'll likely see orderly desks, people in suits, large windows overlooking the city, and a tone that's more "professional."

REMEMBER

Schein groups assumptions into three levels to shed light on why culture is so entrenched and how challenging it can be to change an organization's culture. The most deeply rooted beliefs may be buried under layers of everyday assumptions. An organization can't change its culture simply by revising its mission statement or putting a new organizational framework in place. Changing culture involves changing deeply engrained mindsets.

Avoiding the common mistake of trying to make agile fit your organization

When large organizations start an agile transformation, they often try to bend agile to fit their reality instead of changing their organization to fit agile. Here's an example:

> In many organizations, management defines the product and hands the developers a detailed list of work requirements. The idea is that the more detailed the list of requirements, the more likely the customer will be satisfied with the result. In agile, on the other hand, the developer may start with a *user story* that describes what the user needs; for example, "As a shopper, I want to avoid having to wait in line to check out." The developer is given the creative freedom to come up with a solution.
>
> However, when some companies embark on their agile transformation, they write user stories that read more like work requirements, which completely eliminates the main benefit of the user story.

In this example, the organization adopted the agile practice of user stories, but it changed that practice to conform with the organization's culture (a need to be told what to do). Organizations that are considering the agile method should review their current practices for compatibility Some organizations have characteristics that are easier to support the change, including collaboration between and across business units and departments.

TIP

As you educate and train people in your organization, spend time both on training people what to do and on explaining the reasons why they're being instructed to do things a certain way. When people understand the *why* behind the *what*, they're more likely to "get it." Otherwise, they'll just go through the motions. For example, if people understand that user stories are supposed to give the developer more creative freedom, they're less likely to write user stories that read like requirements.

Identifying Your Organization's Culture Type

One of the first steps in changing anything is to identify what you're changing. You need to know what you have to work with. In the case of transforming corporate culture, you first need to recognize the nature of the existing culture.

Thankfully, William Schneider's book *The Reengineering Alternative* serves as a great resource for identifying organizational culture types. In his book, Schneider presents the following four culture types (see Figure 2-2):

- Control
- Collaboration
- Cultivation
- Competence

TIP

In his book, Schneider provides a questionnaire you can pass around your organization to help determine which of the categories best describes your organization.

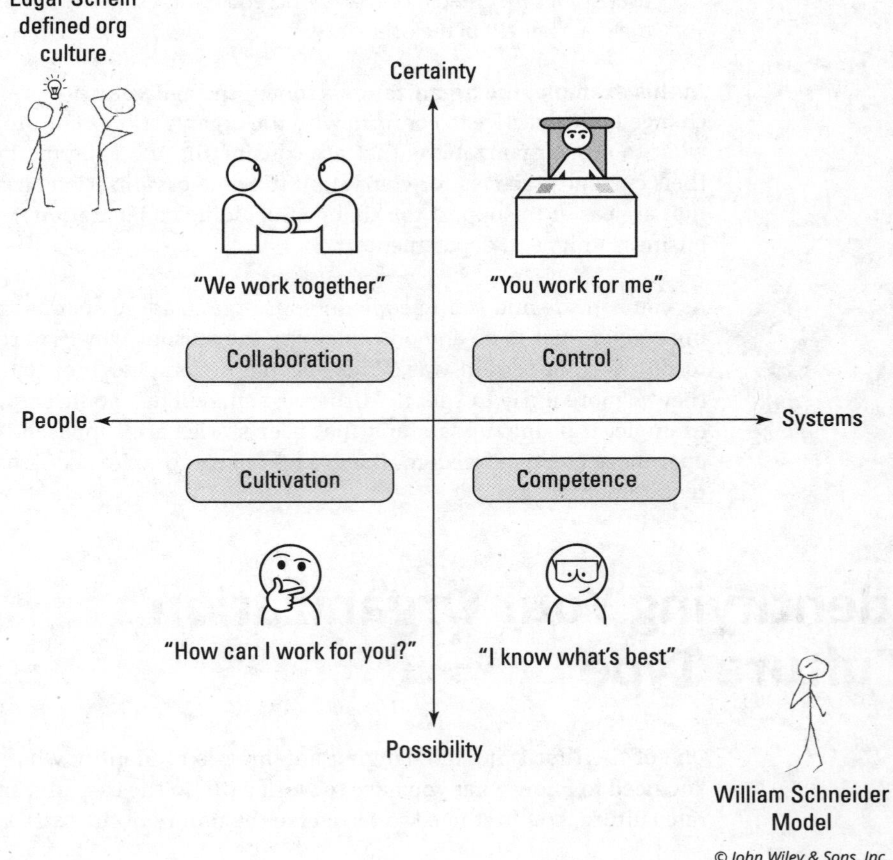

© John Wiley & Sons, Inc.

FIGURE 2-2: Four organizational culture types.

This section describes each of the four types, so you can figure out which of the categories best describe your organization's culture. Your organization's culture may fit in more than one category. It may value competence highly, but also value collaboration, for example. Also, different divisions or departments in your organization may fit in different categories; for example, your warehouse may operate in a culture of collaboration, while sales functions more in a culture of control, and the overall organization operates mostly in the spirit of cultivation.

Each one of these cultures has strengths and weaknesses. One culture may readily accept change, while another fights even the most sensible change but is highly efficient. The key is to understand the various cultures at work in your organization, so you can more easily determine the changes required to transform your organization's mindset and anticipate the challenges in making these changes.

A BLENDED FAMILY

One organization was closely connected to a branch of the military. Many of the top employees were retired officers or career military specialists. You could see that most of these top managers were comfortable in a strong control culture. They knew who worked for them, and they maintained a simple hierarchy.

If you looked at this organization, you'd immediately assume it had a strong control culture. Yet the founders of the organization made a special effort to stress the value of collaboration. The teams were required to work together to reach consensus on decisions, which made them much more informal. The top managers had worked together for decades and made decisions in weekly lunch meetings.

Even though this organization looked like a control culture, it was actually much closer to a collaboration culture. Each manager had a personal connection to the team. They interacted like friends and family. They created trusting relationships and tried to collaborate closely on decisions.

When they started their enterprise agile transformation, they needed a key sponsor to drive the change. In this case, it was a longtime employee everyone knew and trusted. They didn't need the large system most control cultures crave. Instead, they focused on a few relationships and relied a great deal on trust.

Think carefully about your organization's culture. It may be more complex than what it appears to be.

Running with the wolf pack in a control culture

The control culture has a tendency to be very authoritarian. Think of it as a wolf pack. Alpha managers set the direction for the entire organization with beta managers following closely behind to keep the rest of the organization moving in the same direction.

These companies tend to have a conservative management style and put a lot of emphasis on hierarchy. Everyone knows his place in the pecking order.

Emphasizing compliance

A control culture emphasizes compliance. The role of the individual is to comply with the requirements stipulated by that person's supervisor. The head of the organization communicates a vision and delegates to others who are responsible for bringing that vision to fruition. Some people in the organization, typically project managers and quality assurance people, make sure everyone follows along and that the resulting product conforms to the vision.

A control culture prefers that individuals stay within their functional areas. People don't usually move around much. If you're a project manager, then you're unlikely to ever move into another area, such as marketing or human resources. Roles and titles tend to determine the pecking order. Directors have authority over managers, and managers have authority over supervisors.

Seeking certainty with decisions

With so much emphasis on compliance, decision-making in this culture has a tendency to be very methodical and slow. The highest levels push for certainty and demand accountability. Although the C-suite leaders and directors may not micromanage, they want reports showing that decisions are being made and their directives are being carried out. They want to know that their employees have "signed off" and taken responsibility for their decisions.

Favoring big systems

Organizations with a control culture tend to be conservative. The rhythm of the organization favors order and certainty, and they rely on large management systems that ensure predictable outcomes. Many of them follow variations of the *Rational Unified Process* (RUP) — a software delivery framework that has a predictable lifecycle and many building blocks. (Several of the enterprise agile frameworks come from contributors to RUP.) An agile framework, such as the Scaled

Agile Framework® (SAFe®), has a built-in advantage in organizations with a control culture; it plays well with organizations that tend to like large complex frameworks with a lot of roles and clear lines of responsibility. These control cultures also tend to like the top-down alignment you see in SAFe.

TIP

If you're in a strong control culture, try to be aware of how your organization deals with big changes. Fight the urge to go big just because you're a big organization. Keep in mind that agile is not about changing everyone's roles. It's about changing a larger organizational mindset. Looking for another big system maybe not be enough to change how people think about their work.

Effecting change in a control culture

TIP

The best way to make big changes in a control culture is to get someone at a high level to sponsor the change. Think of this sponsor as the driver of change. Without a sponsor, conducting an agile transformation will be very difficult, if not impossible, in a control culture.

CULTURAL BIAS WINS OUT

One organization had a strong control culture. Its leaders liked the idea of being agile, but they struggled with some of their agile teams. The product owners couldn't work outside of their departments. The developers couldn't self-organize. All too often their managers would pull them off for other projects.

Even though they struggled with team agile, they decided to scale up to an enterprise agile framework. They wanted to try the Scaled Agile Framework (SAFe). They figured they'd substitute their current set of roles and responsibilities for a more agile set of roles and responsibilities.

In the end, they just ended up going back to their old way of working. They merely called the system something new. It was a little like that old rock 'n' roll lyric, "Meet the new boss/same as the old boss."

They would have been far better off if they had tried to understand why their agile teams were struggling before they tried something new. Bigger isn't always better. Whether this organization tried to be agile on a small scale or a large scale, it was bound to fail, because the organization had a strong cultural bias that favored control — a bias that's difficult to overcome when encouraging a more agile mindset. To succeed, it had to give up its cultural bias and relinquish some control.

Unfortunately, control cultures put so much emphasis on certainty that recruiting high-level sponsors becomes a huge challenge. Big changes involve a high level of uncertainty. The most common motivation for control cultures to make big, risky changes is when they have no viable alternative — when their backs are against the wall, sometimes when it's too late.

Rising with your ability in a competence culture

The competence culture, prevalent in software development companies, develops a hierarchy that's based on expertise. In a typical competence culture, a group of software developers creates a tool that becomes popular, and these developers become *de facto* managers. Because they were developers, they invest all their effort into making sure everyone conforms to their views of technical excellence.

The leadership focus in a competence culture is about setting standards and creating tasks. Leaders delegate tasks based on each employee's perceived competence level, resulting in a task-driven approach to management. As a result, people tend to specialize, which leads to the creation of deeply ingrained silos.

Living in the matrix

Organizations with a strong competence culture have a tendency to be set up like a matrix, with each person having two or more managers. For example, an analyst may have a department manager, such as a manager who oversees testing or analysis, and a project manager who's responsible for delivering a certain product. They approach any big change or challenge like engineers, breaking it down into tasks and distributing the tasks to various specialists. In a competence culture, managing the organization is like handling an engineering problem.

Suppose you're a quality assurance developer, and you report to a quality assurance manager and to a software development manager. Like everyone, you're prone to gaming the system. You don't like having two bosses asking you to perform different tasks, so you specialize in one area — quality assurance *or* software development. In other words, the company rewards employees for becoming highly competent specialists (though nobody in a leadership position is probably aware this is happening).

Managers within this culture tend to be professional, and a strong sense of meritocracy drives promotions. You can start as an intern and if you develop a high level of expertise, you'll quickly move your way up through the organization.

Putting in the hours

Organizations with a competence culture have a tendency to operate at a really intense pace. They're not always the easiest places to work.

Effecting change in a competence culture

Competence cultures can have a difficult time embracing an agile mindset, because agile teams favor generalization over specialization. On an agile team, you may have people who know how to both develop and test software. A product owner may also work in sales or marketing. (A *product owner* is a Scrum role responsible for representing the end user to determine what features will be in a product release. Find out more about scrum in Book 5.) You don't see that kind of fluidity in a competence culture. In addition, agile promotes open communication and knowledge sharing, which contradicts what's rewarded in the competence culture.

A CASE OF CULTURE CONTROLLING BEHAVIOR

One company, started by two engineers while they were still in grad school, fostered a strong competence culture. Their organization didn't have as much direct authority as you see in a control culture. The founders had a glass office, and you could see them pacing in their white socks. Anyone could walk into their office with new ideas and suggestions.

Still, the organization struggled with many different managers and areas of control. It was a great example of Conway's Law, which states that a technology company's management structure is often set up the same way as its software: It had a different department for the database, web front end, and testing — each with its own managers.

Even with this strong emphasis on software development, the organization struggled to have a more agile mindset. The best software developers had to be shared across many different teams. They also didn't take the time to teach others their expertise. They knew that if many people shared their level of competence, it would give them less authority. No one on the agile teams knew what the other developers were working on.

The managers wanted their agile teams to share knowledge, but the culture made the developers focus on their own expertise. Since they had this culture without thinking about the consequences, the managers struggled to make changes.

TIP

If you have a strong competence culture, you must find ways to encourage organizational learning; for example, you can create communities of practice (CoPs) in which different developers share their knowledge and expertise. These CoPs may meet every week or so to share their work and build up their organizational knowledge. Without some way for knowledge sharing, competence cultures will usually end up with superstar developers who jump from team to team.

In addition, competence cultures are likely to have some characteristics of a control culture, as well, such as top-down management. If your organization is a blend of competence and control cultures, you'll also need to recruit a sponsor from a high level of leadership to drive your enterprise agile transformation.

Nurturing your interns in a cultivation culture

In a cultivation culture (the rarest of the four culture types), leaders focus on empowering and enabling people to become the best possible employees. The managers like to make sure everyone is happy being part of the organization.

These organizations have a tendency to be set up like an authority wheel with the employee in the center surrounded by managers and resources to support the employee's success. Each manager is a spoke in the wheel.

In a cultivation culture, employees are encouraged to express themselves, so the culture places a lot of emphasis on employee surveys. These surveys enable managers to perform their primary function — employee development and growth. In this culture, managers want to bring someone into the organization, hold them up, and then build them up.

Using your smile, charm, and team-building skills

The leadership in a cultivation culture is typically based on how well you're able to convince people to follow your lead. If you're a charismatic person in a cultivation culture, you can become an authority very quickly — even if you're someone who's just started at the company in a low-level position. Managers focus on cultivating the strengths of other people, and they rise in the organization according to their ability to build teams and harness a team's talent to solve a problem quickly.

Embracing generalists

A cultivation culture is a good culture to belong to if you're a generalist. If someone with a problem knocks on your door, you never want to send him away disappointed. You solve the problem, refer him to someone else who can solve the problem, or assemble a team that's qualified to solve the problem.

Other characteristics of a cultivation culture

In addition to favoring generalists and charismatic individuals, the cultivation culture has several other identifiable characteristics, including the following:

- **The focus is on the people over the system.** People who thrive in large, complex systems (typical of control cultures) and are unable to adapt generally do poorly in a cultivation culture.
- **Departmental divisions are less relevant.** Employees are encouraged to work together to solve problems, even if they have to consult with other departments.
- **Employees are not always required to follow procedures.** If an employee has a better way to achieve the same or a better outcome, he's encouraged to do so.
- **The organization is probably a fun place to work.** Growth and development are encouraged, and employees are free to make mistakes on their paths to success.
- **Decision-making relies on consensus.** Decision-making can be difficult and slow, because it is highly participative and organic. As you can imagine, big groups of people can take a long time to achieve consensus.

REMEMBER

True cultivation cultures are rare. Some organizations may think they have a cultivation culture, but if you look closely, you'll see that they're control cultures with a thin coating of people-focused practices.

Millennials and other people under the age of 30 tend to be successful in cultivation cultures, because they often require more cultivation, and they typically seek consensus when making decisions. Organizations run by young entrepreneurs often operate in a cultivation culture.

Effecting change in a cultivation culture

People in a cultivation culture are more likely than those in other cultures to embrace change and adapt to new ideas, because change is part of the cultivation process. They have participatory meetings during which people talk about change, and after they reach consensus to make a change, they quickly embrace it.

Members of a cultivation culture tend to be more receptive to adopting an agile mindset. In many cases, as soon as the organization decides to transform, employees will self-organize into teams with a focus on learning more about agile. However, due to the slow decision-making process characteristic of the cultivation culture, expect to run into some delays.

TIP

Look to enterprise agile frameworks that focus on development practices and software craftsmanship. Some of these elements are in Large-Scale Scrum (LeSS), Disciplined Agile (DA), and the Spotify Engineering Culture.

Working it out together in a collaboration culture

In a collaboration culture, leaders are team builders and coaches, and generalists are favored over specialists. Management style is democratic, but it's not quite as fluid as in a cultivation culture. And while success in a cultivation culture is measured by how well you work with others, in a collaboration culture, success is often based on how long you've been with the company.

In a collaboration culture, the organization has less need to reach consensus when making decisions. Managers work closely together like a small group of friends to make decisions and to build and lead teams. Small clusters of coworkers are likely to form loose social networks.

Collaboration cultures are almost as scarce as cultivation cultures. You rarely see such a culture in software development organizations; it just doesn't play to that industry's leadership style. You see it more often in schools and professional training organizations.

Honoring the family

The big difference between the collaboration and the cultivation cultures is that the authority in collaborative cultures comes from long-term relationships. Organizations are run almost like a family business. The closer you are to people at the head of the organization, the more authority you have. The top people collaborate closely on the overall direction. Think of it like a classic crime family. You have a few older founders at the top and then their trusted group of friends and family all the way down.

These organizations tend to make decisions via brainstorming meetings and through some experimentation. They're a little more open to change than the control or competence cultures, which helps when the organization is trying to embrace an agile mindset. If you have a collaborative culture, it's usually easy for your organization to accept change.

However, some key components of an agile mindset may be difficult to adopt. An agile team must have the authority to pursue new ideas and make mistakes. That authority is pushed down to the team level. However, collaboration cultures tend to cluster the authority at a high level. They're more democratic, but only slightly more.

THAT'S NO WAY TO DEVELOP SOFTWARE!

A group of private preschools was trying to create an in-house, web-based student management system. They had a strong collaboration culture. The owner founded the schools as a family business. Its top managers had been with the school for decades. They all went to each other's houses for the holidays.

The software project was driven by one of its earliest employees, now a manager. The owner and this manager would go to lunch and plan the software on napkins using crayons. Then the manager would come back and give the napkins to the product owners. When the product owners had questions, the manager had few answers. They could never meet with the owner directly because they weren't comfortable working with the newer employees.

The agile teams ran into the same challenges as they would in a strong control culture. They didn't have the authority to make their own decisions, so they had to rely on the owner and manager (two people outside the team) to design the software, and these people were often unavailable to provide feedback.

REMEMBER

Even with their family appeal and open collaboration, this culture has many of the same challenges as a classic control culture. You still have a concentration of authority that makes embracing an agile mindset more difficult.

Effecting change in a collaboration culture

Although a pure collaboration culture is rare, many organizations have some aspects of it. Typically, what happens is that a company starts as a family business or partnership and grows to become a large company in which that culture can no longer operate, but remnants of the culture still exist near the top.

When transitioning a collaboration culture to enterprise agility, consider the following:

- **Look for key aspects of a collaboration culture to adopt.** The collaboration culture has many characteristics that support an agile mindset, including collaborative teams, a preference for generalists over specialists, and a democratic management style. Leverage these characteristics as you move the organization to a more agile mindset.
- **Recruit a sponsor from the top ranks.** This is the same approach recommended for control cultures (described earlier in this chapter). To get anything done in a collaboration culture, you must get leadership's endorsement. They are the only ones with the authority to approve the change, and they need to

loosen the reigns to give development teams more freedom to make decisions. More important, they're the only people the rest of the organization will follow.

WARNING

- **Watch out for family arguments.** When you're transforming an organization with a collaborative culture into an agile enterprise, you may encounter competing visions among the "family members" regarding the end product — the organization's structure and function after the transformation. When visions clash, you're likely to get caught up in family squabbles that can slow and even undermine your efforts and make your job that much more difficult.

You're unlikely to have an organization that's large enough to deliver enterprise software but still runs like a family business. However, parts of your organization may have certain elements of this culture, so be prepared to address the challenges that this culture type presents.

Laying the Groundwork for a Successful Transformation

In general, organizations fail to make real changes for three reasons:

- **The organization's leadership doesn't fully understand the purpose of the change or appreciate its value, or they do a poor job of communicating it to others in the organization.** As a result, they meet with a lot of resistance. After all, why would you change what you're doing if you don't think the change is necessary or beneficial?
- **The organization's leadership doesn't have a clear vision of what the organization will look like after the change has been successfully implemented, or they have the wrong vision.** In other words, they have no goal or the wrong goal. An example of a wrong goal in an agile transformation would be trying to maintain a strict top-down organizational structure to micromanage the development teams.
- **The organization's leadership doesn't have a plan for implementing the transformation, so they fail to "pack for the long journey."** They expect the transformation to occur over days or weeks, when it requires months to years. As a result, they often give up prematurely before they have a chance to capitalize on the many benefits that the big change has to offer.

REMEMBER

Note that none of these challenges references agile practices, such as user stories, 15-minute stand-up meetings, or planning poker (all described in Chapter 1 of Book 6). Adopting these practices is relatively easy. The difficult aspect of any agile transformation is not in changing what people do on a daily basis, but in changing the organization's structure and the way it operates, and in changing how people approach their work and how they work together. Replacing a control culture that has clearly demarcated departmental boundaries with cross-functional, self-managed teams is much more challenging than having your developers play a round of planning poker to estimate their workloads.

This section offers guidance on how to prepare the foundation for a successful enterprise agile transformation by avoiding these common mistakes.

Appreciating the value of an agile organization

People don't change unless they have good reason to do so. Many organizations fail to implement major change initiatives simply because management wasn't fully convinced of their benefits or failed to communicate those benefits to the people in the organization who needed to implement the change. As a result, everyone made half-hearted or symbolic attempts to change, failed, and then concluded that the change was simply a bad idea.

REMEMBER

Prior to embarking on your journey to transform your organization into an agile enterprise, make sure the benefits are clear in your own mind and in the minds of everyone in your organization who will be leading the change:

- **Collaborative excellence:** In agile enterprises, everyone, including management, employees, customers, and stakeholders, collaborates to create and deliver value. You don't have just a few people at the top of the organization determining what's best for the customer and the organization.
- **Continuous improvement:** Agile enterprises embrace continuous improvement in both the product and the process for creating it. Over time, the organization evolves, often with little, if any, management oversight.
- **Improved transparency:** Enterprise agility drives a culture of transparency that increases visibility of obstacles and dysfunction in both products and processes. After adopting an agile framework, you may be surprised at the number of problems your organization has. In most cases, the transformation didn't create the problems, it merely exposed them.
- **Increased business value:** With enterprise agility, the entire organization focuses on delivering value to customers and to the organization. The emphasis is on eliminating or at least significantly reducing anything in the organization that doesn't contribute value.
- **Ability to exceed customer expectations:** By involving customers in product development, the organization is better equipped to meet customer needs and exceed their expectations.

- **Enhanced innovation:** Enterprise agility encourages teams to experiment and to learn from success and failure, promoting a spirit of innovation that gives agile enterprises a competitive edge.
- **Ability to adapt quickly to changing conditions:** By localizing decision-making and accountability, teams can adapt more quickly to take advantage of emerging technologies and respond to changes in the marketplace. Enterprise agility essentially gives large organizations the agility often seen in startups and other small businesses.

Clarifying your vision

Before you try to initiate any big change, develop a clear vision of what your organization will look like or how it will operate differently after the change is in place. Your vision should include the purpose for making the change; for example, "To improve our product delivery agility, so we can deliver greater value to our customers faster." Here's one approach for developing a vision for enterprise agility:

1. **Gather all stakeholders or reps from different stakeholder groups in a room for a brainstorming session.**

   This is a great opportunity to bring in people who are likely to resist change, so they have a voice, and you can address any concerns they may have.

2. **Highlight the problems or limitations with the way your organization currently delivers value/product to customers.**

   Ask participants to point out other limitations or challenges in the current system.

3. **Present agile as a solution, pointing out specifically how it can address the limitations or challenges on the list.**

   Ask participants for their input. This is a good opportunity to identify any pockets of resistance you're likely to encounter.

4. **Ask participants to suggest vision statements that describe the way the organization needs to change to more effectively overcome the challenges it faces and to achieve its goal of increasing its enterprise agility.**

   Write down suggested vision statements on your whiteboard.

5. **Engage the group in a discussion until you arrive at a general consensus on the vision statement.**

   Your goal is to walk out of the brainstorming meeting with a vision statement that everyone in the group accepts. An inability to reach consensus on the vision is usually a sign that your transformation will have a difficult time succeeding.

WARNING

Starting without a clear vision guarantees failure. Many organizations don't have a sense of their own culture. They can't envision how agile will fit with their larger organizational mindset. They haven't even considered whether their organization is open to change. Without a clear vision, you're unlikely to be able to overcome the resistance that always accompanies a major change.

Planning for your transformation

After analyzing your existing culture and developing a clear vision of what you want your organization to look like after the change, you have points A and B — your point of departure and point of arrival. All you need now is a map (a plan) that connects the two points. Chapter 3 in Book 6 provides detailed guidance on how to develop a plan for implementing an enterprise agile transformation. Your plan may look something like this, which is based loosely on the six-step adoption plan for Large-Scale Scrum (LeSS):

1. **Choose or develop your own enterprise agile framework.**

   You can review some enterprise agile frameworks in Chapter 1 of Book 6, and choose the framework that's best suited to your organization's existing culture. You generally want to choose the framework that you think your organization will transition to easiest.

2. **Develop an overall strategy for implementing the change.**

   For example, many organizations start small, with a single product and two or three teams. After these teams have successfully adopted the new approach and are satisfied with the results, the change can be extended out to other products or product lines or to other teams.

3. **Establish a time frame for implementing the change.**

   Keep in mind that large organizations tend to take a long time to adopt any new approach. Think in terms of months and years, not days and weeks.

4. **Create a consensus document for everyone who will be involved in implementing the change.**

   Your consensus document must clearly describe the vision and provide all involved with a list of priorities they need to focus on when addressing their changes locally. (See Chapter 3 in Book 6 for details.)

5. **Provide education and training to everyone in the organization who will be involved in and affected by the agile transformation.**

   Your approach to education and training depends on your strategy for implementing the change. If you're planning to roll out the change to the entire organization, everyone needs to receive agile education and training. If you're starting with one product and only a few teams, focus on training those who will be involved from the start.

Education and training are important in changing the way people in your organization think about the way they do their work. As they begin to understand and experience the benefits of enterprise agility, they will begin to share their experience with others in the organization, which will help drive the cultural change that delivers the greatest improvements.

6. **Build cross-functional teams.**

   The team is the fundamental unit in agile. Teams must be cross-functional, meaning they have all the knowledge and skills required (design, development, analysis, testing, and so forth) to deliver a product end-to-end to the customer.

7. **Define "product."**

   Your product is anything of value delivered to the customer. Identify the value you deliver to the customer and use it to formulate your definition of "product." Everyone must agree on what the product is before your organization can begin to work on delivering it more effectively to the customer.

8. **Define "done."**

   The definition of "done" (DoD) is a term from Scrum software development that refers to a set of criteria that must be met for a product to be considered satisfactorily completed. For example, a DoD may state that "done" means a feature has been tested and successfully integrated into a working version of the product. Without an agreed-upon DoD, teams may never be able to tell when a product is ready for delivery. (Flip to Book 5 for an introduction to running a scrum project.)

9. **Provide teams with the resources they need to complete their work.**

   In agile, the role of organizational leadership shifts from manager to leader-servant. Leadership sets the mission and overall vision, provides the teams with the resources they need, and then steps out of the way, trusting the teams to deliver the highest quality product to the customer.

In Scrum, teams conduct two-part sprint planning meetings where they first figure out what needs to be done and then determine how they will get it done. Approach your agile transformation plan the same way. First, figure out what your organization needs to do (or be) and then how your organization will do it (or be it). The vision statement describes what your organization must do. Your plan describes how to do it.

» Using Kotter's eight-step change model for a top-down change

» Changing from the bottom up with the Fearless Change approach

» Overcoming common obstacles to big change

Chapter 3
Driving Organizational Change

Organizations are like cruise ships — they set their course and when they reach cruising speed are slow to change direction. They're likely to remain on course unless a significant amount of directed energy is applied to make them change direction. In an organization, this impetus typically comes from the leadership of the organization (at the top) or from one or more highly motivated and influential groups or individuals working at lower levels of the organization (from the bottom). Ideally, forces at the top and throughout the organization drive the change.

This chapter provides the guidance you need to determine whether a top-down or bottom-up approach to organizational change management is likely to be most effective for your organization, and it describes two formal change management approaches: the eight-step change model designed by John Kotter for driving change from the top and the Fearless Change approach to drive change from the bottom. Finally, this chapter addresses the obstacles you may encounter as you try to implement a major organizational change (such as enterprise agility) and offers suggestions on how to overcome these obstacles.

Choosing an Approach: Top-Down or Bottom-Up

When you're transforming your organization into an agile enterprise, you have two approaches from which to choose:

- **Top-down organizational change** is driven by the business owner, C-suite executives, or top-level managers — an individual in the organization who has a lot of authority. Choose a top-down approach if your organization has a strong control culture and a leader near the top of the organization who's committed and has the authority to drive the change.
- **Bottom-up organizational change** is driven by teams, individuals, mid-level managers, or outside consultants — an individual or a group that believes passionately in the potential benefits of the change. Choose a bottom-up approach if you're having trouble getting support from your organization's leadership.

Start the process by trying to understand your organization's culture, as explained in Chapter 2 of Book 6. A top-down approach is generally effective regardless of culture, but if you're unable to recruit an influential advocate at the top of the organization, your only option may be to start small and demonstrate agile's value locally before introducing it to the entire organization.

Soon after the Agile Manifesto, most agile transformations started from the bottom up with software developers who knew about the benefits of agile teams from their colleagues. Most managers stepped back and allowed the agile teams to take the lead, because they saw no reason to resist if the teams improved product delivery. Because enterprise agility requires more coordination among teams, managers have a greater incentive to get involved early on, so enterprise agile transformations are commonly driven from the top down.

Top-down and bottom-up organizational change are not about who's involved in making the change. Both approaches are effective regardless of whether the transformation is initiated at the top or bottom of the organization. An organization may even use both approaches in tandem; for example, a change leader near the top of the organization may decide that the best way to implement the change is to take a gradual approach with a few teams in one area of the organization and extend it after these initial teams experience some degree of success and are able to serve as evangelists and provide training.

Don't underestimate the work and persistence required. Many organizations approach their agile transformation as a pep rally, bringing in one or more consultants or coaches to communicate their passion for enterprise agility, as if that will be enough to drive the change. That's not how most large organizations change. Instead, they change direction only through a relentless pursuit of small improvements and over communicating the changes they are making. It's less like a pep rally and more like training for a marathon. You can't run a marathon just by being excited about it; you have to hit the pavement every day (maybe twice daily) regardless of the weather, adopt a healthier diet and lifestyle, and build on small improvements. Likewise, transforming an organization into an agile enterprise involves the day-to-day work of pushing the organization in a new direction. Enthusiasm is great for motivation, but it needs to be combined with hard work.

Driving Change from Top to Bottom with the Kotter Approach

You can find plenty of top-down approaches to organizational change, but a recommended approach is Kotter's eight-step change model:

1. **Create a sense of urgency around a Big Opportunity.**

   Identify a risk or opportunity and then examine how your organization will be impacted if it fails to respond.

2. **Build and evolve a guiding coalition.**

   Assemble a group with a commitment to change and the authority to lead the effort. This team should work independently of other power structures in the organization.

3. **Form a change vision and strategic initiatives.**

   Envision your organization as one that has the ability to take full advantage of the Big Opportunity you identified, and then develop a strategy for transforming your organization from its current state to your vision of the ideal.

4. **Enlist a volunteer army.**

   Create a group to spearhead the change both by advocating for the change and by adopting and then demonstrating the value of the change. This group needs to lead by example.

5. **Enable action by removing barriers.**

   Remove organizational obstacles standing in the way of change, encourage risk taking, and get people talking about agile.

6. **Generate (and celebrate) short-term wins.**

   Create opportunities to show improvement. For example, you can create a new metric and then work to show improvement on meeting that metric. Recognize and reward others for being part of the improvement.

7. **Sustain acceleration.**

   Build on short-term wins and try to use them as evidence that you can make further changes. Try to create momentum to change structures and remove policies that could undermine the vision.

8. **Institute change.**

   Make the connection between the successful changes and the organization's success. Promote employees who share the vision and are helping to generate the wins into management positions, so they have more authority to drive change.

The creator of this approach, John Kotter, referred to the steps collectively as XLR8 (accelerate), with each step serving as a change accelerator. Kotter's early book was called *Leading Change*. He refined his approach in a later book titled *Accelerate: Building Strategic Agility for a Fast-Moving World (XLR8)*. Each step flows to the next, almost like a classic waterfall model (see Chapter 1 in Book 6). Most organizations that try the Kotter approach think of it as a big one-time event. It's used as an organizational shakeup, which is why many companies take this approach only if they feel their core business is in danger.

REMEMBER

Change is not a one-time event. As shown in Figure 3-1, change is an ongoing process, and the steps, though sequential, form an ongoing cycle.

Step 1: Create a sense of urgency around a Big Opportunity

For the Kotter approach to be successful, you must be or recruit a strong leader at the top of the organization who has the authority to drive the change, and this leader needs to create a sense of urgency. This person has to convince the rest of the organization that the change being proposed is essential to the organization's continued success. In many ways, the change leader serves as a field commander, rallying the troops and then providing direction, so that they can implement the change.

The problem is that most organizations don't have field commanders with free time. The types of leaders who need to drive this change are usually CEOs or high-level managers. In large organizations, leadership is almost always tied up with strategic initiatives and financial concerns and is often unaccustomed to leading what they view as changes to operations — something they delegate to lower-level management. As a result, top-level leaders try to outsource this leadership role to outside consultants or change-management firms. Unfortunately, these outsiders, while they certainly have the required expertise, lack the recognition and authority to drive the change.

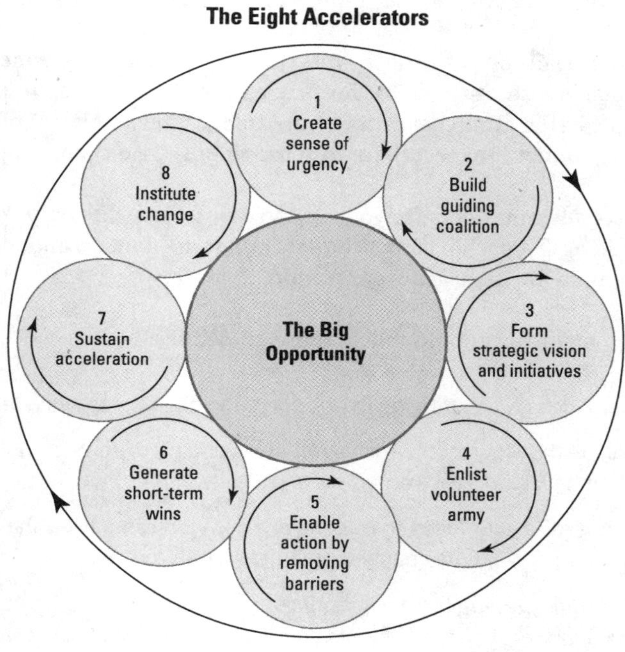

FIGURE 3-1: Kotter's eight-step change model.

© John Wiley & Sons, Inc.

REMEMBER

Don't try to delegate change leadership to someone outside your organization, such as an Agile Coach. Instead, choose a leader or build a coalition within your organization and give it the authority to drive the change. This same individual or group will take the lead on all eight steps of the Kotter change management approach.

Step 2: Build and evolve a guiding coalition

A *guiding coalition* is a powerful, diverse, enthusiastic team of volunteers from across an organization that serves as the social leaders of the change initiative. In enterprise agile transformations, the guiding coalition is typically called a center of excellence (CoE). The Scaled Agile Framework® (SAFe®) calls this the Lean-Agile Center of Excellence (LACE).

TIP

Expect your guiding coalition to represent roughly 5 percent of the overall transformation. For example, if you have 100 people involved in product delivery, the coalition may include about 5 people. If 1,000 people are involved, you'll want about 50 people in the coalition, but a group of 50 probably won't get much done, so break them up into smaller groups of no more than 9 people per group.

Divide the coalition into those who contribute ideas (everyone in the coalition) and a small subset responsible for driving the change. Keep in mind that most of the people in the group have other full-time responsibilities. You want to get their opinions, but don't expect them to serve as full-time change agents.

TIP

As you recruit volunteers for your CoE, try to achieve diversity. You want your CoE to include Agile Coaches, practitioners, and some domain and technical experts to connect agile to the larger organization.

Coalition members should follow these guidelines:

- Share ideas without trying to position yourself as an agile leader.
- Work with fellow members to craft ideas and try to solve complex problems about how to increase organizational agility.
- Standardize your ideas so that the organization can have a shared understanding of what the changed organization will look like.
- Align with Lean-Agile principles of continuous improvement and inspecting and adapting. The team should come up with an initial plan that everyone knows will evolve through its implementation.

WARNING

Watch out for HiPPOs (highest-paid-person's opinions)! The CoE's focus should be on learning and on reaching consensus regarding the change initiative. The coalition shouldn't be merely an extension of management that does what the CEO instructs it to do.

Step 3: Form a change vision and strategic initiatives

The first order of business for the CoE is to create a mission statement. Keep it short and simple, as in the following example:

> Sandwich Shop Enterprises is an organization that develops a software program to compare the menus of different restaurants. We've created a Lean-Agile Center of Excellence (LACE), which is a full-time, cross-functional, self-organized team that is driving the change to improve our organization's Lean-Agile mindset. We will provide guidance on Lean-Agile to the rest of the organization related to training, process improvement, tools, culture, and governance.

Next, create a whiteboard with the following three columns and brainstorm the CoE's scope of responsibility in each area:

- **Doing:** List everything the CoE plans to do to achieve its mission; for example, leadership and team training.
- **Not doing:** List areas that are outside the coalition's sphere of responsibility, such as managing teams.
- **Success metrics:** List measurements of success, such as the percentage of people who received agile team training or the number of agile teams.

REMEMBER

Reach a high level of agreement on any major decision, such as the mission statement and the coalition's responsibilities. Strong agreement among coalition members ensures consistent messaging to the rest of the organization.

Step 4: Enlist a volunteer army

Kotter's fourth step is about creating a mass movement around your change initiative. How you accomplish this goal largely depends on the size of your organization:

- **Small organizations:** If your organization is small, consider hosting monthly "lunch and learns" — optional meetings during which coalition members give presentations about the overall change vision. Free pizza or sandwiches are usually an excellent motivator to help increase attendance.
- **Large organizations:** In a larger organization (thousands of people), communicating a clear vision across several CoEs can be challenging. Consider establishing a guiding CoE in the largest location, preferably the location with the most managers (not necessarily the most practitioners). Note that the Kotter approach is top-down, so work on coaching more managers to drive change. The guiding CoE can standardize the ideas among all CoEs to ensure consistency across the group.

TIP

Try to keep your CoE meetings fun and informal. Lunches and morning breaks are usually the best times to have productive, creative discussions about organizational change management. Keep meetings festive, as you would an office birthday party, substituting the cake with bagels, pizza, or sandwiches. Avoid scheduling meetings late in the week or late in the workday. Late Wednesday mornings are often a good choice, because they provide everyone with a break in the middle of the workweek.

REMEMBER

Don't overtax your army of volunteers. You're asking people to add to their workload without shirking their regular job responsibilities. They may need to expand their energy and expertise to 120 to 150 percent above current levels, which is what often happens in a well-functioning system, but try to remain consistent with an agile mindset — respect your people, give them the freedom to be creative, and enable them to make an impact.

Step 5: Enable action by removing barriers

When you're driving a change initiative, remove any barriers that may get in the way, including hierarchies and inefficient processes. Kotter recommends creating a dual operating system (see Figure 3-2):

> The basic structure is self-explanatory: hierarchy on one side and network on the other. The network side mimics successful enterprises in their entrepreneurial phase, before there were organizational charts showing reporting relationships, before there were formal job descriptions and status levels.
>
> — Excerpt from *Accelerate: Building Strategic Agility for a Faster-Moving World* by John P. Kotter

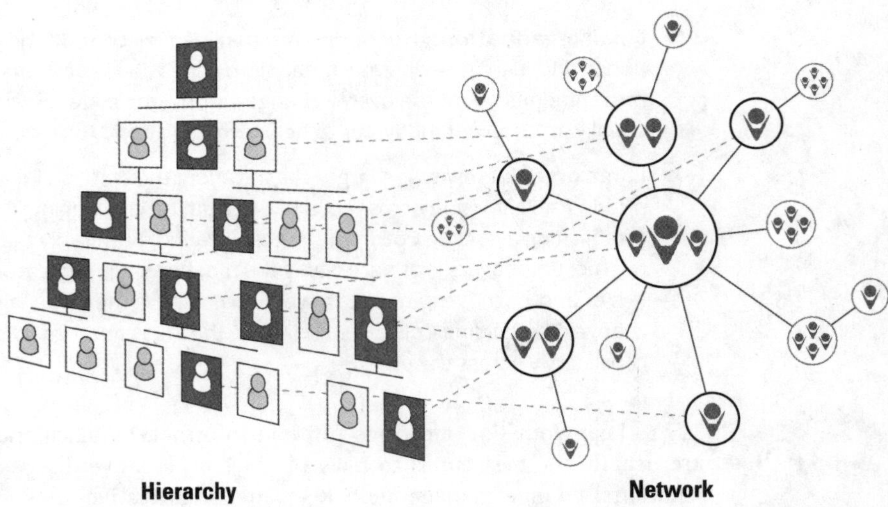

FIGURE 3-2: A dual operating system.

Your organization can maintain the traditional hierarchy while your CoE, army of volunteers, and influential members of the hierarchy form a network of entrepreneurs and leaders who work to make large-scale changes. This strategic network doesn't have a typical command-and-control structure. Instead, it focuses on individuality, creativity, and innovation.

In a sense, Kotter is suggesting that you split your organization in two. The one side holds your management, organizational structure, and legacy ideas (hierarchy). The other side should run like a startup organization (network). It should be free to make, and to some extent, break the rules.

REMEMBER

The CoE is part of the network, but be sure to include people who have the authority to make changes.

WARNING

Although you want corporate leadership to be part of the network, don't let the network become the executive arm of the hierarchy, merely following orders. People will be willing to volunteer and take on extra duties when they believe that their ideas will have a real impact on the success of the organization, but they'll be less likely to volunteer if they're being "voluntold" what to think and do.

Step 6: Generate (and celebrate) short-term wins

John F. Kennedy popularized the saying that "victory has a thousand fathers but defeat is an orphan." In most organizations, everybody wants to be on the winning team. In fact, if you have a lot of wins, you'll have an easier time recruiting volunteers, even those who were early skeptics. Nobody wants to miss out on a chance to contribute to the organization's success in capitalizing on a Big Opportunity.

Whenever your organization makes even the smallest step forward on its path to becoming more agile, celebrate. This is no time to be modest. On the contrary, have an "arm in the air" fireworks display to communicate your win to the rest the organization. Don't be afraid to fist pump even your modest wins. People have a much higher tolerance for listening to good news and self-promotion than you might think.

Also celebrate individuals and not just the entire team. Call out some of your most valuable contributors as a way to reinforce their commitment to the change. Acknowledging people's contributions is one of the easiest ways to keep people motivated and engaged.

Step 7: Sustain acceleration

After a few wins, a team begins to gain momentum, but many CoEs become satisfied with their contributions and take their foot off the accelerator. They may even disband before they make a real impact on the organization. It's at this stage where Kotter pushes for getting everyone thinking about sustained acceleration.

In fact, this is one reason he made "accelerate" such a big part of his updated change management approach. Sustained acceleration is about maintaining a steady string of wins, which Kotter refers to as "sub-initiatives."

Celebrate wins but never declare victory. You don't want to be the team to throw a party with the big banner that says "Agility accomplished!" Instead, focus on smaller, more discrete wins and act as though victory is just beyond your grasp. Celebrate when someone in your organization has received agile leadership training or when you release your first product delivered using an agile mindset. You need to celebrate a steady stream of these sub-initiatives as fuel that will accelerate your overall agile transformation.

Step 8: Institute change

As the network part of your dual operating system gathers momentum, point out the connections between the new ways of thinking and working and the organization's success, so the changes you've implemented become strong enough to replace old habits. It's at this point your change initiative transitions from becoming a movement to becoming the organizational culture. Think of it as achieving critical mass — the minimal size or amount of something to spark change and maintain its momentum. Your CoE should begin to push these agile principles, values, practices, and behaviors into the very culture of your organization.

Maintain your organization's dual operating system. You can keep your organization's hierarchy in place while nurturing networking through communities of practice to ensure that the dialog that drives change in your organization continues. If the networking part of your organization's operating system disbands, all you'll be left with is a hierarchy, which tends to lean toward a control culture that resists change.

Organizational changes are always uphill and against the wind. The best change agents usually have more patience than passion. Respect others and work to make small incremental improvements. Above all, enjoy the process and remain positive and upbeat. People are much more likely to join your effort if they see you having a good time.

Improving your odds of success

If your organization is using the Kotter approach or something similar, here are a couple of tips for improving your odds for success:

» Make sure the agents of change have the authority to make changes. What often happens is that an executive delegates the change initiative, which works only if the organization has a strong control culture. If your organization is more collaborative, people will have a tough time accepting one person as the change leader.

» Think of change as ongoing. People who use the Kotter approach often think of it as eight sequential steps at the end of which you have a big change, almost like a deliverable. In reality, change is something that constantly churns throughout an organization.

REMEMBER

Don't think of change as one big event; think of it instead as a part of the normal workflow.

Driving a Grassroots Change: A Fearless Approach

In their book *Fearless Change: Patterns for Introducing New Ideas*, Linda Rising and Mary Lynn Manns examine several different patterns that emerge when large organizations try to implement major changes. They point out that one of the big sources of resistance is fear — fear of the future and of the unknown. Their Fearless Change approach recommends that organizations try to instill faith in the organization — a belief that the change will be good for the organization and good for its employees.

People mistakenly think change requires a strong leader with a clear vision. They think everyone will listen to the leader and bravely fall in line behind the change. In reality, an organizational change is more like group therapy. You have large groups of people who fear the change. They're not afraid for the health of the organization; they're afraid for themselves. Organizational change often casts doubt on the employee's future, making the person wonder how the change will impact his job.

People don't want to be fearful. They want to feel empowered to move forward, even if they have to do so unwillingly at first. Instead of a strong leader, you may need a leader who's empathetic and reassuring.

WARNING

Don't ignore the fear factor. If you do, you'll be blindsided by those who want to stall or undermine your change initiative.

Recruiting a change evangelist

To take a fearless approach to change, you need to recruit a change evangelist who can establish an emotional connection with the others in the organization the change will impact most. Look for someone who has the following characteristics:

- Someone within the organization, not an outside coach or consultant. An insider is much better positioned to connect emotionally with others in the organization.
- Empathizes with those who may be the biggest skeptics. Someone who has a history with the organization, has seen changes succeed and fail, and understands the emotional factors that have led to past success and failure is likely to have the requisite empathy.
- Is respected and well-liked by her peers.
- Is passionate and enthusiastic about the change being considered (in this case, transforming the organization into an agile enterprise).

A change evangelist makes an emotional connection. She understands both why people are likely to resist the change and why they should embrace it. She acts as a bridge from skepticism to faith, which is a difficult role to play.

Changing without top-down authority

In many ways, Fearless Change is much more realistic than top-down methods, regardless of whether the change is being driven from the top or bottom. Why? Because top-down change often fails for the following reasons:

- **Lack of executive buy-in:** Other members of the leadership team don't believe in the change, so the change initiative lacks impact. One of the only surveys on this topic suggests that the lack of executive buy-in is one of the most common reasons for a failed transformation. (See the later section "Seeing how culture can sink agile.")
- **Lack of follow-through:** The CEO or other change leader initiates the change and then gets busy doing other things. With nobody in place to drive the momentum, the change stalls. Even in a strong control culture, people respond to change on an emotional level. The people who have the authority to make big changes don't have the time to evangelize to individual teams.

  Your change may be at great risk if a champion goes missing!

- **Unaddressed fears:** Even when you have a strong change leader rallying the troops, that person may encounter resistance at all levels of the organization due to fears among employees and leadership regarding how the change will impact their jobs.

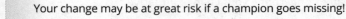

Regardless of whether you have a strong change leader in the upper echelon of the organization, Fearless Change may be the best approach. You can connect with people on an emotional level and use that connection to gain acceptance and start to recruit advocates.

LEVERAGING FEAR TO OVERCOME IT

A large retailer was trying to start a change to enterprise agility. This organization had a strong control culture. Each department had dozens of different roles that created a very clear hierarchy of managers and employees. Everyone knew for whom he worked and everyone knew who worked for him. Each group sat together in clusters of power.

Many managers quickly realized that the more people they had, the more influence they had. This led to bloated departments and almost comically confusing titles. The person who was responsible for the agile transformation had the title "Lead Assistant Senior Special Director for Business Quality Assurance."

This organization had failed a dozen times trying to start a change. The main reason was fear. The organization spent decades creating complex hierarchies and convoluted management structures. There was a lot of organizational "cruft" (a term used in software development to describe overly complicated or badly designed code that often festers over time). There were countless roles that managers created as a way to increase their influence. The people in these roles were afraid. They understood that positions could easily be consolidated and their position eliminated.

The meetings they had about the agile transformation were very intense. How do you explain to a team of 40 business analysts the benefits of having one product owner? Even more challenging, how do you explain the benefits of a self-organized team to a group of mid-level managers?

Many people believed that the best way to confront the challenge was with communication, flexibility, and courage. The problem, however, was that many people were understandably afraid. The organization couldn't become lean and remain bloated at the same time, and trimming the fat was going to impact their positions. Telling them not to be afraid would only deepen their fears.

Instead, they leveraged that fear. They identified the people who were most afraid of the change (those who had the most to lose). Then they created a transformation workgroup that laid out plans for how the organization could move forward. The workgroup focused on taking that negative energy from their fear and turning it into positive energy to drive the plan. They were writing a future for themselves, which helped eliminate their own fears and doubts.

Making change a self-fulfilling prophecy

Ovid's *Metamorphoses* includes a poem about a young sculptor named Pygmalion, who created a statue so beautiful that he fell in love with it. When he tried to kiss the statue, the goddess Aphrodite willed his beautiful sculpture to life. In the poem, Pygmalion created something beautiful, and his expectations brought the sculpture to life.

When you're making a large organizational change, you can benefit from the same "Pygmalion" effect. You can create a self-fulfilling prophecy where your enthusiasm helps recruit others to make changes. This is one of the key roles of change evangelists. They need to have a contagious excitement that wills the change into existence.

REMEMBER

Your change evangelist is the key player in Fearless Change. Look for someone who has the enthusiasm to bring the vision to life.

Looking for change patterns

In their book *Fearless Change*, Rising and Manns describe several *change patterns* — how people respond to change — and they present various techniques to address these patterns. The following sections present two common change patterns.

Accepting change at different rates

People accept change at different rates. You may present an idea to a large group and have people leave the presentation with varying degrees of enthusiasm. Some in the audience will be convinced after seeing the first two slides, while others will see the full fireworks show and still walk away unimpressed.

REMEMBER

Connect with both fans and skeptics. If you talk only to the people excited about the change, you'll get the mistaken impression that the transformation will be easy. Even worse, you won't know the source of resistance.

The diffusion of innovations theory

Fearless Change relies on a 50-year-old diffusion of innovations theory created by Everett Rogers, an assistant professor of rural sociology at Ohio State University. He identified five groups of people who respond differently to innovations:

- **Innovators** quickly embrace new ideas.
- **Early adopters** are interested in new ideas but like to hear a little more before they decide.
- **Early majority** like to see what other people think before they make up their minds.

- **Late majority** accept an idea only after the majority of people accept it.
- **Laggards** must be dragged kicking and screaming into any new change.

REMEMBER

These groups aren't good or bad. An organization needs laggards as much as it needs early adopters. The company would be in chaos if everyone adopted every new change. At the same time, the company would probably not be around very long if it didn't make any changes. You shouldn't try to sort these groups into good and evil. There are no heroes and villains, but you need to take a different approach when introducing the change to each group.

Recruiting innovators and early adopters

TIP

One strategy to accelerate change is to recruit innovators and early adopters and have them convince the late majority and laggards. The late majority is usually swayed by greater numbers of people, but anyone who resists change is likely to be more receptive when hearing about it from an enthusiastic supporter.

After turning a skeptic into a believer, recruit your new convert to become an advocate for change. Newly converted employees may be your most enthusiastic supporters.

Tailoring your message

As you speak with different groups and individuals, tailor your message to your audience. Don't continue to sell to innovators and early adopters who are already on board. You may need to shift from sales to education and training or to recruiting your new advocates to help spread the word.

When presenting to the late majority and to the laggards, find out why they're resisting the change. Maybe similar initiatives have failed in the past and they're convinced that "nothing's going to change," or they're afraid of how the change will impact them. After figuring out the reason behind their resistance, tailor your message to show that you understand and empathize and then present information that addresses their concerns. Let them know that it's okay to be hesitant about the change.

Don't ignore, dismiss, or make light of people's concerns. However unrealistic the concerns, they're still valid, because they reflect how people feel. Your job is to provide information and insight that alleviates the concern.

TIP

You can help convince the doubters by showing them that the proposed change is actually the best option (or the least unpleasant option).

Steering clear of change myths

In *Fearless Change*, Rising and Manns present several change myths (misconceptions) that can impair your ability to transform your organization. This section presents six change myths you're likely to encounter as you start to transform your organization into an agile enterprise.

REMEMBER

Keep these change myths in mind when you're starting your enterprise agile transformation so you'll be less likely to succumb to their influence.

Thinking change sells itself

The first change myth is the notion that if you have something that adds value to the organization, it'll be easy to convince others to accept the change. To avoid falling victim to this myth, keep in mind the following two points:

- Not everyone will see value in your change.
- Even those who see value in the proposed change may not agree that the change is right for the organization; for example, someone may say something like, "I'm sure agile works fine for companies like Google, but this is an office supply business."

REMEMBER

The change won't sell itself. You need a change evangelist to sell it and to keep selling it until you get enough people on board and enough energy to overcome any remaining resistance to the change. You may give yourself a headache repeating the value of the change, but that's a necessary discomfort of being a change evangelist. You may not convince everyone that the proposed change is best, but it will at least give people the opportunity to oppose it for the right reasons.

Thinking people knowing about the benefits is enough to change

Educating people on the benefits of change isn't always enough. Some organizations encounter this challenge with their Agile Coaches. The coach spends considerable time training and developing an effective plan but far too little time giving employees a forum for expressing their concerns. The employees end up knowing what to do, but having little motivation to do it.

REMEMBER

Organizational change requires a combination of training and group therapy. Big change results in emotional upheaval as much as it requires a reorientation to process. If you fail to address the emotional factors, you'll end up with well-trained employees who are reluctant to change.

Believing change requires charm and PowerPoint

Agile transformations have failed in several large organizations because the most influential people were apathetic about the change. They would respond to presentations about the agile mindset like Bill Murray in the movie *Groundhog Day*, in which his character was forced to live the same day over and over again. They'd seen it all before. They wouldn't oppose the change, but they weren't excited about it either.

TIP

If you're the change agent, try not to rely too much on personal charm and PowerPoint presentations. Instead, position yourself as an approachable outsider — someone who's knowledgeable but not overly friendly. Let people know you're aware of their concerns. For example, you may say something like, "I know you've probably heard this all before and nothing ever seems to change, but . . . ." Then try to recruit these longtime employees and see if you can drum up some excitement.

Trying to steamroll over skeptics

Many change leaders try to steamroll over the skeptics to push change through the organization without addressing their concerns. This approach often increases resistance instead of reducing it. When you're starting an organizational transformation, try to see your skeptics as a positive force in the organization. In many organizations, the skeptics are the ones who are most likely to be right. Always try to engage them in open forums. In most organizations, skeptics are like icebergs. The ones you see often represent a small portion of the group that's actually there.

Encourage the skeptics to open up, so you know the source of their resistance and can address their concerns. Your skeptics can be a valuable resource in helping you choose changes that have the highest chance for success.

Relying too much on one change agent

Rarely can a single change leader push change through an organization, even in an organization that has a strong control culture. The myth that a single person can make or break an organization comes from stories about legendary executives who turned their companies around, such as Steve Jobs (Apple), Lee Iacocca (Chrysler), and Dan Hesse (Sprint).

The problem with these stories is that very few executives have what it takes to become a legend or they're working under entirely different circumstances. Effecting big change as an individual requires a rare combination of vision and authority. Most change evangelists will never enjoy anything close to that level of authority.

Believing people will stay convinced

Perhaps the most dangerous change myth is that once you convince people they'll stay convinced. An agile transformation is almost like trying to maintain a healthy lifestyle. You may lose 50 pounds, but trying to keep it off requires persistence. You may convince most people in your organization that change is needed, but they may have deeply ingrained work habits that take a long time and a lot of effort to change. If you stop pumping energy into your change initiative, people are likely to drift back to comfortable behaviors.

Overcoming Obstacles Related to Your Organization's Culture

Your organization's existing culture can create a great deal of inertia that your organization needs to overcome in order to change direction. In fact, an inability to change an organization's culture is one of the leading causes of failed enterprise agile transformations. This section explains how cultural factors can undermine an enterprise agile transformation, and it provides guidance on how to overcome cultural inertia.

Seeing how culture can sink agile

According to an annual survey conducted by VersionOne on the state of agile, the number one challenge companies face when they attempt an enterprise agile transformation is "Company philosophy or culture at odds with core agile values" (see Figure 3-3). Number four on the list is a "General organization resistance to change." Further down at number six is "Insufficient training."

FIGURE 3-3: The top challenges in an agile transformation.

© John Wiley & Sons, Inc.

Most organizations understand and are willing to embrace a more agile mindset. The real challenge is overcoming cultural inertia. The organization wants to adopt enterprise agility, but agile conflicts with a deeply engrained incompatible mindset.

Acknowledging the challenge

The first step to overcoming cultural inertia is to confront it. Many teams try to change culture through training. They think that once individuals understand agile they'll be more likely to embrace it. Unfortunately, more training is rarely the solution. Even when all employees in the organization understand agile and appreciates its potential benefits, they often feel that it's not a solution that'll work in their organization. They lack *faith.*

If you think about it, this feeling makes a lot of sense. A lot of organizations have a strong control culture. Some of agile's key values may be in direct opposition to long-established practices. A culture that puts a lot of emphasis on hierarchy and accountability, for example, is going to have a tough time embracing self-organized teams and distributed authority.

TALK IS CHEAP, TRAINING ONLY SLIGHTLY LESS SO

One organization was starting out with enterprise agility. It spent the majority of its budget training on an enterprise framework. It figured that if everyone in the organization knew more about enterprise agility, excitement would overcome any cultural inertia, and the cultural challenges would just drift away.

Unfortunately, the opposite happened. People were excited about the idea of trying the new system. They just didn't believe it would work for them. One common theme overheard was "This is absolutely a great way to work, it will just never work here."

The organization would have been better off learning less and doing more. Its approach was, "Let's all learn enterprise agility and see if it works for us." A better approach would've been "We're making this cultural change, now let's work together to make it happen."

Prioritizing the challenge

When you start your agile transformation, make culture your number one priority. Agile teams always begin with the highest value items first. Training is number six on the list of common challenges, and culture is number one. It's clear that you need to start with culture. Your effort here will make or break your enterprise agile transformation.

TIP

Build on your success. If you're considering an enterprise agile transformation, you already have at least one agile team in your organization, and now you're looking to scale agile to work on larger projects. Leverage the success of your existing agile team(s) to drive cultural change throughout the organization.

Gaining insight into motivation

Managers and developers often clash on the enterprise agility battlefield because their motivations differ. While management often embraces big organizational change and enterprise agile frameworks that promise improved productivity, quality, and customer satisfaction, developers often want management to get out of their way so they can do their best work.

Management

High-level managers are the first to embrace big changes. It's not because they're less conservative or more adventurous. It's because they're evaluated by how well they improve the organization's processes. When they can take a group of people and change the process to improve results, they see that as good management and strong leadership. Large frameworks, such as Scaled Agile Framework (SAFe) and Large-Scale Scrum Huge (LeSS Huge) are like catnip for these high-level managers.

Developers

On the other side, software developers and engineers see themselves as craftspeople. They want to build something that's elegant and satisfying, and they often view a large framework as a way for management to gain more control over their work. If you're a craftsperson, the last thing you want to do is create something ugly because someone forces you to make a quick fix.

Large-scale organizational changes often create a tension between managers who want to rewire the machine and developers who want to create a world with fewer wires. Developers want agile, and they may think of enterprise agile as an attempt by management to make them *less* agile.

When you're starting your enterprise agile transformation, take a long objective look at each of these groups' motivations. If you have a manager who wants to make big changes, prepare yourself for a lot of communication and pushback from many of the developers. If the change is driven by developers, be prepared to convince the managers that this is a worthwhile change.

REMEMBER

People often assume that others share their motivation. Managers assume everyone wants a big framework, while developers assume that everyone in the company wants (or should want) to deliver beautiful, elegant software. The truth is that the two aren't mutually exclusive. You can have a large framework that provides developers with the creative freedom they crave.

Whether you try the Kotter approach or Fearless Change, think about your particular organization and how each group feels about the change. Both of these approaches push you to better understand everyone's motivations so you can mitigate resistance and avoid unpleasant surprises.

- » **Tackling the cultural aspect of a big change**
- » **Getting everyone in your organization to start thinking Lean**
- » **Selecting an enterprise agile framework**
- » **Making lasting changes**

Chapter 4

Putting It All Together: Taking Steps toward an Agile Enterprise

Enterprise agile transformations involve numerous variables, including the size of the company, its culture, the framework it chooses, the products it creates, and its existing agile competency, so each organization may approach its transformation in a unique way. However, if you're not sure how to get started, consider the following ten-step approach:

1. Identify your organization's culture.
2. List the strengths and challenges with changing your culture.
3. Select the best approach to organizational change management.
4. Train managers on Lean thinking.
5. Start a Lean-Agile Center of Excellence (LACE).

6. Choose a high-level value stream.
7. Assign a budget to the value stream.
8. Select an enterprise agile framework.
9. Shift from detailed plans to epics.
10. Respect and trust your people.

This chapter explains each of these steps in detail.

REMEMBER

Think of these steps only as a great way to get started. After you have an enterprise agile framework in place, any additional changes to improve the system will be more targeted to address areas that need improvement.

Step 1: Identifying Your Organization's Culture

The first step toward transforming your organization into an agile enterprise is to size up its existing culture, so you know what you're up against. Chapter 2 of Book 6 describes the four corporate culture types presented by William Schneider in his book, *The Reengineering Alternative* — control, competence, collaboration, and cultivation. However, placing your organization into one of those four culture types is challenging for two reasons:

- **As an insider, you may not be the best judge.** You may see your organization as you want it to be instead of as it really is, or you may be unable to see how your organization differs from others.
- **Your organization may have elements of two or more cultures.** For example, your organization may have a control culture with pockets of collaboration and cultivation cultures. What's most common is to have a dominant culture type and then a few characteristics of another type.

TIP

Often you can figure out your organizational culture model by touring your organization, observing behaviors, and asking yourself the following questions:

- **What's the office dress code?** For example, a formal dress code is more characteristic of a control culture.
- **How do people decorate their work area?** For example, if people hang copies of their diplomas, certifications, and awards, you're probably dealing with an organization that has a strong competence culture.

» **Where are people sitting?** If people are working in cubicles, then you're likely looking at a competence or control culture. If the cubicle area is surrounded by offices with doors, you're most likely looking at a control culture. If groups share work areas and can see one another's screens, you're probably dealing with a collaboration culture.

» **Where are people meeting?** If people are meeting in groups in the middle of an open floor plan, the organization probably has some aspects of a collaboration culture.

» **Who's calling the shots?** Do employees make decisions or do they receive their marching orders from the top down (as in a control culture)?

» **Do people look happy?** People are generally happiest when they're able to contribute to express themselves and when their opinions matter, as in a collaboration culture. In a strictly controlled environment, people show up for work, put in their time, and go home.

» **What's the noise level?** A noisy environment is more typical of a collaboration culture, but you can have a very noisy office in which everyone is working independently; for example, an office full of real estate brokers.

TIP

As you gather and analyze your evidence, follow these tips and cautions to make a more objective assessment:

» Gather plenty of evidence and look for patterns of behavior. Don't draw your conclusion based on only one or two pieces of evidence.

» Assemble a group of three or more people to make the assessment, so it's not based on one person's opinion. Make sure everyone agrees about the evidence, and then have everyone cast a ballot for the culture type he thinks is predominant in the organization. Approach this vote as you would play a round of planning poker: Vote and then discuss the reasons each person voted the way he did. Continue this cycle of voting and discussing until you reach consensus. Work toward ranking the four culture types from strongest to weakest in the organization.

» Keep in mind that your organization may have one dominant culture with characteristics of other culture types.

» Beware of *confirmation bias* — interpreting data based on preexisting beliefs. For example, everyone in your group may think your organization has a strong collaboration culture, so it gathers evidence and analyzes it in a way to show that the organization has a collaboration culture, even though the organization actually has a strong control culture. Make a conscious effort to be objective.

TIP

Chances are good your organization has a control culture or at least some elements of a control culture, because it's the most prevalent culture type. In fact, most organizations have to work hard to adopt something other than a control culture. Up until recently most of the largest companies relied on a pretty strict hierarchy, which spawns some habits that are tough to break.

REMEMBER

No culture is good or bad, better or worse. Every culture is just an underlying system the organization decided to create and reinforce, and it may have a valuable role to play in the organization's success. What's important is that you understand the culture you're dealing with, so you can implement your agile transformation more effectively and efficiently.

Step 2: Listing the Strengths and Challenges with Changing Your Culture

Different elements of your organization's culture may accelerate or hinder your change initiative, so try to identify these elements early on. One way to identify potential assets and liabilities within your organization is to assess your culture's strengths, weaknesses, opportunities, and threats (SWOT). You can then take advantage of your strengths and try to minimize the impact of your weaknesses.

Create a SWOT diagram as shown in Figure 4-1. At the top of the diagram, write the dominant culture in your organization followed by the secondary culture type (if any). Create a box for each of the SWOT categories — Strengths, Weaknesses, Opportunities, and Threats.

Collaborate with your group to identify specific strengths, weaknesses, opportunities, and threats inherent in your organization's culture that are relevant to your enterprise agile transformation. Record the items your group identifies in each of the relevant boxes, as shown in Figure 4-1.

Your SWOT diagram can be a valuable tool in your agile transformation. For example, one of the strengths identified in the SWOT diagram shown in Figure 4-1 is "Strong PMO" (*PMO* stands for project management office). You can leverage the power of a strong, supportive PMO by using it to drive your enterprise agile transformation.

Dominant Culture: Control

Cultural Elements: Competence

Mandatory Training Executive Buy-in **Strengths** Strong PMO	Risk Averse **Weaknesses** Next-New-Thing Fatigue
New CIO **Opportunities** Great Coaches	Well-Established Hierarchy **Threats** Functional Managers

FIGURE 4-1: A SWOT diagram of your company's culture.

© John Wiley & Sons, Inc.

WARNING

Keep in mind that one organization's strengths may be another organization's weaknesses. If your PMO doesn't support agile, then "Strong PMO" would go in the Threats box, and you'd have to figure out a way to address this potential source of resistance.

TIP

Spend extra time on the Opportunities category, because opportunities often provide the impetus to overcome resistance within the organization. Opportunities give people a good reason to embrace change. Look for opportunities in your agile transformation that failed change initiatives from the past didn't have. When you present your SWOT analysis to the organization, you can then use these opportunities to answer the question, "Why will this change initiative succeed when so many others have failed?" You may even want to address specific change initiatives from the past to explain why they failed.

REMEMBER

Think of your SWOT diagram as an analytical tool for developing your game plan. You're identifying your team's strengths and weaknesses, so you can leverage your strengths and minimize the impact of your weaknesses. For example, if you identify strong corporate leadership as a threat and your development teams as a strength, you may decide that a bottom-up approach to your agile transformation would be best, as explained in Chapter 3 of Book 6.

A MISTAKEN CULTURAL ASSESSMENT

One organization was convinced it had an open collaboration culture even though the evidence suggested it had a well-established control culture. The organization was divided into functional areas, and each person knew her place in the organization. Managers were often promoted based on the number of "direct reports" they had on their teams. But the people on their agile transformation team had a very strong confirmation bias. They thought that a control culture sounded too cold and harsh. It didn't reflect their values as an organization.

The agile transformation team created a SWOT diagram of the organization's strengths and challenges, but it didn't reflect the reality in the organization. Team members thought that their primary challenge was getting everybody through training and that their strength was working together in teams.

When the time came to choose a change management strategy, they based their choice on a lot of misinformation. They chose to go with Fearless Change, because they thought it was the best approach for collaborative organizations with a strong drive to work together in teams.

When they started their agile transformation, they quickly encountered serious obstacles. Many of the managers didn't want to loan out their team members to this grassroots effort. The managers were afraid that if they were stripped of their direct reports they would not be promoted (or worse), so they only allowed team members to participate only when they had nothing else on their plates. Of course, for many of the team members that was just a euphemism for *never.*

This organization would have had a much easier time had it matched its change management strategy with the reality of the organization and chosen the Kotter approach. The agile transformation team could've worked with executives to create a top-down change management strategy. Executives could've collaborated closely with managers to maintain their functional hierarchy. In Kotter's language, they could still run their own organizational "operating system."

The moral of this story is that you must be very careful when you identify your culture and your organization's strengths and challenges. If you're mistaken in your cultural assessment, you're likely to choose the wrong change management strategy and doom your transformation in the earliest stages.

Step 3: Selecting the Best Approach to Organizational Change Management

After you've identified your organization's culture and conducted a SWOT analysis, choose a change management technique, such as one of the two approaches presented in Chapter 3 of Book 6:

- **Kotter's eight-step change model (top down):** If your organization has strong leadership that supports the enterprise agile transformation, the eight-step Kotter approach is probably best.
- **Fearless Change (bottom up):** If you have influential groups within the organization that enthusiastically embrace enterprise agility and resistance or apathy at the top, driving change from the bottom up may be the most effective approach.

For example, if your organization has a strong PMO, the Kotter approach is likely to be best. A strong PMO has the logistics in place to drive a major transformation, including the reporting structure, in-house training, and relationships with key executives. The PMO would be well-positioned to create and maintain a dual operating system (see Chapter 3 in Book 6) that maintains the functional hierarchy while creating a more flexible team-based network.

On the other hand, if your organization has a stronger competence culture, you may be better off trying Fearless Change. Note that competence cultures value knowledge and skills. A highly competent culture is likely to have more authority to make big changes, so an enterprise agile evangelist can have significant impact. She could become an expert in enterprise agility and convince others to make big changes.

REMEMBER

Your decision is not an either/or choice. Although the Kotter approach initiates change from the top, it includes bottom-up support through the use of an "army of volunteers." Likewise, although Fearless Change drives change from the bottom up, it relies on a change leader with some level of authority. You can certainly mix and match, choosing elements from both approaches. Your decision is whether to initiate change *primarily* from the top or bottom.

Step 4: Training Managers on Lean Thinking

For any enterprise agile transformation to succeed, top-level managers need to understand that enterprise agility is built on the foundation of Lean thinking — organizing activities in a way that eliminates waste to deliver optimum value. You can use the Simple Lean-Agile Mindset (SLAM) to show the system-level optimizations that are essential to successful enterprise agile transformations.

The Simple Lean-Agile Mindset (SLAM) is a conceptual construct for understanding how agile enterprises function regardless of which enterprise agile framework they adopt. Think of SLAM as an overall description of a game, such as Monopoly, and look at the enterprise agile frameworks (introduced in Chapter 1 of Book 6) as various ways to play the game. SLAM is a high-level view of what the different enterprise agile frameworks and practices are trying to accomplish.

SLAM breaks down enterprise agility into the following four areas:

- **System-level optimization:** A collection of eight methods for improving the way people work alone and together in an organization to achieve any given objective and to engage in continuous improvement.
- **Strategic vision and execution:** The organization's unifying vision, along with the three-step process for executing that vision: (1) Break it down, (2) prioritize, and (3) pull work into the teams.
- **Empirical process control:** The system for ensuring continuous improvement: (1) Deliver in small batches and (2) gather and respond to feedback.
- **Business agility:** The extension of agility throughout an organization. While enterprise agility focuses on product delivery, business agility makes every part of the organization more lean and agile, including human resources, accounting, marketing, sales, purchasing, and production. Small teams, autonomous but aligned, work toward delivering the highest value to the customer and to the organization.

Your organization should always look for ways to reduce waste, improve efficiency, and eliminate defects. Many parts of system-level optimization support continuous improvement, including shortening the cycle time, clearing communication channels, encouraging transparency, working in cross-functional teams, and removing fear of failure.

REMEMBER

Discourage your organization's leadership from thinking of enterprise agility as just a few new process improvements or as a collection of practices, such as small teams and daily stand-up meetings. Enterprise agility is bigger than that. By focusing on Lean thinking, you increase the scope of enterprise agility beyond processes and practices to a mindset. The focus is on delivering value to the customer in the most efficient manner possible.

One fact that top managers often have difficulty accepting is that local optimization differs from system-level optimization. For example, a super-productive employee can actually slow down a system, just as a star player can ruin a team. Instead of hiring and rewarding superstars, organizations need to look for people who have the knowledge, skills, and characteristics to complement the team.

Executives and directors are accustomed to thinking of the organization as broken into different functional areas with each functional area broken down into teams. They may have a difficult time imagining a team of superstars being slower than several teams of average performers. One team turning out too much work too fast can actually create a bottleneck that slows the entire process. Having a balanced system with everyone working at the same pace is most efficient.

REMEMBER

Many of the organizational improvements behind your enterprise agile transformation include system-level optimization, so managers need to grasp the concept and appreciate the value of system-level improvements. Be prepared to spend plenty of time training managers, so they understand the benefits and are ready to make big changes.

Step 5: Starting a Lean-Agile Center of Excellence (LACE)

Whether you initiate change at the top or bottom, create a Lean-Agile Center of Excellence (LACE) to transition the entire organization to a Lean-Agile Mindset (see Chapter 3 in Book 6). A Center of Excellence (CoE) is a group of enthusiastic and knowledgeable people who promote change throughout the organization.

To create your LACE, recruit an individual within the organization who has the knowledge, enthusiasm, and charisma to bring others on board. (This may be you.) Provide this individual with the resources she needs, including a meeting room, a budget, and, most important, the authority to make changes.

As you form your LACE and run your meetings and events, follow these guidelines:

- Create a fun group that's passionate about improving the organization. Recruit the type of people who are always looking for new ways to shorten their commute to work and to manage their email more efficiently.
- Recruit doers, not just talkers. Look for people who persevere in the face of adversity. Impatience is okay, but they need to be in it for the long haul.

» Develop a LACE mission statement, goal, and objectives. Formulate a vision of what the organization will look like after it becomes an agile enterprise, and develop a plan for how your LACE will help the organization achieve that vision.

» Charter the group with authority from the top to spearhead change. Your LACE will disintegrate quickly if all its efforts are shut down by middle managers. The LACE should realize that it will encounter some resistance, but its members shouldn't begin to feel that their endeavors are fruitless.

» Maintain a meeting and event calendar with a cadence of regularly scheduled meetings and events. Without a schedule, people are likely to lose interest and stop attending meetings. A predictable cadence helps people plan other commitments around these events, reducing potential conflicts.

» End every event with consensus and an action plan. Never "agree to disagree." Instead, give all participants the opportunity to argue their ideas, but at the end of the event, the group should have consensus and an action plan. Feel free to have a show of hands if you can't reach consensus.

TIP

Find the sweet spot between fun and effective. Keep in mind that most of the people in your LACE are volunteers. They could be working on other projects, and they have a life outside of work. They usually join the LACE out of an interest in improving the organization. Make events festive and productive, so your volunteers look forward to meetings and feel as though the LACE is making a positive impact on the organization. If you give a one-hour PowerPoint presentation about the benefits of the Lean-Agile Mindset, you'll quickly find yourself with many empty seats.

REMEMBER

If your CoE is staffed with volunteers, know that getting real work done with a volunteer army is always a challenge, especially when you're working on an initiative that's likely to encounter resistance. By finding the sweet spot between fun and effective, you can draw the crowds while making a rewarding impact.

Step 6: Choosing a High-Level Value Stream

Your LACE should collaborate with upper management to identify value streams. (A *value stream* is a series of steps for building solutions that deliver value to a customer continuously.) Value streams come in two types:

- **Operational value streams:** Steps to provide goods or services to customers internally or externally to generate revenue for the organization. For example, an organization may have a value stream for selling and delivering a product to a customer.
- **Development value streams:** Steps to design and build new products, systems, and services capabilities, such as a software application, a driverless car, or an internal process. For example, the process used to create a product sold to a customer would be a development value stream.

REMEMBER

To make your organization Lean, you eventually want to optimize both operational and development value streams, but consider starting your agile transformation with a development value stream for two reasons:

- Optimizing a development value stream is easier, because you can focus on a system for developing a single product.
- Your work will be more interesting and rewarding, providing greater motivation for everyone involved in your enterprise agile transformation.

Focus on a development value stream that's a key part of the business. Look for a value stream that meets the following four overlapping criteria:

- **It has leadership's support.** You're more likely to rally leadership support for your enterprise agile transformation by improving development of a product that leadership values.
- **It is clearly high level.** Choose a value stream that everyone in the organization understands and appreciates. If people know the product and appreciate its value to the organization, explaining the benefits of enterprise agility will be easier, and your wins will be more visible.
- **It crosses functional areas.** Choose a product that requires collaboration across functional areas, such as business analysis, design, programming, and testing, so you'll need to create one or more small, cross-functional teams.
- **It poses a real challenge or opportunity.** Choose a value stream that has an opportunity for significant improvement, so that your success delivers real value to the organization. A big win will rally the entire organization around future extension of enterprise agility to other areas of the organization.

Step 7: Assigning a Budget to the Value Stream

Most organizations still budget their work as *projects*. They have a budget based on the *project management triangle* (also referred to as the *iron triangle*):

- **Scope:** The product's features or requirements
- **Resources:** Money, personnel, equipment, and so on
- **Time:** The schedule or deadline

Each of these three points in the iron triangle is a constraint. Generally, a change in any of these constraints impacts the other constraints and the overall quality of the product. For example, if you broaden the scope by adding features, the product is likely to cost more and require more time to complete.

With enterprise agility, you need to stop budgeting for projects and start budgeting for value streams. Instead of carefully defining the scope of a project, as is common with project budgeting, the scope remains flexible, and the development team integrates functionality into the product incrementally according to an ever-evolving *product backlog* (a prioritized list of work items).

REMEMBER

Value stream budgeting moves away from focusing on what the project will do and instead puts all the emphasis on what *value* the product provides.

Think of it this way. Sometimes you walk into a restaurant and you have a complete notion of what you want to order. Maybe you have a favorite sandwich or a dish you've ordered in the past. Other times you walk into the restaurant with a set budget in mind (maybe you don't want to spend more than $30) and a general notion that you just want to get something delicious to eat. In the first example you're funding a project. You know exactly what you want to buy and you know how much it will cost. In the second example you're funding your value stream. It's valuable to you to have something delicious to eat. When you went to the restaurant you don't really know the final product, you just want it to be delicious.

REMEMBER

The advantage of value stream budgeting is that it more closely aligns with the enterprise agile mindset. You're giving the teams flexibility to narrow down the highest-value features and work to deliver a high-quality product. You don't have a complete picture of what their product will be when it's finished. Instead, your teams work closely with the customers to zero-in on what they want. Your aligning your organization and agreeing on the highest-value parts of your product.

SHIFTING BUDGETS FROM PROJECTS TO VALUE STREAMS

One organization developed a payroll processing system. It wanted to increase its organizational agility, but was accustomed to funding projects, not value streams. It would work with the customer to develop a list of requirements and a schedule for delivery. Then, it would develop a budget based on the resources and the amount of time required.

Budgeting was a major challenge, because the organization operated in silos, and each project required pulling people from different functional areas. They needed developers, database engineers, business analysts, graphic designers, testers, and so on. The team had a project manager, and each team member had a manager from his own functional area. To get people to work on a project, the project manager had to coordinate with the functional area manager, and if the project took longer than expected, the project manager had to struggle to keep the person on the team before that person got pulled to work on another project.

When the customer requested a new feature (a way for employees to view their paychecks from their smartphones), the organization decided to budget for the value stream instead of for the project.

The organization created a cross-functional team to deliver the new feature and assigned it a budget based on the team's estimate of how long it would take to deliver. The team figured it could deliver a solution in four weeks, so the budget needed to account only for the cost of the team over that four-week time frame. The team had no list of requirements, because the solution was uncertain; for example, the team could create an app or just add an area to the customer's website that employees could access using a mobile web browser.

The organization assigned a budget to the value stream and left it up to the customer and cross-functional team to develop a satisfactory solution.

Step 8: Selecting an Enterprise Agile Framework

Prior to initiating your enterprise agile transformation, choose one of the agile frameworks introduced in Chapter 1 of Book 6, or mix and match elements from various frameworks to tailor your own solution. Refer to Figure 4-2 for guidance:

- **Along the horizontal x-axis:** From left to right, frameworks range from highly prescriptive to more empirical. A highly prescriptive approach, such as the

Scaled Agile Framework® (SAFe®), has more roles, practices, and guidance. More empirical frameworks, such as Large-Scale Scrum (LeSS) and the Spotify Engineering Culture, encourage experimentation, measurement, and learning.

- **Along the vertical y-axis:** From bottom to top, frameworks differ depending on the change management strategy — whether change is initiated at the bottom (team) level or is driven from the top (enterprise) level down. Note that SAFe, Disciplined Agile Delivery (DAD), and LeSS all tend to be frameworks that require a top-down change management style to implement.

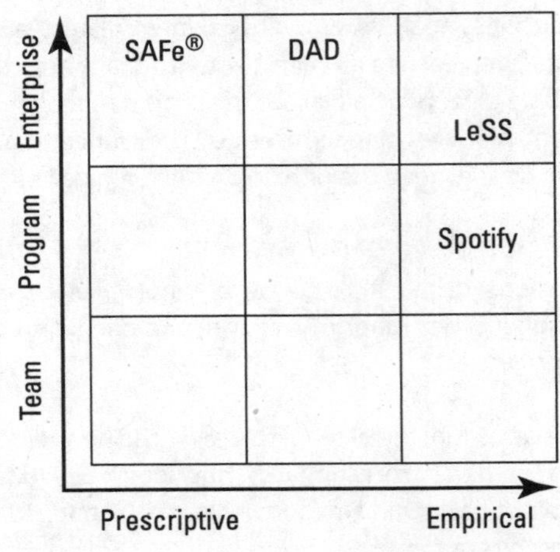

FIGURE 4-2: Characteristics of the top enterprise agile frameworks.

Use Figure 4-2 to match your organization's existing culture to a suitable framework. For example, if you have a strong control culture, consider a prescriptive framework that you can use to drive change from the top down, such as SAFe. On the other hand, if you have a strong competence culture, you may be better off using a more empirical framework with a greater emphasis on teams, such as LeSS, which gives teams more flexibility in how they do their work and enables you to leverage their expertise in improving the process.

WARNING

Choosing an enterprise agile framework that clashes with your organization's culture can lead to disaster. For example, trying to force the Spotify Engineering Culture on an organization with a strong hierarchy would be very disruptive. A company with a deeply ingrained hierarchy is likely to resist a system that reorganizes everyone into squads, tribes, chapters, and guilds. Such a change would also push a lot of responsibility for process improvement down to small squads of employees, which would introduce far too much uncertainty for high-level management to accept.

WARNING

Don't choose a framework just because it worked well for an organization you admire, because that framework may not be the right match for your organization. For example, many organizations choose a framework merely because it worked for Google, Facebook, Apple, or Microsoft, but when they try the same approach, they fail miserably, because the framework clashes with their organization's existing culture. To make it even more tempting, many consulting firms that promote a given framework try to sell it on the basis that it worked for a few top-performing and well-known companies. Avoid the temptation. Think instead about how suitable the framework is for *your* organization.

REMEMBER

Also be sure to choose a framework based on the type of organization you are, *not* the organization you want to be. Compare your transformation to performance training. If you're terribly out of shape, you don't adopt a training program designed for world-class, long-distance runners. Instead, you choose a training program that's better suited to your existing physical condition. After you achieve a certain fitness level, you can step up to a more aggressive program.

Step 9: Shifting from Detailed Plans to Epics

Large enterprises favor predictability, so before developing a product, they insist on having a detailed plan. Enterprise agility runs counter to this traditional approach. Instead, agile teams work with the customer to identify what the customer needs, and then they innovate, experiment, and adjust to develop a solution. Many organizations have difficulty transitioning from detailed planning to a more creative agile approach, because they're afraid of the potential for negative outcomes. However, to become more innovative, organizations must reduce their aversion to risk and place greater trust in their product developers.

TIP

If people in your organization apply pressure to produce a detailed plan, push back. Encourage them to focus on the value stream and give the agile teams creative license to innovate solutions. For example, suppose your organization manufactures breakfast cereals. Your customer wants a tasty low-carb alternative. Leadership demands research and planning. They want a complete list of ingredients, nutritional values, and even the name of the new cereal before even one flake is toasted. But that's not agile. In such a case, you need to push back and have the organization turn the project over to the team in the form of an *epic* — a lightweight business case for creating the product.

Instead of handing the team a detailed list of product requirements, you give the team an epic, such as "Create a nutritious and delicious low-carbohydrate breakfast cereal that will blow the competition off the shelves." The team can then start experimenting with different recipes to lower the carbohydrate content while improving the cereal's flavor and texture. The customer would taste each product increment and provide feedback about how to improve it. The team may even send samples out to some of the customer's more influential social media fans to obtain additional feedback. Over the course of several product iterations, the team would eventually arrive at the winning recipe, and the customer could deliver the product to its market.

REMEMBER

The whole point to having agile teams is to optimize value by allowing teams to innovate. Giving teams detailed product requirements undermines the purpose of enterprise agility — to improve value through innovation.

Step 10: Respecting and Trusting Your People

As organizations strive to become more agile enterprises, they often focus on frameworks, roles, and practices and lose sight of the more important aspects of enterprise agile transformations — principles and people. Innovation is a product of the mind. It's the ideas people come up with when they have the knowledge, skills, and resources to do their jobs and the respect and trust to think independently. Otherwise, people simply do what they're told, which stifles innovation.

As your organization embarks on its agile transformation, remind everyone of the Agile Manifesto (see Chapter 1 in Book 6). Highlight the first value: "Individuals and interactions over processes and tools." Reinforce that value among executives and all levels of management, so they know that the source of innovation is found in the organization's employees and their interactions with one another and with the organization's leaders and its customers.

REMEMBER

Respect for people is more than just an organizational optimization. It's a wholesale rewrite of how many executives view their workforce. In his book *Drive*, Daniel Pink highlights the three elements that motivate people at work:

» **Autonomy:** Most employees have an inherent desire to do quality work and have a positive impact on the organization's success. They need to feel that they're trusted to do a good job without a great deal of oversight and management intrusion. Unfortunately, many organizations value predictability over autonomy, and they end up stifling innovation and discouraging employees from taking initiative.

- **Mastery:** People like to feel as though they're great at their jobs, and most are willing to spend time outside of work and even invest in their own professional development to achieve mastery. Your organization's leadership would be wise to feed this desire for mastery by supporting personal and professional development.

  Your organization can encourage mastery by supporting communities of practice, a center of excellence (see Chapter 3 in Book 6), and guilds. For an additional investment, your organization may consider paying for employees to attend seminars or conferences, and it may provide tuition reimbursement for certain classes. The return on investment in terms of increased employee retention and improved knowledge and skills is well worth it.

- **Sense of purpose:** Employees want to feel as though they're having a significant positive impact on the organization's success. Seeing an idea come to life and significantly improve the end user's experience is a huge reward. It's what makes people want to jump out of bed in the morning eager to get to work.

Enterprise agility requires a culture of mutual respect and trust, and it nurtures such a culture. As soon as you transition to small, self-organized, cross-functional teams and stop providing teams with detailed product requirements or specifying *how* to build the product, employees naturally begin to look for ways to improve the product and the process for creating it. Management can help in two ways:

- **Get out of the way.** Although management traditionally assigns and supervises work, in an agile enterprise, it needs to get out of the way. The product owner maintains a product backlog (a prioritized list of work items), and the team draws from this list to determine what must be done. How it gets the work done is up to the team.
- **Serve the teams.** Management should regard themselves as *enablers.* They should provide the teams with whatever they need to excel, whether it's hardware and software, training, agile coaching, specialized tools, or something else entirely. That kind of support will maximize the potential value created by the team.

REMEMBER

Look for ways to continuously improve your organization's workforce and the systems it uses to deliver value to the customer. These two Lean-Agile practices will drive much of your organization's continuous improvement.

7

Making It Official: PMP Certification

Contents at a Glance

IN THIS CHAPTER

» Checking out the PMP exam blueprint

» Delving into the exam domains

» Understanding the application and scheduling process

» Getting ready for and taking the exam

Chapter 1
Introducing the PMP Exam

So you decided to take the Project Management Professional Certification Exam. That's a big step in moving forward in your profession.

The Project Management Professional (PMP) certification is developed by the Project Management Institute (PMI), which has more than 500,000 members worldwide. Its credentialing program is designed to ensure competence and professionalism in the field of project management. PMI offers several credentials, and the PMP certification is the most well known by far. In fact, the PMP is the most widely recognized project management certification in the world, and there are approximately1 million certified PMPs around the globe.

REMEMBER

Adding this certification to your resume is important in the growing and competitive field of project management. A PMP certification gives employers confidence that existing employees have the level of knowledge to do their jobs well. It also gives employers a yardstick with which to measure new hires. And your project stakeholders can have confidence in your proven knowledge and experience when you have a PMP credential. Bottom line: With a PMP certification, you have more opportunities in your career path.

This chapter walks you through some information about the exam and the application process.

Going Over the PMP Exam Blueprint

The exam content is based on an exam blueprint that defines the domains that should be tested as well as the percentage of questions in each domain. The domains and percentages for the current exam are in the following table:

Initiating the project	13%
Planning the project	24%
Executing the project	31%
Monitoring and controlling the project	25%
Closing the project	7%
Total	**100%**

Knowledge and skills

Each domain has tasks associated with it as well as the knowledge and skills needed to carry out the task successfully. For example, you might see something like this:

- **Task:** Analyze stakeholders to identify expectations and gain support for the project.
- **Knowledge and skills of:** Stakeholder identification techniques

In addition to knowledge and skills specific to a domain, you need cross-cutting skills. A *cross-cutting skill* is one that goes across all domains (such as soft skills, problem solving tools and skills, and leadership tools and techniques). Always keep in mind that cross-cutting skills go across all domains.

Code of ethics and professional conduct

The PMI Code of Ethics and Professional Conduct ("the Code") identifies four ethics standards — responsibility, respect, honesty, and fairness — and divides them into *aspirational* standards (those that project managers we strive to achieve) and *mandatory* standards (those that project managers must follow). Both standards use statements that describe behavior, such as "We negotiate in good faith" or "We listen to other's points of view, seeking to understand them."

TIP

The PMP exam does not test on the Code of Ethics and Professional Conduct explicitly the standards are integrated into the test questions; therefore, you must know and understand the Code to do well on the exam. Chapter 3 of Book 7 addresses the Code specifically. By spending time with the Code, you will be familiar with the ethical context of the questions you encounter on the exam.

Exam scoring

The PMP exam has 200 questions, and you are allowed four hours to complete all 200 questions. Of the 200 test questions, only 175 are scored. The other 25 questions are "pre-test" questions, which is a bit of a misnomer because they don't come before the other questions but are sprinkled in with them. Those 25 unscored questions are a trial. PMI is looking at the performance of those questions to see whether they can eventually be integrated into the exam as scored questions. That's actually a good quality control process and good news for you because you can be assured that only questions that have been through a rigorous validation process are actually on the exam.

In addition to receiving a pass/fail for the exam overall you will attain one of three proficiency levels for each domain:

- **Proficient:** Your performance is above the average for the domain.
- **Moderately proficient:** Your performance is average for the domain.
- **Below proficient:** Your performance is below the average for the domain.

Digging into the Exam Domains

The five domains on the exam have specific topics that they test. The following sections summarize the topics by domain. Books 1 and 2 go into detail on these domains.

Initiating the project

The initiating domain is worth 13 percent of the exam score. This domain comprises the initial project definition, identifying stakeholders, and getting project approval. You will see information about

- Evaluating project feasibility
- Defining high-level scope and related success criteria

- Identifying and analyzing stakeholders (see Chapter 2 in Book 1)
- Proposing an implementation approach
- Completing a project charter
- Gaining project charter approval

Planning the project

The planning domain is worth 24 percent of the exam score. Topics in this domain include the knowledge areas that are listed below and cover all aspects of developing the project management plan.

- Developing the integration plan: Identify and coordinate all the processes and activities within the project management process groups.
- Developing the scope management plan: All work required — and only the work required — to complete the project successfully.
- Developing the schedule management plan: Manage the timely completion of the project.
- Developing the cost management plan: Manage and control cost so the project can be completed within the approved budget.
- Developing the quality management plan: Incorporate the organization's quality plan to meet product standards and stakeholders' requirements.
- Developing a communications management plan: Dispersion of project information/documentation to team and stakeholders.
- Developing a stakeholder management plan: Identify, manage, and engage stakeholders.
- Developing a resource management plan: Identify, acquire, and manage the resources necessary to complete the project.
- Developing a risk management plan: Identify and rank risks and then develop mitigations.
- Developing a procurement management plan: Purchase or acquire products/services outside of the project team.
- After the project management plan is developed,
  - Obtaining project management plan approval
  - Conducting a project kick-off meeting

Executing the project

The executing domain is worth 31 percent of the exam score. These questions deal with the day-to-day management of the project after the majority of the planning is done — in other words, executing the work defined in the project management plan to satisfy the project requirements.

- Managing internal and external resources and stakeholders to perform project activities
- Following the quality management plan
- Following the change management plan
- Executing the project management plan while managing risk
- Providing leadership, motivation, and other skills to maximize team performance to satisfy the project requirements

Monitoring and controlling the project

Monitoring and controlling questions make up 25 percent of the test. The questions are about managing activities required to track, review, and regulate the progress, performance, and any changes in the project.

- Measuring project performance
- Applying change management
- Controlling quality for project deliverables
- Conducting risk management
- Managing issues
- Communicating status
- Managing procurements

Closing the project

This domain makes up 7 percent of the questions. The questions deal with closing a phase, a procurement, contracts, or the overall project (see Chapter 4 in Book 2).

- Closing contracts
- Gaining final acceptance

» Transferring ownership and management
» Conducting a project review
» Documenting lessons learned
» Writing the final project report
» Archiving project records
» Measuring customer satisfaction

Applying for and Scheduling the Exam

The *PMP Certification Handbook* has all the information you need to apply for, pay for, and schedule the exam. It includes information on cancelling and rescheduling, the audit and appeals processes, and the continuing certification requirements. This section touches on a few highlights from the handbook, but it doesn't cover everything. For that, you need to download and review the handbook. Go to `www.pmi.org` and click the Certifications tab. In the Certification Types menu, click Project Management Professional (PMP). A link to the handbook is at the bottom of the page.

To take the exam, you need to meet the following qualifications:

» **A four-year college degree**

TIP

If you don't have a four-year degree, you can take the exam if you have 7,500 hours of project management experience over at least five years.

» **At least three years of experience managing projects**
» **At least 4,500 hours of experience managing projects**
» **35 contact hours of project management education**

WARNING

PMI audits a percent of the applications submitted for the exam. If your application is selected for audit, PMI may call your employer to validate your hours, or you may have to produce evidence to validate the information on the application. If you cannot validate the information, you cannot take the exam.

Surveying the application process

You can fill out your application online at the PMI website (`www.pmi.org`).

WARNING

Filling out the entire application is time consuming. The easy stuff is the demographics and contact information. Even the education and training sections are relatively quick to fill out. But then you need to document your 4,500 hours of experience. That's right: You have to answer questions about projects you've worked on and fill in the number of hours until you reach that 4,500-hour milestone. That can take a long time, so be prepared!

Then there is that not-so-small issue of payment. If you're a PMI member, your exam fees are currently $405 US. If you're not a PMI member, you pay $555 US.

TIP

To become a PMI member, just go the PMI website (`www.pmi.org`). Click the Membership tab to get all the information you need to join. The price for a one-year membership is currently $129.

After you start your application process, you have 90 days to submit the application. Then, PMI has five days to review your application for completeness. To make sure your application isn't returned to you, follow these steps:

1. **Write your name exactly as it appears on your government-issued identification that you will present when you take the examination.**

   Read more about the acceptable forms of ID in the upcoming section "Exam day."

2. **Ensure the application includes your valid email address.**

   This is PMI's primary way of communicating with you throughout the credential process.

3. **Document your attained education and provide all requested information.**

4. **Document 35 contact hours of formal project management education in the experience verification section of the application.**

   REMEMBER

   You must have completed the course(s) you're using for this eligibility option before you submit your application.

5. **Affirm that you have done the following:**

   - Read and understand the policies and procedures outlined in the certification handbook.
   - Read and accept the terms and responsibilities of the PMI Code of Ethics and Professional Conduct. This is included in the *PMP Certification Handbook.*
   - Read and accept the terms and responsibilities of the PMI Certificate Application/Renewal Agreement.

6. **Affirm that you provided true and accurate information on the entire application, understanding that misrepresentations or incorrect information provided to PMI can result in disciplinary action(s), including suspension or revocation of your examination eligibility or credential.**

Make sure you fill out your application early enough to leave yourself time to go through the application and acceptance process and schedule your exam. It's recommended that you give yourself at least six weeks prior to when you want to take the exam.

Scheduling your exam

After your application is accepted and you submit payment for the exam, you can schedule your exam. You have one year from the date your application is approved to take your exam.

PMI will direct you to the Pearson Vue website (`https://home.pearsonvue.com/pmi`) to schedule your exam date. Pearson is the PMI preferred vendor.

Scheduling your exam is a simple process. On the Pearson Vue website, you will log in and follow the prompts. The scheduling process should take less than five minutes.

Do not misplace the unique PMI identification code you receive when PMI notifies you that your application was approved. This code will be required to register for the examination. In addition, you should print and save all examination scheduling verifications and correspondence received from Prometric for your records.

Because PMI cannot guarantee seating at the testing centers, PMI recommends that you schedule your exam six weeks prior to when you want to take the test and at least three months before your eligibility expires.

If you're scheduling your exam around the time a new exam is coming out, you should give yourself at least four months prior to the exam cut-over date. Many people try to get in before the new exam comes out!

Taking the Exam

Taking the PMP exam can be stressful, to say the least. To help ease the stress a bit, here are five tips to keep in mind for the 24 hours before the exam.

- **Don't cram.** The night before the exam, you should know everything you need to know for the exam. Try to have a nice evening.
- **Get plenty of sleep.** "Have a nice evening" doesn't mean you should go out and stay up late. Your mind will be much clearer if you get a good rest.
- **Leave plenty of time to arrive at the exam site.** You cannot take the exam if you are late. Build in plenty of time for traffic snarls, getting lost, and so forth. Beforehand, perhaps take a practice test drive at the time of day you're scheduled to take the exam, just to see how long it takes.
- **Don't drink too much caffeine.** Or any kind of liquid for that matter.
- **Use the restroom before you start the exam.** After you start the exam, don't count on leaving the room until you finish.

Arriving on exam day

When you get to the exam site, you need to show a valid and current form of government-issued identification with your photograph and signature. The name on the ID must exactly match the name on your application. You also have to show them your unique PMI identification number. The following are acceptable forms of government-issued identification:

- Valid driver's license
- Valid military ID
- Valid passport
- Valid national ID card

WARNING

The following *are not* acceptable forms of identification:

- Social Security cards
- Library cards

There are serious restrictions on what you can bring into the testing areas. You *may not* bring anything into the testing area or to the desk where you take the exam, including

- Purses
- Food and beverages
- Book bags

- Coats or sweaters
- Luggage
- Calculators
- Eyeglass cases
- Watches
- Pagers
- Cellphones
- Tape recorders
- Dictionaries
- Any other personal items

Also, you may not bring anyone into the testing area, including

- Children
- Visitors

Calculators are built into the computer-based training (CBT) exam. The testing center administrator provides scrap paper and a pencil to all credential candidates on the day of the exam.

You take the exam on a computer. When you go into the exam testing area, you have the opportunity to take a tutorial and a survey. These are optional. You have 15 minutes to do this.

TIP

Use this time to do a memory dump on your scratch paper. Write down equations, tips, the process matrix, and any other memory joggers that will help you during the exam.

During the exam, you have the opportunity to flag questions to come back to them. Make sure to first go through and answer all the questions you're sure about and relatively sure about. For those questions that you're not sure about, flag them to return to later.

Looking at types of questions

The exam has several types of questions:

- **Situational:** The majority of questions are situational. In other words, you need the experience to know what they are talking about. These can be difficult. They start something like this:

  Assume you are the PM on a project to upgrade the physical security on a university campus.

  Then you review a situation:

  The Dean of Students wants to make sure that all campus housing can only be accessed by the student, faculty, or staff ID cards. The Security Director states that the only way to provide 100% security is to use a biometric scanner. The Finance Director doesn't care what you do as long as you reduce the current operating costs by 15%.

  Finally, the question:

  What document should you use to record the expectations of each of these stakeholders?

- **Only one possible correct answer:** Some questions appear to have two correct answers; however, the exam allows only one correct answer per question. For those questions, ask yourself, "What is the first thing I would do? What is the best thing to do?" Keep in mind that the *Project Management Body of Knowledge (PMBOK) Guide* is the source for many exam questions, so think of the PMBOK-ish response. (Find out more about this guide in the later section "Preparing for the Exam.")
- **Distracters:** *Distracters* are a technique that test questions writers use to, well, distract you. In other words, they put in extra information that you don't need to answer the question.
- **MSU (made stuff up):** You might see some cool words slung together and think it makes sense. If you haven't heard of it before, it probably doesn't exist: for example, "charter initiation process." There are initiating processes, and one of the outputs of the initiating processes is a charter, but there is no charter initiation process.
- **Calculations:** There are a fair number of calculation questions. At least About 8 to 10 questions will have earned value (EV) information and equations, and about 8 to 10 questions will have other types of calculations. If you know your equations, these are some of the easiest questions on the test.
- **Identifications:** Expect about 20 to 25 questions where you have to know a specific process name, input, tool, technique, or output.

Some tests are *adaptive*. That is, the more questions you get right, the harder the questions become. If you miss questions, the easier the questions become. The PMP is not adaptive. The questions are not adjusted based on your answers.

Trying some exam-taking tips

TIP

These tips should help you when the going gets tough:

- **Keep moving.** Don't spend a lot of time trying to figure out one question. You could lose the opportunity to answer many others.
- **Skip to the end of a question.** If you get a lengthy question, read the end of the question first. That usually tells you the question you need to answer. The rest of the information is just background.
- **Go with your instincts.** Your first choice is usually correct, so don't second-guess yourself! Change your answer only if you're certain that it should be changed.
- **Think in broad terms.** The exam is global and across all industries. If you apply too much of what you do on a day-to-day basis, you could miss some of the questions. Think about the questions from a global cross-industry perspective.

Getting your results

When you're done with the exam, you submit your test at the computer. This is a scary moment! To make it worse, the computer will ask you whether you are sure. (And, no, the computer isn't hinting that you failed.) Select Yes, and *voilà!* You're informed whether you passed or failed. (Be confident; you will pass!) The exam administrator will hand you a printout of your exam results, indicating your pass/fail status. The printout will also give you an analysis of your results indicating by area whether you are proficient, moderately proficient, or below proficient.

About six to eight weeks after passing the exam, you will receive a congratulations letter, a certificate, and information on how to maintain your certification.

In the unlikely event that you do not pass the exam, you may take the test up to three times during your one-year eligibility period. If you do not pass within three attempts, you need to wait for a year to reapply. There is more information on this in the *PMP Certification Handbook.*

Preparing for the Exam

In addition to the PMP certification, PMI also puts out the *Guide to the Project Management Body of Knowledge*, or the *PMBOK Guide*. While information in the exam blueprint overlaps information in the *PMBOK Guide*, the exam blueprint identifies tasks, knowledge, and skills, and the *PMBOK Guide* identifies the *artifacts*, or the "what" of project management. Let me show you what I mean.

Earlier in this chapter, you see how the exam blueprint might address information about stakeholders:

- **Task:** *Analyze stakeholders to identify expectations and gain support for the project.*
- **Knowledge and skills of:** Stakeholder identification techniques

The *PMBOK Guide* doesn't discuss knowledge and skills the same way that the exam blueprint does. The *PMBOK Guide* identifies the outputs needed to fulfill the task, such as a stakeholder register and a stakeholder management strategy.

REMEMBER

Although the *PMBOK Guide* isn't the only source of information for the PMP exam, it is the primary source. The *PMBOK Guide* describes project management practices that, generally, are considered good for most projects. That means there is wide agreement that the outputs from the processes are appropriate and that the tools and techniques used to develop the outputs are the correct tools and techniques. It does not mean, though, that you should use every input, tool, technique, or output on your project. The *PMBOK Guide* is just a guide, not a methodology or a rulebook.

Additionally, the *PMBOK Guide* provides a common vocabulary for project management practitioners. For example, when you want to "decompose" your project into a set of deliverables, you use a "work breakdown structure" (WBS). You don't use a "scope management plan" or a "requirements traceability matrix." By having a common set of terms with an agreed-upon meaning, you can communicate better with your project stakeholders. By becoming familiar with the *PMBOK Guide* and using this book to help you study, you'll be in good shape to pass the exam.

It's time to get started. Good luck!

» **Discovering the process groups**

» **Getting acquainted with the knowledge areas**

» **Mapping all the processes in a table**

Chapter 2

It's All about the Process

This chapter corresponds to the information in Annex A1 of the *Project Management Body of Knowledge (PMBOK) Guide*, which identifies the processes needed to manage a project and the inputs and outputs associated with each process.

Although the information in the Annex isn't very exciting, it is important because it establishes the framework for the *PMBOK Guide* and provides the architecture of the processes used in managing a project, by introducing the five process groups and the ten knowledge areas that the project management processes belong to.

TIP

You find a lot of information in this chapter. Don't expect to absorb it all in one sitting. Come back to this chapter every so often. By the time you're ready to take the exam, the information here should make sense. In fact, you should be able to re-create it for yourself. After you can do that, you are ready for the exam!

Managing Your Project Is a Process

REMEMBER

A *process* is a set of interrelated of actions and activities performed to create a pre-specified product, service, or result. You manage projects via a series of processes, which have *inputs* that are needed to initiate the process. Then you apply tools and/or techniques to transform the inputs into outputs.

A simple example is making a cup of coffee. The inputs are the beans, water, a grinder, a pot, a heating mechanism, a filter, and a cup. The techniques you use are grinding the beans and boiling the water. The output is a cup of coffee.

REMEMBER

Here are the *PMBOK Guide* definitions for these terms.

- **Input.** Any item, whether internal or external to the project, that is required by a process before that process proceeds. May be an output from a predecessor process.
- **Tool.** Something tangible, such as a template or software program, used in performing an activity to produce a product or result.
- **Technique.** A defined systematic procedure employed by a human resource to perform an activity to produce a product or result or deliver a service, and that may employ one or more tools.
- **Output.** A product, result, or service generated by a process. May be an input to a successor process.

TIP

Inputs can be outputs from previous processes, and outputs can become inputs to subsequent processes.

The Project Management Institute (PMI) defines 47 project-related processes used to manage projects. Each process is part of one of five process groups:

- Initiating processes
- Planning processes
- Executing processes
- Monitoring and Controlling processes
- Closing processes

In addition, each process belongs to one of the ten knowledge areas:

- Project Integration Management
- Project Scope Management
- Project Schedule Management
- Project Cost Management
- Project Quality Management
- Project Human Resource Management

» Project Communications Management

» Project Risk Management

» Project Procurement Management

» Project Stakeholder Management

The following section talks about the process groups, and you discover the knowledge areas later in this chapter.

TIP

You also need to apply product-related processes to your project, but those are dependent upon the nature of the product and thus are not covered by the *PMBOK Guide*. An example of a product-related project might be integration testing prior to deploying a new system, or editing before printing a technical manual. Those processes are dependent upon the nature of the work and are governed by your organization's policies.

Understanding Project Management Process Groups

The project management process groups (hereafter referred to as *process groups*) of Initiating, Planning, Executing, Monitoring and Controlling, and Closing interact with each other in each project phase and throughout the project as a whole.

REMEMBER

A **project management process group** is a logical grouping of project management inputs, tools and techniques, and outputs. The project management process groups include Initiating processes, Planning processes, Executing processes, Monitoring and Controlling processes, and Closing processes. Project management process groups are not project phases.

TIP

Notice that the domains tested on the PMP are the same as the process groups identified in the *PMBOK Guide*. This means that the exam is based around your skills and knowledge in the various process groups, even though most of the information presented in the *PMBOK Guide* is presented by knowledge area.

Many people make the mistake of thinking that the process groups are a project life cycle. They are not. Rather, they are a way of categorizing the various processes by the nature of the work involved in the process. Chapter 1 in Book 1 describes the project life cycle.

You apply each process group in each phase of the project life cycle although to varying degrees. Figure 2-1 shows how the process groups interact.

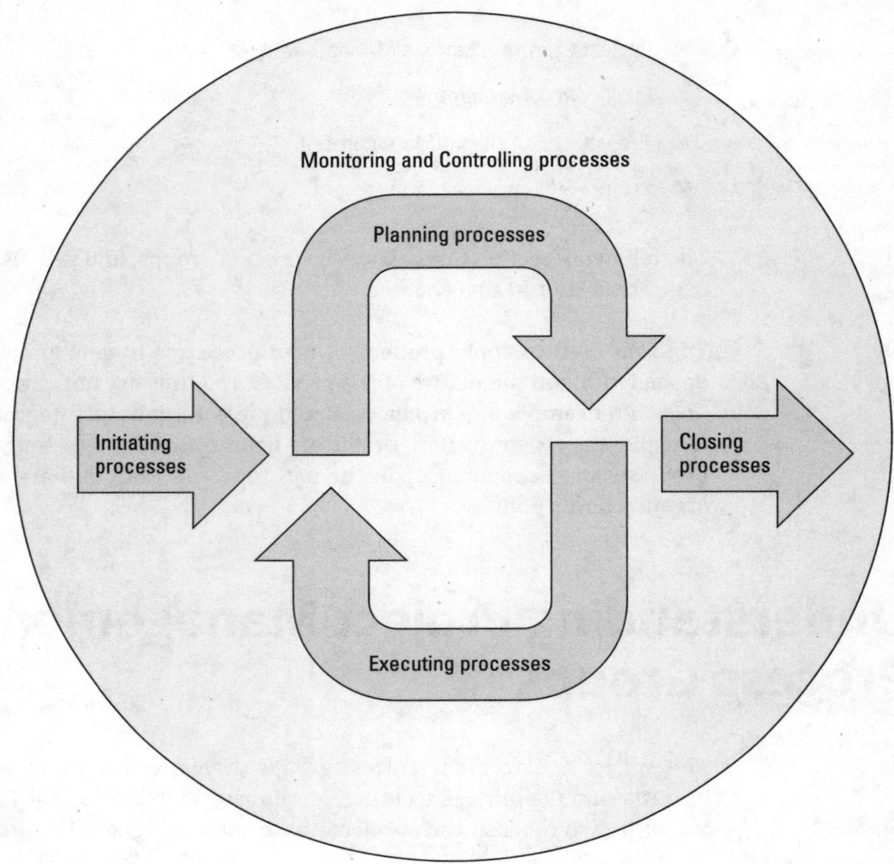

FIGURE 2-1: Process group interactions.

© John Wiley & Sons, Inc.

You can see that when you enter a phase of a project, you go through the Initiating processes. After that is complete, you begin the Planning processes, which lead to Executing processes. However, along the way, you will likely have to replan or progressively elaborate your plans. Therefore, you are planning and executing throughout the majority of the project. Throughout all the processes groups, you conduct activities from the Monitoring and Controlling processes to make sure that the results from the Executing processes are on track with the plans from the Planning processes. When the project objectives have been met, you close out the phase or the project. Figure 2-2 shows how the process looks with a project with three phases.

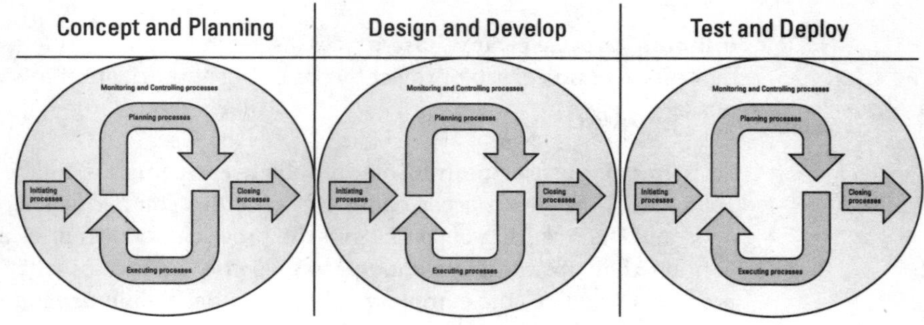

FIGURE 2-2: Project life cycle and process groups.

© John Wiley & Sons, Inc.

Before the Project Begins

Projects are initiated for many reasons: a customer request, regulatory reasons, a technological advance, and so on. Typically, one of the following entities has the authority to initiate a project based on the preceding needs: a program, a portfolio, or a Project Management Office (PMO).

REMEMBER

The decision to initiate a project isn't made in a vacuum. Several steps occur before a project is initiated. Here is a brief generic summary of some of the activities that take place:

1. Someone defines a need or proposes a concept.
2. Some high-level project definition is done, and alternatives to meet the need are developed and discussed.
3. A business case is put together, which can include market opportunity, financial investment, payback period, net present value, and other financial metrics.
4. The business case is presented to the person or group with the authority to initiate projects.

TIP

You might see a couple of questions on the exam that ask where projects come from, or about the work done prior to project initiation. Keep in mind that some work is done prior to authorizing a project.

Initiating processes

Initiating processes happen at the beginning of a project and are revisited at the start of each project phase.

Initiating Processes are those processes performed to define a new project or a new phase of an existing project by obtaining authorization to start the project or phase.

To help you absorb the information about each process in the process groups, Table 2-1 shows the process name, the activities you perform as part of that process, and the resulting outputs from the process. The activities aren't a complete list, but they are complete enough to give you the idea of what happens in each process. Of course, the complete list of activities would depend upon the specific project. The outputs aren't the full list of outputs, but they are the major outputs from each process. However, the information listed is a solid summary of the information for each process.

TABLE 2-1 Initiating Processes, Activities, and Outputs

Process	Activities	Output
Develop Project Charter	Assign a project manager (PM). Identify objectives. Identify stakeholders. Identify stakeholders' needs and expectations. Turn stakeholder needs and expectations into high-level requirements. Define high-level project scope. Review information from similar previous projects. Identify order of magnitude budget. Identify summary milestones. Define success criteria. Use organizational policies, procedures, and templates to develop the project charter. Present the charter for approval and formal authorization.	Project charter
Identify Stakeholders	Identify stakeholders. Determine how to manage stakeholders. Communicate how the project is aligned with the organizations' strategic goals.	Stakeholder register

TIP

Use the information in all the process group tables to quiz yourself. Try to look at the process and identify the activities and outputs.

Planning processes

Planning processes occur throughout the project. The bulk of your time planning will occur right after the project charter is approved. At some point, you will have done sufficient planning to finalize the project management plan and the baselines contained within it. At that point, you begin managing your performance according to those baselines.

However, planning doesn't end after you baseline. You will need to replan based on changes, risk events, and performance. For large projects, you should be engaged in *rolling wave planning,* where you have details for work in the near future and higher-level information for work later in the future. A good time to develop detailed plans for the upcoming phase is when you're closing out one phase and initiating another.

REMEMBER

Rolling wave planning is an iterative planning technique in which the work to be accomplished in the near term is planned in detail, while the work in the future is planned at a higher level.

REMEMBER

Planning processes are those processes performed to establish the total scope of the effort, define and refine the objectives, and develop the course of action required to attain those objectives.

Table 2-2 shows planning processes, activities, and outputs.

You can see that a lot of work goes on in the planning processes!

Table 2-2 doesn't show the loops and iterative nature of planning. However, considering that you're at the point of taking the PMP exam (or at least thinking about it!), you've been managing projects long enough to know that you go through many iterations of planning before you reach a point where the key stakeholders can reach an agreement. For example, you might go around several times in the scope, schedule, cost, and risk processes to find an agreeable approach.

REMEMBER

All plans are preliminary until you do a thorough risk analysis and incorporate the risk management activities, risk responses, and contingency reserves into your scope, schedule, and cost documents. Only then can you baseline.

TABLE 2-2 Planning Processes, Activities, and Outputs

Process	Activities	Outputs
Develop Project Management Plan	Determine how to manage scope, schedule, and cost for the project and document the information in a management plan. Determine how to manage change for the project and document the information in the change management plan. Determine the appropriate level of configuration management and document it in a configuration management plan. Document the project life cycle. Determine how performance will be measured and reviewed. Determine which processes are needed for the project and the degree of rigor. Review information from past projects. Identify and follow organizational policies, procedures, processes, and templates used for planning. Identify EEFs* that will influence your project. Identify organizational interfaces and other projects you need to integrate with. Determine the methods used to monitor and control the project. Negotiate and prioritize project constraints. Baseline the plan. Get formal approval and sign-off on the project management plan. Hold a team kick-off meeting.	Project management plan
Plan Scope Management	Document the approach to develop a scope statement and WBS.** Describe how the WBS will be maintained and approved. Describe how formal acceptance of deliverables will take place. Determine how scope changes will be integrated with the project change control system. Describe how requirements activities will be planned, conducted, and documented. Document how configuration management for requirements will be carried out. Define requirements prioritization. Identify the metrics and acceptance criteria for requirements. Determine the requirements traceability structure.	Scope management plan Requirements management plan

Process	Activities	Outputs
Collect Requirements	Employ brainstorming, role playing, negotiating, facilitating, interviewing, and consensus-building skills to identify and agree on project requirements. Document and prioritize project and product requirements.	Requirements documentation Requirements traceability matrix
Define Scope	Document what is in and out of scope. Describe project deliverables and their acceptance criteria. Document assumptions. Document constraints.	Project scope statement
Create WBS	Decompose work into deliverables. Describe each work package.	WBS dictionary Scope baseline
Plan Schedule Management	Document how the schedule will be developed and managed throughout the project.	Schedule management plan
Define Activities	Identify activities needed to create deliverables.	Activity list Activity attributes Milestone list
Sequence Activities	Put activities in order.	Network diagram
Estimate Activity Resources	Determine resource requirements.	Resource requirements Resource breakdown structure
Estimate Activity Durations	Estimate project duration.	Duration estimates
Develop Schedule	Develop preliminary schedule.	Project schedule Schedule baseline
Plan Cost Management	Document how cost estimates will be developed. Describe how contingency funds will be determined and managed. Describe how the project budget will be developed. Identify the control mechanisms that will be used to monitor and control the project budget.	Cost management plan

(continued)

TABLE 2-2 ***(continued)***

Process	Activities	Outputs
Estimate Costs	Estimate project costs.	Cost estimates
Determine Budget	Develop project budget.	Cost performance baseline Project funding requirements
Plan Quality Management	Document project quality standards and requirements.	Quality management plan Quality metrics Quality checklists Process improvement plan
Plan Human Resource Management	Document project roles and responsibilities. Develop project organization chart. Determine how to manage project staff.	Human resource plan
Plan Communications Management	Document who needs what information, in what format, and how often.	Communications management plan
Plan Risk Management	Document approach to risk management.	Risk management plan
Identify Risks	Interview stakeholders for threats and opportunities. Document project threats and opportunities.	Risk register
Perform Qualitative Risk Analysis	Assess probability and impact of risks.	Risk register updates
Perform Quantitative Risk Analysis	Apply simulation, expected monetary value, decision trees, and other quantitative analysis techniques to risk events.	Risk register updates

Process	Activities	Outputs
Plan Risk Responses	Brainstorm risk responses and develop strategies to effectively manage threats.	Risk register updates
Plan Procurement Management	Document approach to procurements. Select contract types. Develop procurement documents, including an SOW.***	Procurement management plan Make-or-buy decisions SOWs Procurement documents Source selection criteria
Plan Stakeholder Management	Identify and documents methods to effectively engage stakeholders in the project. Determine how to manage stakeholder expectations.	Stakeholder management plan

* *EEF: enterprise environmental factor*

** *WBS: work breakdown structure*

*** *SOW: statement of work*

REMEMBER

Planning goes on throughout the project. You can and will revisit any or all of these processes and activities at various points in the project.

Executing processes

The Executing processes are where the majority of the project budget is expended and the majority of time is spent. This is where the project team creates the deliverables and meets the requirements and objectives of the project. See Table 2-3.

REMEMBER

Executing processes are those processes performed to complete the work defined in the project management plan to satisfy the project objectives.

TABLE 2-3 Executing Processes, Activities, and Outputs

Processes	Activities	Outputs
Direct and Manage Project Work	Coordinate people and other resources to execute project activities. Problem-solve issues and risks, and analyze the best approach to them. Implement changes, corrective and preventive actions, and defect repairs. Implement risk responses as required.	Deliverables Work performance data
Perform Quality Assurance	Audit utilization and effectiveness of the quality plan.	Change requests
Acquire Project Team	Negotiate and influence to ensure the appropriate type and number of resources are assigned to the team.	Staff assignments
Develop Project Team	Motivate, team build, and mentor to improve individual and overall team performance.	Team performance assessments EEF updates
Manage Project Team	Manage and lead team throughout the project. Resolve conflicts and solve problems.	EEF updates Organizational process asset updates Change requests Project management plan updates
Manage Communications	Develop communications. Collect and distribute information.	Project communications
Conduct Procurements	Negotiate contract elements, terms, and conditions.	Selected sellers Contracts/agreements
Manage Stakeholder Engagement	Document, negotiate, and resolve issues and conflicts. Facilitate meetings and present information to ensure a common understanding among stakeholders. Communicate to manage stakeholder expectations.	Issue logs Change requests Project management plan updates Project document updates

Monitoring and Controlling processes

Monitoring and Controlling processes measure the performance of the project, take action based on the performance analysis, and maintain the integrity of the baseline by ensuring that only approved changes are integrated into the project management plan.

Monitoring and controlling processes are those processes required to track, review, and regulate the progress and performance of the project, identify any areas in which changes to the plan are required, and initiate the corresponding changes.

Almost every process in this process group has the following outputs:

- Change requests
- Project management plan updates
- Project document updates
- Organizational process asset updates

Table 2-4 lists the four consistent outputs only once, but you should know that they are common outputs from the Monitoring and Controlling processes.

TABLE 2-4 Monitoring and Controlling Processes, Activities, and Outputs

Processes	Activities	Outputs
Monitor and Control Project Work	Measure and analyze project performance to identify any variances from plan.	Organizational process asset updates
	Problem-solve to determine appropriate corrective and preventive action.	Project management plan update
	Perform a root cause analysis of variances.	Project document updates
	Manage time and cost reserve allocation.	
Perform Integrated Change Control	Evaluate change request impacts.	Approved change requests
	Negotiate competing constraints with stakeholders for requested changes.	
	Maintain baseline integrity by ensuring only accepted changes are integrated into the project.	
	Communicate status of project changes to all impacted stakeholders.	

(continued)

TABLE 2-4 *(continued)*

Processes	Activities	Outputs
Validate / Verify Scope	Inspect deliverables for acceptance.	Accepted deliverables
Control Scope	Measure performance against the baselines.	Work performance information
Control Schedule	Perform EV* analysis.	
Control Cost	Calculate estimates to complete.	Forecasts
Control Quality	Inspect and review all deliverables for compliance with specifications. Apply control charts, histograms, cause-and-effect charts, and other quality control tools to deliverables. Identify areas to improve project and product performance.	Quality control measurements Verified deliverables
Control Communications	Determine the effectiveness and efficiency of the communications management plan and update it as necessary.	Work performance information
Control Risks	Continually monitor status of existing risks. Identify new risks to the project. Negotiate risk response strategies with stakeholders. Problem-solve to identify appropriate risk responses. Evaluate effectiveness of risk management processes and risk responses.	Risk register updates
Control Procurements	Inspect vendor work and work sites.	Procurement documentation
Control Stakeholder Engagement	Determine the effectiveness and efficiency of the stakeholder management plan and update it as necessary.	Work performance information

* *EV: earned value*

REMEMBER

Monitoring and controlling processes are applied throughout the project. They are conducted for each phase and for the project as a whole.

Closing processes

Even though there are only two processes in the Closing process group, several activities occur. See Table 2-5.

TABLE 2-5 **Closing Processes, Activities, and Outputs**

Processes	Activities	Outputs
Close Project or Phase	Review project management plan to ensure all aspects of the project are complete. Follow all organizational policies regarding phase exit criteria or project closure. Evaluate and document team member performance and update information on new skills as appropriate. Interview stakeholders and document lessons learned. Objectively evaluate project performance and write a project closeout report. Present final project results. Collect, compile, and organize all project records for archives. Interview and survey stakeholders to analyze and rate customer satisfaction. Acknowledge team members with rewards and/or celebrations. Release and return all project resources.	Final product transition Organizational process assets updates
Close Procurements	Review contracts to ensure all contractual obligations have been met. Negotiate and manage conflict to resolve any open issues or claims associated with procurements. Manage and coordinate relationships with internal procurement resources and vendors. Obtain sign-off from legal and the vendors to close contracts. Organize all procurement documentation for archives. Conduct a procurement audit to improve the procurement process in the future.	Closed procurements Organizational process assets updates

REMEMBER

Closing processes are those processes performed to finalize all activities across all project management process groups to formally close the project or phase.

TIP

Figure A1-2 in the Annex of the *PMBOK Guide* has a high-level view of how the various process groups interact with one another. You should study this and make sure you understand it and can explain the interactions.

The Ten Knowledge Areas

Another way of looking at the project management processes is by grouping them in knowledge areas. There are ten knowledge areas.

REMEMBER

A **project management knowledge area** is an identified area of project management defined by its knowledge requirements and described in terms of its component processes, practices, inputs, outputs, tools, and techniques.

The following sections give you the *PMBOK Guide* definition of the knowledge area, and then list the processes contained in that area.

Project Integration Management

This knowledge area is the centerpiece of project management: Here's where you combine and coordinate the work of all the processes so they flow smoothly.

REMEMBER

Project integration management includes the processes and activities needed to identify, define, combine, unify, and coordinate the various processes and project management activities within the project management process groups.

- Develop Project Charter
- Develop Project Management Plan
- Direct and Manage Project Work
- Monitor and Control Project Work
- Perform Integrated Change Control
- Close Project or Phase

Project Scope Management

Scope management is the backbone from which all the rest of the knowledge areas build. Scope processes are concerned with requirements, defining project and product scope, creating the work breakdown structure (WBS; see Chapter 3 in Book 1), getting acceptance of the scope, and managing changes to the scope.

REMEMBER

Project scope management includes the processes required to ensure that the project includes all the work required — and only the work required — to complete the project successfully.

- Plan Scope Management
- Collect Requirements
- Define Scope
- Create WBS
- Validate Scope
- Control Scope

Project Schedule Management

Project schedule management processes create and control the schedule. The processes needed to create a reliable schedule can be done at one time, especially for smaller projects, but they are presented here as discrete processes because the skills and techniques used are distinct for each process.

REMEMBER

Project schedule management includes the processes required to manage the timely completion of a project.

- Plan Schedule Management
- Define Activities
- Sequence Activities
- Estimate Activity Resources
- Estimate Activity Durations
- Develop Schedule
- Control Schedule

Project Cost Management

The cost estimates and project budget are some of the most closely scrutinized elements in the project management plan. Estimating costs can be one of the more challenging activities you undertake. This knowledge area looks at estimating and budgeting costs. It also looks at controlling them and introduces earned value (EV) management.

REMEMBER

Project cost management includes the processes involved in planning, estimating, budgeting, financing, funding, managing, and controlling costs so that the project can be completed within the approved budget.

- Plan Cost Management
- Estimate Costs
- Determine Budget
- Control Costs

Project Quality Management

If project scope is about what the project and product are supposed to deliver, project quality is about how good it has to be. These processes look at project and product quality from the perspective of planning, maintaining, and controlling.

REMEMBER

Project quality management includes the processes and activities of the performing organization that determine quality policies, objectives, and responsibilities so that the project will satisfy the needs for which it was undertaken.

- Plan Quality Management
- Perform Quality Assurance
- Control Quality

Project Resource Management

Much of the *PMBOK Guide* is about the techniques and outputs associated with managing a project. For this knowledge area, the most important component of performing the work is the people. This knowledge area focuses on the tools you use as well as many of the interpersonal skills needed to effectively manage the project team.

REMEMBER

Project resource management includes the processes that organize and manage the project team.

- Plan Human Resource Management
- Acquire Physical Resources
- Utilize Physical Resources
- Manage Physical Resources

Project Communications Management

Project Communications Management is where you make sure the right people get the needed information in the most effective and efficient way and at the appropriate time.

REMEMBER

Project communications management includes the processes required to ensure timely and appropriate planning, collection, creation, distribution, storage, retrieval, management, control, monitoring, and ultimate disposition of project information.

- Plan Communications Management
- Manage Communications
- Control Communications

Project Risk Management

You can have the best plans in the world, but if you don't incorporate risk management into your project planning, your plans can all go down the tube in an instant. This knowledge area defines the processes needed to keep project risk to an acceptable level.

REMEMBER

Project Risk Management includes the processes concerned with conducting risk management planning, identification, analysis, responses, and monitoring and control on a project.

- Plan Risk Management
- Identify Risks
- Perform Qualitative Risk Management
- Perform Quantitative Risk Management

- Plan Risk Responses
- Control Risks

Project Procurement Management

In many projects, your organization won't have the skills or capacity to perform all the activities or create all the deliverables necessary. Therefore, procurement management is an important part of managing your projects.

REMEMBER

Project procurement management includes the processes to purchase or acquire the products, services, or results needed from outside the project team to perform the work.

- Plan Procurement Management
- Conduct Procurements
- Control Procurements
- Close Procurements

Project Stakeholder Management

You can meet every milestone, have a fully functioning product, and come in on budget, but if your stakeholders are not happy, you can't really call your project a success. The larger your projects are, the more important it is to manage your stakeholders.

REMEMBER

Project Stakeholder Management includes the processes required to identify all people or organizations impacted by the project, analyzing stakeholder expectations and impact on the project, and developing appropriate management strategies for effectively engaging stakeholders in project decisions and execution.

- Identify Stakeholders
- Plan Stakeholder Management
- Manage Stakeholder Engagement
- Control Stakeholder Engagement

Interestingly enough, the *PMBOK Guide* presents the project management processes by their knowledge areas. However, the PMP exam evaluates exam performance based on process groups. Because the exam is based on process groups, this chapter presents the information by process group and then by knowledge areas in the process groups.

Mapping the Processes

Because each process is part of a process group and part of a knowledge area, it's useful to see how those intersect. Table 2-6 shows how each process maps to a knowledge area and a process group.

TIP

One of the best study tips you can get is to create a table like the one shown in Table 2-6 and fill it in with the processes. Being able to identify the process, the process group, and the knowledge area will help you recollect the information you will need as you take the exam. In fact, when you get into the exam, take a moment and re-create that chart on a piece of paper to reference during the exam.

TABLE 2-6 Project Management Process Groups and Knowledge Areas

	Initiating	Planning	Executing	Monitoring and Controlling	Closing
Integration	Develop Project Charter	Develop Project Management Plan	Direct and Manage Project Work	Monitor and Control Project Work Perform Integrated Change Control	Close Project or Phase
Scope		Plan Scope Management Collect Requirements Define Scope Create WBS		Validate / Verify Scope Control Scope	
Schedule		Plan Schedule Management Define Activities Sequence Activities Estimate Activity Resources Estimate Activity Durations Develop Schedule		Control Schedule	

(continued)

It's All about the Process

TABLE 2-6 ***(continued)***

	Initiating	Planning	Executing	Monitoring and Controlling	Closing
Cost		Plan Cost Management Estimate Costs Determine Budget		Control Costs	
Quality		Plan Quality Management	Perform Quality Assurance	Control Quality	
Resources		Plan Human and Physical Resource Management	Acquire, Utilize, and Manage Physical Resources Develop Project Team Manage Project Team		
Communication		Plan Communications Management	Manage Communications	Control Communications	
Risk		Plan Risk Management Identify Risks Perform Qualitative Analysis Perform Quantitative Analysis Plan Risk Responses		Control Risks	
Procurement		Plan Procurement Management	Conduct Procurements	Control Procurements	Close Procurements
Stakeholder	Identify Stakeholder	Plan Stakeholder Management	Manage Stakeholder Engagement	Control Stakeholder Engagement	

IN THIS CHAPTER

» Starting with the basics of the Code

» Focusing on responsibility, respect, fairness, and honesty

» Noting a few important terms

Chapter 3
Reviewing the PMI Code of Ethics and Professional Conduct

The Project Management Institute (PMI) has developed and published a Code of Ethics and Professional Conduct ("the Code") that describes the expectations of project management practitioners. The Code articulates the ideals that project managers should aspire to, and those behaviors that are considered mandatory. The purpose of the Code of Ethics and Professional Conduct is to instill confidence in the project management profession and to help an individual become a better practitioner.

This chapter presents the standards in one place to give you further understanding of how they might be integrated into exam questions. There are no exam objectives associated with the information in this chapter. Rather, you'll see questions that incorporate situations that would require you to apply standards from the Code along with the technical information from the process groups and knowledge areas.

The Code focuses on four areas: responsibility, respect, fairness, and honesty. This chapter looks at each of these four elements and how they apply to projects and the Project Management Professional (PMP) exam.

Beginning with the Basics of the Code

The Code describes the ideals for project management and the appropriate behaviors in the roles of project managers. It can also be used as a reference to guide project managers' behavior when they are faced with difficult situations. The Code applies to the following groups of people:

- All PMI members
- Anyone who holds a PMI certification (including the PMP)
- Anyone applying for a certification
- Anyone who volunteers with PMI

The Code was developed when PMI asked practitioners from around the globe to identify those values that were most important in decision making and guiding their project management actions. Based on the feedback from the global community, the four values that the Code is based on were identified as

- Responsibility
- Respect
- Fairness
- Honesty

There are two aspects to each value: aspirational standards and mandatory standards. And the standards are not mutually exclusive. An act or omission can be both aspirational and mandatory:

- **Aspirational standards:** Those standards that describe the conduct people should strive to uphold as project management practitioners.
- **Mandatory standards:** Those standards that are firm requirements. They may limit or prohibit behavior.

WARNING

Practitioners whose conduct is not in accordance with the mandatory standards are subject to disciplinary procedures before the PMI Ethics Review Committee.

TIP

You can find the Code at the PMI website: `https://www.pmi.org/about/ethics/code`. A copy is also integrated into the PMP Certification Handbook, also found on the PMI website at `https://www.pmi.org/-/media/pmi/documents/public/pdf/certifications/project-management-professional-handbook.pdf`.

The Code is not copyrighted. This chapter quotes the description of the value and the aspirational and mandatory standards verbatim.

Responsibility

The responsibility standards are about taking ownership for actions, decisions, and the consequences that result from them. Here is the definition of responsibility from the Code.

REMEMBER

Responsibility is our duty to take ownership for the decisions we make or fail to make, the actions we take or fail to take, and the consequences that result.

Responsibility aspirational standards

REMEMBER

The following are the six aspirational standards under responsibility. Keep in mind that aspirational standards are standards that project managers strive to uphold. The following is from the Code of Ethics and Professional Conduct:

1. We make decisions and take actions based on the best interests of society, public safety, and the environment.
2. We accept only those assignments that are consistent with our background, experience, skills, and qualifications.
3. We fulfill the commitments that we undertake — we do what we say we will do.
4. When we make errors or omissions, we take ownership and make corrections promptly. When we discover errors or omissions caused by others, we communicate them to the appropriate body as soon they are discovered. We accept accountability for any issues resulting from our errors or omissions and any resulting consequences.
5. We protect proprietary or confidential information that has been entrusted to us.
6. We uphold this Code and hold each other accountable to it.

As you look at the standards here, see whether you can think of the type of questions you would see on the exam. For example, you might see questions that ask what you should do if what is in the best interest of the project schedule is to move forward without another round of testing even though the safety director has recommended it. In this situation, you're looking at the good of the project schedule and probably some stakeholder satisfaction issues and weighing them against the need for public safety.

Regardless of what you would do in real life, for these questions, you want to stick with the Code and select the answer that indicates that if safety issues were at stake, you would run the extra round of testing.

Another area you need to watch in this section is not taking on projects that you're not qualified to manage. If there is a project with a type of technology, or regulations that you're not familiar with, you're probably not qualified to manage that project. At the very least, you're obligated to disclose your concerns over your lack of experience.

The standard about not disclosing proprietary and confidential information is a pretty black-and-white issue. You shouldn't have any problem with those questions. A more difficult question is what to do if you see someone else not behaving in concert with the Code. It can be very hard to "make waves" if you see someone behaving inconsistently with this Code. However, if that person is a PMP and not in alignment with the values, you are required to hold him accountable to the Code.

Responsibility mandatory standards

The two types of mandatory standards for responsibility are regulations and legal requirements, and ethics complaints.

There are two mandatory standards for regulations and legal requirements. Keep this in mind: *Mandatory requirements are not negotiable!* The following is from the Code of Ethics and Professional Conduct:

1. We inform ourselves and uphold the policies, rules, regulations, and laws that govern our work, professional, and volunteer activities.
2. We report unethical or illegal conduct to appropriate management and, if necessary, to those affected by the conduct.

The ethics complaint standards have to do with violating the Code and reporting violations by others. The following is from the Code of Ethics and Professional Conduct:

1. We bring violations of this Code to the attention of the appropriate body for resolution.
2. We only file ethics complaints when they are substantiated by facts.
3. We pursue disciplinary action against an individual who retaliates against a person raising ethics concerns.

For regulations and legal requirements, make sure that you understand the policies, regulations, and rules associated with the work you're doing. In addition, if you see someone behaving unethically or illegally, you are required to report her.

REMEMBER

The section on ethics complaints will govern your relationship with PMI after you apply to take the exam. If you see a violation of this Code, you must report it to the Ethics Review Committee. However, make sure that you can substantiate the facts of the case. Bringing an ethics violation to the committee is a serious undertaking. People can have their memberships and their certifications revoked if their behavior is egregious enough. In the event of an investigation, you have the responsibility to cooperate with PMI in obtaining the facts about the case.

Respect

REMEMBER

Respect is our duty to show a high regard for ourselves, others, and the resources entrusted to us. Resources entrusted to us may include people, money, reputation, the safety of others, and natural or environmental resources. An environment of respect engenders trust, confidence, and performance excellence by fostering mutual cooperation — an environment where diverse perspectives and views are encouraged and valued.

Respect aspirational standards

REMEMBER

The respect aspirational standards are about appreciating diversity in culture, opinion, and points of view. They also address the professionalism with which we conduct ourselves. The following is from the Code of Ethics and Professional Conduct:

1. We inform ourselves about the norms and customs of others and avoid engaging in behaviors they might consider disrespectful.
2. We listen to others' points of view, seeking to understand them.

3. We approach directly those persons with whom we have a conflict or disagreement.
4. We conduct ourselves in a professional manner, even when it is not reciprocated.

When the exam asks questions about culture, many times we think about different cultures as representing people from different countries — but that isn't the only scenario in which we experience diverse cultures. Here are some other examples:

- Differences in ages or generations can mean different means of communication and different work ethics.
- If you change jobs and go to a different company, or even just a new department, the work rules and norms may be different.
- Different geographical areas, even if they are in the same country, have different work styles.

TIP

You might see the term *ethnocentrism* on the exam. This term means the tendency to see the world from one's own ethnic perspective and not understand that there are alternative world views. The majority of the questions having to do with different cultures can be correctly answered by embracing diversity and having an open mind and tolerance for different points of view.

You might see questions on the exam that provide a scenario wherein a team member complains about your management style. The proper response is to approach that person directly and seek to understand what is causing the conflict. However, sometimes, people shy away from direct contact, or they are inclined to complain about the team member to others. For this section of the exam, you have to aspire to be more communicative and direct than you are accustomed to.

Regarding professionalism, perhaps when someone is treating you disrespectfully or unprofessionally, you have a hard time responding professionally. This is something you need to keep aspiring to! This includes gossip! Not only do you have an ethical obligation to not participate in gossip, but you should also actively discourage others from this behavior.

Respect mandatory standards

REMEMBER

The following mandatory respect standards have to do with power, influence, and behavior. The following is from the Code of Ethics and Professional Conduct:

1. We negotiate in good faith.
2. We do not exercise the power of our expertise or position to influence the decisions or actions of others in order to benefit personally at their expense.

3. We do not act in an abusive manner toward others.
4. We respect the property rights of others.

You might see some questions about contracts and procurements that talk about negotiating in good faith. Some of these questions might even state that the person with whom you're negotiating has adopted a win-lose attitude to the negotiation. Regardless, you're required to negotiate in good faith and mutual cooperation.

Contracts aren't the only place where you need to negotiate on your project. Sometimes you need to negotiate the competing constraints, or negotiate with functional managers for resources. In these situations, you have to assume that the person you are negotiating with is doing his best, and approach the situation from a win-win perspective.

Other standards in this area require that you influence with integrity, and not with power or to the detriment of others. It's pretty obvious treating others unfairly, disrespectfully, or abusively is not okay. Nor is it okay to disrespect the personal, intellectual, or real property of others. By the way, this includes copyrighted material. It is against the Code to copy and use others' work without their express permission.

TIP

Many of the questions about respect will be situational. You will have to assume you are in the position of the project manager and select the appropriate response.

Fairness

REMEMBER

Fairness is our duty to make decisions and act impartially and objectively. Our conduct must be free from competing self-interest, prejudice, and favoritism.

Fairness aspirational standards

REMEMBER

The aspirational fairness standards are concerned with making sure that all relevant parties have equal opportunities. This will be especially prevalent in procurement questions. The aspirational standards also address impartiality and transparency in decision making. The following is from the Code of Ethics and Professional Conduct:

1. We demonstrate transparency in our decision-making process.
2. We constantly reexamine our impartiality and objectivity, taking corrective action as appropriate.

3. We provide equal access to information to those who are authorized to have that information.

4. We make opportunities equally available to qualified candidates.

One way to demonstrate transparency in decision making is to develop a decision-making process and establish decision-making criteria. You can see this as developing and applying source selection criteria. This can apply to other types of decisions as well.

The other standards in this section can be easily applied to procurements and hiring or promoting team members.

Fairness mandatory standards

The mandatory fairness standards address objectivity, conflicts of interest, favoritism, and discrimination. The following is from the Code of Ethics and Professional Conduct:

1. We proactively and fully disclose any real or potential conflicts of interest to the appropriate stakeholders.
2. When we realize that we have a real or potential conflict of interest, we refrain from engaging in the decision-making process or otherwise attempting to influence outcomes, unless or until
   - We have made full disclosure to the affected stakeholders.
   - We have an approved mitigation plan.
   - We have obtained the consent of the stakeholders to proceed.
3. We do not hire or fire, reward or punish, or award or deny contracts based on personal considerations, including but not limited to, favoritism, nepotism, or bribery.
4. We do not discriminate against others based on, but not limited to, gender, race, age, religion, disability, nationality, or sexual orientation.
5. We apply the rules of the organization (employer, Project Management Institute, or other group) without favoritism or prejudice.

The Code has two key definitions in the first mandatory standard.

» **Conflict of Interest.** A situation that arises when a practitioner of project management is faced with making a decision or doing some act that will benefit the practitioner or another person or organization to which the practitioner owes a duty of loyalty, and at the same time will harm another person or organization to which the practitioner owes a similar duty of loyalty. The only way practitioners can resolve conflicting duties is to disclose the conflict to those affected and allow them to make the decision about how the practitioner should proceed.

» **Duty of Loyalty.** A person's responsibility, legal or moral, to promote the best interest of an organization or other person with whom she is affiliated.

The rules about conflicts of interest apply to actual and perceived conflicts. Here's an example: Say that you're an officer in a PMI chapter, you happen to provide training, and the board is looking at offering a training course. You should excuse yourself from the discussion because you could be perceived as having a conflict of interest even if you didn't promote yourself at the expense of others.

REMEMBER

For conflict of interest situations, be as conservative as possible by disclosing information even if you think it not relevant to the situation. Better to over-disclose than be accused of conflict of interest.

TIP

The remaining standards are about not showing favoritism and not discriminating in any way, shape, or form. Exam questions that address these standards are fairly easy to spot — and as long as you choose the answer that shows the high moral ground, you will do fine on these questions.

Honesty

REMEMBER

Honesty is our duty to understand the truth and act in a truthful manner both in our communications and in our conduct.

Honesty aspirational standards

REMEMBER

The aspirational honest standards are about keeping our word and fully disclosing all relevant information. The following is from the Code of Ethics and Professional Conduct:

1. We earnestly seek to understand the truth.
2. We are truthful in our communications and in our conduct.
3. We provide accurate information in a timely manner.
4. We make commitments and promises, implied or explicit, in good faith.
5. We strive to create an environment in which others feel safe to tell the truth.

Think about your performance reports or your status reports. You want to put the best information forward. You want to talk about the good things that have happened on the project. After all, not many people want to discuss risks and challenges, especially if you think you can correct them before someone finds out, or if you have a plan to make things right again. However, this behavior goes against the honesty standards.

In addition, if a team member gives you information you believe might not be wholly true, you have a duty to find out the truth. You also need to make sure to not penalize team members for coming to you with risks or challenges. You need to create an environment where people can tell you the truth without fear of abusive responses. These standards are probably some of the same rules you had growing up: Tell the truth, be on time, and keep your promises.

Honesty mandatory standards

REMEMBER

The mandatory honesty standards take the aspirational standards one step further by stating that we must not engage in deceptive or dishonest behavior. The following is from the Code of Ethics and Professional Conduct:

1. We do not engage in or condone behavior that is designed to deceive others, including but not limited to, making misleading or false statements, stating half-truths, providing information out of context or withholding information that, if known, would render our statements as misleading or incomplete.
2. We do not engage in dishonest behavior with the intention of personal gain or at the expense of another.

These mandatory standards carry over from the aspirational standards in the preceding section. In addition to telling the truth, you can't commit the sin of omission or misleading someone, or not speaking up if someone misinterprets what you told her. It can be difficult to confess that your projects are in trouble, especially if you expect a punitive response. However, you have a duty and an obligation to disclose the whole truth.

This concept applies to estimating and planning as well. If you're given an unrealistic deadline from your sponsor, you have an obligation to inform her that the deadline is unrealistic — and tell her why it is unrealistic. If your team members are giving you optimistic estimates and you know about it, you have an obligation to discuss the situation with them and get more realistic estimates.

TIP

Some of these standards might be easier than others to apply, but they all represent the high moral ground. Keep that in mind when you come across these questions on the exam.

Keeping Key Terms in Mind

TIP

Although you may not see the majority of these terms on the exam, you may see ethnocentrism, conflict of interest, and duty of loyalty on the exam. However, you need to be familiar with all the terminology in the context of behaving ethically and in accordance with the Code:

- Code of Ethics and Professional Conduct
- Responsibility
- Respect
- Fairness
- Honesty
- Aspirational standards
- Mandatory standards
- Ethnocentrism
- Conflict of interest
- Duty of loyalty

Index

A

B

C

D

E

F

G

H

I

J

K

L

M

N

O

P

Q

R

S

T

U

V

W

X

About the Authors

Nick Graham is the founder and managing director of Inspirandum Ltd., a small and specialized company focused on achieving excellence in project management and in the related areas of project governance and program management. He's also a director of Anglo-Swiss Projects, the company that manages the new PRIME project management method of which Nick is also co-author. Nick is a member of the Institute of Directors (MIoD) and of the Association for Project Management (MAPM). He is the author of *Project Management Checklists For Dummies.*

Mark C. Layton, known globally as Mr. Agile, is an executive and board of directors advisor with over 25 years in the project/program management field. He is the Los Angeles chair for the Agile Leadership Network and is the founder of Platinum Edge, LLC — an organizational improvement company that supports businesses making the waterfall-to-agile transition. Mark holds MBAs from the University of California, Los Angeles, and the National University of Singapore; a B.Sc. (*summa cum laude*) in behavioral science from University of La Verne; and an A.S. in electronic systems from the Air Force's Air College. He is also a distinguished graduate of the Air Force's Leadership School, a Certified Scrum Trainer (CST), a certified scaled agile program consultant (SAFe SPC), a certified Project Management Professional (PMP), and a recipient of Stanford University's advanced project management certification (SCPM). He is the coauthor of *Agile Project Management For Dummies* and *Scrum For Dummies.*

David Morrow is an Executive Agile Coach, helping leadership and scrum teams work through their roles in ensuring agile transformation success. David is a Certified Scrum Professional (CSP) and Certified Agile Coach (ICP-ACC), and he has more than two decades of experience building and coaching teams to be more powerful and successful. David served as the CEO of Devnext for 15 years before moving into coaching full-time for Platinum Edge. He is the coauthor of *Scrum For Dummies.*

Steven J. Ostermiller is a coach, mentor, and trainer empowering leaders and teams to become more agile. He holds CSP and PMP designations. He is the coauthor of *Agile Project Management For Dummies.*

Stan Portny, president of Stanley E. Portny and Associates, LLC, is an internationally recognized expert in project management and project leadership. During the past 35 years, he's provided training and consultation to more than 200 public and private organizations in consumer products, insurance, pharmaceuticals, finance, information technology, telecommunications, defense, and healthcare. He has developed and conducted training programs for more than 100,000 management and staff personnel in engineering, sales and marketing, research and development, information systems, manufacturing, operations, and support areas. A Project Management Institute–certified Project Management Professional (PMP),

Stan received his bachelor's degree in electrical engineering from the Polytechnic Institute of Brooklyn. He holds a master's degree in electrical engineering and the degree of electrical engineer from the Massachusetts Institute of Technology. Stan has also studied at the Alfred P. Sloan School of Management and the George Washington University National Law Center. He is the author of *Project Management For Dummies.*

Doug Rose has been transforming organizations through technology, training, and process optimization for more than 20 years, and he now specializes in providing agile coaching and training for teams, programs, and organizations. Author of the Project Management Institute's (PMI) first major publication on the agile framework, *Leading Agile Teams,* Doug helps his clients improve their organizational agility by coaching, instructing, and facilitating on the Scaled Agile Framework (SAFe), scrum, Extreme Programming (XP), Kanban, Lean Software Development, Iterative Project Management, User Stories, Use Cases, and Retrospectives. Doug has a master's degree (MS) in information management, a law degree (JD) from Syracuse University, and a bachelor of arts degree (BA) from the University of Wisconsin–Madison. He's also a Scaled Agile Framework Program Consultant (SPC), Certified Technical Trainer (CTT+), Certified Scrum Professional (CSP-SM), Certified Scrum Master (CSM), PMI Agile Certified Professional (PMI-ACP), Project Management Professional (PMP), and Certified Developer for Apache Hadoop (CCDH). He is the author of *Enterprise Agility For Dummies.*

Cynthia Snyder Dionisio is a well-known project management speaker, consultant, and trainer. She was the project manager of the team that updated PMI's *Project Management Body of Knowledge,* Sixth Edition, and she is the author of many books, including *A Project Manager's Book of Forms: A Companion to the PMBOK Guide,* and *A Project Manager's Book of Tools and Techniques* (all from Wiley). Her books have been translated into several languages. Cynthia provides consulting services focusing on project management maturity, and she is a much-sought-after trainer in the private, public, and educational sectors. She is the author of *Microsoft Project 2019 For Dummies* and *PMP Certification All-in-One For Dummies.*

Publisher's Acknowledgments

Senior Acquisitions Editor: Tracy Boggier

Compilation Editor: Georgette Beatty

Editorial Project Manager and Development Editor: Christina Guthrie

Technical Editor: Katherine Tuttle, MS, PMP

Production Editor: Tamilmani Varadharaj

Cover Image: © mattjeacock/Getty Images

Take dummies with you everywhere you go!

Whether you are excited about e-books, want more from the web, must have your mobile apps, or are swept up in social media, dummies makes everything easier.

Find us online!

dummies.com

Leverage the powe

Dummies is the global leader in the reference category and one of the most trusted and highly regarded brands in the world. No longer just focused on books, customers now have access to the dummies content they need in the format they want. Together we'll craft a solution that engages your customers, stands out from the competition, and helps you meet your goals.

Advertising & Sponsorships

Connect with an engaged audience on a powerful multimedia site, and position your message alongside expert how-to content. Dummies.com is a one-stop shop for free, online information and know-how curated by a team of experts.

- Targeted ads
- Video
- Email Marketing
- Microsites
- Sweepstakes sponsorship

20 MILLION PAGE VIEWS EVERY SINGLE MONTH

15 MILLION **UNIQUE** VISITORS PER MONTH

43% OF ALL VISITORS ACCESS THE SITE VIA THEIR MOBILE DEVICES

700,000 NEWSLETTE SUBSCRIPTION TO THE INBOXES OF *300,000* UNIQUE INDIVIDUALS EVERY WEEK

# of dummies

Custom Publishing

Reach a global audience in any language by creating a solution that will differentiate you from competitors, amplify your message, and encourage customers to make a buying decision.

- Apps
- Books
- eBooks
- Video
- Audio
- Webinars

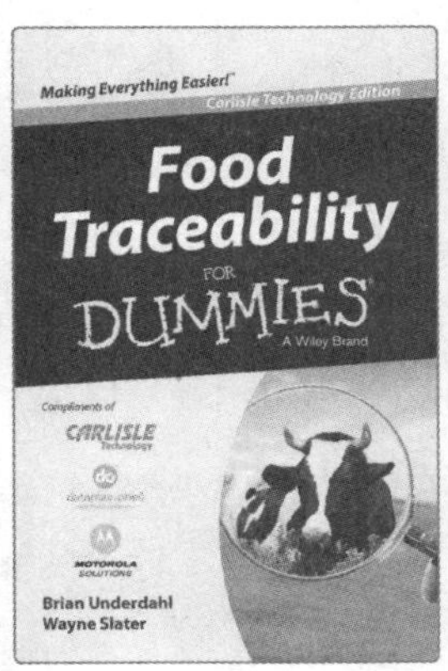

Brand Licensing & Content

Leverage the strength of the world's most popular reference brand to reach new audiences and channels of distribution.

For more information, visit dummies.com/biz

PERSONAL ENRICHMENT

9781119187790
USA $26.00
CAN $31.99
UK £19.99

9781119179030
USA $21.99
CAN $25.99
UK £16.99

9781119293354
USA $24.99
CAN $29.99
UK £17.99

9781119293347
USA $22.99
CAN $27.99
UK £16.99

9781119310068
USA $22.99
CAN $27.99
UK £16.99

9781119235606
USA $24.99
CAN $29.99
UK £17.99

9781119251163
USA $24.99
CAN $29.99
UK £17.99

9781119235491
USA $26.99
CAN $31.99
UK £19.99

9781119279952
USA $24.99
CAN $29.99
UK £17.99

9781119283133
USA $24.99
CAN $29.99
UK £17.99

9781119287117
USA $24.99
CAN $29.99
UK £16.99

9781119130246
USA $22.99
CAN $27.99
UK £16.99

PROFESSIONAL DEVELOPMENT

9781119311041
USA $24.99
CAN $29.99
UK £17.99

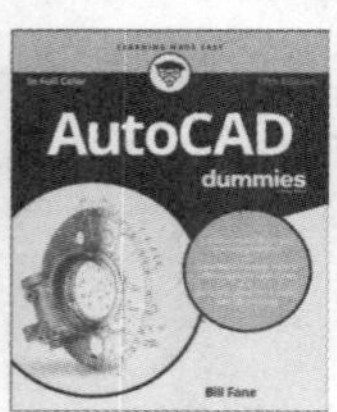

9781119255796
USA $39.99
CAN $47.99
UK £27.99

9781119293439
USA $26.99
CAN $31.99
UK £19.99

9781119281467
USA $26.99
CAN $31.99
UK £19.99

9781119280651
USA $29.99
CAN $35.99
UK £21.99

9781119251132
USA $24.99
CAN $29.99
UK £17.99

9781119310563
USA $34.00
CAN $41.99
UK £24.99

9781119181705
USA $29.99
CAN $35.99
UK £21.99

9781119263593
USA $26.99
CAN $31.99
UK £19.99

9781119257769
USA $29.99
CAN $35.99
UK £21.99

9781119293477
USA $26.99
CAN $31.99
UK £19.99

9781119265313
USA $24.99
CAN $29.99
UK £17.99

9781119239314
USA $29.99
CAN $35.99
UK £21.99

9781119293323
USA $29.99
CAN $35.99
UK £21.99

dummies.com

dummies®
A Wiley Brand

Learning Made Easy

ACADEMIC

9781119293576
USA $19.99
CAN $23.99
UK £15.99

9781119293637
USA $19.99
CAN $23.99
UK £15.99

9781119293491
USA $19.99
CAN $23.99
UK £15.99

9781119293460
USA $19.99
CAN $23.99
UK £15.99

9781119293590
USA $19.99
CAN $23.99
UK £15.99

9781119215844
USA $26.99
CAN $31.99
UK £19.99

9781119293378
USA $22.99
CAN $27.99
UK £16.99

9781119293521
USA $19.99
CAN $23.99
UK £15.99

9781119239178
USA $18.99
CAN $22.99
UK £14.99

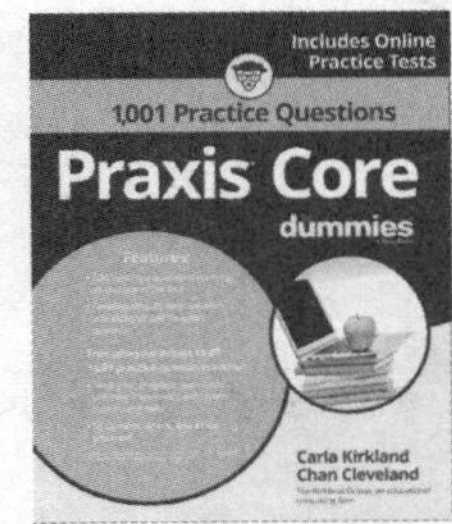

9781119263883
USA $26.99
CAN $31.99
UK £19.99

Available Everywhere Books Are Sold

dummies.com

Small books for big imaginations

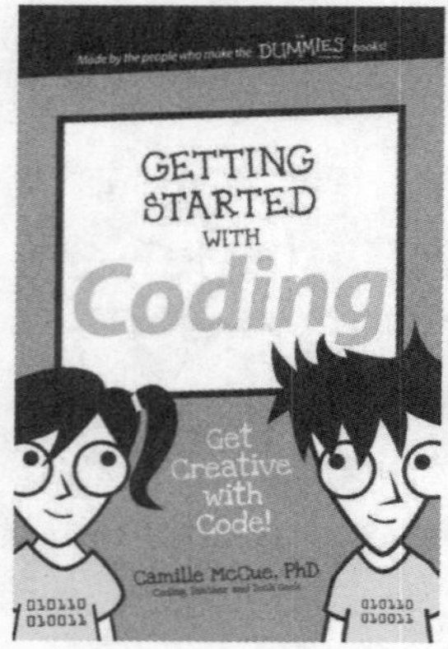

9781119177173
USA $9.99
CAN $9.99
UK £8.99

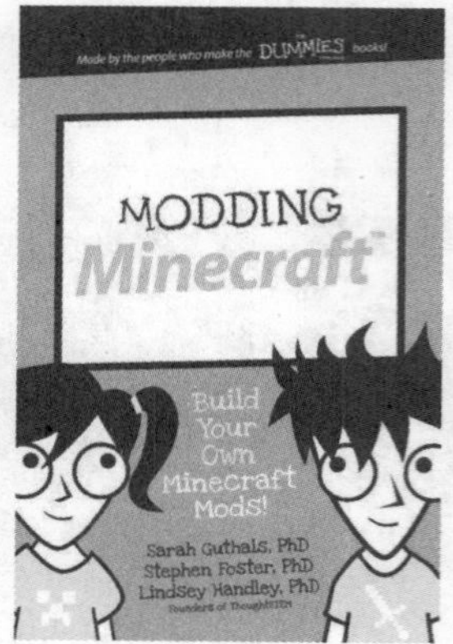

9781119177272
USA $9.99
CAN $9.99
UK £8.99

9781119177241
USA $9.99
CAN $9.99
UK £8.99

9781119177210
USA $9.99
CAN $9.99
UK £8.99

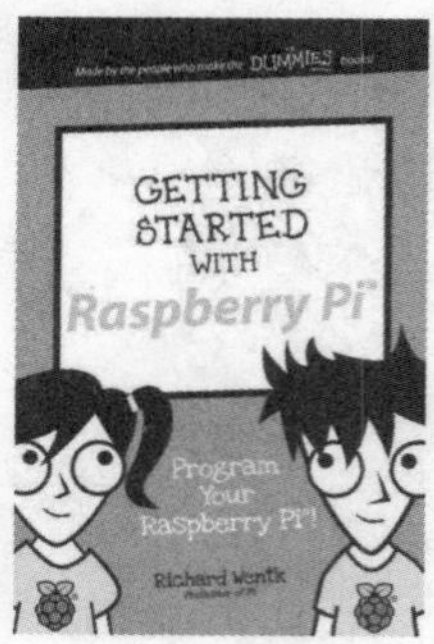

9781119262657
USA $9.99
CAN $9.99
UK £6.99

9781119291336
USA $9.99
CAN $9.99
UK £6.99

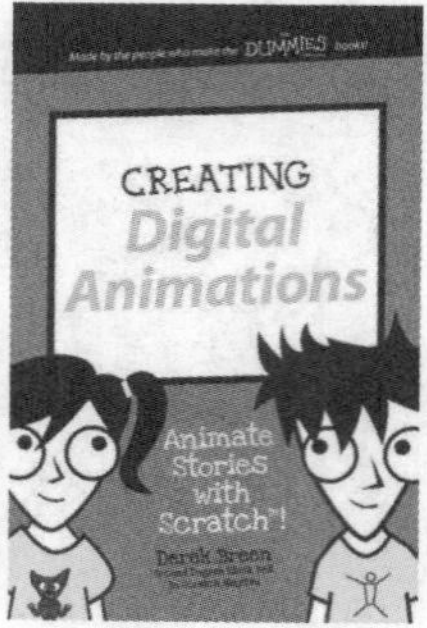

9781119233527
USA $9.99
CAN $9.99
UK £6.99

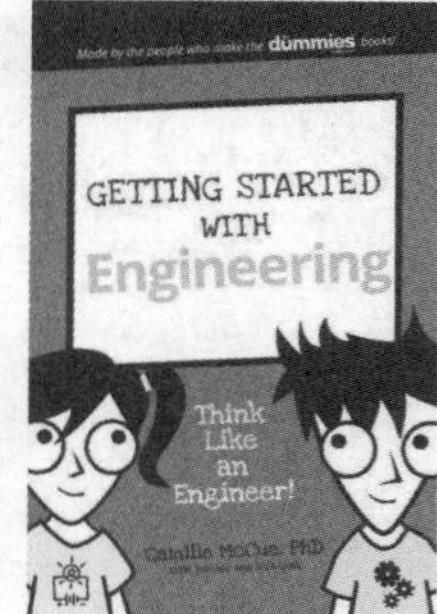

9781119291220
USA $9.99
CAN $9.99
UK £6.99

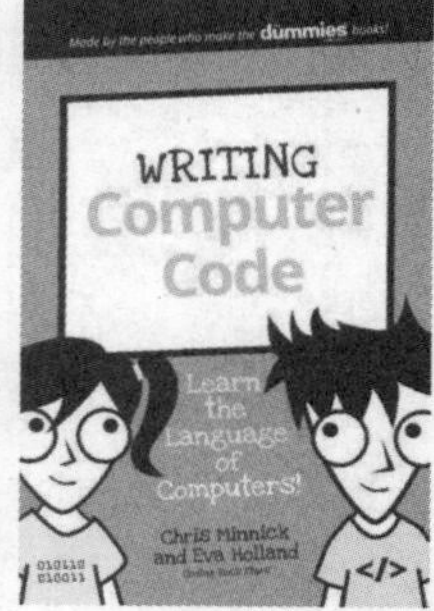

9781119177302
USA $9.99
CAN $9.99
UK £8.99

Unleash Their Creativity

dummies.com

dummies®
A Wiley Brand